Roots and Branches

Selected Papers on Tolkien

by Tom Shippey

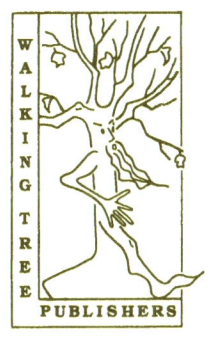

2007

Cormarë Series

No 11

Series Editors

Peter Buchs • Thomas Honegger • Andrew Moglestue

Editor responsible for this volume:
Thomas Honegger

Library of Congress Cataloging-in-Publication Data

Shippey, Tom A.

    Roots and Branches:
    Selected Papers on Tolkien by Tom Shippey

    ISBN 978-3-905703-05-4

Subject headings:

Tolkien, J. R. R. (John Ronald Reuel), 1892-1973 – Criticism and interpretation
Tolkien, J. R. R. (John Ronald Reuel), 1892-1973 – Language
Fantasy fiction, English – History and criticism
Middle-earth (Imaginary place)
Literature, Comparative.

Ilustrations by Anke Eißmann.

All rights reserved. No portion of this book may be reproduced, by any process or technique, without the express written consent of the publisher.

Table of Contents

Introduction

The Roots: Tolkien and his Predecessors

Tolkien and the *Beowulf*-Poet	1
Tolkien and the Appeal of the Pagan: *Edda* and *Kalevala*	19
Tolkien and the West Midlands: The Roots of Romance	39
Tolkien and the *Gawain*-Poet	61
Grimm, Grundtvig, Tolkien: Nationalisms and the Invention of Mythologies	79
The Problem of the Rings: Tolkien and Wagner	97
Goths and Huns: The Rediscovery of Northern Cultures in the Nineteenth Century	115

Heartwood: Tolkien and Scholarship

Fighting the Long Defeat: Philology in Tolkien's Life and Fiction	139
History in Words: Tolkien's Ruling Passion	157
A Look at *Exodus* and *Finn and Hengest*	175
Tolkien and Iceland: The Philology of Envy	187
Tolkien's Academic Reputation Now	203

The Trunk: The Lord of the Rings, The Silmarillion

Light-elves, Dark-elves and Others: Tolkien's Elvish Problem	215
Indexing and Poetry in *The Lord of the Rings*	235
Orcs, Wraiths, Wights: Tolkien's Images of Evil	243
Heroes and Heroism: Tolkien's Problems, Tolkien's Solutions	267
Noblesse Oblige: Images of Class in Tolkien	285
"A Fund of Wise Sayings": Proverbiality in Tolkien	303

Twigs and Branches: Minor Works by Tolkien

Tolkien and 'The Homecoming of Beorhtnoth'	323
The Versions of 'The Hoard'	341
Allegory versus Bounce: (Half of) an Exchange on *Smith of Wootton Major*	351
Blunt Belligerence: Tolkien's *Mr Bliss*	363
Another Road to Middle-earth: Jackson's Movie Trilogy	365
List of Abbreviations and References	387
Index	403

Series Editor's Preface

It was in July 1992. I was attending a conference at Trinity College, Dublin, and had brought along a copy of the recently published second edition of Tom Shippey's *The Road to Middle-earth* for 'leisure time reading'. I don't remember much of the conference – but I remember vividly how I often played truant and spent my time sitting in pubs or cafes, reading and re-reading this astonishing book. I have been aware of Tolkien's 'medieval roots' ever since my own studies, but my recognition of Tolkien's debt to Philology and medieval literature had been patchy, haphazard and limited. Tom Shippey's book was 'like lightning from a clear sky'. It not only elucidated the philological details with authority and acumen but, which is an invaluable achievement, was able to impart some of Tolkien's 'philological passion' to the reader. Lady Philology was revealed in all her splendour and glory. My own years of study of the Germanic languages at university suddenly became part of a greater, daring enterprise, with *The Lord of the Rings* at its centre.

The Road to Middle-earth has deservedly remained in print over the decades and is now available in its 3rd edition – and remains, in my opinion, still the best monograph on Tolkien's work. Yet although *The Road to Middle-earth* and *J.R.R. Tolkien. Author of the Century* are undoubtedly the two most prominent studies in the field, they are not the only contributions by Professor Shippey. Over the years, he has written and lectured widely on Tolkien-related topics and many of his essays are, though still highly topical, no longer readily available. It was this unsatisfactory situation which prompted Walking Tree Publishers to approach Tom Shippey and propose to him the re-publication of his older essays – to which Professor Shippey readily agreed, adding some new and as yet unpublished items.

We are grateful to Tom Shippey for the care and labour he devoted to this volume, to all editors and publishers mentioned in the respective footnotes for permission to reprint, and are proud to offer the reader a rich, varied and nourishing banquet of Tolkien-related essays.

Thomas Honegger
Jena, December 06

Introduction

The twenty-three essays in this volume were produced over a period of some twenty-five years, and I am most grateful to Thomas Honegger and his colleagues at Walking Tree Publishers for the opportunity to print, reprint, and amplify them. Four of them were written from the outset as academic articles for journals or collections, but the majority began either as lectures delivered to university audiences or, even more often, as talks to meetings of a Tolkien Society. I am grateful, too, to the organisers of both lectures and talks, which have enabled me to meet admirers of Tolkien, and to attempt to convert some of his critics, in England, Holland, Denmark, Norway, Spain, Iceland and the USA. Something which has struck me most forcibly is the genuine, widespread, and passionate interest in Tolkien, in language and in literature more generally which I have encountered again and again on these occasions, an interest entirely without self-interest: members of Tolkien Societies are not there because it will help them to get a PhD and an academic appointment, but because they want to know. That is what university teaching is supposed to be like, but, as Tolkien knew, far too often isn't.

The differences of original production have left their mark, in spite of my attempts to move the essays towards consistency. In some the signs of original oral delivery may still be present, and annotation varies from academically heavy to informally (almost) non-existent. I fear that I have also too often repeated my asides or illustrations, as one can see by looking at the 'Index' under 'woses' or 'Lancashire Fusiliers.' But I have resisted the temptation to airbrush out all mistakes or omissions. In 1982 I thought that the discovery of the etymology of the name 'Attila' was one of the most exciting and thought-provoking successes of comparative philology, but did not know, at that time, that Tolkien had thought so too: see, again, the 'Index' under 'Attila.' Checking the 'Index' under 'noodles' will furthermore make the point that even after twenty-five years, and more, of reading Tolkien, it is still possible to find out something quite unexpected and unknown to scholarship.

This raises the question of what more there is to be done. If there are leading themes in this volume – none was intended, but inevitably what one does reflects one's own experience and interests – it seems to me that there are two, again inevitably connected. The positive one is the idea of continuity from the far past, the 'roots of romance.' As I say repeatedly, Tolkien was convinced that he was living on and in the site of ancient legend, and that the legends and the words and attitudes and even literary-genres associated with them remained alive and present, if gone underground and no longer attended to. Very often they had become *déclassé*, present only in forms (like place-names and proverbs and fairy-tales) long regarded as beneath the notice of the educated or too familiar to be worth attention. Bringing them back to notice was part of what I repeatedly indicate as the intrinsic democracy of philology.

My other leading theme is regrettably negative, and stems from the élitism which has marked literary studies in the English-speaking world for centuries, and which has only become more powerfully marked, in reality, when associated with its current rhetoric of diversity, inclusion, rescuing silenced voices (etc.). My former colleague John Carey, like Tolkien once a Merton Professor of Oxford University, has argued caustically (Carey 1992) that the drive for literary 'modernism' in the twentieth century was created by the urge of the *haute bourgeoisie* to differentiate themselves from a new, literate, lower middle-class readership and authorship whom they felt to be usurping their places and their privileges; he goes on to argue that late twentieth-century and twenty-first century 'postmodernism' has just been a raising of the stakes – with the result, though this is my argument not his, that one needs a PhD from an approved élite institution to understand postmodern literary discussion, and (not at all co-incidentally) that major presses now find difficulty in selling two hundred copies of many critical works, while English departments in US universities have lost some two-thirds of the share of student majors which they had thirty years ago. In this way the dying curse of that great green dragon Comparative

Philology – slain by the critics long ago – becomes ever more evidently operative. But things do not have to be that way, and Tolkien and associated studies are one way of reversing a sad trend.

One area where I feel there is much more to be said is that of Tolkien's literary relationships. There was fantasy before Tolkien, and indeed a powerful Victorian and Edwardian fairy-literature and folktale-scholarship, both of them largely forgotten but both perhaps leaving more of a mark on Tolkien than we have realised (see, for instance, in very different ways, Bown 2001, Collingwood 2005, Fimi 2006, 2007). There was furthermore a deep and widespread fascination with theories of comparative mythology, quite clearly stimulated by the successes of comparative philology, but ending in failure: this too has left its mark on Tolkien and perhaps even more on C.S. Lewis, but the history of what one might call Victorian mythography remains to be written. Meanwhile, if one reads Tolkien and Lewis and Charles Williams and Barfield, and the other Inklings, and the works they refer to, all together, one may frequently pick out hints of what I have called 'Inkling conversation' – the topics they must have discussed among themselves, and often disagreed about, and sometimes converted into fictional settings to try out their point. See, once more and for example, 'Index' under 'virtuous paganism' and 'Manichaeanism.'

Another literary relationship is the adversarial one. Between the wars the Inklings must collectively have been aware of their own unfashionable state, and the literary dominance of groups such as the 'Bloomsberries' and what Martin Green has dubbed the *Sonnenkinder*. Lewis in particular often seems to me to be 'counterpunching' against a literary and academic orthodoxy: but the history of its dominance has again not been written, and the texts once fashionable have drifted towards oblivion. Tolkien too, though famously not open to influence, must at least have known of, and been in general agreement with his friend's concerns.

One final area for study has struck me while preparing entries for Michael Drout's forthcoming *Tolkien Encyclopedia*. There is a very great deal of writing on Tolkien nowadays, but hardly anyone has cared to probe the notes to Tolkien's editions (*Exodus*, *Finn and Hengest*), or works such as W.E. Haigh's *New Glossary* of the dialect of Huddersfield, which Tolkien clearly influenced, and from which he surely drew such data as Sam Gamgee's first name, probably Barliman Butterbur's second name, and (see above) the word 'noodles.' These data of course come very often in the form of glosses, comments on single words, and are not formed into connected arguments; but as I have said again and again, that is the way Tolkien's mind worked. Nor is the activity of the glossator (which is what Tolkien started as) to be despised.

Much more could be said also, I feel, about Tolkien's early poems and their repeated rewritings, as also about his experiments with alliterative and other metres, most notably in *The Lays of Beleriand*: though Tolkien wrote modern alliterative poetry better than anyone (even W.H. Auden), the special merits of this mode have been little understood. The same goes for Tolkien's repeated but never entirely successful attempts to find a 'Lost Road' back through early English and Germanic myth. This is all detailed work, not lending itself (at least initially) to dramatic generalisation, but there is a forest beyond the trees, and hints of a mountain-range rising even beyond the forest.

Speaking of which, one area where Tolkien has become ever more relevant is that of ecology: see in this instance Dickerson and Evans 2006, Gee 2004, and in more personal style Blackham 2006. But once one starts recommending works on Tolkien, so many are the perspectives he opens that there is just no end to it. As the Old Norse hero said (slightly adapted) *orþz þiccir enn vant oss hváro*, 'each of us thinks there is more to be said.' And so there is, as twenty-five years have repeatedly shown me.

Tom Shippey

The Roots

Tolkien and his Predecessors

Tolkien and
the *Beowulf*-Poet[1]

Did Tolkien ever wonder whether he might possibly be the *Beowulf*-poet reincarnated? If the question had ever been put to him, he would certainly have answered 'No.' Indeed, it is said that on one occasion a similar question *was* actually put to him, 'Do you believe in reincarnation?', and he answered, 'No, I am a Christian.' Nevertheless, though he may have rejected the idea of reincarnation as a possibility for real people in real life, Tolkien several times introduced it into his fiction. The Dwarves, we are told, "have many strange tales and beliefs concerning themselves and their fate in the world," and one of them is that on five occasions a child has been born to the house of Durin their ancestor "so like to his Forefather that he received the name of Durin" and "was indeed held by the Dwarves to be [Durin] the Deathless that returned" (*LotR*, 1046). Tolkien was concerned also about the recurrence of the name Glorfindel. In *The Lord of the Rings* he is the elf-lord who appears to help the hobbits escape the Nazgûl and reach Rivendell; in *The Silmarillion* he is a hero of Gondolin who is killed by a Balrog in the pass of Cirith Thoronath thousands of years before. There is a simple answer to this repetition ready to hand, which is that there are many more people than there are names, and that it is common for people to be called after heroes or legendary figures of the past. But Tolkien continued to think it was more than a coincidence, and some years after *The Lord of the Rings* was published wrote a long explanation of elvish naming-habits and especially 'Of Rebirth' (*Morgoth*, 220-53, 300): the second Glorfindel was the first Glorfindel reborn. Finally, the most prominent of all the human characters in *The Silmarillion* is of course Beren, who alone among

---

[1] This essay began as a paper given by invitation at Truman State University, Missouri, on March 30th 2001. I am grateful to Dr Christine Harker for the opportunity to speak, and to develop some thoughts.

mortal men was allowed to return after his death; and Beren and Lúthien are the names on the Tolkiens' own tombstone.

Reincarnation in the modern Western world, moreover, has an air of the alien and Oriental about it, which might well have led someone like Tolkien to reject it. But he knew that there were indeed hints of such a belief in the old traditions of England and Scandinavia. It may account for the custom, in old times – it is still not entirely dead – of calling children after former members of a family, but never after living members. If, in an Icelandic saga, one encounters a character called, for instance, Véstein Vésteinsson, it is a natural inference to conclude that he was born after his father's death, a conclusion which has a bearing on the vexed interpretation of *The Saga of Gísli Súrsson* (see Kroesen 1982). Reincarnation to Tolkien, then, was a familiar idea, not an unwelcome one, and one with native roots.[2]

That still does not mean that he applied it to himself. Just the same, Tolkien's published comments on the *Beowulf*-poet make it clear that he felt a relationship with his long-dead and completely anonymous predecessor which was, to say the least, much closer than one merely scholarly. There was a strong element of fellow-feeling, and a certain readiness to dispense with argument on the grounds that Tolkien, after all, *knew what the poet had been thinking*. In his famous 1936 lecture on the poem Tolkien summed up generations of scholarship with the words:

> Slowly with the rolling years the obvious (so often the last revelation of analytic study) has been discovered: that we have to deal with a poem by an Englishman using afresh ancient and largely traditional material. ('Monsters,' in *Essays*, 9)

But the description of the poet would do almost as well as a description of Tolkien. "An Englishman": there is no doubt about that. Tolkien was well

---

[2] Tolkien further offers a guarded defence of reincarnation as a possibility "for certain kinds of rational incarnate creatures" in a letter to a Catholic inquirer (see *Letters*, 189).

aware that his name had a German derivation (just as many scholars of the past had tried to make out that *Beowulf* was German, or Danish, or Frisian); but he also knew that the derivation was centuries old (just like the story of *Beowulf*), and insisted repeatedly that he felt himself to be in all essentials an Englishman of the West Midlands, of old Mercia, where his mother's family, the Suffields, had been entrenched since literally time immemorial (see *Letters*, 54). "Using afresh ancient and largely traditional material": this would be an excellent description of what he did again and again in *The Lord of the Rings*, and even in 1936, when that work was not yet thought of, it is not a bad description of what Tolkien was doing in the various extant versions of the 'Silmarillion,' which he was at such pains to root in ancient if too-often forgotten English tradition.

The self-referential quality of Tolkien's lecture was indeed so marked that he sometimes had to disguise it. At one point, defending the importance of dragons against the critics, he said of the *Beowulf*-poet, "He esteemed dragons, as rare as they are dire, *as some do still* (*Essays*, 12, my emphasis). Who were the 'some'? A few pages later he adds:

> Even today (despite the critics) you may find men not ignorant of tragic legend and history, who have heard of heroes and indeed seen them, who yet have been caught by the fascination of the worm. More than one poem in recent years [...] has been inspired by the dragon of *Beowulf,* but none that I know of by Ingeld son of Froda. (*Essays*, 16)

Michael Drout's publication of Tolkien's early drafts of this lecture enable us to see that when Tolkien claimed "More than one poem" for the dragons, he meant, in fact, exactly two, his own 'Iumonna Gold Galdre Bewunden' and C.S. Lewis's 'Once the worm-laid egg …' (Drout 2002: 56-8, 110-14) – not very convincing evidence of a general modern taste, which was what Tolkien was trying to prove, but evidence maybe of a taste shared with the author of *Beowulf*. As for "men not ignorant of tragic legend and history," to whom does that apply better than to Tolkien? And "those who have heard of heroes and indeed seen them"? As he was well aware, Tolkien's own regiment, the Lancashire Fusiliers, had the distinction of winning more Victoria Crosses during World War I (17) than any other in the British and Imperial armies. So Tolkien had seen heroes and served with them, and so, perhaps, had the *Beowulf*-poet. Both men, though, preferred to write also about 'monsters,' or the non-human, about myth rather than history; and Tolkien thought, very convincingly, that he was accordingly just the man to explain why.

These are not the only examples of disguised self-reference in Tolkien's essays, which has only become more and more obvious with time. When, jocosely, Tolkien remarked to the audience of his lecture, later essay, 'On Fairy-Stories' that just as the fairy-stories of humans are often about the Escape from Death, so "[t]he human stories of the elves are doubtless full of the Escape from Deathlessness" ('OFS,' in *Essays*, 153), no-one present can have had any idea of what he was talking about: as far as anyone knew, there were no "human stories of the elves." But we now know that there were: the story of Beren and Lúthien already existed in several different versions, known only to Tolkien and a very few friends. In scholarly writing, however, as in the record of scientific experiments, one is by old convention supposed to conceal personal feeling, and – to return to *Beowulf* – Tolkien did this fairly well in his three major published comments on the poem: namely the lecture of 1936, the essay 'On Translating *Beowulf*' prefixed to the 1940 translation of the poem by Clark Hall and C.L. Wrenn, and the 1963 lectures published posthumously as *Finn and Hengest* (ed. A.J. Bliss 1982).

These have met astonishingly different fates. The 1936 lecture is generally accepted as the starting-point for almost all modern criticism of the poem, and may well be the most-often cited scholarly paper in the humanities of all time; there is a small scattering of references to Tolkien's thoughts on translation; the learned world has effectively ignored the 1982 publication. All this is normal for Tolkien (see further the essay on 'Tolkien's Academic Reputation Now' in this volume): a few of his papers – perhaps three – deserve to be called 'field-defining,' the rest would have sunk without trace if it were not for their connection with his fiction. Nevertheless, what energised all his scholarly writings, whether on *Sir Gawain* or *Ancrene Wisse* or fairy-stories or *Beowulf*, was a conviction that his close identification with the ancient writers, who he believed passionately to have sprung from the same soil and talked the same (ancestral) language as himself, gave him a privileged insight into what they meant and what they thought. In no case was this identification closer than with the unknown poet of *Beowulf*.

On the face of it, this identification does not make a great deal of sense. *The Lord of the Rings* is one of the most successful single works in the whole history of fiction, having sold hundreds of millions of copies – no-one knows the exact figure, in any case now much inflated by the number of viewers of the recent film versions – and was visibly if not prodigiously successful from the moment it was first published. By contrast the poem of *Beowulf* survived for close on eight hundred years only as a single manuscript copy, looked at during that time, as far as we know, by only four people, of whom three ignored it.[3] Yet the contrast is not as enormous as it seems. On the one hand *Beowulf* is now one of the best-known works in the history of literature, translated into many languages, existing once more in millions of copies (something its forgotten author could never even have imagined); it is said that more learned articles have been written about it in the past two hundred years than about any other literary work in English, even *Hamlet*, though it could also be said that we still know almost nothing for sure about its purpose or origins. On the other hand, one has to remember that for most of his life Tolkien also thought of his own works, including *The Silmarillion* and *The Lord of the Rings*, as being one-copy

---

[3] See Shippey and Haarder (1998: 1-2).

manuscripts, which might never find their audience. At the start of 'The Notion Club Papers' he imagines a future in which his work, like *Beowulf*, has become a dusty anonymous manuscript, its author forgotten, being studied by scholars who try to trace its provenance by examining the paper, the handwriting, the internal references that may help to date it (see *Sauron*, 155-8). For most of his life Tolkien, like the *Beowulf*-poet, was a largely unread author. He must have hoped for the same change of fortune as his predecessor, which indeed he received.

Points like this may explain a certain sympathy, a fellow-feeling, between Tolkien and the poet. But are there any deeper connections between them? At this point one has to confront the central problem of *Beowulf* studies, which is that what we (think we) know about the poem, and what it seems to say about itself, do not correspond at all. To put it bluntly, almost all critics now agree, following Tolkien, that it is the work of a literate, Christian, Englishman. But the poem, to general embarrassment, never once mentions England, or Britain, or anyone English, apart from two doubtful and marginal cases – the characters Hengest and Offa – about whom one thing is certain, which is that they are still living on the mainland of Europe, whatever may happen to them later or whoever their descendants may be. Furthermore, though the poem refers to the Bible, and frequently to God, the references are always to the Old Testament, never the New, and there is no mention of Christ or any of his standard Old English epithets, such as 'the Redeemer,' 'the Healer,' etc. Specifically Christian reference seems to have been deliberately avoided. Finally, though the poet knows the verb 'to write,' OE *wrítan*, and uses it twice, on one occasion it definitely, and on the other quite probably, does not mean 'write' but has its older meaning of 'to cut,' or 'to engrave runes.' Similarly, the poem uses the loan-word *(for)scrifan*, from Latin *scribere*, which in German, for instance, becomes *schreiben*, the normal word for 'write.' But in *Beowulf* it means 'condemn.' On internal evidence, then, the poem was not written by a literate Christian Englishman, but orally composed by one or more illiterate pagan Scandinavians. Almost no-one has believed this since Tolkien's 1936 lecture, but before that time variations on such an opinion were common. The most direct approach may have been that of Gregor Sarrazin, a German professor who argued that the poem was an Old English translation of a lost Old Norse poem, which he called the *Byggviskviða Grindilsbana*. This is a logical answer to a genuine problem, but there is absolutely no evidence for it at all.

Tolkien had a different answer, which he put carefully if circuitously in his 1936 lecture. The problem with this – if one manages to pick one's way through Tolkien's immensely complex and engaging rhetoric – is that it depends on Tolkien's conviction that he knew exactly when the poet was writing, and why, and what the poet was thinking when he wrote. When was he writing? Tolkien says that he will "accept without argument throughout the attribution of *Beowulf* to the 'age of Bede'" (*Essays*, 20), that is to say approximately 700-730 AD. There has been much argument about this, and the general consensus at the moment puts the poem as much as 250 years later.[4] But Tolkien thought that the poem must have come from a time when conversion to Christianity had taken place, and the new religion was solidly established, but not so solidly that memory of pagan times had faded – and, though Tolkien does not say this, perhaps there were still memories of grandparents who had died as pagans and so, in a strict view, had no chance of salvation. Tolkien keeps on calling this a "time of fusion," "a fusion that has occurred *at a given point* of contact between old and new," "a pregnant moment of poise" (*Essays*, 20, 23). Quite when this was would depend on where this was, for conversion took place at different times in different parts of England, roughly 600-700 AD, and Tolkien offers no opinion on that, but he is quite clear about "the mood of the author, the essential cast of his imaginative apprehension of the world" (*Essays*, 20); he

---

[4] I think Tolkien was right, and the modern consensus is wrong, for reasons given in part in Shippey 2005d.

was "looking back into the pit [...] perceiving [the old tales'] common tragedy of inevitable ruin, and yet feeling this more *poetically* because he was himself removed from the direct pressure of its despair" (*Essays*, 23). The poet was, then, looking backwards; aware of a kind of anachronism, a contrast between his own time and the time he was writing about; and he was, in particular, a Christian looking back with love and sympathy at people he knew to have been pagans, and whom he would have liked to view as 'virtuous pagans.'

The issue of the salvation or otherwise of virtuous pagans seems to have been a topic of Inkling discussion – Lewis offers views on the subject in the last of the 'Chronicles of Narnia,' *The Last Battle* (1956), and more indirectly in his last novel, *Till We Have Faces* (also 1956). But one may well ask, what has their situation got to do with Tolkien? Surely he was not in a similar situation to the *Beowulf*-poet, "looking back into the pit." In Tolkien's time England had been entirely Christian, even after the backsliding of the Viking period, for almost a thousand years. Yes, but what of the future? Tolkien might not be looking back into the pit of heathenism, but in 1936 he could well be looking forward into it. As he said himself (though we cannot be sure how far he was thinking about Nazi ideology in particular), the northern heathen imagination "has power [...] to revive itself even in our own times" (*Essays*, 26). And in this Tolkien was a better prophet than he would have wanted to be: seventy years later England is for all intents and purposes a 'post-Christian' country, even more than the rest of Europe. One may say, then, that while in Tolkien's view the old poet was a Christian, looking back with admiration and pity at a heathen age, and (though he did not know it), on the brink of a new and much more dangerous heathen challenge, so Tolkien was a Christian, also looking back at heathen tradition (though from much further away), and on the brink of new and dangerous heathen challenges, both internal and external, which were still to be resisted.

Both men furthermore responded in very similar ways. Both created an anachronistic world, populated by virtuous pagans, whose paganism is never – or in both cases almost never – openly confronted. Both worlds are in a way 'bowdlerised,' i.e. they have had removed elements which one might have expected to exist, but which would be distressing, make the characters seem less virtuous. There are no slaves in *Beowulf*. Though recent excavations have revealed a clear and gruesome case of human sacrifice at Lejre itself,[5] the traditional site of the poem's great hall Heorot, there is no human sacrifice in *Beowulf*. Indeed there is only one mention of pagan deities, idol worship, and sacrifice to the devil, and that is in a passage, lines 175-88, which Tolkien wrote off explicitly as not genuine (*Essays*, 42-44). In fact *Beowulf*, for all its many mentions of God, presents the world of its characters as having effectively no organised religion at all. It is a pagan world with no real pagans in it.

Tolkien did not think this was an accident (as some continue to do), and his heroic Middle-earth is very similar to the heroic Never-Never Land imagined by his predecessor. His Riders of Rohan, semi-barbaric though they are, also do not have slaves. Though there are faint hints of some kind of pagan religion in the background, in place-names like Harrowdale (the valley of the *hearh*, the pagan temple), or Halifirien (the holy mountain), there are no priests, and no-one is seen practising any kind of religion. At the funeral of Théoden one sees aspects of recorded pagan ritual, the great mound raised, the circling riders, the minstrel who sings a dirge, the burial with weapons and treasure – all very similar to the burial of Beowulf, though that also contains a cremation, of which Tolkien did not approve – but, again just as with Beowulf, there is no mention of the other pagan element, the killing of horse, hawk, hound and slave to go with their master. The Riders, and the heroes of *Beowulf*, don't do things like that, though

---

[5] It has only just been discovered, see the report by Tom Christensen on recent excavations in Niles (forthcoming 2007). But Tolkien would have known of similar discoveries.

real-life old Germanic pagans certainly did. Tolkien furthermore signals a kind of awareness of the unrealistic and imaginary nature of the world he created by building into it a strong element of deliberate anachronism, seen especially in the hobbits, with their 'pipeweed' (tobacco), their 'taters' and 'potatoes,' their 'rabbits' and 'coneys,' all things unknown to the real ancient world.

The most important connection between the two writers, though, is this. Faced with a complex problem of sympathy for one tradition combined with commitment to another, they reacted in the same way. Each man – so Tolkien said – constructed an artefact to suit himself, an artefact very likely to be misunderstood. In his extended allegory of the hall and the tower, Tolkien suggested that the scholars trying to understand the *Beowulf*-poet saw him as having built a tower when they would have preferred him to rebuild the old hall from which he took the stone for it, and could not imagine why he had done so. "But from the top of that tower," said Tolkien, "the man had been able to look out upon the sea" (*Essays*, 8). In much the same way Tolkien's character Niggle, in 'Leaf by Niggle' – an especially obvious self-presentation by Tolkien – devotes himself to painting first leaves and then a Tree. But no-one understands or values his work, and the last word said about him in the real-life world is, "Niggle! ... Never knew he painted" ('Leaf,' in *Reader*, 119). Niggle, the old poet, Tolkien: all of them (he suggested) would only be understood in the hereafter.

Did *Beowulf* affect Tolkien other than as a very general, if welcome, role-model? His fictional involvement with the poem lasted for at least fifty years, and one chapter of *The Two Towers* derives in outline and in detail from it: the approach of Aragorn and his companions to Meduseld in 'The King of the Golden Hall' follows the etiquette of *Beowulf* lines 229-405 almost exactly: first challenge, leavetaking by the first challenger, second challenge by the doorwarden, piling of arms outside the hall, reception standing in front of the throne. Hama's proverbial decision about Gandalf's staff, "in doubt a man of worth will trust to his own wisdom" is at once a translation and a commentary on the Danish coastguard's obscure and usually misunderstood proverb in lines 287-9 of the poem.[6] The name 'Meduseld' itself merely adds a capital to a word used in the poem at line 3065, where *mid his mágum medúseld búan*, 'to inhabit the mead-hall with one's kin,' means simply, 'to live.'[7] Tolkien took from the poem, then, a clear view of the nature of heroic behaviour. But one can point to at least five or six further ways in which it suggested important ideas to him, some of them based on uniquely close and serious study of its wording (Tolkien was on this topic, never forget, the most learned person in the world).

One I have hinted at already. It may be a coincidence, but probably is not, that both *Beowulf* and *The Lord of the Rings* use the word *hǽðen*, or 'heathen' (of human beings), exactly twice. Using the word of course implies that the user is himself a Christian, and also has an inevitable derogatory sense. The *Beowulf*-poet knew that his old-time characters had been heathens (so Tolkien thought), but did not want to appear to condemn them for it; so while he used the word to describe Grendel, and to describe the dragon's treasure, twice each, he deliberately avoided using it of people – except that twice again there is a crack in the façade. At line 179 sacrificing to idols is condemned as *hǽþenra hyht*, 'hope of the heathens'; at line 1983 Beowulf's aunt Hygd carries round the drinking-bowl *hǽðnum to handa*, 'to the hands of the heathens,' i.e. Beowulf and his relatives. But in the second case, someone has scratched out the second letter of the word *hǽðnum*, if that is indeed what it was, as if disapproving or correcting. Tolkien thought, in 1936, that the first case might be an interpolation, not what the poet wrote at all. Yet it is odd that *The Lord of the Rings*, like

---

[6] For a discussion of the scholarly issue, see Shippey (1978: 12-14).

[7] Meduseld is Théoden's hall, Edoras is the name for the courts and other buildings which surround it (see *LotR*, 496). The latter name is also formed by capitalising a word in *Beowulf*, this time at line 1037, and incidentally changing it slightly from its West Saxon form to a Mercian one. As often, Tolkien clarifies the meaning of words in old poems by integrating them into his fiction: see also the essay 'A Look at *Exodus* and *Finn and Hengest*' in this volume.

Beowulf, normally abstains carefully from saying that its characters are heathens, though they must be, with, again just like *Beowulf* two exceptions. Denethor, intent on killing himself and taking his son Faramir with him, says, "We will burn like heathen kings" (807), and Gandalf, reproving him, says much the same thing, "only the heathen kings, under the domination of the Dark Power, did thus, slaying themselves in pride and despair, murdering their kin to ease their own death" (835). Tolkien may have come to think that the references in *Beowulf* were not a mistake, and should be imitated: in both works one can see a Christian writer looking back at virtuous pagans or not-quite-heathens, with real and definitely non-virtuous heathendom dimly perceptible even further back, behind or opposed to the main characters.

Tolkien may have picked up another hint from *Beowulf* of how to deal with the difficult negotiation between Christian and pre-Christian, and this has to do with the Valar. It has been pointed out that when Tolkien first started writing about these, in *The Book of Lost Tales*, they seemed much more like the deities of the pagan Norse or Celtic or Classical pantheons:[8] Tolkien increasingly toned this down in later life, since after all the appearance of definite deities would contradict the First Commandment. By the time of *The Silmarillion* they have become firmly subordinate to the One. But are even demi-gods really acceptable in the work of a Christian writer? Tolkien may have been consoled to think that the *Beowulf*-poet was once again there before him, with what may have been a similar solution. At the start of the poem the Danish people is bereft, left without a king; Scyld Scefing comes to them over the waves in some miraculous way, re-establishes the kingdom, and dies; his people put him in a boat, laden in true pagan fashion with treasure, and entrust the boat to the waves, as if

---

[8] See Hutton 2003. Professor Hutton develops his views further in a paper on 'The Pagan Tolkien,' read at the Tolkien Society Conference in Aston, Birmingham, on August 12th, 2005, of which he has kindly allowed me to see a copy. We hope it will appear in the volume of conference proceedings.

expecting him to return to wherever he came from. With characteristic English understatement, the poet says that the Danes 'did by no means provide him with lesser gifts […] than those did who sent him forth in the beginning.' Who are 'those'? The poet offers no further clue, indeed denies knowledge, but there is no doubt about the word 'those,' *Þá* in Old English. The word is used 62 times elsewhere in the poem, but this is the only time in which it takes stress and alliteration, as if the poet wanted to pick it out: he could have written 'He,' and ascribed the miracle to God, but for whatever reason he preferred to ascribe it to an unknown group of beings, possessed of supernatural powers and using them, very occasionally and selectively, for the benefit of humanity. They seem very like the Valar.

It must have been noticed already that while Tolkien read *Beowulf* very carefully, he did not read it like a literary critic, but like a philologist. His insights tended to be drawn from tiny details, often very technical ones. Yet one may say that one of the grandeurs of philology has always been the way in which tiny details can open up great vistas of suggestion and, furthermore, find a natural connection between ancient and modern, and even with the facts of one's own life. Tolkien certainly found this to be the case. It must have increased what I have called above a relationship much closer than one merely scholarly. Of this process I can give three further examples.

One is the idea of 'the dragon-sickness.' Tolkien uses this term on the last page of *The Hobbit*, to describe the fate of the Master of Lake-town, who "being of the kind that easily catches such disease […] took most of [Smaug's] gold and fled with it, and died of starvation in the Waste, deserted by his companions." 'Dragon-sickness' is evidently avarice, but it is a specialised form of it, passive rather than active – its sufferers want to hoard rather than spend or display – and strongly connected with love of metal. Though the phrase is only used of the Master, it has clearly also affected Thorin Oakenshield, and of course Smaug. There seems to be something contagious about it: Bilbo "did not reckon with the power that gold has *upon which a dragon has long brooded*" (*Hobbit*, 237, my emphasis). In the end both Tolkien and his friend Lewis were to see this as one of the characteristic if unrecognised vices of the modern world, but its origin is in *Beowulf*, and Tolkien was thinking about it long before he wrote *The Hobbit*. In 1923 he published a poem called 'Iumonna Gold Galdre Bewunden' (see the essay on 'The Versions of 'The Hoard'' in this volume for its rather complex history). In all its versions, though, the poem traces the history of a hoard as it passes from elf to dwarf to dragon to hero, and in each case corrupts and betrays its owner. The poem's title is line 3052 of *Beowulf*, it means 'the gold of men of old, wound round with spell,' it refers to the dragon's treasure just won at the cost of his life by the hero, and in context it implies – though as always with *Beowulf*, interpretations are disputed – that the hoard may have had a curse on it, or a spell like the ones which the dwarves put over the treasure taken from the trolls, which may or may not have caused Beowulf's decision (brave? rash? greedy?) to fight the dragon alone.

There is another issue connected with treasure in *Beowulf*, and that arises from the word *searu*, with its various compounds. I have discussed this at more length elsewhere (Shippey 2003a: 170-72), so I say here only that its meanings and associations in the poem, and elsewhere in Old English, include 'treasure,' 'armour,' 'craft, especially smithcraft,' and 'betrayal.' On the face of it, these meanings hardly fit together, and the word is regularly translated different ways in different places by modern translators. But Tolkien thought there was a clear logic in it, and tried to show that logic by rolling all the meanings together into a portrayal of dwarvish psychology, as he puts it near the start of *The Hobbit* (15), "the love of beautiful things made by hands and by cunning and by magic," a phrase which covers treasure, and *mithril*-armour, and craft, and *galdre* all at once, and which in context already carries a hint of greed and ferocity and jealousy, the germ of 'dragon-sickness.'

It is not just dwarves and dragons who suffer from it, as Tolkien's poem made clear in all versions from 1923, it affects elves too, and also humans. The name Saruman is only the Old Mercian form of *searu-man*, and it carries the same set of Beowulfian implications: cunning first and foremost, having "a mind of metal and wheels," as Treebeard puts it (*LotR*, 462), greed and desire for mastery, slow corruption from original good intentions, and – here Tolkien has added to the recorded Old English meanings – hatred of the natural world, especially trees. Tolkien took this, however, from his own experience. As is well known, in his childhood he played round Sarehole Mill, was frightened by the two millers there, 'the White Ogre' and 'the Black Ogre,' and eventually saw the pastoral and idyllic landscape of rural Worcestershire (as it was then)[9] swallowed up by industrial Birmingham. Saruman came from Sarehole Mill, and Sarehole Mill was a centre for one form of 'dragon-sickness.' Did Sarehole Mill have anything to do with *Beowulf*? And is the first element really the word *searu-*, or (in Worcestershire) *saru-*? *The Oxford Dictionary of Place-Names* suggests that the first element is either a personal name, or the ancestor of the modern word 'sere,' meaning 'grey, withered,' when applied to vegetation the opposite of 'green,' and nothing to do with treasure, mills or machinery at all. But Tolkien would have seen a very clear and meaningful connection. The 'dragon-sickness' ages and withers its sufferers, in the same way as they destroy their environment. The hints of *Beowulf* were, then, absolutely applicable to the modern world, and gave a strong line for development in Tolkien's fiction.

One could say the same of another word in *Beowulf*, *sceadu*, modern English 'shadow' (the words are pronounced almost exactly the same way, regardless of their spelling). In *The Lord of the Rings* Tolkien frequently capitalises this to become "the Shadow," and uses it in brief for the power of Mordor. There is something challenging about this, for shadows do not exist – surely they are an absence, not a presence? – and one might say that

---

[9] It is in Warwickshire now, but only because the county boundary was changed in 1911 (see Bratman 1999).

therefore they can have no power. The Old English poem *Solomon and Saturn* however asks the riddling question, 'What things were not that were?', and answers, still riddlingly, 'shadow', as if the poet thought they could be both an absence and a presence (Shippey 1976: 94). That is the case in *The Lord of the Rings*: compare "the land of Mordor where the Shadows lie" in the Rings-verse (49) with, even more ominously, "Mordor where the shadows are" in Sam's 'The Fall of Gil-galad' (181). Shadows are like wraiths, there and not-there, dead and not-dead. The ominousness of the idea is hinted at, once again, by two difficult passages in *Beowulf*. In lines 705-7 the poet says, of Beowulf and his retainers waiting in Heorot for the arrival of the man-eater Grendel:

	þæt wæs yldum cúþ,
þæt hie ne móste,	þá Metod nolde,
se synscaþa	under sceadu bregdan.

'It was known to men, that when God did not wish it, the sinful ravager was not permitted to draw them under shadow.' What does 'draw them under shadow' mean? Even more significant, though the poet seems to mean to be reassuring, he isn't. Grendel was not allowed to draw men under shadow *as long as God did not wish it*, but that implies that sometimes God *does* wish it, as has been the case with Grendel in the past, and is furthermore common experience. 'Shadow' in *Beowulf* is a power, and it may be an active and even a physical power. In line 650 King Hrothgar vacates his hall, for he knows that with the fall of night, *scaduhelma gesceapu scríðan cwóman*, literally 'the shapes of shadow-helms came striding.' Translators deal with this different ways, often opting for something like 'under the cover of darkness' to explain or paraphrase 'shadow-helms.' Tolkien thought that Old English poets usually meant what they said: 'shadow-helms' form part of his image of the Ringwraiths. But more significant is the combination, in the *Beowulf* line, of 'shape' and 'shadow.' It is when the shadows take on shapes that they become most deadly, turn from being absences to being presences, and this is once again a vital part of Tolkien's image of the Ringwraiths: individual, original, inimitable, but at the same time with a root in the wording of old poetry.

My last example long escaped me, despite a direct hint from Tolkien himself. In his much-neglected *Finn and Hengest* Tolkien considered the relationship between the 'Finnsburg Episode' in *Beowulf*, an account there of a poem said to be sung in Hrothgar's hall after the defeat of Grendel, and the *Finnsburg Fragment*, some fifty lines surviving of an independent Old English poem on the same subject. Tolkien's explanation of the two is complex, and on an entirely different line from his 1936 lecture, but it centres on the heroes Hnæf, Hengest, and a Jutish hero Gárulf, described in the *Fragment* as *déormód hæleþ*, 'fierce-minded hero.' The second of these remains in memory as the legendary founder of Kent and England – if the poem's Hengest is the same as the legendary Hengest, as Tolkien thought he was. The first has been almost completely forgotten, and the last is rarely remembered or mentioned even by scholars of Old English. Tolkien, however, thought that they still had connections with his immediate environment and even his personal life. The place-name Hinksey, just outside Oxford, is explained by *The Oxford Dictionary of Place-Names* as deriving from *hengestes-ieg*, 'the island of the stallion.' But Tolkien thought it could as easily have been named for the ancient hero. Meanwhile he thought that the name Hnæf survived in the modern surname 'Neave,' borne by his own Aunt Jane Neave, who lived at Bag End. Aunt Jane's village, in Worcestershire, is Darmston, and *The Oxford Dictionary of Place-Names* derives this without qualification from Old English *Déormódes-tún*, 'dwelling-place of Déormód.' Déormód here is a personal name, whereas in the *Finnsburg Fragment* it is taken to be an adjective describing Gárulf. But in Old English personal names and adjectives are hard to tell apart (Anglo-Saxons did not use capital letters as we do), and the history of Old English poems, *Beowulf* especially, is full of uncertain, disputed, or unrecognised cases.

Tolkien mentioned the cases of Hinksey and Neave to me in a conversation some time in the last year of his life, but not Darmston. It is odds-on, however, that he looked the name up in *The Concise Oxford Dictionary of English Place-Names* (names were perhaps Tolkien's most enduring fascination), and odds-on again that he noted the connection with the *Finnsburg Fragment*. What he thought about that particular case I do not know. In general, though, I think that the conclusion he drew from such continuities between ancient poetry and modern life is perfectly clear. He thought that the heroes of antiquity *had not gone away*. They were still there, in the landscape, in names, and probably in the gene-pool. They and the poetry about them and the concepts which that poetry had embodied might not be well-known or well-recognised any more, but the concepts at least were still a living force and very much part of his, Tolkien's, personal experience, and of other people's too if they would only realise it. As for *Beowulf*, it was wiser and more meaningful than even scholars had realised, and that wisdom and meaning were perfectly capable of being reproduced for and understood by a twentieth- or twenty-first century audience. Indeed, the wisdom of the poem could be neglected only at one's peril. And Tolkien's insight into that wisdom suggested, to repeat a phrase used twice already, a relationship between him and the poet much closer than one merely scholarly – even if one could not quite call it innate, or hereditary.

Tolkien and the Appeal of the Pagan: *Edda* and *Kalevala*[1]

Works Rooted and Uprooted

"It is an interesting question: what is this flavour, this atmosphere, this virtue that such *rooted* works have." Tolkien posed the question near the start of his 1953 lecture on *Sir Gawain and the Green Knight* (*Essays*, 72), but then confessed that it was not his business to answer it that day, or, alas, any other. Nevertheless it remains an interesting question, not least because Tolkien so clearly devoted much of his lifelong writing effort to attempting to duplicate, or emulate, or counterfeit, whatever the secret ingredient was. It may seem that this was wasted effort. If 'rootedness' comes from having deep roots in old and half- or more than half-forgotten myth, as Tolkien thought was the case with *Sir Gawain* and *Beowulf* and Shakespeare's *King Lear* and *Hamlet*, then no work of fiction individually created by a modern author can hope to match it. It could also be said that a committed Christian author like Tolkien ought not to be rummaging in the depths of mythologies which were evidently pagan, at best misguided, at worst soul-destroying. Tolkien countered the first objection by keeping open the possibility that the quality he admired so much in *Beowulf* was indeed "largely a product of art" ('Monsters,' in *Essays*, 7); and the second by his developed theory of 'mythopoeia,' the right to create, or sub-create.[2] In any case, the whole issue of relations between individual authors and the roots of their tradition may well be a complex one, as the cases to be considered here will show.

---

[1] This piece appeared first in Jane Chance (ed.), *Tolkien and the Invention of Myth: A Reader* (Lexington, KY: University Press of Kentucky, 2004), 145-61. I am grateful to editor and publisher for permission to reprint.

[2] For which see 'On Fairy-Stories,' cited here as reprinted in *Essays*, 109-61. Tolkien's discussion of 'sub-creation' comes mainly on pp. 139-45. For 'mythopoeia,' see the poem of that name printed in later editions of Tolkien's *Tree and Leaf*.

In searching for this unknown quality which Tolkien saw and admired, I will examine in particular two works which Tolkien certainly knew and used from an early date: the *Prose Edda* of Snorri Sturluson, and the *Kalevala* of Elias Lönnrot. Proving that he knew and used them is now hardly necessary. If there were any doubt left after repeated demonstrations, then the essays of Marjorie Burns, Richard West, and several others in *Tolkien and the Invention of Myth* (Chance 2004), in which this essay also first appeared, would answer it. The issue I wish to take up here starts by noting that when one writes, as I just have, "the *Prose Edda* of Snorri Sturluson, and the *Kalevala* of Elias Lönnrot," the word 'of' has two quite distinct meanings.

Snorri Sturluson was an Icelandic writer and politician, born in 1179, murdered by his enemies in 1241. The work we know as the *Prose Edda* is essentially a handbook written by him to instruct poets wishing to continue the complex tradition of Norse skaldic poetry, which Snorri evidently felt was slipping out of cognizance. In order to do this he not only wrote a section on skaldic meters, the *Hattatal* or 'list of meters,' but also one on 'poetic diction,' the *Skáldskaparmál*, which explains the complex allusions to mythic events once part of the skaldic vocabulary. He preceded both of these, however – though the sections now go *Gylfaginning, Skáldskaparmál, Hattatal*, they may have been written in reverse order[3] – with the *Gylfaginning* or 'Deluding of Gylfi,' an extensive and coherent account of the pagan Norse mythology, some 20,000 words in length, set in the form of a conversation between the deluded Gylfi and three divine or semi-divine beings. There is no doubt that Snorri was the author of this work in an entirely modern sense. However, its accepted modern title, the *Prose Edda*, sometimes the *Younger Edda*, indicates a problem, though it may be ours, not Snorri's. It is used to distinguish Snorri's work from the *Elder* or *Poetic Edda*, a collection of poems now found primarily in two manuscripts

---

[3] See Faulkes (1987: xi-xii).

separate from Snorri's work. It is certain, though, that Snorri knew these poems, and some which are not contained in surviving manuscripts, as he quotes from them freely in what is, after all, a manual on poetry. The mythological stories in the *Prose Edda*, then, are certainly not Snorri's own, nor can one tell how old they are. The word 'edda,' used previously in the Middle Ages to refer to Snorri's work, could meanwhile mean one of several things: 'the book of Oddi' (Snorri was brought up there), 'the book of poetry' (from *óðr*, 'poetry,' which is cognate with the name of the god Odin, patron of poets), 'great-grandmother' (so, as it were, 'tales from long ago'), or just 'composition' (from the Latin word *edo*, 'I compose').[4] *Edo*, however, also gives us the word 'edit,' and Snorri can be seen as having in some ways the function of an editor of poetry rather than a straightforward composer of prose. There is no doubt, then, about the 'rootedness' of the *Prose Edda*. It goes back to a pagan age which had been officially terminated in Iceland more than two hundred years before Snorri wrote, and draws on material which must be, in essence and perhaps in actual wording, even older.

The case of the *Kalevala* is entirely different, but even more complex. Briefly, during and after the Napoleonic wars the nations or protonations of Europe became engaged in what was almost an 'arms race' to provide themselves with national literary traditions which would cement their claim to having always existed, a desire especially strong among nations such as Germany whose claim to existence was in fact shaky or threatened. One early manifestation of this, for instance, was the craze for the works of 'Ossian.' From 1760 onwards a Gaelic-speaking Highlander named James Macpherson – it will be remembered that the rebellion of Bonnie Prince Charlie had been defeated and Highland tradition all but crushed in and after the Battle of Culloden in 1746 – created a sensation in England and eventually across Europe with his translations from the Gaelic

---

[4] The varying theories are summarized in Faulkes (1987: xvi).

of fragments, and then of entire epic poems, centered on the hero Ossian, or Oisín. Macpherson, however, despite increasing pressure and skepticism, refused to produce the manuscripts from which he claimed to have drawn, and opinion eventually hardened into a belief that he had never had any. His work, in other words, was a fake, however damaging this might be to Scottish *amour propre*. Recent opinion has tended to rehabilitate Macpherson slightly, and to see him as an improver, compiler, and editor of what was then still a living tradition of Gaelic poetry.[5] But this was not the view of, for instance, Jacob Grimm, the great philologist, author of the *Deutsche Mythologie* or *Teutonic Mythology*, and collector with his brother Wilhelm of *Grimm's Fairy Tales* – another work allegedly 'rooted' in antiquity, but one in which the Grimms have been repeatedly accused of going beyond the proper limits of collectors and editors and turning into rewriters. Grimm nevertheless made sharp distinction between what he saw as a genuine work of antiquity like the *Poetic Edda* and a 'phony' one like the Ossian cycle. Indeed, prefiguring Tolkien, he saw the distinction as one of basic quality, to be felt by anyone with any sense for authenticity at all. How could one possibly mistake a work like the *Elder Edda*, he asked rhetorically, a work whose plan, style, and substance breathe the remotest antiquity, whose songs lay hold of the heart in a far different way from the extravagantly admired poems of Ossian?[6] The one was rooted, the other a mere modern fad.

Grimm never made any further comparison with Elias Lönnrot's *Kalevala*, but its existence adds a further complication to the whole issue of 'edition' as opposed to 'composition.' Lönnrot, a Finnish doctor working in remote areas of Karelia, took an interest in the traditional songs of the area, and made a collection of them. In doing so he did no more than the

---

[5] For an account of the history and current state of opinion, see Fiona Stafford's 'Introduction' to Gaskill (1996: v-xxxi).
[6] I here paraphrase Stallybrass (1882-8: III, v-vi), translating Grimm (1875-8: II, v).

Grimms, for instance, collecting folktales, or Walter Scott collecting ballads. Lönnrot, however, went on to arrange the songs into a connected cycle, or even epic, which he published in twenty-five *runos* or cantos in 1835, expanded to fifty in 1849. In doing this Lönnrot was in line with the contemporary doctrine of *Liedertheorie*, first propounded in 1795 by F. A. Wolf, which held that even the great classical epics of Homer had begun as short, independent, anonymous, nonliterate *Lieder*, or 'lays,' or 'ballads,' which had then been, so to speak, stitched together into a connected whole by a single named poet. It was then an entirely appropriate activity for any would-be creator of a national epic to arrange and connect up traditional songs into an epic cycle, just as Homer had, especially if he believed, like Lönnrot, that he was really reassembling something which had once already taken epic shape. Conversely it became the characteristic activity of critics, especially German critics, to dissect epic poems like *Beowulf* or the *Nibelungenlied* back into their original allegedly separate *Lieder* or ballads. Or one might, like Lord Macaulay, take a familiar Roman historian like Livy and write versions of the ballads his histories might be thought to have been based on: these are Macaulay's *Lays of Ancient Rome*, which Tolkien began his poetic career by imitating.[7] The distinction between the genuine and the phony, which both Grimm and Tolkien were so sure of, accordingly became a matter of inner quality, not to be decided on purely objective criteria: though it deserves to be said here that Lönnrot kept particularly accurate records of what he had collected and what he had himself added or changed. His work has been reedited to the highest scholarly standards in the thirty-three volume *Suomen Kansan Vanhat Runot*, 'The Ancient Runes of the Finnish People.'[8]

---

[7] In his poem 'The Battle of the Eastern Field,' published in his school magazine, *The King Edward's School Chronicle*, in 1911, when he was 19 (see Carpenter 2000: 266). For discussion of Macaulay's relation to *Liedertheorie*, and Tolkien's response to it, see Shippey (2000a: 233-36).

[8] I owe these remarks to Dr Osmo Pekonen of the University of Helsinki.

Meanwhile Lönnrot's *Kalevala* became, as intended, the Finnish national epic, the date of its publication still a national holiday, and it could be argued that Finland owes its current existence as an autonomous and prosperous state to it and to the national spirit it invigorated. Tolkien would unquestionably have wished to do the same for England, a nation whose ancient traditions, he felt, had been even more thoroughly suppressed than those of Macpherson's Scottish Highlands, and whose autonomy had (and has) been subsumed into the United Kingdom of Great Britain and Northern Ireland, to which Tolkien felt little loyalty.[9] But he had nothing like the resources that Lönnrot had to work with, or even what was available to Snorri: England had no living native mythical tradition, nor any poetic corpus based on it. Nevertheless, the *Prose Edda* and the *Kalevala* had a quality he admired, and which he perhaps thought they shared, in spite of the very different circumstances of composition outlined above. In what follows I try to set out what this quality was and how it was created, so that the rest of this essay becomes in large part a critique of *Edda* and *Kalevala*, and of their reception, seeking however always to identify the elusive 'flavour of rootedness' which Tolkien himself detected.

Norse Tradition and the Prose Edda

The exact chronology of the rediscovery of Snorri's *Prose Edda* remains obscure. Unlike *Beowulf*, for instance, it does not seem to have burst upon the learned world all at once, though there was a Latin edition by the Danish scholar Resenius (Peder Resen) as early as 1665, which, however, had limited circulation. Rather, as with the *Elder Edda*, knowledge of it seems to have leaked out in selections and paraphrases. An important step was Paul Henri Mallet's *Introduction à l'histoire de Danemarck*, with its second volume of translations, *Monumens* [sic] *de la mythologie et de la poésie des Celtes et particulièrement des anciens Scandinaves* (1755-56), translated

---

[9] See, for instance, Tolkien, *Letters*, 131, 144, 180.

into English by Thomas Percy (discoverer of the Percy Manuscript, another manuscript whose existence was long in doubt) as *Northern Antiquities* (1770). These and a succession of other mythological guides and handbooks made familiar to the world stories which are now known worldwide, if only at comic book level: the Chaining of Fenris-Wolf, Thor's trip to Útgartha-Loki, Thor's fishing for the Midgard-Serpent, and a score of others. By Tolkien's time there was a definitive edition by Finnur Jónsson, and English translations by Sir George Dasent (1842) and A.G. Brodeur (1916). A long selection from the *Prose Edda* forms the first item in E.V. Gordon's *Introduction to Old Norse* (1927), compiled at a time when Tolkien and Gordon were close collaborators.

The very familiarity of these stories has, however, overlaid the shock-effect which they had on the literary world when they first began to appear in print. They introduced an entirely new mythology, which had been completely forgotten everywhere except in remote outposts like Iceland. To someone brought up on classical epic and Bible story, they furthermore introduced an entirely new worldview, or mind-set, or as Tolkien might say, literary 'flavour.' And yet, on further inspection, English readers might start to think it was not so absolutely unfamiliar after all. Snorri's readiness to treat themes of the utmost importance, such as Old Age and Death and the End of the World, with a pervasive humor, while strange to and indeed forbidden by classical literary theory, was just what Shakespeare had been accused of by generations of French critics. Snorri's Old Icelandic still translates very easily into colloquial modern English. Perhaps the worldview had not gone away after all; it had just been dropped by the literary caste, the media people, the teachers and arbiters of literature – people who, as Tolkien would readily have agreed, had consistently rejected any form of native popular culture, whether *Grimm's Fairy-Tales* or Shakespeare or Tolkien himself, coming around only slowly and reluctantly in a whole series of rearguard actions. What, we should ask, were the surprising or shocking novelties in Snorri's matter and method?

One is his remarkable laconicism, a habitual use of understatement. When the Æsir bind Fenris-Wolf, he refuses to allow them to put the fetter Gleipnir on him, fearing treachery, unless the god Tyr will stand with his hand in Fenris's mouth as a guarantee of good faith. Once it is clear that Fenris cannot escape from the fetter, "[All the gods] laughed, except for Tyr. He lost his hand" (Faulkes 1987: 29). A little earlier, as Snorri runs through a list of the Norse pantheon, he says of Tyr, "he is one-handed and he is not considered a promoter of settlements between people" (Faulkes 1987: 25). This latter statement means that he is the god of war, and stirs up fighting. But it is characteristic of all Norse tradition to play down demonstrations of emotion, and to speak in terms of opposites. The trait remains perfectly familiar: in some English social groups, including Tolkien's, 'not bad at all' is about the highest compliment that can be paid. Tolkien certainly aimed at similar effects from the start of his writing career. See, for instance, his description of the Valar in *The Silmarillion*, which clearly imitates Snorri's account of the pantheon, and of Tulkas in particular, the Vala equivalent of Tyr: "He has little heed for the past and the future, and is of no avail as a counsellor" (*Silm*, 29). More strikingly, one might note the end of chapter 2 of the 'Quenta Silmarillion,' when Yavanna warns Aulë that trees now have protectors (the Ents): "Now let thy children beware! For there shall walk a power in the forests whose wrath they will arouse at their peril." Aulë says only, "Nonetheless they will have need of wood," and goes on with his work (*Silm*, 46). The remark prefigures millennia of conflict leading all the way to Gimli and Treebeard, but no more is said. No more needs to be.

Scenes like this furthermore indicate another element in the *Prose Edda*, and in Norse tradition as a whole, which was early identified as 'fatalism.' It was rather a strange sort of fatalism, for it was anything but resigned. Norse heroes appeared able to be quite sure they were doomed, while making violent efforts to avert that doom. In Snorri, even the gods are constantly under threat, from the giants, from old age (when the giant

Thiassi makes off with Idun's apples of immortality), from death (for Balder is killed and sent down to Hel and Odin, his father, has no power to rescue him). They are also well aware that at Ragnarök they will be defeated and killed by their enemies, though once again this does not stop Odin from continually recruiting warriors to join his Einheriar, live in Valhalla, and fight with him in the Last Battle. But while this incompatibility may be illogical, it is also both attractive and, in a way, realistic. 'Fate often spares the man who is not doomed, as long as his courage holds,' says Beowulf at one point (lines 572-3), and while this makes no sense, viewed analytically – could Fate spare the man who *was* doomed? aren't fate and doom much the same thing? – it remains an excellent guide for future conduct. Keep your spirits up, as no one can be sure what is fated: this is advice often given by Gandalf. Tolkien clearly pondered extensively on the whole question of fate, doom, chance, and luck, and the relation of these powers to individual free will, building his answers into the whole structure of *The Lord of the Rings*, and especially into the repeated expansions of the Tale of Túrin.[10] In doing so he was trying, I believe, to retain the feel or 'flavour' of Norse myth, while hinting at the happier ending of Christian myth behind it.

His reason for doing this, I would further suggest, was a wish to retain the heroic quality of his Norse sources. Tolkien made his thoughts on this clear in his famous lecture on *Beowulf*, where he argued, for one thing, that while ancient English mythology had all but totally vanished, it could not have been very different from Norse – and here he meant predominantly the two *Eddas*, prose and poetic. The striking fact about this shared mythology, he said, was its "theory of courage [...] the great contribution of Northern literature" ('Monsters,' in *Essays*, 20). By the 'theory of courage' he did not mean that in Norse mythology courage was admired, as it is in all human traditions. He meant that Norse mythology was unique in confronting certain and ultimate defeat, but regarding that neither as an excuse for

---

[10] See Shippey (2000a: 143-47) and (2000a: 249-54) respectively.

giving up, nor as a logical refutation of one's position. Evil will triumph, but it will still be evil; and those killed resisting it, even those killed beyond death like Odin's Einheriar, will still be in the right. This is not a consolation, but it is a fact. Tolkien did not go on to say this, but one might add that it is then not so surprising that the pagan English were converted so readily to a religion of hope; and Tolkien did say that as soon as that conversion took place, the old stories, not yet forgotten, were "viewed in a different perspective" (*Essays*, 21). That is the perspective of the *Beowulf*-poet, writing about pagan times and heroes but a Christian himself; of Snorri Sturluson, in exactly the same position but with both a stronger tradition of paganism and a longer tradition of Christianity; and of Tolkien as well, writing in a society with a far longer history of Christianity, but also one under renewed and different threat.

A last point about the 'flavour' of Snorri and of Norse tradition as a whole, and an especially surprising one in view of what has just been said, is its endemic good humor. The world of Snorri's myth is the exact opposite of a *divina commedia*, but Snorri writes habitually as a comedian. Thor repeatedly loses his dignity in his encounters with the giant Skrymir, striking him three times while he is asleep with the lightning-hammer Miöllnir, only for Skrymir to wake each time and wonder vaguely if something has fallen on his head – a leaf? an acorn? bird-droppings? "Thor backed away quickly and replied that he had just woken up" (Faulkes 1987: 40). There is grotesque farce in the tests of strength which Útgartha-Loki sets for Thor, draining a horn (connected to the sea), picking up a cat (it is really the Midgard-Serpent), wrestling an old crone (she is Elli, Old Age), and marked ribaldry in Loki's defeat of the giant contracted to build Ásgarth – he entices away the giant's draught-stallion in the shape of a mare. The gods laugh as Tyr loses his hand, and think it good sport to throw and shoot at Balder, confident in his invulnerability. Strong and fierce amusement runs through the *Poetic Edda* as well, as in the mythological poem *Þrymskviða*, which E. V. Gordon selected for his Norse reader – it tells a story not included in Snorri, of how a giant stole Thor's hammer to ransom it for Freyja, only for Thor to disguise himself as Freyja and turn up for the wedding. It is normal for saga heroes to die with a wisecrack of some kind. The last line of one of the first Norse poems to be translated, the *Krakumál* or 'Death-Song of Ragnar Lodbrog,' is *hlæjandi skal ek deyja*, 'I shall die laughing.' All this was quite seriously offensive to many educated tastes as Norse became familiar. Not only was laughter itself thought to be vulgar by many eighteenth-century ladies and gentlemen (Ragnar's last line was habitually toned down in translation to a mere smile, see Shippey 1999a), there was a strong feeling against mixing laughter with anything serious. It contradicted notions of stylistic decorum. Tragedy was high-style and comedy was low-style, and the two should be carefully separated (his failure to do this was one of the French arguments against Shakespeare, while later on Dickens remained in the critical wilderness for generations because comedy could not be taken seriously). But Norse writers seemed to have no feeling for decorousness. As mentioned above, Snorri was ready to combine themes of the utmost importance with a pervasive humor. And this too is a part of the heroic temperament and the 'theory of courage.' Indeed, everything that has been said here about Snorri can be seen as part of a coherent philosophy. The laconicism connects to the fatalism: If things are fated, there is no point in talking about them. Both connect further with the cult of 'naked will': The hero cannot be defeated, even by fate, if he refuses to give up or yield, while he shows the self-control that is most admired by refusing to speak, or groan, like Gunnar in the snakepit and his brother Högni having his heart cut out. Laughter like Ragnar's, also in a snakepit, shows the ability to rise above mere personal circumstance.

These qualities together not only form a coherent philosophy, they also mark a quite distinctive literary style – one which, I repeat, had been lost to the world. And this perhaps gives us one answer to Tolkien's question about 'rootedness.' What distinguishes rooted works like Snorri's *Prose Edda* is the fact that even what may seem accidental or minor qualities, like the pervasive humor, are there because they fit an entire worldview, and the mythology it generated, unless, indeed, the mythology generated the worldview. In a 'rooted' work one may not be able to separate one from the other, or from the story – so that the story may continue to embody aspects of a mythology and a worldview long dead, and so (Tolkien's words) compensate for "the inevitable flaws and imperfect adjustments that must appear, when plots, motives, symbols, are rehandled and pressed into the service of the changed minds of a later age" ('Sir Gawain,' in *Essays*, 72).

Indeed, those rehandlings themselves may possess their own charm, just because they demonstrate a disjunction between author and material, and so open up the sense – Tolkien uses the word 'flavour' once again – of "a great abyss of time" ('OFS,' *Essays*, 128). A final point to remember about Snorri's *Prose Edda* is that it is basically an epitome. Snorri is not telling stories, but summarizing them for the benefit of apprentice poets, secure in the knowledge that they exist already, often as well-known poems (even if we no longer happen to have them). What is *The Silmarillion* but an epitome? As Christopher Tolkien says, "My father came to conceive *The Silmarillion* as a compilation, a compendious narrative, made long afterwards from sources of great diversity (poems, and annals, and oral tales) that had survived in agelong tradition" (*Silm*, 8). And he goes on to say that to some extent that was how it was actually written, with prose tales from *The Book of Lost Tales* turned into extensive poems in *The Lays of Beleriand*, and then epitomized in their turn in various versions, including annals in different languages (see Noad 2000). Perhaps another characteristic of a 'rooted' work is simply that it can survive as an epitome, for (to quote Tolkien once again) "myth is alive at once and in all its parts" ('Monsters,' *Essays*, 15). The air of summarizing much more extensive knowledge is another feature of Snorri's work which Tolkien spent great effort in trying to recapture, in many versions of *The Silmarillion*, and which was to bear fruit in the continual allusiveness of *The Lord of the Rings*.

Lönnrot and the Kalevala

Tolkien's interest in the *Kalevala* is even better recorded than his interest in Snorri's *Edda*. He had discovered W. F. Kirby's translation of it before he left school in 1911, and tried to read it in the original Finnish the following year. In 1914 he began work on 'The Story of Kullervo,' a retelling of one of the *Kalevala*'s main sections. Though never completed, this was to become the germ of the story of Túrin, one of the Great Tales, as Tolkien called them (Carpenter 2000: 57, 66-67, 81, 104). Nevertheless, though Tolkien's interest is well-known, the reasons for it have not been discussed. They deserve consideration, especially as, with Tolkien's normal finickiness over what was authentic and what was not, he might have been expected to show a certain skepticism about its origin. Tolkien was very ready to dismiss other nineteenth-century rewritings of mythical stories, such as Wagner's *Ring*, as Ossian-style fakes. What did he see, and value, in the *Kalevala*?

One very evident answer is its pathos. Old Norse literature is notoriously the most hard-hearted in Europe, its very emblem the heart which is cut from Högni and brought to his brother Gunnar. Gunnar looks at it approvingly – his captors have earlier tried to fool him by bringing a base-born heart and passing it off as Högni's – and recognizes it by its lack of (literal) trepidation:

> "Here I have the heart of Högni the brave,
> Not like the heart of Hjalli the coward.
> Little does it tremble as it lies on the plate.
> It trembled much the less when it lay in his breast."[11]

There is no room for sentiment in the heroic tradition.

---

[11] My translation of lines 2-5 of stanza 25 of the Eddic *Atlakviða* (Neckel and Kuhn 1962: 244).

By contrast the *Kalevala* is strongly marked by pathos, and often by sympathy for the fate of females – the girl Aino who drowns herself rather than face an unwanted marriage, the Maiden of Pohja weeping as she prepares to leave home for an unknown husband, a series of anxious mothers wondering whether their sons will return from expeditions, repeated allusions to wife-beating and rape. Children also come into the story. And here anyone aware of the facts of Tolkien's life would find it hard not to see a personal motive in his selection of 'The Tale of Kullervo.' This, *runos* 31-36 in Lönnrot's extended version of 1849, is the most easily detachable of the ten or eleven interlinked sections which make up the *Kalevala*. It tells the story of two brothers, who fall out over fishing and grazing. One of them, Untamo, then wipes out the whole family of the other, Kalervo:

> Left of Kalervo's folk only
> But one girl, and she was pregnant.
> (Kirby 1907: II, 40)

She gives birth to Kullervo, who is born in slavery. Untamo repeatedly tries to murder him without success, but eventually sells him cheaply to Ilmarinen the smith, in exchange for a few worn-out tools, "For a slave completely worthless." Kullervo is then ill-treated by Ilmarinen's wife, once the Maiden of Pohja. She bakes a stone into his bread, on which his knife-point breaks. Kullervo takes this especially hard:

> "Save this knife I'd no companion,
> Nought to love except this iron,
> 'Twas an heirloom from my father."
> (Kirby 1907: II, 94)

He revenges himself by sending bears and wolves to kill the wife, after which he escapes into the forest. There – very strangely – he is told that his family are in fact still alive, is reunited with them, but once again spoils matters by his violence and clumsiness, which terminate in a (euphemistically described) rape of his unrecognized sister, and her suicide. Kullervo also considers suicide, is dissuaded by his mother, and takes delayed vengeance on Untamo instead. He returns to find his family once more dead, and eventually kills himself with his own sword on the spot where he met his sister. This last motif, and the motif of the sword replying to him when he asks whether it will kill him, were to remain the ending of Tolkien's 'Tale of Túrin' through all revisions.

The faults of this story as a narrative are easy to see, and in some ways Tolkien set himself to cure them, but parts of it must surely have struck a particular chord with him. Tolkien's father had died when he was four, his mother when he was twelve, after which, estranged from other members of his family, he lived in a succession of lodgings, student rooms, camps, barracks, and bedsitters, literally without a home of his own for the following twenty years (Carpenter 2000: 25-114 *passim*). Kullervo's laments, then, could easily be applied to himself (indeed, they fit Tolkien rather better than Kullervo):

> "I was small, and lost my father,
> I was weak, and lost my mother,
> Dead is father, dead is mother,
> All my mighty race has perished."
> (Kirby 1907: II, 102)

Tolkien must also have felt sympathy with the moral pronounced at the end by 'the aged Väinämöinen':

> "Never, people, in the future,
> Rear a child in crooked fashion,
> Rocking them in stupid fashion,
> Soothing them to sleep like strangers."
> (Kirby 1907: II, 125)

Children reared in this way will not get over it.

Tolkien, of course, did very sucessfully get over the traumas of his childhood and the further traumas of his young maturity, but the pathos of the *Kalevala* may have done more than catch his eye and his sympathies. The whole structure of the *Kalevala* is, in a way, a sad one. The fifty *runos* of the 1849 version are divided, as has been said, into about ten loosely-linked sections of two to eight *runos* each, with several connecting themes and characters running through them, but for all the exuberance of the narrative, the thematic trend is downward. The *sampo*, mystic source of prosperity, is forged by Ilmarinen as payment for the Maiden of Pohja; but the Maiden is killed by Kullervo, and when Ilmarinen and his companions recapture the *sampo*, it is broken in the resultant fighting. Väinämöinen regards this as a benefit, for the fragments of the *sampo* will remain in Finland, and beats off repeated revenge attacks from Pohja; even the theft of the Sun and Moon is cancelled out by the relighting of a new Sun and Moon with magic fire. Nevertheless, Väinämöinen is superseded in the end, and sails away to an unknown country, leaving behind only his harp and his songs as a consolation. The story opens with Väinämöinen trying to find a bride, but he is never successful. Ilmarinen also fails, first in his attempt to make a bride out of gold, then in his attempt to replace his wife by her sister. Lemminkainen too, despite his many exploits and adventures, fails to carry off a bride, while his marriage with Kyllikki founders. There are repeated scenes thoughout the *Kalevala* of heroes returning to discover their homes laid waste, as there are of suicide, and of aged mothers weeping. All round, one can see why Longfellow, attempting to produce an American national epic (difficult for a country with no Middle Ages), should have picked *Kalevala* as a model for his epic of dispossession and replacement, *The Song of Hiawatha*. *Kalevala* ends, finally, with an apology from the imagined poet, which repeats the grief of Kullervo, "I was small when died my mother," but also presents the poet as an outcast, abused and unwanted:

> Even now do many people,
> Many people I encounter
> Speak to me in angry accents,
> Rudest speeches hurl against me,

>   Curses on my tongue they shower.
>   (Kirby 1907: II, 274)

Tolkien perhaps remembered this self-characterization many years later, when he came to write the poem 'Looney,' rewritten in *The Adventures of Tom Bombadil* as 'The Sea-Bell,' where it is also alternatively titled 'Frodos Dreme.' The self-images scattered through his work show a persistent streak of alienation – Niggle, Ramer, Smith of Wootton Major[12] – while the quietly sad ending of *The Lord of the Rings* echoes the departure into exile of Väinämöinen. But the example of the *Kalevala* may further have allowed Tolkien to see that a national epic need not be triumphalist (though all too often they are). It can be about loss as well as gain, loss of the *sampo*, loss of the silmarils;[13] it can be about partial success, with Sun and Moon replacing the Light of the Trees in *The Silmarillion* rather as the new Sun and Moon replace the old ones in *Kalevala*; it can confront an ultimate failure.

This last point may have grown to be especially important to Tolkien. In his youth he remarked that "[t]hese mythological ballads are full of that very primitive undergrowth that the literature of Europe has been steadily cutting and reducing for many centuries":[14] the word 'primitive' is surprising, for the *Kalevala*, as said above, is as it stands a work of the nineteenth century, and by Tolkien's standards modern literature. But one of its remarkable features, for a poem from a country nominally Christian for centuries, is the absence from it of any obvious Christianity. Some characters wear crosses, and there is a supreme deity called Ukko, who, however, rarely intervenes. W.F. Kirby, the translator, wrote (1907: I, ix), "The religion of the poem is peculiar; it is a Shamanistic animism, overlaid with

---

[12] Niggle is the main character of 'Leaf by Niggle,' as Smith is of *Smith of Wootton Major*. Ramer is one of the members of the Notion Club, see 'The Notion Club Papers' (in Tolkien, *Sauron*, 145-327), and the discussion of that work in Shippey (2000a: 287-88).

[13] See further Senior 2000 on this theme.

[14] The only known source for this remark is Carpenter's (2000: 67) citation from unpublished papers.

Christianity," but he may have been writing defensively: the overlay is barely visible. Once again this may have given Tolkien a hint, a glimpse of a genuinely pre-Christian atmosphere – one not exactly of gloom, for the heroes and heroines of *Kalevala* are too boisterous and resourceful for that, but one which accepts ultimate defeat and finds victory only in song, in recreation. This is very much the atmosphere of Middle-earth, both in *The Lord of the Rings* and *The Silmarillion*. Despite all the efforts and successes of the characters, everything is slowly winding down, being lost, heading for extinction. That is the best that human beings or Hobbits can do, without the Divine Redemption from outside of which characters in Middle-earth have only the faintest of inklings.

Conclusion

If Snorri's *Edda* is an epitome, the *Kalevala* is an edited anthology, and its collective origins are betrayed at every turn. Even in paraphrase, as given above, the story of Kullervo does not make good sense. His family is wiped out in *runo* 31, and it is very clear that he is a posthumous child, but they are alive again in *runo* 34, without explanation for the discrepancy. It makes good sense for Kullervo to be surly and violent while carrying out the tasks set for him by his hostile uncle Untamo, but he repeats this behavior when working for his father, against whom he has no apparent grudge. Kullervo's incestuous rape of his sister can only be excused, even within the morality of the poem, by not knowing who she is; but in order for him not to know that, she too has to be separated from her family, in a repeat of the 'lost child' motif. Any German *Liedertheorist* of the nineteenth century would have had no hesitation in pointing out the doublings and contradictions, and deducing the multiple authorship which we know at bottom to be the case. Retelling the story as that of Túrin, Tolkien explained away all such problems with great care, keeping the major scenes of bereavement, disobedience, rescue, heartbreak, and suicide, but embedding them in a quite different framing narrative. This too gives his work a kind of 'rootedness.' One can see Tolkien doing his best to compensate for (repeating his own words) those "inevitable flaws and imperfect adjustments that must appear, when plots, motives, symbols, are rehandled [in this case by Lönnrot] and pressed into the service of the changed minds of a later age" [both Lönnrot and Tolkien]. Even flaws and discrepancies can serve a purpose.

More generally, though, what Snorri's *Edda* and the *Kalevala* did for Tolkien was to give him two quite different but complementary views of a pre-Christian age, both the product of Christians looking back at but still in touch with pagan imaginations. The fierce and uncompromising Norse mythology gave Tolkien Gandalf, the divine messenger with a short temper, heavy hand, and strong if unpredictable sense of humor. The romantic and mysterious Finnish mythology contributed a sense of grief and loss, together with a powerful foundation in natural beauty and love of the native land. Snorri and Lönnrot must certainly have been among Tolkien's major role models, along with the anonymous poets of *Beowulf* and *Sir Gawain*, the Worcestershire poet Layamon, and the great philologists Grimm and Grundtvig. As for what gives the 'flavour,' the 'atmosphere,' the 'virtue' of 'rootedness,' several suggestions have already been made in this essay, but surely the most vital one must be the sense of many minds, not just one, pouring their thought and emotion into the greatest issues of human life, and death. Ramer, one of the characters in 'The Notion Club Papers,' already mentioned as a particularly likely representative of Tolkien himself, tells his colleagues:

> "I don't think you realize, I don't think any of us realize, the force, the daimonic force that the great myths and legends have. From the profundity of the emotions and perceptions that begot them, and from the multiplication of them in many minds – and each mind, mark you, an engine of obscure but unmeasured energy."
> (*Sauron*, 228)

Mythologies, like languages, can never be entirely individual productions, not even when (as with Quenya and Sindarin and the myths of Middle-earth) we know quite certainly who invented them, for they are always built on a foundation, in Tolkien's case a foundation of deep philological knowledge. But he would never have done the work to acquire that knowledge if he had not first been stirred by the appeal of works like these, the appeal of the pagan.[15]

---

[15] For further views on this theme, see essays by Burns, Drout, Flieger, all in the volume edited by Chance 2004; see also Burns 2005 and Hutton 2007 (forthcoming).

Tolkien and the West Midlands: The Roots of Romance[1]

What we are doing today is strange, or at least unexpected. I believe there is a case for saying that the Old Edwardian whose centenary we are celebrating, John Ronald Reuel Tolkien (1892-1973), had more single-handed influence on the literary world than anyone else this century. You could dispute this claim in several ways:

- you could say that what he did was not literature. (He would have agreed with this, very probably adding 'Thank God!' For Tolkien's attitude to the word 'literature,' see the comments in the first few pages of any edition of my *The Road to Middle-earth*.)
- or you could say that however great his influence, it has been absolutely deplorable. (Many of my colleagues in the field of 'literature' would certainly say that, and I have seen more than one of them make themselves quite sick with bad temper just thinking about it.)
- or you could try saying that his influence, however great, was not exactly single-handed. (I have suggested this myself, in my 'Introduction' to the World's Classics edition of William Morris's *The Wood beyond the World* (1980: xvii-xviii), but the suggestion is no more than a slight footnote or correction to an otherwise clear picture.)

---

[1] This piece was first given as a lecture at King Edward's School, Birmingham (which both Tolkien and I attended, respectively 1900-11 and 1951-60) on October 22nd, 1992. It was then printed in *Lembas Extra* (1995), 5-22. My thanks are due to the *Lembas* editors for permission to reprint, and further to Mr A.J.E. ('Tony') Trott, for the initial invitation to speak, and for far more than I can indicate here in terms of initial inspiration. I have, however, made major changes to the piece for this volume, cutting out as much repetition as possible, and inserting a good deal of material, now deeply academically unfashionable, on the provincial literary culture of the early West Midlands.

The underlying facts to support my statement at the start are these. In the first place, according to Tolkien's publishers, *The Hobbit* (1937) is the most successful children's book there has ever been. Meanwhile *The Lord of the Rings* (1954-5) reintroduced to the literary world a genre which had been thought to be dead beyond revival: namely, romance; and at the same time created a new literary mode of expression: namely, the fantasy trilogy. How many of these were there before Tolkien? As far as I know, none. How many are there now? Any large bookstore will supply sets or units of at least a dozen, with many more out of stock or out of print. All round, it is said that some five per cent of literary production these days – several hundred volumes a year – is fantasy, almost all of it is Tolkien-derived, and some of it quite slavishly or fanatically so, as one can see from the titles alone. And in addition there's the whole 'Dungeons and Dragons' phenomenon, now extended into the field of electronic games, much of it very clearly Tolkien-derived in its personnel ('orcs' are now standard, but this is a word introduced to modern English by Tolkien alone).

That's the situation now. For a sense of how Tolkien changed the literary world, think how things looked when, in 1937, Tolkien's publisher Sir Stanley Unwin asked for a sequel to *The Hobbit*, and Tolkien sent him the unfinished *Silmarillion*. It must have looked like one of the least likely and least possibly publishable works ever received. We do in fact know now what the publisher's reader Edward Crankshaw said, for it has been printed in *The Lays of Beleriand*, 365. Crankshaw wrote as follows, with my comments inserted:

> I am rather at a loss to know what to do with this – it doesn't even seem to have an author! – or any indication of sources, etc. Publishers' readers are rightly supposed to be of moderate intelligence and reading; but I confess my reading has not extended to early Celtic Gestes, [what Tolkien sent in was neither Celtic nor a Geste], and I don't even know whether this is a famous Geste or not [it wasn't], or, for that matter, whether it is

> authentic. I presume it is [it wasn't], as the unspecified versifier has included some pages of a prose-version (which is far superior).

The reader was baffled. But who can blame him? Tolkien had to change the literary world and its expectations even to get a reading.

I have said Tolkien was the most influential and successful author of the century: and I now ask, what were the roots of that success? Where were the roots of romance? And I am at least quite sure that I know where they weren't. This came to me some 22 years ago, in 1970, when I addressed a Tolkien conference at the Cannon Hill Centre on Pershore Road.[2] It was a one-day event. I was down to talk about 'Tolkien and Philology.' I was the last speaker of the day. And I went on after several speakers had discussed Tolkien and philosophy, Tolkien and sociology, Tolkien and Jungian psychology (etc.). By the day's end the prospect of one more -ology had the audience heading for the rear exit in droves. Fortunately it was 1970, I had been a lecturer at Birmingham University during the student 'troubles' of that era, and I was well used to dealing with mutinous audiences. I got up to the front of the platform, told them to sit back down again, and told them philology was different from other -ologies, because it was based on fact; and I proposed to tell them the facts they needed to know, both about Tolkien's words and Tolkien's world. This approach went down particularly well, Tolkien's secretary was in the audience, and passed on my typescript to him, which he read and liked enough to send me an encouraging letter. But that's the gist of what I have to say today: the roots of Tolkien's romance are in philology. And philology takes in both literature and language, as well as illuminating corners of history for which we have no other evidence.

My view remained for a long time a minority one, though people have come round to it more recently, and Tolkien criticism has often

---

[2] A mile or so from King Edward's School, as the 1992 audience knew perfectly well.

continued to play around with subjects more congenial to the modern academic mind. But I will waste no time on that. Let us consider instead where the roots of romance actually *were*. This audience will have no trouble in accepting the thesis that they were in the West Midlands. But let us consider first where the West Midlands are – what are the natural, historical, linguistic, and literary boundaries of the region?

Tolkien was pretty clear about where he thought its and his heartland were. In one letter he declared that in spite of his German-derived name, "I am in fact far more of a Suffield (a family deriving from Evesham in Worcestershire)," and in another, "I am a Suffield by tastes, talents, and upringing, and any corner of that county [Worcestershire] (however fair or squalid) is in an indefinable way "home" to me, as no other part of the world is" (*Letters*, 218, 54). In yet another letter written to W.H. Auden he also declared, "I am a West-midlander by blood (and took to early west-midland Middle English as a known tongue as soon as I set eyes on it," as if language were something genetically passed on; he extended the claim to "Anglo-Saxon […] and alliterative verse" in one of the letters already cited (*Letters*, 213, 218). To him, then, and passing over the idea about linguistic genetics, Worcestershire was above all 'home.' But it is well-known that the most idyllic period of Tolkien's life, which he never forgot, was when he lived at Sarehole, now in King's Heath, which as we all know is in Warwickshire. Does this not contradict what I have just said? No – and here I am indebted to the researches of David Bratman (see Bratman 1999) – because the county boundary was changed after Tolkien left Sarehole. It was in Worcestershire when he lived there, and is in Warwickshire now.[3]

---

[3] One odd survival can be seen on the wall of the old drill hall, now expensive apartments, in Mossfield Rd., King's Heath, now in Warwickshire. This commemorates its use by the *Comitatus Wigornensis*. *Comitatus* is the word now used by the learned to indicate the Anglo-Saxon *heorðwerod*, or 'hearth-troop,' a king's or a lord's personal bodyguard. *Wigornensis* means 'of Worcester,' and the whole phrase is a learned way of saying 'the Worcestershire Yeomanry.' With all proper respect to the Lancashire Fusiliers, if Tolkien had been able to choose, I am sure he would have opted to serve with the *comitatus* of Worcestershire.

But it is probably fair to say that Tolkien recognized Warwickshire as also part of the heartland, of the West Midlands. Indeed I would go on and say that for Tolkien the West Midlands consisted of the three shires which meet in Birmingham, Worcestershire, Warwickshire and Staffordshire; with in addition the English shires to the west of them, Herefordshire and Shropshire. These five shires, it could be argued, form a cultural unit with deep roots in history.

David Bratman, in the piece mentioned, has suggested however that we ought to count nine shires, adding to the ones I have listed Gloucestershire, Oxfordshire, Cheshire, and (south) Lancashire. These, he argues, are the counties recognized as 'Mercian' by the Anglo-Saxon kings of Wessex. Mercia was, under its most famous and powerful king, Offa, who had his capital at Tamworth (Staffs.) and tried to make Lichfield England's third archbishopric, much larger than that, taking in by my count some 20-odd counties, though only 16 or 17 by Dr. Bratman's. But the situation was much altered, and for good, by the Viking wars of the ninth through eleventh centuries, which separated 'Danish Mercia' from 'English Mercia,' and led to the latter being taken over by the last remaining native Anglo-Saxon dynasty, the kings of Wessex aforesaid. This meant that the counties of the North Midlands, north and east of Staffordshire, i.e. Derbyshire, Nottinghamshire, Leicestershire, Lincolnshire, came under Danish control as the 'Five Boroughs,'[4] with lasting effects on their dialects, to which Tolkien was especially sensitive. Further north than that and one passes into Northumbria, never part of Mercia: those are the 'Six Northern Counties,' Cumberland, Westmoreland and Lancashire west of the Pennines, Northumberland, Durham and Yorkshire east of them. Tolkien was again very aware of the peculiarities of far-northern dialect.[5]

---

[4] The fifth borough was Stamford, which did not become the center of a shire.

[5] As one can see from his appreciative 'Foreword' to Haigh 1928, and his long article on northernisms in Chaucer, 'Chaucer as a Philologist: The Reeve's Tale,' *Transactions of the Philological Society* (1934), 1-70.

But what about the counties which border the five I have identified as 'heartland'? Every English county of course has its own history and deserves individual attention, but I would say first that while Tolkien lived in Oxford most of his life, he still felt a difference between it and Warwick to the north-west. Oxfordshire is closely connected with Buckinghamshire – the two counties share a regiment, which used not to be usual in England, the 'Ox and Bucks Light Infantry' – and this seems to be the area of 'the Little Kingdom' in *Farmer Giles of Ham*, which eventually declares its independence from 'the Middle Kingdom,' which is pretty clearly Mercia, with a capital left unidentified but suspiciously close to Tamworth (see Shippey 2003a: 97-8 for some calculations). Tom Bombadil, meanwhile, was identified by Tolkien as representing the "spirit of the (vanishing) Oxford and Berkshire countryside" (*Letters*, 26). Ox, Bucks and Berks – Tolkien liked them, but they were their own place. Briefly, I think the same is true of Gloucestershire (and vanished Winchcombeshire). And as for Cheshire, there is a case to be made for it as part of the West Midlands, but it was for a long time a peculiar county, one of the two medieval English Counties Palatine (where the inhabitants enjoyed peculiar tax privileges); and even by English standards there was serious neighbourly antipathy between Cheshire and Staffordshire, eventually decided at the Battle of Shrewsbury in 1403, where the two counties fought it out bitterly and determinedly, and Staffordshire rather unexpectedly won. So I would stick to my nominated five; and I would add – and here we get to 'the roots of romance,' as advertised – that arguably we are now looking at a collective literary and poetic tradition, now almost completely obscured, but to which Tolkien attached great importance. Briefly, if English literature had stuck to the traditions of the West Midlands, it would have done a great deal better than it has.

With what literary works would Tolkien have identified my five 'heartland' counties, and do they have anything in common? In answering this question, I should say here that the most interesting period to Tolkien, if only by default,[6] was the period of 'Middle English,' which I would define roughly as the period between the Battle of Hastings (1066) and the Battle of Flodden Field (1513). Both these battles were important historically, but it could also be said that each marked the end of a literary (and linguistic) era. What did Tolkien think about them? The answer here must inevitably be very potted, but in the first place Tolkien certainly thought Hastings was a disaster. It took England forever out of the Germanic world. It did so linguistically: Tolkien might not have gone so far as the author of *Gunnlaugs saga Ormstunga* (The Saga of Gunnlaug Wormtongue), who declared (in Icelandic) "Ein var þá tunga á Englandi sem í Noregi ok í Danmörku. En þá skiptust tungur í Englandi, er Vilhjalmr bastarðr vann England" ['there was then one tongue in England as in Norway and in Denmark. But then the tongues in England shifted when William the Conqueror – note that 'Conqueror' is not quite an exact translation of the Icelandic – won England'] (Foote and Quirk 1974: 33, my translation); but he could not fail to note the major grammatical and lexical changes which have made Old English to us so much of a foreign tongue. The Conquest also took England out of the Germanic world in a literary way: no more *Beowulf*, no more poems about monsters, just dream-poems, love visions, rhymed verse and romantic nightingales. But it also meant that the English language was downgraded to subordinate status, so that no matter what people actually said, all over England they stopped writing English and turned instead to French and Latin. I will comment more on the literary associations of Flodden Field below, but it could be said that this was the last thoroughly medieval battle fought on English soil, fought out by foot-soldiers in armour with edged weapons; and at very much the same time

---

[6] He would no doubt have been even more interested in West Midlands literature from the Old English or Anglo-Saxon period, but hardly any survives. Even works which may originally have been Mercian – and Worcester is known to have been an important center for writing – are nearly always preserved in Late West Saxon. It was once thought, erroneously, that *Beowulf* might have had a connection with Lichfield (Staffs.), but Tolkien wisely chose never to remark on it.

Middle English turned into early Modern English, with linguistic standardization further reinforced by the beginnings of print culture.

In between, there was no standard English, only dialects; and English furthermore, for most of the period and over most of the country, was downgraded to subordinate status, so that no matter what people actually *spoke*, all over England they stopped *writing* English and turned instead to French and Latin. But not quite all over England. Tolkien's first major philological discovery was his demonstration in 1929 that two manuscripts of Middle English *in different handwriting* were nevertheless written in identical English, down to spelling, and even more remarkable, down to tiny points of grammar – tiny points not identical with Old English (and so not just copied) but rigorously developed from it. What did this mean historically? Well, people do not spell the same way by accident. They have to be taught. So even in the early Middle Ages *someone* was teaching English people how to write English, in a real school. Or to put it Tolkien's way, my comments again inserted:

> There is an English older than Dan Michel's and richer, as regular in spelling as Orm's [these are two other relatively consistent writers of Middle English] but less queer; one that has preserved something of its former cultivation [i.e. before the Norman Conquest]. It is not a language long relegated to the 'uplands' struggling once more for expression in apologetic emulation of its betters [i.e. French and Latin] or out of compassion for the lewd, but rather one that has never fallen back into 'lewdness,' and has contrived in troublous times to maintain the air of a gentleman, if a country gentleman. It has traditions and some acquaintance with the pen, but it is also in close touch with a good living speech – a soil somewhere in England. ('AW,' 106)

Where in England was the soil and where did these two manuscripts come from? The answer is almost certainly Wigmore Abbey in Herefordshire.

According to more exact theory (see Dobson 1976) the *Ancrene Wisse* itself was written for three ladies living in the Deerfold, at map reference 395685. But I will not pursue dialect and manuscript studies further. I will just say that the striking things about Herefordshire in the Middle English period were:

- it preserved Old English literary and linguistic tradition
- it was the forgotten shire; the last of Old England; what England ought (without the Conquest) to have been
- and if you were to try to locate the hobbits' forgotten Shire on the map, you would do well to think of it as Herefordshire (and its neighbours) or, as medieval poets themselves put it, the little world 'between Wye and Wirral.'

However, as David Bratman points out (1999: 10), the hobbits' Shire is much bigger than any English county, and so should not be confined to just one. What did the West Midlands counties as a group contribute to English literature, and English continuity, in Tolkien's view? I will take them one at a time.

Herefordshire, to begin with, gave us not only the *Ancrene Wisse*, on which Tolkien worked for more than thirty years, but also its associated texts, known as 'the Katharine group.' They consist of the female saints' lives, *Seinte Katharine*, *Seinte Iuliene*, *Seinte Marherete*, the treatise on virginity called *Hali Meiðhad*, the allegorical work *Sawles Warde*, and some five other devotional works "which would provide highly suitable reading for women in religion, such as those for whom *Ancrene Wisse* was intended" (Shepherd 1959: xii). The *Ancrene Wisse* itself is a spiritual guide written, as said above, for three ladies who had chosen to live enclosed lives. What probably struck Tolkien most about these works – though I am sure he also sympathised with their content – was first, the clear, fluent, unembarrassed, efficient, idiomatic English in which they were written, something not matched in prose for at least another three hundred years;

and second, the traces they all bore of awareness of an older world of belief and superstition and even mythology, since irretrievably lost. Two of Tolkien's earliest academic works try to recover fragments of this 'lost world' from single words and textual cruxes in these texts.[7]

The same is true of another work closely contemporary with the *Ancrene Wisse* (both are early thirteenth century), the *Brut* written by Layamon, the priest of Areley Regis, also known as Areley Kings, or Areley Redstone, in Worcestershire on the west bank of the Severn just below Stourbridge, where the little river Gladden, or Gladdon (a name Tolkien remembered and used) flows into the Severn.[8] The *Brut* is in a way a derivative work (showing once again the subordinate status of English in this period), being very largely a translation of the *Roman de Brut*, or legendary history of Britain, written in Anglo-Norman by Wace, a native of Jersey. But just as in the *Ancrene Wisse*, things keep bobbing up, for Layamon is also still in touch with native English belief, and vocabulary, and narrative style: his *Brut* is in some ways much more like *Beowulf* than it is like Wace. From Layamon also Tolkien took the word 'dwimmerlaik,' though characteristically he reformulated it to be the word he thought Layamon meant, and perhaps the one he wrote – for words like this, preserving ancient belief, were especially likely to be misunderstood by later copyists.

Yet a third preserver of old habits, old words, and old styles of writing, is the enormous macaronic manuscript now labeled as Harley MS 2253. As a result of the researches of Carter Revard – who has found

---

[7] They are 'Some Contributions to Middle English Lexicography,' and 'The Devil's Coach-Horses,' in *Review of English Studies* 1 (1925): 210-15 and 331-6 respectively. The author of *Seinte Marherete* also explains at one point that the month of July *[on] ure ledene, Þet is ald englis, [is] efterliÞe inempnet*, 'is called Afterlithe in our language, that is old English.' The name is used also in the Shire calendar (*LotR*, 1079). Tolkien would also have appreciated the author's stubborn refusal to accept that 'Old English' was over.

[8] He comments on the meaning of the word itself in Old and modern English in *Letters*, 381.

literally scores of datable manuscripts in the same handwriting – we can now pin this down even more definitely than Layamon: the man who copied the manuscript, including many high-quality poems in Middle English of quite unusual type, worked in Ludlow, Shropshire, between 1314 and 1349, and may have written the manuscript for Sir Laurence Ludlow of Stokesay Castle, eight miles away (see Revard 2000). It should be noted that one of the other works he copied – and in this case perhaps wrote – is the *Roman de Fouke Fitz Warin*, a prose romance in Norman French which shows quite unusual awareness of the local geography and family feuds of the Herefordshire/Shropshire border.[9] But perhaps the most engaging aspect of Harley 2253, for Tolkien, was that so many of the poems in it are just plain funny. They are hobbit-poems, written for people like Farmer Maggot and Gaffer Gamgee, as also more upscale people like the Tooks and the Brandybucks: they complain about the government, poke fun at their friends, imagine what boys and girls say to each other, or simply freewheel imaginatively. One of the most striking is the poem 'The Man in the Moon,' which perhaps got Tolkien thinking about his two 'Man in the Moon' poems (see Shippey 2003a: 37-8).

Continuing my county-by-county progression, Tolkien's other major early philological work was his edition, with E.V. Gordon, of the poem *Sir Gawain and the Green Knight*, of 1925. Where does this poem come from? Modern dialect research puts it – you can see there is no iffing and butting among philologists – at map reference 393364, in the valley of the River Dane, the border between Staffordshire and Cheshire. I would add that although dialect study puts it just on the Cheshire side of the border, there is an admitted five-mile margin of error, and there is some sign that the dialect of the poet was very slightly further south than that of his one copier (see Duggan 1997). I accordingly take it to be a Staffordshire poem and one

---

[9] There appear to have been both a French verse version of it, and one in English alliterative verse, though neither has survived except fragmentarily, see Hathaway *et al.* (1975: xix-xxvi): another case of 'the lost literature of medieval England.'

which again affected Tolkien because he thought it had held on to true tradition (a quality he valued above almost all else, see *BLT 2*, 290). I have said elsewhere in this volume what I think this poem (and the three others by the same poet) contributed to Tolkien's recovery of ancient belief – most notably the idea of the 'wood-wose,' like 'dwimmerlaik' a word that had to be rescued from misunderstanding and near-oblivion, preserved only in *Sir Gawain* and street-names like Woodhouse Lane in Leeds, where his office used to be – so I will not repeat myself here. I will just say that in fourteenth-century Staffordshire, as in fourteenth-century Shropshire and thirteenth-century Herefordshire and Worcestershire, native English tradition was still alive, powerful, and remarkably sophisticated: even if they didn't know about it in London.

And what about Warwickshire? It has no great medieval work to point to, but it was of course the county which produced England's national poet, Shakespeare, in the early modern period. Tolkien's view of Shakespeare, I think, was that he could have been *good* – if he had not made the mistake of going to London and going commercial. Shakespeare wrote, or co-wrote, some thirty-eight plays. Of these, however, it seems that only two did not have borrowed plots, were Shakespeare's own idea, and these two are *A Midsummer Night's Dream* and *The Tempest* – the two plays about magic, one set in an enchanted wood dominated by Puck and the fairies, the other on an enchanted island dominated by the wizard Prospero and his servants Ariel and Caliban.[10] Left to himself, Shakespeare wrote about wizards and elves. Now, why did he not do more of that, and spare us the propaganda history plays, the laborious comedies? – so Tolkien may have thought. It is not as if there were not flashes of awareness in other plays too. *King Lear* tells an old story from the *Brut*, and in an exceptionally irritating way starts to recount a ballad about 'the Dark Tower,' only to break off;

---

[10] Another that might be considered original is *The Merry Wives of Windsor*, with its subplot about the figure from Warwickshire folklore, Herne the Hunter.

Macbeth strangely preserves a great deal of Old English phrasing, in the one play which brings on-stage an Anglo-Saxon king, and was obviously read by Tolkien with care and attention; perhaps most strikingly, at the end of *Love's Labours Lost*, Shakespeare suddenly breaks into pure hobbit-poetry, carefully imitated by Tolkien in Bilbo's 'Warning of Winter' (*LotR*, 266). Certainly, then, Shakespeare knew more than he ever showed.

My argument has been that the five 'heartland' counties preserved most of what was for Tolkien the 'true tradition' of English mythology and English poetry, elsewhere overpowered and brushed out of memory by alien invasions. The list of works above could readily be extended. The greatest alliterative poet of the fourteenth century, other than the unknown *Gawain*-poet, was William Langland. His own statements in *Piers Plowman*, narrowed down by modern dialect research, place his home town as Hanley Castle in Worcestershire, stronghold of the Despensers; Tolkien wrote a brief parody of Langland titled 'Doworst,' which has never been published in full (see article on 'Alliterative verse by Tolkien' in Drout 2007). A stray poem of exactly the same type as the comic lyrics of Harley MS 2253 turned up in the 20th century in a lawyer's safe in Bridgnorth, Shropshire – what was it doing there? – was taken to London for safe keeping, edited under the title of 'Papelard Priest' by A.H. Smith, who also brought out Tolkien and Gordon's *Songs for the Philologists*, and was then destroyed in the Blitz: only Carter Revard has ever taken any notice of it. Other poems of the fourteenth century 'Alliterative Revival' – it was really a Survival – can be linked with Staffordshire, such as *Winner and Waster* and *Parlement of the Three Ages*.

Shropshire also provides one of the strangest examples of continuity from medieval to modern. Thomas Percy, born in Bridgnorth, tells a story that some time in (perhaps) the 1740s or 1750s he was staying with a friend in Shifnal, also in Shropshire, when he observed a maidservant using an old manuscript to light the fire. He begged the manuscript, and on it he based his edition, much later, of *Reliques of Ancient English Poetry* (1768). The

Percy manuscript, as it has become known, contained other, unknown alliterative poems of traditional type, and one of the two surviving manuscripts of the last poem known to have been written in the old traditional form, 'Scottish Field,' a poem about the Battle of Flodden Field: the other manuscript of this, once again showing ancient continuity, remains to this day in the possession of the descendants of the author, one of the Legh family of Baguley, Cheshire, whose boast it is that his family had lived there since even before William the Conqueror (and so much for the Norman Conquest):

> He was a gentilman, by Jesu, that this Jest made,
> which said but as ye see, for soth, and no other.
> At Baguley that burne his biding place he had;
> his auncetors of old time haue yerded their longe,
> before William conquerour this Countrey Inhabited.
> (Baird 1982: 16-17, lines 418-22)

Percy's heavily-edited and much-expanded *Reliques* furthermore changed the course of English poetry, inspiring the *Lyrical Ballads* of Wordsworth and Coleridge – Wordsworth was another poet from a backward province, who knew more about traditional (ballad) poetry and the rhythms and phrasings of old English than he admitted. Finally, one might say – and Tolkien would probably have agreed – that place has its own power. John Milton had nothing to do with the West Midlands by birth or upbringing. But just once he wrote a work to be performed nowhere else than Ludlow Castle, the masque of *Comus*, which at once echoes *A Midsummer Night's Dream* and foreshadows Tolkien's slowly developed 'myth of stars and shadows.' It is one of the great English forest-poems: Milton must have drawn inspiration from his surroundings.

It is striking how little interest any of the above has aroused in the modern academic world of literary study. The 'AB language' of the *Ancrene Wisse* group continues to be worked on, in a somewhat marginal way (see Zettersten 2006), but there is still no full modern edition of most of the associated works, except for the edition of *Seinte Iuliene* brought out by Tolkien's pupil Simonne d'Ardenne (1961); there is a translation of *Ancrene Wisse*, with a 'Preface' by Tolkien, by another of Tolkien's pupils, Mary Salu (1955). The edition of Layamon's *Brut* eventually undertaken by the Early English Text Society came out as volume 1 in 1963, as volume 2 in 1978; volume 3, with the notes and introduction, has never appeared, and both editors have died. Carter Revard's highly significant researches, one of the few positive identifications made in the medieval English area, and appearing in print from the late 1970s, do not receive *a single word* in the recent and designedly authoritative Cambridge volume on *Medieval English Literature* (which in general ignores all 'provincial' English productions); the same volume shows no awareness that there are two manuscripts of 'Scottish Field' (see Wallace 1999: 710-11). 'Papelard Priest' might as well have stayed in the lawyer's safe in Bridgnorth, for all the notice taken of it. Only *Piers Plowman* (studies of which remain in an extremely confused state) and the works of the *Gawain*-poet (very largely as a result of the Tolkien and Gordon editions) have managed to get on to the academic curriculum in any established way; and there is a strong tendency to try to remove them from the West Midlands environment, and see them in one way or another as London poems.[11] I do not think Tolkien would have been surprised by any of this. He thought native English tradition had always been unwelcome to and suppressed by the authorities, ever since 1066. Modern times were no different.

What does what I have just said tell us about 'the roots of romance'? One thing is that you don't need a story to generate it. You can make do with suggestive scraps – with a *word*, like 'dwimmerlaik' or 'wood-wose.' Or maybe even (see Tolkien on 'AB language') a *part of speech*, or *the*

---

[11] For *Sir Gawain* transposed to a metropolitan milieu, see Putter (1996: 23), responded to in Shippey (2000c: 93-4). Langland of course, like Shakespeare, did move to London, but the readiness to see him there and reluctance to follow the connections with Hanley Castle are commented on in Shippey 1997a and 1999b.

inflection of a verb. But what these can create, via the philological imagination, includes:

- the Shire (of the hobbits, but also the forgotten shires of Hereford, Worcester, and Shropshire in the post-Conquest Dark Age).
- the Woses (of Drúadan Forest, but also of the badlands above the Aire in Yorkshire, or in the thickets of medieval Cheshire / Staffordshire).
- and the Mark: I mean the Riddermark of the Riders of Rohan, but this too is, or ought to be, a totally familiar English location. Where is 'the Mark'? We are in it. Birmingham was all through the Anglo-Saxon period near the heart of 'Mercia,' Offa's kingdom with its capital at Tamworth and its cathedral at Lichfield. But Mercia is a Latinism. What did the English inhabitants of Mercia call their own country? They never wrote the term down, but their neighbours to the South in Wessex called them the *Mierce* – pronounced with a '-che' at the end. This must mean the inhabitants of the *Mearc, -ea- changing to -ie- by a familiar Old English sound-change. But then the inhabitants of the South (as you must have noticed) have long had a habit of gargling simple words like, for instance, 'a bottle of milk' ('bo'ul a' mi-ulk' in London English). Clearly the plain-spoken inhabitants of Mercia, in essence the English Midlands (East and West, but firmly ruled from the West) would simply have said that they were the *Merche, and they lived in the *Mark. And what was the sign of the Mark (as the sign of Wessex was the Golden Dragon)? We don't know, because of the Wessex bias of all our historical sources, but Tolkien made the sign of his Mark the white horse on the green field. I think he took this from the White Horse of Uffington, not far south of Oxford and close to the Mercia-Wessex border. And I think it comforted Tolkien in exile in Oxford to think that he might no longer be in the Shire, or in the

West Midlands, but at least he was still inside the ancestral Mark of Mercia.

Perhaps it is now clearer what I meant by 'philology.' It is the scientific study of historical language, in which language and literature are inextricably connected (which is why Tolkien was so reluctant to talk about 'literature,' or take it seriously as a separate subject in practice opposed to language). But besides illuminating literature, philology also illuminates history, and indeed modernity. What it tells you is at one and the same time:

- real (it is about real places, for instance)
- made-up (because you have to make up the 'reconstructed' forms)
- fantastic (it is about wood-woses and giants, *etaynes* and ogres and wood-trolls)
- everyday (like place-names and surnames).

Place-names themselves repay study very quickly. People tend not to think about them, assuming they are just that way because they always have been. But this is not so. What does Edgbaston mean? It must come from **Ecgbaldes stan*, 'Edge-bold's stone.' Where the stone is we no longer now – maybe in someone's back garden, or part of a wall. What about Birmingham? This is probably **Beorn-inga-ham*, 'the home of the followers of Beorn.' Remember Beorn? He has a major role in *The Hobbit*, triggered perhaps by Tolkien wondering what the founder of the city was like (his name also means 'bear'). What about Umberslade Road, not so far away from where we are now? Slade is an old word for 'dell' or 'valley.' But Umber-? This looks like a learned Latinism, from *umbra*, 'shade,' so 'the shady valley.' But why should anyone talk Latin about Umberslade Road? A word Tolkien was fond of is the rare word 'umbel,' usually applied by him to 'hemlocks.' This has caused a good deal of confusion (see Gilliver *et al.* 2006: 141-2), but Tolkien used the word in defiantly native fashion to indicate plants like 'Queen Anne's lace,' 'cow parsley' or 'traveller's joy':

so, 'valley where the cow parsley grows.' Maybe Tolkien took the word from the etymology of the road, as he took the 'Woses' from Woodhouse Lane. Finally, a place we know Tolkien knew and which he brought into his fiction, Sarehole Mill Road, the inspiration for Ted Sandyman's mill in Hobbiton. What does Sarehole mean? The first bit could be from Old English *sear*, 'grey, withered.' Or it could be from a personal name which *The Oxford Dictionary of Place-Names*, with its usual unthinking Southern bias, gives as **Searu* – obviously, in Mercian, **Saru*. 'The mill at Saru's hole'? Tolkien evidently did create a character, Saruman, who takes over the mill and is responsible for the industrial pollution of the Shire associated with it. Again, name has led to reconstruction, and the two together have created story. Tolkien, I would suggest, was a brooder. He brooded on names, including the names of Old Edwardians.[12] The great advantage of this is that names are real, but they are also unexpected. They rely on a whole process of naming and thinking which is greater than any single person could ever invent.

Tolkien's fascination with the West Midlands, its history, philology and literature, has only become clearer and clearer over the decades. We see it especially strongly in his posthumously-published works, edited by his son Christopher from 1975 to now. In these perhaps the most surprising thing to emerge is this: Tolkien wanted to equate Elfland with Birmingham. Perhaps not quite Birmingham, but anyway with the area where Warwickshire, Worcestershire and Staffordshire meet (which is much the same as Birmingham). Thus, in Tolkien's early *Book of Lost Tales* – the original form of *The Silmarillion*, and so deep in the background to *The Lord of the Rings* – we see him developing a long fiction that the 'lost tales' themselves were told to an Englishman, an Anglo-Saxon indeed, on the elvish isle of Tol Eressëa. But in later years, in this fiction (for which see *BLT 1*, 24-5)

---

[12] He was very interested in Peter Neave, who used to play wing three-quarter for the Second XV. Of course 'Neave' was also the name of his favourite Aunt Jane.

Tol Eressëa would become England. Kortirion, the main town of the elvish isle, would become Warwick. Alalminorë, the 'land of elm-trees' surrounding Kortirion, would become Warwickshire. And in the most striking personal identification, Tavrobel, the place where Eriol the Englishman was told the tales, would in the end turn into the Staffordshire village of Great Haywood, where Tolkien spent some of his Great War convalescence. In a further footnote in *The Lost Road* (page 413), Christopher Tolkien notes that even the house where the stories were told is capable of being identified. Tolkien called it, in his fiction, the house of the Hundred Chimneys, and put it near a bridge where two rivers joined. This looks very like Shugborough Hall, home of the Earls of Lichfield, near the end of the old packhorse bridge that also crosses two rivers in Great Haywood. Christopher Tolkien says, "It seems very likely that it was my father's sight of the great house through the trees and its smoking chimneys as he stood on the bridge that lies, in some sense, behind the House of the Hundred Chimneys of the old legend."

And there is a further irony which I am sure Tolkien would have relished. What does 'Shugborough' mean? I haven't looked this up in *The Oxford Dictionary of Place-names* because I don't need to.[13] The first element of Shugborough must come from Old English *scucca* (pronounced 'shooker'), 'goblin' or 'demon.' Could it ever have meant 'elf' – in which case 'Shookers' Town' would be a very good name for a place in which the elves passed on their stories? You would think not, goblins and elves being very different in Tolkien's universe. But if you remember characters like Éomer, with his deep doubt and distrust of the elves, his equation of them with the other dangerous non-humans, you can see how mistakes in later tradition could arise. All the non-humans could end up lumped together under an all-purpose name like *scucca*. Once again, I suspect the

---

[13] I did eventually look it up, to discover that it wasn't listed. Shuckburgh in Warwickshire however has exactly the same etymology for the first element, the second perhaps being *beorg*, 'hill' rather than *burh*, 'town,' so 'goblin hill.' See Ekwall (1977: 421).

place-name with its unexpected roots caught Tolkien's ear and led him on to story. He saw fantasy in perfectly everyday words, names and places – and he did so because, to the philological ear, it is there.

A major advantage of philology (unlike, as far as I can see, Jungian psychology) is that it takes you outside yourself, to look at things outside your own head. It has of course by now been almost totally abandoned as a subject at British universities; it was never very popular; in 1991 Tolkien's own Chair of Anglo-Saxon at Oxford was itself (so the rumour ran) slated to be lapsed (till an anonymous donor re-endowed it, or so the rumour goes again). All this is a pity, a triumph for what Tolkien called in his 'Valedictory Address' to Oxford in 1959 "the misologists" – the haters of words, as the philologists are the lovers of words. My own view is that the roots of romance in Tolkien's work (and in all that emanates from it) were:

- first, his own deeply sad early life, which left him in permanent emotional exile. In view of the occasion I would add that while Tolkien, fatherless from the age of three and an orphan at twelve, was shuffled from one often depressing location and lodging after another,[14] King Edward's School remained, entirely to the credit of the school and his teachers, his main refuge, if not his home. But the friends he made there, R.Q. Gilson (son of Cary Gilson) and Geoffrey Bache Smith, were killed in Flanders in 1916;
- second, his image of the West Midlands, Herefordshire, Worcestershire and even Birmingham, which in later life came to seem a form of paradise from which he was forever excluded;[15]

---

[14] 9 Ashfield Rd., King's Heath; 5 Gracewell, in Sarehole, Hall Green; in a house in Moseley now pulled down and another behind King's Heath Station; in 26 Oliver Rd. Edgbaston, and in the Oratory Cottage in Rednal; in Stirling Rd. and in Duchess Rd., Edgbaston. All these places were familiar to the audience at KES.

[15] A feeling which is also very strong in the poetry of A.E. Housman (1859-1936). Housman was born at Fockbury in Worcestershire, but is most famous for his collection *A Shropshire Lad* (1896). His work became popular, however, in the early 1920s, when Tolkien was struggling to be a poet, with a second collection, *More Poems* (1922), fol-

- but third and most important, the way that both the above were altered and refashioned by the philological imagination.

Well, the 'misologists,' as Tolkien called them, have by now very largely hijacked the study of English literature in British universities. They were horrible to Tolkien all through his professional life, and they hate and resent his memory and his legacy even now. Still, there is at least this consolation: there can now be no doubt at all – no doubt at all – about who had the last laugh! And it is a proof of the strength of the West Midlands literary tradition that it has managed to survive, and to keep on throwing out shoots from the dead stock, or if one prefers Bilbo's image, fire from the ashes: like Layamon's *Brut* in the thirteenth century, or *A Midsummer Night's Dream* in the sixteenth, or Percy's *Reliques* in the eighteenth, or Tolkien's work itself in the twentieth and twenty-first.

---

lowed by *Last Poems* (1936). Housman was furthermore one of the great Classical philologists – all reasons for Tolkien to have read him with close attention.

Tolkien and
the *Gawain*-Poet[1]

Tolkien's involvement with the *Gawain*-poet lasted almost the whole of his professional or writing life. Before proceeding, I should explain that by 'the *Gawain*-poet' I mean not only 'the man who wrote *Sir Gawain and the Green Knight*,' but also 'the man who wrote the four anonymous poems now preserved in Cotton MS. Nero A.X, i.e. *Sir Gawain*, *Pearl*, *Purity* and *Patience*.' All four are written in the same distinctive dialect. It is true that this need not mean they were written by the same hand, for the person who copied them all might for instance have 'translated' poems in different dialects into his own; while, as Tolkien himself showed in his 1929 essay on '*Ancrene Wisse* and *Hali Meiðhad*,' even in the Middle Ages, different people could under some circumstances have been taught at school to write the same English, no matter where they came from. So the four poems *could* all have had different authors. There has at least been a suggestion that a fifth poem, *St. Erkenwald*, in a closely similar dialect but a different manuscript, is also by 'the *Gawain*-poet.' I do not propose however to consider these issues. It is clear from note 13 of his 1953 essay on the poem (details given below) that Tolkien thought it "beyond any real doubt" that the man who wrote *Sir Gawain* "also wrote *Pearl*, not to mention *Purity* and *Patience*" (*Essays*, 107), while he offered no view on *St. Erkenwald*. 'The *Gawain*-poet,' then, meant to Tolkien the unknown author of the four late fourteenth century poems in MS. Nero A.X.

As said at the start of this essay, Tolkien had the *Gawain*-poet in mind for at least fifty years. His first work on him was the joint edition of *Sir Gawain and the Green Knight* produced by Tolkien and his Leeds colleague E.V. Gordon, published by the Clarendon Press in 1925. It was an

---

[1] This piece appeared first in Patricia Reynolds and Glen H. GoodKnight (eds.). 1995. *Proceedings of the J.R.R. Tolkien Centenary Conference*. Milton Keynes: Tolkien Society, and Altadena, CA: Mythopoeic Press. 213-9.

enormously successful book, which altered the whole current of English medieval studies – till then heavily Southern and Chaucerian in bias, at least at non-specialist level – and which is still the standard edition (as revised and updated in 1967 by Tolkien's pupil Norman Davis). Its success led to an immediate suggestion that the same pair should go on and edit *Pearl* from the same manuscript. Almost as soon as the first edition appeared, however, Tolkien and Gordon ceased to live close together, as Tolkien went off to Oxford while Gordon took over Tolkien's Leeds chair. In Humphrey Carpenter's *Biography* (2000: 112), Tolkien is cited as referring rather ruefully to Gordon as "an industrious little devil"; it seems likely that Gordon wanted to press on with *Pearl* in the late 1920s while Tolkien (whose fears about his own lack of discipline can be glimpsed in 'Leaf by Niggle') had turned much of his attention to other things. Time went by. Gordon died prematurely, in 1938; and when the edition of *Pearl* eventually appeared in 1953 it was signalled on the title page as "Edited by E.V. Gordon," but actually brought out by his widow Ida L. Gordon, a considerable medieval scholar in her own right. In her 'Preface' to that work Mrs. Gordon records the original start as a joint product; mentions Tolkien's withdrawal from the project "when he found himself unable to give sufficient time to it"; and goes on to give "warmest thanks […] to Professor Tolkien, who had the original typescript for some time and added valuable notes and corrections." One can probably conclude in the end that while the edition of *Pearl* is indeed largely E.V. Gordon's work, there are also substantial contributions by Ida Gordon, with in all probability both an initial input and later additions by Tolkien: some of the notes in the edition (as I indicate below) do seem resonantly Tolkienian.[2]

In addition to these two works Tolkien also devoted the W.P. Ker Memorial Lecture of 1953 to 'Sir Gawain and the Green Knight,' eventually printed in *Essays* 72-108. Christopher Tolkien's 'Foreword' to that

---

[2] See further Anderson 2003, and the entry on *Pearl* in Drout 2007.

volume makes it clear that Tolkien had in 1953 just completed his alliterative verse translation of *Sir Gawain* into modern English, but that the version existing then was repeatedly altered and emended. It came out in final form in 1975, along with the translations of *Pearl* and *Sir Orfeo*. The publishing history of Tolkien on the *Gawain*-poet then runs from 1925 to 1983, while Tolkien, as far as we know, did not cease to think and comment on the poet's works from the 1920s till his own death in 1973. References to the *Gawain*-poet in fact crop up in unexpected places in Tolkien's scholarly works; the poet's influence on Tolkien's fiction is considered further below.

Why did Tolkien feel this attraction to the poems of Nero A.X? Since I have said repeatedly in my book *The Road to Middle-earth* that philology is "the only proper guide to a view of Middle-earth 'of the sort which its author may be supposed to have desired'" (Shippey 2003a: 8),[3] it is not surprising that I see Tolkien's interest in the *Gawain*-poet as primarily philological. I would separate it into three strands, those of class, place and tradition.

To deal with class first: it is obvious that the dialect of the *Gawain*-poet was in no way an ancestor of modern Standard English. All the poems are full (much fuller than Chaucer's) of words now found only, if at all, in non-standard dialects. One could say indeed that the modern descendants of the *Gawain*-poet's dialect are among the least-regarded and lowest-status dialects of modern England. At one point in *Sir Gawain* the Lady, flirting with Sir Gawain, tells him he ought to be eager to teach 'a ȝonke þynk' about love. The addition of an extra 'g/k' sound in words like 'young, thing, ring, finger' is still common in areas of the North-West Midlands; it is however a feature which ambitious parents and schoolteachers try hard to stamp out.

---

[3] The phrase in single inverted commas comes from the 'Preface' to the Tolkien and Gordon edition of *Sir Gawain*, where the editors use it to describe their own intentions as regards the poet.

Yet in spite of these and other marks of modern low-status, the *Gawain*-poet, most surprisingly to a modern ear, betrays not the slightest sign of linguistic self-consciousness or inferiority. His language is indeed in other areas almost haughtily high-status, as in his careful and zestful descriptions (full of technical vocabulary) of the upper-class sport of hunting. Tolkien certainly appreciated this clash of linguistic indicators. In 1928 he wrote a 'Foreword' to Walter E. Haigh's *A New Glossary of the Dialect of the Huddersfield District*, in which he said that Haigh's work was valuable "not only to local patriotism, but to English philology" generally. He picked out words showing sound-changes dating back to Old Germanic; noted also the way in which learned words were naturalised in a powerful local speech;[4] and went on to say that there was particular interest in the study of dialects of the North-West because of the signs in them of competition and cohabitation between Old English and Old Norse. Furthermore, he remarks, in the fourteenth century this north-west area was to become:

> the centre of a revival in vernacular speech, of which the most interesting examples preserved are poems in an alliterative metre descended from the old verse of Anglo-Saxon times, though clothed in a language now difficult to read because of its strong Scandinavian element and its many other peculiar and obscure dialectal words. These texts do not all come from the same part of the North-West, and where each was written is still in debate, but their connexion with the modern dialects, of which that of Huddersfield is an interesting example, is immediately apparent to any one glancing at this glossary. Indeed, such books as this one sometimes throw valuable light on the meanings or forms of words in

---

[4] As for instance the word 'auction.' I have commented on Tolkien's playing with the two meanings of this in Shippey (2003a: 93n.). See also the essay 'History in Words' in this volume, and further the entry on *New Glossary* in Drout 2007 – where at last a solution is found, in Haigh, for the etymology of Sam Gamgee's self accusation, "Noodles!".

> these old poems, such poems as the romance *Sir Gawain and the Green Knight*, [and] the beautiful elegiac sermon known as *The Pearl*. (Haigh 1928: xvi)

On the next page Tolkien picks out a particularly unexpected case of close resemblance between the aristocratic medieval *Gawain*-poet and Haigh's working-class modern informants. The *Gawain*-poet appears at one point to make a 'mistake' in English, when the Green Knight, their challenge settled, asks Sir Gawain "to com to þy naunt," i.e. 'to come to thine aunt.' It looks as if someone, poet or scribe, has mixed up "þyn aunt" (used at line 2464) with "þy naunt" (line 2467), both forms deriving properly from Old French *aunte* (as the Tolkien-Gordon glossary says). But was this a 'mistake'? Mr. Haigh's informants made it spectacularly clear that they used both words, in their pronunciation *ænt* and *nont*. However they regarded *nont* as normal, and *ænt* as affected. Haigh cites a man saying teasingly to his daughter, thought to be trying to ingratiate herself with her (rich) aunt Sally by talking a form of standard English:

> Thæ thinks thi nont Sally'll bau thi e niu frok if thæ toks faun (polite) to er – imitating her – 'ænt Sarah are yo goin' out? au'll mind th'ouse for yo waul yo kum back'. It's '*ænt* Sarah' this en *ænt* Sarah' t'tuther; bet thi nont Sally'll maund er bræss muer ner tha maunds other *or*, er *er ees*.[5]

Tolkien would I am sure have preferred it if a West Midlands form of English had become standard, instead of the South-East Midlands form which

---

[5] In this quotation I have not reproduced several of the marks used by Haigh to indicate pronunciation. It should be noted that in this dialect the diphthong 'ai' is changed to 'au.' It is part of the father's teasing imitation of his daughter's accent that he has her say 'mind' for 'maund' – though not 'I' or 'while.' A translation would run: 'You think your aunt Sally'll buy you a new frock if you talk fine to her. "Aunt Sarah, are you going out? I'll mind the house for you till you come back." It's "Aunt Sarah" this and "Aunt Sarah" the other; but your aunt Sally'll look after her money more than you look after either her or her house.'

actually did so. He was probably attracted on one level to the *Gawain*-poet's works by their demonstration that great poetry could be written without strain in what would now be regarded as a 'vulgar' or 'ugly' dialect. But which dialect is it, exactly? In the 'Foreword' to Haigh Tolkien suggested that *Sir Gawain* was probably written "to the west of Huddersfield" (Haigh 1928: xvii n.), while he and Gordon declared in their 1925 edition (p. viii) that "the Lancashire character of the language is perfectly preserved." Tolkien himself was mistaken here, though in a way which I am sure he would be glad to have demonstrated. Later research since 1925 – of course conducted with the advantage of many more located texts than were available to Tolkien – puts the *Gawain*-poet a county and a half further south, in the valley of the River Dane, on the boundary between Cheshire and Staffordshire, and indeed (one can see there is no needless shilly-shallying among philologists) at map-reference 393364 on the Ordnance Survey charts, a location reckoned as correct to within a hundred yards.[6] Further corollaries of this very precise location[7] are that the poet was probably connected with Dieulacres Abbey near Leek in Staffordshire, that he may have imagined the castle of Sir Bertilak as being located at Knight's Low in Swythamley Park, and most relevantly for Tolkien that – writing in a local dialect for a local audience – he encouraged his hearers to imagine his Arthurian romance as set in a landscape they knew, and which they could name. Thus, as the huntsmen set out to hunt the wild boar (perhaps at Wildboarclough, just above the Dane), the poet says:

> þenne such a glauer ande glam of gedered rachcheȝ
> Ros, þat þe rochereȝ rungen aboute (ll. 1426-7)

---

[6] See McIntosh *et al.* (1986, 1: 178 and 3: 37, where a misprint has crept in over the map-reference).

[7] The points below are made by Elliott 1984. Elliott's location of the poem is strikingly confirmed by McIntosh *et al.* in the study cited above.

Tolkien and Gordon in 1925 gloss 'rocher' as "rock [Old French *roch(i)er*]" – one of the strong points of their edition was that it showed immediately which language words in the poem were derived from, Old English, Old Norse or Old French – and Tolkien's translation of 1975 accordingly reads:

> Then such a baying and babel of bloodhounds together
> arose, that the rock-wall rang all about them.
> (*SGPO*, 60)

But if one is gathering hounds at Swythamley or Wildboarclough in the Dane valley, the rock-wall that is likely to be resounding is not 'the rocheres,' but 'the Roaches' – the steep jagged hills overlooking the valley, still called 'the Roaches,' and with a name which derives from the Old French root *rocher* just as certainly as Tolkien and Gordon's proposed reading. I have remarked elsewhere how Tolkien liked in *The Hobbit* "to make names out of capital letters" – turning 'the hill' into 'The Hill,' the stream at its foot into 'The Water,' and so on (Shippey 2003a: 96). I am sure Tolkien would have been delighted to see the *Gawain*-poet doing in a sense the opposite – turning 'the Roaches' into 'þe rochereȝ,' the Flash brook three lines later into 'a flasche' – but in the secure knowledge that his local audience would very probably as it were insert their own capital letters once more, and feel sure that they were living (as Tolkien thought we all do) on the site of ancient legend and romance.

This close equation by the *Gawain*-poet of legendary past and real present, of which Tolkien was not aware, is nevertheless corroborated by features of the *Gawain*-poet's dialect of which Tolkien was very well aware, namely its deep tap-root into old and largely forgotten tradition. Tolkien comments on this quality in the poem at the start of his 1953 essay ('Sir Gawain'), regrettably going on to say he is at present concerned with other matters (see Shippey 2003a: 308-9). I do not think, though, that there is any difficulty in tracing what Tolkien meant, providing always that one looks at the *Gawain*-poet with a philological eye. Consider for instance lines 720-5 of the poem, describing Sir Gawain's adventurous ride from Camelot (evidently somewhere down South) into the wilderlands of the Pennines:

> Sumwhyle wyth wormeʒ he wereʒ, and with wolues als,
> Sumwhyle wyth wodwos, þat woned in þe knarreʒ,
> Boþe wyth bulleʒ and bereʒ, and boreʒ oþerquyle,
> And etayneʒ, þat hym anelede of þe heʒe felle;
> Nade he ben duʒty and dryʒe, and dryʒtyn had serued,
> Douteles he hade ben ded and dreped ful ofte.

Tolkien translated this passage as follows:

> At whiles with worms he wars, and with wolves also,
> at whiles with wood-trolls that wandered in the crags,
> and with bulls and with bears and boars too, at times;
> and with ogres that hounded him from the heights of the fells.
> Had he not been stalwart and staunch and steadfast in God,
> he doubtless would have died and death had met often.
> (*SGPO*, 43)

But it is essential for a philological understanding to go back to the original, or indeed to go back and forward between original and translation, for (to quote Tolkien again), "a good translation is a good companion of honest labour, while a 'crib' is a (vain) substitute for the essential work with grammar and glossary, by which alone can be won genuine appreciation of a noble idiom and a lofty art" ('On Translating *Beowulf*,' *Essays*, 50-51).

If one looks at the original poem, and then at the Tolkien/Gordon glossary, several words in these six lines should catch the eye: for instance, 'dreped.' The Tolkien and Gordon glossary says "dreped, pp., slain, killed, 725. [OE. *drepan*, smite; ON. *drepa*, kill]." So, is the word an Old English or an Old Norse one? As one can see from his 1975 translation, Tolkien definitely took the word in its Old Norse sense, not its Old English one. "Ded and dreped" to him was a tautology, the line meaning 'he would have been dead and killed time and time again.' Why then give both etymologies (if the Old English one is irrelevant), and why convict the poet of repeating himself? The answer as usual is a philological one: I have no doubt that yet another of the points which drew Tolkien to the *Gawain*-poet was his dialect's unusual fusion of the two languages Tolkien studied most, Old English and Old Norse – a fusion so intimate that one could have an Old English past participle form (the Old Norse form would have given 'drepen' not 'dreped') with an Old Norse meaning. Even modern Standard English is to an extent not often realised a mixture of English and Norse. For the *Gawain*-poet's ancestors that mixture had been even deeper and more thorough. Though the poet was also extremely familiar with French, his language showed clearly an old and stubborn resistance to Latinate forms, southern influence, and Standard English. The point about 'ded and dreped' is (in a way) a trivial one. But Tolkien thought such points could not be faked. They were the linguistic guarantors of true literary tradition: part of "this flavour, this atmosphere, this virtue that such *rooted* works have," to quote the first page of his 1953 essay on *Sir Gawain* (*Essays*, 72).

In any case there are more significant details in lines 720-5. The word 'etayneȝ' certainly caught Tolkien's eye. It is glossed "ogre, giant [...] [OE. *eoten*]." Tolkien and Gordon obviously knew that the parallel word *iötunn* is extremely common in Old Norse – Tolkien uses it freely in his scholarly work. But the point here is first, that this time the form 'etayn' *must* come from Old English, not Old Norse; and second, extremely significantly, that while *iötnir* are common in Norse literature, *eotenas* or 'etayneȝ' are extremely rare in English. The word is found some half-dozen times in Middle English (see *Oxford English Dictionary* [*OED*] under 'eten'), and just once in Old English: indeed, in *Beowulf* (not cited by the *OED*). Had the *Gawain*-poet got the word from *Beowulf*? Almost certainly not.[8] To him, as to

---

[8] In Tolkien's time it was thought that the first person known to have owned *Beowulf* was Lawrence Nowell, Dean of Lichfield, the traditional heart of the West Midlands, and less than fifty miles from the River Dane. See (if with some scepticism) Kenneth Sisam,

the *Beowulf*-poet, it was not an antiquarian word to be snuffled out of a library, but a word from living speech, preserved (like the *ænt/nont* distinction) over centuries innocent of books. The fact that we rarely encounter the word only shows that in the Middle Ages the best stories were rarely written down. Nevertheless the survival of such words indicates a true tradition of giant-stories lasting from *Beowulf* to *Sir Gawain*, or to use Tolkien's dates, from about 725 AD to about 1375 – a longer interval than that which separates the *Gawain*-poet from us.

And then there are the 'wodwos' of line 721. I have discussed the survival of this word up to the present day, indeed to the address of Tolkien's Leeds office and my own (Shippey 2003a: 65n.), so I will say here only that it repeats the pattern of true tradition surviving in altered and in this case genuinely 'mistaken' form. 'Wodwos' is here clearly plural; its singular (in the *Gawain*-poet's mind) would presumably be 'wodwo'; but the Old English word from which it should be derived, as Tolkien and Gordon record, would be *wudu-wása*, whose plural would be *wudu-wásan*. The *Gawain*-poet ought to have written 'wodwosen' (and maybe he did). But somewhere down the line the true historical form was forgotten, except in place and personal names, no doubt because the stories and the concept of the 'trolls of the forest' were being forgotten – till revived, of course, in the Woses (NB plural form), the 'Wild Men of the Woods' of Druadan Forest in *LotR* (Book 5, chapter 5, 'The Ride of the Rohirrim').

Even the 'mistakes' of the *Gawain*-poet, it will be seen, tell a story to the philological mind, of which Tolkien was the twentieth century's most prominent example. 'þy (n) aunt' bears witness to the naturalisation of French and the survival of living speech. 'Dreped' and 'etaynez' in their different ways tell us about the relations of Englishmen and Norsemen off the normal historical map; 'etaynez' and 'wodwos' between them hint at a

---

'The Beowulf Manuscript,' in Sisam (1953: 61-4). We now know that the first owner was the Dean's first cousin, also called Laurence Nowell. Where he obtained it is completely unknown.

great but lost tradition of story-telling, again off the normal literary and critical map. Yet more details could be picked out of the same six lines. A common 'vulgarism' much reproved by schoolteachers is 'dropping your aitches.' Did the *Gawain*-poet drop his aitches? In line 723 'etayneʒ' alliterates with the second syllable of 'anELede' and is obviously meant to alliterate with 'heʒe.' Should the latter then not be pronounced 'eʒe'?[9] One cannot be sure, but in his translation Tolkien scrupulously follows the 'error' of his original: the only way to get the traditional and correct three alliterations out of Tolkien's line is to read it as: 'and with Ogres that 'Ounded 'im from the 'Eights of the fells' – a perfectly plausible pronunciation in the area, just as good as Standard English, and backed up not only by the *Gawain*-poet but once more by the *Beowulf*-poet, whose aitches are not above suspicion either.

Nevertheless, one may say in the end, words, etymologies and glossaries apart, what did Tolkien make of the *Gawain*-poet as a thinker, a poet, a story-teller: not just a language-user, a 'set text,' and a subject for budding philologists to cut their teeth on! We have substantial evidence here in the 1953 essay to which I have already referred. This is no easier to paraphrase than any other of Tolkien's scholarly works. But one conclusion I would venture to draw from it is that Tolkien saw the *Gawain*-poet – as he had earlier presented the *Beowulf*-poet – as an artist in vital respects much like himself: someone deeply embedded in a Christian and Catholic tradition, but nevertheless (if in definitely subordinate fashion) ready to make use of the lost, popular, monster-creating, 'fairy-tale' traditions which we can infer from his very vocabulary.

Tolkien's main point about *Sir Gawain* is thus that in it "the temptations of Sir Gawain, his behaviour under them, and criticism of his code, were for our author his story, to which all else was subservient" (*Essays*, 83). "All else," one should remember, includes many of the most dramatic

---

[9] One of the rules of alliterative verse is that all vowels may alliterate with each other.

and mythically-suggestive scenes in the poem: the appearance of the fearsome Green Knight with axe and holly-branch at Arthur's court, his beheading by Sir Gawain, his instant resurrection, the long journey of the knight into the wilderness as quoted above, and the 'trial-and-repayment' scene in the midwinter snow at the eerie Green Chapel. All interesting, says Tolkien, but "subservient," even (*Essays*, 74) by comparison "perfunctory." Rather than expanding on any or all of these, Tolkien prefers to spend a high proportion of his essay discussing a scene so seemingly underweighted in the poem as to have received almost no critical discussion, and that discussion in his view entirely mistaken; i.e., stanza 75 of the poem, in which Sir Gawain (having resisted the Lady's sexual temptations, but accepted from her a girdle as a gift) goes to confession and is absolved. On this stanza, Tolkien says, "the whole interpretation and valuation [of the poem] depends." Either the poet meant it, in which case it is to be taken seriously, or he was "just a muddler" and his story "just a fairy-story for adults, and not a very good one" (*Essays*, 87).

Tolkien's opposition here is a highly aggressive one, showing how very much he wanted to see the poet not only as an orthodox Catholic with strong awareness of the sacraments, but as a conscious ethical thinker. If one takes this scene Tolkien's way, then the poet makes his character go to confession and *either* not mention his retention of the girdle *or* be told by his confessor that retaining it, against the compact he has made with the Lady's husband, is not a sin. Tolkien prefers the second option, which involves him conceding that much of the action of the poem in the Beheading Game and the Exchange of Winnings compact is in a way not serious – though potentially fatal – but just "a game with rules" (*Essays*, 89). It is these rules Gawain is breaking by retaining the girdle, not a moral commandment. The moral code *would* have been broken, however, if Gawain had stooped to adultery with the Lady, and that is why the temptation scenes are the centre. One might sum up by saying that Tolkien views the poem as bringing two systems into conflict with each other, a Christian moral code and an aristocratic code of honour: the conflict being decided very definitely, by such scenes as the 'confession' stanza, in favour of the former.

I am bound to say at this point that I disagree with Tolkien over some though not most of his interpretation.[10] I agree about the conflict of codes, but feel that the poet exerts his energies to reconcile them, rather than subordinating one to the other: in which case, to take up Tolkien's dilemma over the nature of Gawain's confession, the poet's intention was to suggest the former, not the latter, of Tolkien's alternatives – Gawain did not mention retention of the girdle any more than a modern would feel obliged to confess a foul at football or perhaps a post-dated cheque in business. It is true that I am not a Catholic, and so may underrate the force of what the poet shared with Tolkien. On the other hand, when Tolkien at the end puts the poem into elaborately but not ironically modern terms of "the School Tie" and "the colours of the First Eleven" (*Essays*, 100), I can perhaps speak as one who shared an Old School Tie with Tolkien, and deep interest in the same First Elevens and Fifteens, and so may stress only to a greater degree than he does the real importance of 'games with rules' and 'codes of honour.'

It seems to me, indeed, that by stressing the poet's moral Catholicity Tolkien put himself into a difficult position, which he himself recognised, over the very nature of the temptation. For if the castle is "a courteous and Christian hall" (*Essays*, 78), as I agree it is, what are we to think of the Lady's repeated temptations to adultery? What would have happened if Gawain had succumbed? Would his only problem then, in the Exchange of Winnings plot, have been keeping to the letter of his compact with the castle Lord? Surely not. Tolkien in fact refuses to pursue this line of thought, urging that all this is unthinkable, and not to be explained away by any of those "ancient and barbaric customs" (i.e. wife-swapping) against which

---

[10] My views are explained in Shippey 1971.

C.S. Lewis also reacted,[11] or by "tales in which memory of them is still enshrined" (*Essays*, 82). In saying this Tolkien once again abjured a whole tradition of ancient story of a kind he himself, in fiction, repeatedly used: a whole *legendarium* of ettens and woodwoses and soulless, dangerous elf-maidens. Yet despite abjuring it with the words "we are not in that world," Tolkien nevertheless finds suggestions of that world indispensable. The reason we do not wonder about the chances of a 'successful' temptation, Tolkien says, lies in the menacing suggestions left over in the poem of 'fairy story.' If Gawain did respond to the Lady, he would meet something terrible, like the heroine of 'Bluebeard' opening a forbidden door: "hanging in the background, for those able to receive the air of 'faerie' in a romance, is a terrible threat of disaster and destruction" (*Essays*, 83).

The interesting thing for those who, forty years later, are reading Tolkien's fiction is the careful and perhaps compulsive way in which Tolkien presents an image of an artist wholly dedicated to one tradition (the Christian and Catholic one), nevertheless employing echoes of another (the long and originally pre-Christian tradition of native fairy-tale and monster-story), and using both to create a critique of a third (an essentially secular code based on humour, etiquette and good manners). It is hard to resist the thought that Tolkien read the *Gawain*-poet this way because it resembled his own experience: though one might well put Tolkien a good deal closer to fairy-tale than his predecessor, if at the same time no further away from Catholicity. Perhaps the vital point, however, is that even in his strong advocacy of the one tradition Tolkien is unable to do without the other. Just as I see Tolkien's fiction as in several senses a 'meditation' between a Christian world and a heroic pagan one (Shippey 2003a: 208, 219-22), so Tolkien sees the *Gawain*-poet as understanding and drawing on both those worlds, while in this case 'subordinating' one to the other. And, just

---

[11] Lewis's essay 'The Anthropological Approach,' first published in Tolkien's 1962 *festschrift* and reprinted in Lewis 1969, is in large part a reaction to interpretations of *Sir Gawain* such as Tolkien is here rejecting.

as I argue that this 'mediation' between two worlds gives *The Lord of the Rings* a moral force which would be lacking if it were just "a saint's life, all about temptation [or] a complicated wargame, all about tactics" (Shippey 2003a: 146), so Tolkien says firmly, leading straight on from the quotation above about 'the air of 'faerie',' that in the mixed mode of *Sir Gawain*:

> The struggle becomes intense to a degree which a merely realistic story of how a pious knight resisted a temptation to adultery (when a guest) could hardly attain. It is one of the properties of Fairy Story thus to enlarge the scene and the actors; or rather it is one of the properties that are distilled by literary alchemy when old deep-rooted stories are rehandled by a real poet with an imagination of his own. (*Essays*, 83)

De te narratur fabula, one might say: Tolkien describes himself once again. Nor would he, I feel, view it as anything but a compliment to be fitted into literary tradition in a place similar to that of the *Gawain*-poet. There is furthermore one typically, even pedantically philological point from the passage already cited which once more associates Tolkien with his predecessor. The poet says that Sir Gawain fought many dangerous ventures before he ever got to his temptation:

> Nade he ben duȝty and dryȝe, and dryȝtyn had serued,
> Douteles he hade ben ded and dreped ful ofte.

The first line of these two is, grammatically speaking, a double subordinate clause, if with its doubleness obscured by ellipsis. It means, in full expanded form: 'If he had not been stalwart and staunch, *and* if he had not served the Lord,' then he would doubtless have been dead and killed many times over. Put that way, one might wonder: 'Well – what if he had been one but not the other? What if he had been stalwart and staunch, but not a servant of God? Or what if he had been a servant of God, but a timid and feeble one?' Gandalf would say perhaps that this is a problem best not thought about; but something like it seems to me a major part of the structure of *The Lord of the Rings* (Shippey 2003a: 140-54). And whether that is so or not, it is certainly interesting to see Tolkien himself repeating just such alternative but undecidable conditions. The *Gawain*-poet leaves it uncertain whether it is Gawain's ability or his piety which saves him; the *Beowulf*-poet has his hero similarly leave it undecided whether it is *wyrd* or 'courage' that saves a warrior; and in exactly the same mode Gimli says to Merry and Pippin (at *LotR* 550) that "luck served you there, *but* (my emphasis) you seized your chance with both hands, one might say." In other words luck would *not* have saved Merry and Pippin any more than serving God would have saved Gawain – *on its own*! In all these traditional stories courage and fortitude are as important as morality, piety, or the intervention of higher powers. That is what keeps them stories rather than allegories.

There are other aspects of the *Gawain*-poet's work to which Tolkien would, I am sure, have liked to pay tribute. It should not escape notice, for instance, that the poem *Purity* pays such particular attention to questions of secular good manners (seen at times as superior even to morality, or at least as more irritating when absent) that modern criticism has on the whole preferred to turn a blind eye to them as to the issue of Gawain's confession. Tolkien would certainly also have responded powerfully to the clash of parental grief and Catholic consolation in *Pearl*, a clash perhaps even more powerful emotionally and even harder to 'mediate' than that between knightly manners and Christian duty in *Sir Gawain*. Nevertheless I feel yet once more that the deepest appeal of the *Gawain*-poet to Tolkien lay in the innumerable problems he set for philologists, all of them full of suggestion for the 'philological mind.' At line 115 of *Pearl* the dreaming narrator finds himself in a land by a strange stream where dazzling stones shine, "As stremande sternez, quen stroþe-men slepe," or as Tolkien translates it, "As streaming stars when on earth men sleep." 'Stroþe' however does not mean 'on earth.' The note in Gordon's edition reads:

> 115 *stroþe-men*: of uncertain meaning and derivation. *Strothe* in *Sir Gawain* 1710 appears to be derived from ON. *storð*

> 'stalks of herbage,' but the North-West place-names containing Stroth, Strother [...] point to a native OE. *stroð, *stroðor [...] *Stroð appears to have had the meaning 'marshy land (overgrown with brushwood),' and probably influenced the development of the imported ON. storð. Here stroþe-men is probably used in a generalized poetic sense to mean 'men of this world' [...], but stroþe would probably carry with it also, pictorially, a suggestion of the dark, low earth onto which the high stars look down. (Gordon 1953: 51-2)

One wonders how far credit for this note should be shared between E.V. Gordon, I.L. Gordon, and Tolkien. The philological point about Old English and Old Norse is only a reversal of what is said above about 'dreped,' and could have come from any of the three. The image of the men in the brushwood, asleep and in the dark, yet looked down on by the high, streaming stars *which they cannot see* seems, however, a perfect image of life in Middle-earth as portrayed by Tolkien and as remarked by Gildor or Galadriel. The marshy scrubland where the 'stroþe-men' sleep is the same as *galadhremmin ennorath*, 'tree-tangled' Middle-earth itself, and the 'stremande sternez' are the sign of Elbereth Gilthoniel, 'Elbereth star-kindler.' In this as in many other ways the images of the *Gawain*-poet have been received and transmitted by Tolkien back into living literary tradition.

Grimm, Grundtvig, Tolkien: Nationalisms and the Invention of Mythologies[1]

The most recent event in Tolkien studies has been, significantly, a double one. In the first place, *The Lord of the Rings*'s own first place in the Waterstone's Bookshops poll for 'Most Important Books of the Century'; and in the second place, the predictable outburst of horror and spleen that followed it from the professional interpreters of literature, in particular Germaine Greer and Auberon Waugh.[2] This antithetical response to Tolkien has been going on now for most of my lifetime, and both parts of it become more surprising as they continue. One might have thought by now that Tolkien's fiction, without being disgraced or dethroned in any way, might after more than forty years have slid backwards into that known-but-not-much-read state of perfectly respectable books like, for instance, Aldous Huxley's; while conversely the critical profession might have been able to find some not too threatening place for Tolkien in its collective pantheon, as it has done for other over-popular and initially rejected writers like Dickens and Wells. But neither change has taken place, and we still see the old love/hate response (love/hate, not love-hate) in undiminished vigour. This is, I think, a phenomenon. And phenomena deserve some kind of rational explanation.

I have offered two in the past (Shippey 1982, 1992, 2003a, ch. 1). One is that the critical hatred at least stems from the century-old war in university departments of English between the Philologists and the Critics, in which the Critics, having all but destroyed their enemies, seemed to see victory snatched from their grasp by the secret weapon of fantasy. The other is that outside universities, British literature at least was dominated, in the

---

[1] This piece appeared first in Maria Kuteeva (ed.). 2000. *The Ways of Creative Mythologies: Imagined Worlds and their Makers*. 2 vols. Telford: Tolkien Society Press, I: 1-17.
[2] Germaine Greer in *Waterstone's Magazine*, Winter/Spring 1997, 4; Auberon Waugh in *The Times*, 20 Jan. 1997. I owe these references to an unpublished paper by Patrick Curry, which eventually appeared in revised form as Curry 1999. See also Honegger 1999b, in the same volume.

between-war years when Tolkien's fiction was incubating, by a group labelled by Martin Green as the *Sonnenkinder*, the Children of the Sun (see Green 1977).[3] To these, as to other related literary groups, Tolkien and Lewis and their circle formed a conscious and increasingly effective reaction, for which again they could not be forgiven. Meanwhile Patrick Curry, addressing the same question, has located the antipathy to Tolkien in 'modernism,' with Tolkien as an early 'postmodernist' (or of course anti-modernist), who has once again become increasingly, not decreasingly powerful as a rallying-point for entirely contemporary protest and resistance (see Curry 1997 and 1999). All these explanations could be true at once, and indeed there is not much doubt that they are connected. I would like accordingly to add another, which not only helps to explain the double response phenomenon, but also locates Tolkien in yet another intellectual tradition besides those of philology and fantasy: that is, within mythography.

There is as far as I know no extended study of this available, a fact revealing in itself when one considers the prodigious annual output of books and PhD dissertations on all kinds of literary topics – all kinds, that is, that appear between the invisible blinkers of academic acceptability. But it seems to me that what happened was that Western European scholars during the nineteenth century became involved in at least four connected collective enterprises, which I will number for future reference. One (1) was the rediscovery of ancient languages – languages which, NB, had been completely unknown to and unreadable by even the most learned of their predecessors, so that Gibbon wrote his *Decline and Fall of the Roman Empire* without knowing a word of Gothic, or, probably, knowing that the Goths had left a literary trace behind. I have tried to convey something of the excitement of this movement elsewhere (in chs. 1 and 2 of successive

---

[3] Respectively a minor and a major figure in the group identified by Green were Philip Toynbee, perhaps Tolkien's least perceptive critic (the competition is formidable), and Evelyn Waugh, father of Auberon, still keeping up the feud in 1997.

editions of *The Road to Middle-earth*). Along with this (2) went the scientific study of ancient languages, which added to mere knowledge a method and a confidence in that method which was once again entirely new, and which, as its practitioners were once more well aware, had never been available to anyone before. Note that it might have been possible to have the rediscovery without the scientific study, and indeed in England, with its extremely narrow and conservative two-university élite, there was a doomed and bitter attempt to present the languages without learning the Danish/German method.[4] But (1) and (2) together gave rise to (3), the recovery of ancient texts.

Once again, we still have no extended study of this extraordinarily powerful and mould-breaking phenomenon, the launch of 'medievalism' on the world through ancient poetry. One can only point to some dates: Thomas Percy's *Reliques of Ancient English Poetry* in 1765, with Macpherson's 'Ossian' poems appearing from 1760 onwards – both these precursors of course carried out, like Percy's *Five Pieces of Runic Poetry* from 1763, without the benefit of either stages (1) or (2) above, and vitiated by continuing doubts about the very existence of the manuscripts from which the editors were supposed to have worked. Then the Russian *Song of Igor*, published in 1797, von der Hagen's edition of the *Nibelungenlied* in 1810, the Grimms' edition of the *Elder Edda* in 1812, Grímur Thorkelin's *Beowulf* in 1815, Schmeller's *Heliand* in 1830, Lönnrot's *Kalevala* in 1835 (the date of its publication still a national holiday in Finland), Laing's translation of the *Heimskringla* in 1834, Lady Charlotte Guest's translation of the *Mabinogion* in 1836, the *Chanson de Roland* coming along surprisingly late in 1837.[5] To someone like Jacob Grimm (1785-1863), every year must have

---

[4] This can be seen in the furious correspondence between J.M. Kemble and a string (?) of anonymous reactionaries in *The Gentleman's Magazine* from 1834. For some excerpts and an account of the affair, see Shippey and Haarder (1998: 28-30, 195-200).

[5] Some account of this European movement is given in the last chapter of Quint 1993.

seemed to bring a completely new literary treasure. Poets like Goethe (1749-1832) found the ground shifting under their feet.

But it should also be noted that these literary and linguistic efforts created something like an 'arms race' among the nations of Europe. In order to *be* a nation, it seemed – and this feeling was particularly strong among those language groups which were not nations, the Celts and the Germans – it was vital to have an ancient literary epic as part of one's *raison d'être*. We are often told nowadays that literature and the history of literature are merely concealed meditations on power.[6] But anyone familiar with the history of medievalism will be aware that in the case of the texts above, there was nothing concealed about the power-motive at all. Karl Simrock (1802-76), the great populariser and translator of medieval German poetry, pointed angrily in 1859 to the loss of German provinces across the Rhine (they were soon to be reconquered), and asked himself with bitter sarcasm:

> What does a province matter anyway? And now a poem, even? Every market-fair brings new ones, and they are forgotten before the next. How is a thousand-year glory of our people supposed to depend on an epic? How were the Homeric poems of the Germans, once they had finally been dragged out of the rubble, supposed to be able to contribute to strengthening our self-awareness and making us in the end into a nation?

But then he answered (it was part of his 'take-over bid' for *Beowulf* as a German, not an English poem):

> It is really not over once they have been dragged out. From the rubble of the centuries into the dust of the libraries, that is a step from one oblivion into another: it leads no closer to the goal. This goal is the heart of the nation: if our old poetry once finds its place there, then

---

[6] The idea has become a cliché of the 'New Historicism,' as of the followers of Foucault.

> Sleeping Beauty has woken from her enchanted sleep, then the heroes sleeping in the mountains rise again, then the dry tree buds on the Alpine meadow, then the old Kaiser hangs his shield on the green bough, then the battle is fought, which will bring back the last of our lost provinces to Germany. (Shippey and Haarder 1998: 308, translating Simrock 1859: 161)

Was he talking about provinces or about poems? He saw no distinction between the two. Military and political force rested on national self-confidence, and national self-confidence rested on the secure possession of national epics. Not for nothing did Gaston Paris (shooting back) give his lecture 'La *Chanson de Roland* et la nationalité française' during the siege of Paris in December 1870: the event really happened, but the context, the topic, and the lecturer's name, make it seem very nearly allegorical (see Hult 1996)

*

The point of this essay, though, is to argue that there was yet a fourth parallel and connected movement during the nineteenth century, as intimately connected with power as the one above, but less finished and less recognised: this, number (4), was the recovery and reclassification of ancient mythology. It is easy once again to underestimate the enormous changes this made to European and American 'mental furniture,' both educated and uneducated. Till the nineteenth century 'mythology' meant either Classical or Biblical. Possession of some knowledge of the former was one of the marks of the educated person, while some knowledge of the latter (probably not labeled as mythology) was felt to be essential for everyone. It is astonishing how rapidly both have been eroded, and how much they have been replaced by knowledge of mythologies, especially Norse mythology, which once again were completely unknown to even the most learned scholars not very many generations ago. I would venture the claim that any kind of poll (along the lines of Waterstone's) would show a more dispersed knowledge of Odin and Thor, Loki and Fenris-Wolf and the Mithgarth Serpent, among the modern American and European reading public, than of Jupiter and Juno, Polyphemus and Prometheus and Circe.

However, unlike movements (1), (2) and (3), movement (4) was in a sense not successful. It was expected to be. In George Eliot's *Middlemarch* (first published 1871-2), a major character is Mr Casaubon, an amateur scholar of independent means who has devoted his life to working on a 'Key to all Mythologies.' But as the story goes on – and after Casaubon has succeeded in persuading the intellectually starved Dorothea to marry him – it becomes clear that everything Casaubon has been doing is a waste of time. 'If Mr Casaubon read German he would save himself a great deal of trouble,' says one character dismissively (Will Ladislaw, in ch. 20). Much later, in ch. 48, the narrator herself takes sides against Casaubon. His theory, she says:

> floated among flexible conjectures no more solid than those etymologies which seemed strong because of likeness in sound until it was shown that likeness in sound made them impossible.

What were the German books that Casaubon should have read, one might ask. And what are the ridiculed 'etymologies'? Commentary on this from critics is as usual sparse – "only an editorial Casaubon would wish to pursue the matter further," says one editor, failing to trace a similar reference[7] – but the remark about etymologies disproved by "likeness in sound" probably points to some second-hand awareness of Jacob Grimm and the comparative philologists' insistence on strict phonological correspondences (not identities). George Eliot, herself a skilful Germanist, though not a Germanicist, appears at this point in the 1870s to be convinced of the superiority of German philological method, and to think moreover that the likes of

---

[7] George Eliot. 1965. *Middlemarch*. Edited by W.J. Harvey (Penguin English Library). Harmondsworth, p. 905. The issue is discussed further in Shippey 2005a.

Casaubon were also to be superseded by new discoveries *in the field of mythology*.

But this never happened. We have no science of comparative mythology capable of producing the same results as comparative philology. To put it another way, there can be no doubt of the success of Grimm's *Deutsche Grammatik*. From the appearance of its first volume in 1819 (fourth volume 1837), it was responsible for radical change and improvement in the ability to read texts, at the same time as making it clear that the Germanic languages were not mere barbarian vernaculars spelled and written with casual freedom, but had grammars and morphologies as strict and as rule-bound as the Classical ones. Grimm's *Deutsches Wörterbuch*, which began to appear in 1838, to be completed many years posthumously in 1913, was less successful in the sense of generating the strict semantic rules which were at one time expected to follow the strict phonetic ones, but nonetheless has remained constantly usable to this day. Grimm's third major intellectual enterprise, however, his *Deutsche Mythologie* (first edition 1835, fourth edition posthumously completed in three volumes 1875-8), was a failure.

One could, indeed, use even harsher language than that about it. Although it went into four editions, and was translated into several languages including English – the English translation, in four volumes, is still in print today – the *Mythologie* is in many places in my opinion literally unreadable. This judgement will perhaps only convince those who have tried to work out Grimm's opinion on some particular point through the maze of different editions (as I have, with reference to Grendel, Scyld and Beowulf). Doing this has however given me the opinion, rightly or wrongly, that what Grimm really did was to put all the facts he could collect on index cards, shuffle them into approximate order, and then write out the results; and as more facts became available to him, with more and more ancient texts becoming accessible, he wrote these in on margins or on interleaved sheets, with the intention of eventually incorporating them into new editions. I do not know what the last editor of the *Mythologie* was faced with after Grimm's death (Professor Elard Hugo Meyer), but whatever it was he seems to have decided not to try to sort it out. The last volume of the fourth edition of the *Mythologie* consists only of notes to the preceding three volumes, plus a discarded appendix, with the self-exculpatory explanation from Meyer that he feared that if he began to integrate the later material with the earlier, he 'might do too much' and dilute the pure spirit of Grimm with his own lesser matter. Meanwhile if one dips into any of the earlier volumes, far too often one comes upon stretches like the following:

> With us the word *alp* still survives in the sense of night-hag, night-mare, in addition to which our writers of the last century introduced the Engl. *elf*, a form untrue to our dialect; before that, we find everywhere the correct pl. *elbe* or *elben*. H. Sachs uses *ölp*: 'du ölp! du ölp!' (i.5, 525b) and ölperisch (iv. 3, 95c); conf. *ölpern* and *ölpetrütsch*, alberdrütsch, drelpetrütsch (Schm. 1, 48); *elpentrötsch* and tölpentrötsch, trilpentritsch (Schmid's Schwab. dict. 162); and in Hersfeld, hilpentritsch. The words mean an awkward silly fellow, one whom the elves have been at, and the same thing is expressed by the simple *elbisch*, Fundgr. 365. In Gloss. Jun. 340 we read *elvesche wehte*, elvish wights. (Stallybrass 1883-8: II, 443, translating Grimm 1875-8: I, 366)

The subject being discussed here is highly Tolkienian (elvish wights), as are some of Grimm's preoccupations, like historically correct linguistic forms for non-human races; but the trails of less and less relevant dialectal forms, the barely-comprehensible abbreviations, and the habit of italicising as far as I can tell at random, all clog any sense of intellectual progress beyond recovery. Grimm's *Grammatik*, one may say, imposed order on literally millions of readings, so that one could thereafter detect grammatical pattern and indeed deviation from that pattern. The *Mythologie* just left the data as a heap, wider in scope but (for all George Eliot's hopes) no more testable or contestable than Casaubon's broodings.

There was, however, a thesis buried in Grimm's work, or possibly two theses, even if these are nowhere directly stated. The first thesis is that the various forms of Germanic mythology are the relics of one original consistent whole, now extinct. The second, that that whole is still capable of being recovered, from ancient works but also from relic-forms preserved in modern fairy-tales, like the Grimm brothers' famous *Kinder- und Hausmärchen*, in their many editions from 1812. Both these theses rested on linguistic analogy. If such words as German *zwerg*, English *dwarf*, Norse *dvergr*, could be shown to be phonologically related and to derive from a hypothesised original **dvairgs*, then perhaps the concepts too could be traced back to their original. If theories about the phonology of early Germanic could be tested by the recovery of modern but non-standard dialect forms, then perhaps theories about early Germanic mythology could also be expanded by the search for the non-standard, sub-literary and therefore unspoilt, in such forms as fairy-tale. The analogy was at least not ridiculous, even if it has never been tested. But the real issue was lost sight of too early, as mythology, like poetry, became the theatre of nationalist contests for authority and power.

Grimm's very title, *Deutsche Mythologie*, was provocative in itself. Since much of the material he was dealing with was actually Norse, his work contained the tacit claim that the Scandinavian peoples were really *deutsch*, or German, a claim softened by the English translation into *Teutonic Mythology*. Nevertheless Grimm was quite capable of trying to cut the Scandinavians out. As early as 1823 he can be seen pointing to the just-edited *Beowulf* and insisting that for all its references to Danes and Swedes its mythology was essentially unknown to Scandinavia, and therefore German; and in the same review, incidentally, can be seen 'translating' the name Askr from the better-authenticated Norse mythology into its Old English and Old High German forms, a device at least toyed with by

Tolkien.[8] The political implication of his work was noticed and resented immediately in Scandinavia, and it can come as no surprise that even before Grimm had got into print (though not before he had started to make his views known), he faced challenge and competition from that quarter, and in particular from the Dane, Nikolai Frederik Severus Grundtvig (1783-1872).

Grundtvig's life-work is even harder to summarise than Grimm's, but one can say very briefly that he was for at least thirty years the most knowledgeable *Beowulf*-scholar in the world, in which field his perceptions have sometimes never been surpassed (not even by Tolkien); that he was also the agent of national self-definition for Denmark to a degree equalled only by Lönnrot in Finland; and that his poems and hymns remain a part of living Danish culture to this day (as does the immense collection of *Danske Folkeviser* or Danish ballads made by his son Svend). Grundtvig's *Nordens Mytologi* of 1808, very much expanded in the second edition of 1832, is like Grimm's *Deutsche Mythologie* only a part of his immense output. Nevertheless Grundtvig's *Mytologi* betrays a problem not shared with Grimm, and only partly shared with Tolkien: which is that Grundtvig was a devout and evangelical Protestant pastor, who found himself writing about heathendom. He might love the *Edda* as literature. But could he afford to love it as faith? The problem was shared by many Christian antiquarians in the nineteenth century, from Grundtvig's countryman and antagonist Peter Erasmus Müller – eventually Bishop of Sjælland, who nevertheless published a book 'On the Genuineness of the Asa-Teaching' first in German and then in Danish in 1811/1812, using the terms *Echtheit* and *Asalehre*, *Ægthed* and *Asalæren* respectively – to George Stephens, the passionately anti-German English professor in Copenhagen, who in 1878 published a very strange book indeed, *Thunor the Thunderer carved on a Scandinavian font of about the year 1000: the first yet found god-figure of our Scando-*

---

[8] Grimm's 1836 review of a work by his follower J.M. Kemble can also be found excerpted and translated in Shippey and Haarder (1998: 206-8). For Tolkien's toying with Æsc/Askr, see Christopher Tolkien's note in *Book of Lost Tales 1*, 245.

Gothic forefathers, in which he tried to argue, in curiously roundabout fashion, that Thor, Thunor and Christ were all in some way to be identified. Stephens actually defies paraphrase, but Tolkienists will understand it if I say simply that like Müller he is putting forward a 'splintered light' thesis.[9] Grundtvig, I think, avoided this, but at the cost of retreating into 'mythical allegory': he is one of the "very old voices these and generally shouted down, but not so far out as some of the newer cries," whom Tolkien notes as one of the constituents of the Babel of Beowulfians in '*Beowulf*: The Monsters and the Critics' (*Essays*, 8).

In brief, though, what the Grimm/Grundtvig competition shows is that for the mythographers of the nineteenth century (and their history has still to be written), the major problems were:

(1) to rediscover a lost unity of belief, along the lines of the linguistic science of 'reconstruction' in which they all firmly believed
(2) to press this into the service of their own major or minor language groups: German, Danish, Frisian, Scottish, etc.
(3) to reconcile it with their own Christian professions.

*

A question one can now ask is, how does Tolkien fit into this general picture? And the answer is, amazingly well. Rediscovering a lost unity of belief: this is exactly the aim of Tolkien's two early and still virtually-unread articles on '*Sigelwara land*.' It is comic, if sad, that when he refers to these in '*Beowulf*: The Monsters and the Critics,' helpful glossators still persist in translating the phrase as 'land of the Ethiopians' (for that is what the dictionaries say),[10] when as so often Tolkien's point was that the dictionaries

---

[9] I take the phrase from Verlyn Flieger's book, *Splintered Light* (1983).
[10] As is done in the reprint of Tolkien's essay in Nicholson 1963, a book once very much used.

were wrong. Late Anglo-Saxons might have used *sigelware* as a translation for 'Ethiopians,' but the real meaning of the original word was something like 'fire-giants' – a term from a mythology dead even to Anglo-Saxons, but nevertheless traceable by philology. Meanwhile much of the very core of *The Silmarillion* could be seen as a response to Grimm's extended brooding over the term 'elf.' Grimm derived this in its various Germanic forms from an original *albs, alp*, which he connected to Latin *albus*, to make a contrast between *alfar* and *dvergar*, elves and dwarves, white spirits and black. However he was faced with very clear statements in Norse contrasting *liosalfar*, 'light elves,' with *döckalfar*, 'dark elves,' not to mention *Svartalfaheim*, or 'black-elf home,' which is where the dwarves live. One way of settling this would be to say that elf was a category originally including both elves (light-elves) and dwarves (dark-elves, black-elves); though as Grimm noted this ran into further trouble when one noted dwarves bearing names like Nár or Náin, which seem to mean 'pale.' Grimm in the end characteristically proved unable to come to a conclusion, after amassing all his index cards, tailing off with the feeble remark that maybe *döckr* meant "not so much downright black, as dim, dingy" (Stallybrass 1882-8: II, 445). Tolkien invented a much better resolution of the data, in which one sees 'light-elves' and 'dark-elves' strongly contrasted in spite of an original identity, and in which dark elves and dwarves might be confused by careless (human) observers in spite of a very clear original difference. But sorting out this mythographic puzzle involved him in creating an entire mythological narrative: see further the essay 'Light-elves, Dark-elves, and Others' in this volume. It is still hard to say anything about the chronology of Tolkien's inventions, but this activity – recovering, or creating, a 'lost unity of belief' from later confusions – seems to have been part of Tolkien's method from the very beginning.

How far did Tolkien, then, mean to press this invention into the service of his own language group? One striking fact about the English, as opposed to other Europeans and especially the other inhabitants of the United

Kingdom and the British Isles, is that when it came to national origins, or indeed outer signs of national identity, they could in the nineteenth century hardly have cared less. When the origins of *Beowulf* came to be disputed, it was a fight between Germans and Danes, with English scholars joining in on both sides, but only rarely and perfunctorily putting in any kind of claim for English authorship: Tolkien's weary remark in 1936 about the obvious being discovered "[s]lowly with the rolling years" (*Essays*, 9) was if anything an understatement. To this day there is no specifically English national anthem (only one for the United Kingdom), and till very recently one saw more Union Jacks than St George's Crosses waved by England football supporters (but never by Scots or Welsh).[11] One explanation of this is to say that through the nineteenth century any sense of English national identity was deliberately suppressed, while Scottish, Welsh and Irish identities were deliberately fomented, in the interests of British imperial unity.[12] But whether that is the case or not, one result is that Tolkien, coming into the fields of philology and mythology in the twentieth century, could hardly avoid seeing an immense gap, for his country and language-group, filled for other countries and language groups by the works of men like Grimm and Grundtvig. Did he not set himself to fill this?

The evidence that he did is once again easier to collect the further back one goes in Tolkien's work. As early as 1916, in the 'Story of Eriol's Life' summarised by Christopher Tolkien in his discussion of the sources of *The Book of Lost Tales 1*, 22-7, one can see Tolkien trying to forge a link between his own entirely original and imagined stories of the elves and the traditional tale of the founders of England, Hengest and Horsa, "a matter to which my father gave much time and thought," as Christopher Tolkien says (*BLT 1*, 23). The very early equation of Tol Eressëa with Britain (not England), and Kortirion with Warwick, was eventually dropped, but the

---

[11] Though there has been a remarkable change in this area since this essay was first published, only a few years ago.

[12] As I argue in Shippey 2000b.

idea of dedicating his mythology "to England; to my country" was still remembered by Tolkien many years later.[13] The matter has been discussed at length by Carl Hostetter and Arden Smith (1995), though I would make one alteration to what they say: when they declare that Ottor Wǽfre is "the first mortal 'discoverer' of England [but] could not himself be English," they are putting the matter in an American way which I think Tolkien himself would have corrected. 'England' nowadays is a geographical designation like 'America,' but was not so originally: it is just a shortened form of Old English *Engla-land*, 'land of the English,' and could be applied to anywhere the people or peoples known as *Engle*, 'the English,' happened to live. So I would say that Ottor Wǽfre was conceived as an Englishman, or an Angle, even if (Christopher Tolkien's careful phrase) "he was not an Englishman of England" (*BLT 1*, 24). But all this says, and it is a conclusion which would have been accepted without dispute by Grimm, Grundtvig or indeed Simrock above, is that tribal designations are older than and not the same as modern political boundaries.

Tolkien wanted to stress 'Englishness' from early on. As his first conception proved too complex or too full of contradictions he moved on to others, like the skilful re-invention of the English hero Wade (now very little more than a name), or his careful use throughout *The Lord of the Rings* of Old Mercian rather than West Saxon (a politically pointed decision, in its way, as the orthodox British history of his own day, and ours, prefers to tell itself a story in which national *British* unity, not English unity, derives from a political unification based on the rather doubtful conquests of the West Saxon kings from the late ninth century on). And though the original English connections of his elvish mythology have I think vanished completely from the final versions of both *The Hobbit* and *The Lord of the Rings*, they have been replaced by two very clear national self-images in 'the Shire' and 'the Mark,' both in their different ways identifiably English terms, the one

---

[13] In his 1951 letter to Milton Waldman, see *Letters*, 144.

standing for a modern England, that of Tolkien's youth, the other for the old England of his literary texts, especially *Beowulf* (another English work which never mentions England).[14] In these ways it seems to me that Tolkien was still following what I have suggested as the second aim of his nineteenth-century predecessors, i.e. to press a 'reconstructed' mythology into the service of his own language-group. However, one may also say that one major, indeed vital, difference between Tolkien and his predecessors lies precisely in his internationalism, on which many have commented (e.g. Curry 1997: 132ff.). His variety of nationalism, which he noted himself with a characteristic carefulness of language not always realised,[15] shows neither the aggressive nationalism of Grimm (attempting to bring many national traditions under the hegemony of *deutsch*), nor the defensive nationalism of Grundtvig (insisting on Danish independence from exactly the kind of subordination proposed or implied by Grimm). The difference, of course, may well stem from no more than the obviously different linguistic situation. Long before Tolkien's birth the English language had ceased to be a possession of the English people or a marker for Englishness in any way at all, as was not true of Danish or even German. And in the same way Tolkien's mythology has proved itself to be unconstrained by national boundaries, as insidious and exportable as the language. Just as there are millions of native English speakers now who have no idea where England is, even on the map, so there are millions of readers of Tolkien who have no idea that there is any element in his fiction which might at any time have

---

[14] 'Shire' is a distinctively English territorial designation. Its occurrence in Scotland as well shows only that modern national boundaries have shifted. 'Mark' is much more widespread, as one can see from Denmark or the Mark of Brandenburg, but Tolkien correctly identified it as the Old English term translated into Latin 'Mercia,' and as the native term for his native region. See further the essay on 'Goths and Huns' in this volume.

[15] In the passage cited above from *Letters*, 144-5, Tolkien presents his idea of creating "a body of legend" dedicated "to England" as if it had been abandoned – "my crest has long since fallen" – but at the same time indicates it as still a possibility, "It should possess [...] I would draw [...]." The propositions are not exclusive.

been equated with 'Englishness,' and are none the worse for it. That does not mean that the quality is not there, and intended to be there.

Turning to the third aim of the nineteenth-century mythographer, reconciling a reconstructed and heathen mythology with one's own Christian profession, one can say that Tolkien's predecessors had it relatively easy. Since all those mentioned were Protestants, often aggressive Protestants, they could often say that what they were trying to do was to reach back to an early purity of belief – a 'splintered light' again – which had been blurred by Roman Catholic obfuscation.[16] This was clearly not an option open to Tolkien, and here I can only say that he seems to me to have turned the problem of reconciliation from one of belief to one of literary temper: from considering the *Echtheit* or 'genuineness' of the faith of his heathen ancestors to considering its literary attraction. This is in itself a complex and again critically unconsidered question, but I would suggest that a start could be made by looking for instance at the strange and curious European vogue, from the time of Thomas Percy onwards, of poems like 'The Death-Song of Ragnar Hairy-Breeks.'[17] The ideas behind this are mirrored with some fidelity in familiar parodies like the 'Monty Python' film *Erik the Viking*, a compendium of clichés (Valhalla, berserkers, horned helmets, drinking out of skulls etc.), but clichés which stem from a change of taste as marked and as novel as the rediscoveries of languages and of texts which created it. Poems like the 'Death-Song' or *Krakumál* created for European readers a new image of heroism which, like Gothic, had been simply unavailable to scholars like Gibbon. In many ways this shaped anthologies like the *Introduction to Old Norse* created by Tolkien's friend and collaborator E.V. Gordon (first edition Oxford 1927, but still in print); the

---

[16] A view particularly strongly marked for instance by Ludwig Ettmüller, whose Zürich 1875 edition (or anti-edition) of *Beowulf* was titled *Carmen de Beovvulfi Gautarum regis* [...], *quale fuerit antequam in manus interpolatoris, monachi Vestsaxonici, inciderat*, 'The Song of Beowulf King of the Gauts [...] as it was before it fell into the hands of an interpolator, a West-Saxon monk.'

[17] For the vogue, see Omberg 1976; for that particular poem, see Shippey 1999a.

Grimm, Grundtvig, Tolkien: Nationalisms and the Invention of Mythologies 95

image remained endlessly adaptable and reworkable by Tolkien, carefully divorced by him from the originally pagan contexts which Grimm, in particular, and his many followers sought so continually and in the end so disastrously to recreate, to 'reconstruct.'[18]

*

I hope the above has indicated some ways in which Tolkien was like, and some ways in which he was not like, his predecessors in the study and adaptation of European mythologies. He was squarely traditional in his belief that the data still preserved, sketchy though they were, could be coaxed into revealing concepts and images not present at first-hand (like **sigelhearwan* and **wuduwásan*). His wish to fill the particularly yawning gap in his own native tradition is only remarkable in that he had even less to work with than his Continental colleagues. The problem over reconciling the whole activity with Christian faith had also been faced many times before, again in probably less acute form. Where Tolkien was different – though again, only in degree, not in kind – was in transferring the whole activity from scholarship to narrative. Though one might well say that both mythology and ideology only work if they *are* embedded in narrative; while almost all of us are perfectly capable of pulling ideology at least *out* of narrative, as some of those present when this essay was first read (Patrick Curry and Maria Kamenkovich) could confirm.[19] I would end by returning to where I began and saying that yet another reason for Tolkien's continuing popularity across the world, and his continuing *un*popularity with sections of the literary profession, is that his highly traditional but by no means outdated mythology and ideology, whatever labels one wishes to put on them,[20] have

---

[18] For the fruitless post-Grimm reconstruction of Germanic heathendom, see Stanley 1975, and 'Goths and Huns' in this volume.

[19] See Curry (1997: 55-6), citing Maria Kamenkovich's account of Tolkien's influence on the events of August 19-22, 1991 (Kamenkovich 1992).

[20] I think 'reactionary' is literally true; there is no need to accept the common assumption that reaction against (alleged) progress is always wrong, or always pointless. Curry prefers 'postmodern.' The two labels are connected through their opposition to the view

remained perfectly comprehensible to millions of readers: a source of encouragement to one (much larger) group, a challenge, a menace, and even a reproach to another.

---

that 'modernism' is a correct interpretation of what is/has been happening, and is not to be defied.

The Problem of the Rings: Tolkien and Wagner[1]

"Both rings were round, and there the resemblance ceases" (*Letters*, 306). Tolkien's gruff dismissal of a suggested connection between *The Lord of the Rings* and Richard Wagner's opera tetralogy *Der Ring des Nibelungen* is well-known, and was evidently meant to terminate discussion. However, Tolkien also gruffly dismissed *Macbeth*, and allegory, and the medium of film, and in each case there is at least doubt as to how the dismissal should be taken.[2] There is no doubt at all that Tolkien paid keen attention to Shakespeare, and especially *Macbeth*, for all his professed dislike; his dismissal of allegory is in context a dismissal of a particularly dumbed-down version of it, which does not deny the fact that he frequently and overtly used allegory himself, for particular purposes; and his well-merited disapproval of one particular and extremely bad film script again does not cancel the fact that he approved the idea in principle. His attitude to Wagner was again a response to a dumbed-down (but frequently-repeated) opinion, to the effect that 'Tolkien got it all from *The Ring of the Nibelung*.' We now know, furthermore, that Tolkien did attend performances of Wagner's *Ring*, which was one of his friend C.S. Lewis's favourite works; they both knew it, and they must at least have talked about it.[3] This essay will argue that Tolkien's attitude to Wagner was rather like his attitude to Shakespeare's *Macbeth* and *A Midsummer Night's Dream*, or Edmund Spenser's romance-epic *The Faerie Queen*. All three authors had got on to something seriously impor-

---

[1] This essay has not been previously published, but is based on a paper given at the 18th International 'Studies in Medievalism Conference,' St Louis, Oct. 18th, 2003.

[2] See, respectively, Shippey (2003a: 182-5) and the essays on 'Allegory versus Bounce' and 'Another Road to Middle-earth: Jackson's Movie Trilogy' in this volume.

[3] See Wilson (1990: 30-32) for C.S. Lewis's early love of Wagner, and the BBC TV interview of 30th March 1968, 'Tolkien in Oxford,' cited by Rosebury (1992: 132), for Tolkien's attendance at Wagner operas.

tant, but had then (in Tolkien's view) botched it: it was one of his duties to set matters straight.

One could go further and say that, to Tolkien, Wagner seemed an enthusiastic amateur. He was interested in, indeed fascinated by, the same set of works as Tolkien, but could not read the Old Norse ones, at any rate, in the original language, and furthermore could not follow the involved scholarly arguments about their nature and origin.[4] And this meant (to Tolkien) that he did not show them sufficient respect – reason enough for denying all connection with him. Just the same, it should be said that, just as *The Lord of the Rings* is the most important and influential medievalist work of the twentieth century, so Wagner's opera-cycle was the most important of the nineteenth. And they do both centre on the Ring of Power. The similarities and the differences between them deserve to be drawn out.

This is particularly important because Wagner's work also derives from what has often been called the *Königsproblem*, the 'king problem,' of nineteenth-century comparative philology, Tolkien's professional discipline and major intellectual interest. In brief, the dominant literary work of the Middle Ages in Germany was the long romance, the *Nibelungenlied*: German scholars (who effectively invented comparative philology) naturally took this as their central text. However, at some time – and I have never been able to discover when this was – it was realized that not only did the *Nibelungenlied* have a far-off origin in fifth-century history, the story it contained of the murder of Siegfried and the downfall of the Nibelungs was also told in four other places, some of them older than the *Nibelungenlied* and markedly different from it in detail, in literary form, in general attitude. The question of how these texts related to each other, and what the original story might have been – this was the *Königsproblem*, surrounded often by nationalist passion, for all the other texts were in Old Norse, which meant that on the face of it the *Nibelungenlied*, the German national epic, was not

---

[4] There is a good account of Wagner's life, reading, and knowledge in Björnsson 2003.

a German story at all! And at the heart of all versions was a Ring; or rings; or something to do with rings. But could the true and original line of the story ever be straightened out from all the contending versions? Or – and here Wagner enters the frame – could a better story perhaps be written?

The five most important ancient 'Nibelung' texts are these. First, there are the poems of the *Elder* or *Poetic Edda*, written in Old Norse, and found for the most part in one manuscript known as the Codex Regius. But, alas! at a critical point some eight pages of the manuscript are missing, and these pages seem to have contained the greater part of a long poem, usually called **Sigurðarkviða inn meiri*, 'the Great Lay of Sigurd,' to distinguish it from the 'Short Lay of Sigurd,' which survives along with the 'Fragment of a Sigurd-Lay,' also called 'The Old Lay of Sigurd.' Of all the known lost works of the Norse tradition, this 'Great Lay' must be one of the two most regretted. Much ingenuity has been spent on imagining what it would have contained. We know, however, that Tolkien wrote a poem which he called *Volsungakvitha en nyja*, 'the New Lay of the Volsungs,' in which he attempted "to unify the lays about the Völsungs from the Elder Edda," written in the same metre (and language?) as the original (see *Letters*, 379). The poem has never been published, but it would be entirely characteristic of Tolkien, and of the philological imagination, to try to fill a gap in a manuscript, and solve a scholarly problem, in a creative way as well as an academic one. Perhaps the 'New Lay' was meant to fill out the 'Old Lay,' and the 'Short Lay,' and so replace the 'Great Lay.'

The next main source of the legend, and the one which has become 'canonical,' is the *Prose Edda* of Snorri Sturluson, written probably 1230-40. Snorri knew and quoted from the *Poetic Edda*, and probably had a copy of it which had not lost the vital Sigurd-Lay. Unfortunately his main aim in the *Prose Edda* was to provide a guide to poetic diction and traditional story for budding powers, and he told no more than he had to. His version of the entire Nibelung story, start to finish, is only some six pages long – the *Nibelungenlied*, which tells only a part of that story, is nearly three hundred.

Much more developed is *The Saga of the Volsungs*, written some thirty years later, by an anonymous author, who also had available to him the *Poetic Edda*. Unfortunately this author quite clearly sometimes did not understand the older versions and poems which he was trying to paraphrase, organize, and work into a whole. Although the saga has been much used and much translated, and been an inspiration to many, there are times when the author seems to be groping for a meaning. The fourth Old Norse version is a long and almost encyclopaedic saga, the *Þiðreks saga af Bern*, or 'Saga of Theodoric of Verona,' which collects all kinds of heroic legends, the Nibelung story among them. The date of this is uncertain, but it may have predated both Snorri and the *Völsunga saga*. Even more confusingly, though it survives in Old Norse, it is increasingly thought to be a translation from Low German. Finally, there is the *Nibelungenlied* itself, which probably also predates Snorri and *Völsunga saga*, and which is written in a southern dialect of Middle High German, far away in place and language from all the other versions.

The complex relationship between all these stories has occupied scholars for generations.[5] But the kind of problem they create can be seen by centering on one scene which they all handle (except for the *Poetic Edda*, which is deficient at this vital point). This scene itself centers on rings. Briefly, and ignoring variations of detail, the hero Sigurd, or Siegfried,[6] last of the Volsungs, has killed the dragon Fafnir and gained possession of the treasure of the Nibelungs. In both Snorri and *Völsunga saga*, this treasure includes the magic ring Andvaranaut, 'the possession of Andvari,' taken from the dwarf Andvari by Loki and given successively to Odin, to

---

[5] The best guide to the long debate is Andersson 1980.

[6] It will be seen in what follows that I use the spellings of the names given by the various translators, so that Norse Sigurðr becomes anglicized Sigurd or German Siegfried, Guðrun becomes Gudrun, or Kriemhild, or Grimhild, etc. Wagner's spellings are again slightly different. This very normal feature of ancient stories surviving in different texts may explain Tolkien's readiness to have different names for many of his own characters: changes prove a tale's antiquity/authenticity.

Hreidmar, father of Fafnir, and taken by Fafnir when he kills his father. This ring, which deserves to be called The Ring, gives its possessor enormous powers, but is cursed. In three Norse versions Sigurd then wakes the sleeping Valkyrie Brynhild, and enters into some kind of pact with her. But (in all versions) he then goes to the court of the Burgundian kings, and makes a pact with King Gunnar/Gunther that he will win Brynhild for Gunnar by changing his shape to that of the king. He then marries Gunnar's sister Gudrun, in the *Nibelungenlied* called Kriemhild. The fatal moment comes when Brynhild realizes that she has been mastered, not by Gunnar, but by Sigurd; that she has in fact been deceived, and betrayed, and possibly seduced, and even deflowered, by a man who is not her husband. For this she has to take deadly revenge.

But how does she find out? All surviving ancient sources agree that it is the result of a taunt from her sister-in-law Gudrun/Kriemhild. And they also further agree that the vital proof is a ring. At that point, however, they all tell different stories – *and not one of them makes sense*. This is the very heart of the *Königsproblem*, for scholars like Tolkien and for artists like Wagner. I give the four versions below, making with reference to each the obvious criticism.

In Snorri's *Prose Edda*, Gudrun and Brynhild argue over who has the right to wash her hair further upstream, and who has the more valiant husband. Brynhild says:

> "It was a greater achievement for Gunnar to have ridden the flickering flame when Sigurd did not dare."
> Then Gudrun laughed and said: "Do you reckon it was Gunnar that rode the flickering flame [which guarded the sleeping Brynhild]? I reckon that the one that went to bed with you was the one that gave me this gold ring, and that gold ring that you are wearing and that you received as morning gift, that is known as Andvari's gift, and I reckon it was not Gunnar that won it on Gnita-heath."

> Then Brynhild was silent and went home.
> (Faulkes 1987: 103)

What's wrong with this version? It has *two* rings. The revelation is very destructive, because Gudrun knows that Brynhild received her ring as a 'morning gift,' which was traditionally given to the bride on the morning after the wedding-night, if she has proved to be a virgin and in exchange for her virginity. This suggests that Sigurd did not hand Brynhild over to her husband intact, and has furthermore boasted of the fact to his wife, and even given her the love-token which Brynhild gave him. But more seriously, the big shock is the recognition of the famous ring, the fatal ring, Andvaranaut, known to belong to Sigurd ever since he won it from the dragon. This is what seems to silence Brynhild. But she has had it on her finger all the time! Has she never noticed? If she never recognized it before, then why should she be so shocked by recognizing it now?

Let's try again. In *Völsunga saga*, the two women are again bathing in the Rhine. Brynhild wades further out in the river than Gudrun, and Gudrun asks what this means.

> Brynhild said: "Why should I be your equal more in this than in other matters? I think my father is more powerful than yours, and my husband has accomplished many splendid feats and rode through the burning fire, but your husband was a thrall of King Hjalprek."
>
> Gudrun answered angrily: "It would be wiser for you to hold your tongue than to insult my husband. Everyone agrees that no-one at all like him has come into he world. It is not fitting for you to insult him, because he was your first man [*frumverr*]. He killed Fafnir and rode the wavering flames when you thought it was King Gunnar. He lay with you and took from your hand the ring Andvaranaut, which you can now see here for yourself."

> Brynhild saw the ring, recognized it, and became
> as pale as death. (Byock 1990: 82)

This time there is only one ring, and it is Andvaranaut, and Gudrun has it on her finger. That's why Brynhild has not seen it before. This is a powerful scene in many ways: Brynhild knows that she owned it, she knows who took it – the man she thought was Gunnar. If Sigurd's wife now owns it, then the man who took it must have been Sigurd (unless Gunnar gave it to his sister, not impossible, but pointless). The real objection is, if Sigurd has *taken* the ring Andvaranaut from Brynhild, he must have *given* it to her beforehand, because the ring is known to have come from the hoard of the dragon Fafnir, whom Sigurd killed. So when did he do that? And if he gave it to her as a morning-gift, that means he must have taken her virginity *before* he wooed her for Gunnar – unless he took it back as soon as he gave it to her, which is ridiculous. This version necessitates a kind of plot-doubling.

The author of the *Nibelungenlied*, a courtly poem, found much of this too vulgar and embarrassing to be repeated. For one thing, in his world queens do not wash their hair in the river and argue over precedence about who gets to stand upstream. Accordingly, in his poem Kriemhild and Brunhild argue over who has the right to enter church first, and see it as a matter of social class:

> Brunhild: "A liegewoman may not enter before a queen!"
>
> Kriemhild: "It would have been better for you if you could have held your tongue […] for you have brought disaster on your own pretty head. How could a vassal's paramour [*kebse*] ever wed a King?"
>
> Brunhild: "Whom are you calling a paramour?"
>
> Kriemhild: "I call you one […] My dear husband Siegfried was the first to enjoy your lovely body, since it was not my brother who took your

>maidenhead. Where were your poor wits? – It was a vile trick. – Seeing that he is your vassal, why did you let him love you? Your complaints have no foundation."
>
>Brunhild: "I swear I shall tell Gunther of this."
>
>Kriemhild: "What is that to me?"

Brunhild starts to cry, in a very un-Valkyrie-like way, and Kriemhild enters the minster before her, but on the way out, they start again:

>Brunhild: "Halt for one moment [...] You declared me to be a paramour – now prove it! [...]"
>
>Kriemhild: "[...] I prove it with this gold ring on my finger, which my sweetheart brought me when he first slept with you."
>
>Brunhild: "This noble ring was stolen and has long been maliciously withheld from me! But now I have got to the bottom of it and I know who took it from me."
>
>Kriemhild: "You shall not make me the thief who stole it! [...] As proof that I am not lying, see this girdle which I have round me – you shared my Siegfried's bed!" (Hatto 1965: 113-15)

There are several problems here, of which the first is that this is not the famous ring Andvaranaut (of which the *Nibelungenlied* knows nothing), but just an anonymous ring. Also, it's not clear how Sigurd got it. Logically, Brunhild ought to have given it to him as a token, because then she would know that it must have been passed on by the man she slept with, whoever that was. But Kriemhild never says that is what happened – her remark "my sweetheart first brought [it] me when he slept with you" is obscure, to say the least – and maybe Brunhild is right to say the ring was stolen: in which case it might have been stolen by anyone. The weakness of the motif is shown up by the fact that Kriemhild here has to introduce a second token, the girdle – very often a symbol of sexual conquest.

Finally, consider number four, the *Þiðreks saga*. In this, Brynhild asks why Grimhild is sitting in her high seat in her hall; Grimhild says, because both are rightfully hers:

> Brynhild said: "Even if your mother did have this seat and your father this castle and this land, now I own them and not you, rather should you wander in the woods and frequent unknown paths with your husband Sigurd. That is more suitable to you than being queen in the land of the Niflungs."
>
> Then Grimhild said: "Why do you scorn me and cast reproaches and dishonor at me, when I thought I should have honor and fame, that my husband is Sigurd the warrior. Now you are starting this game because you want us to talk further, whether it is for your honor or your disgrace. Answer me this first question I ask you: Who took your virginity, and who was your first man [*frumverr*]?"
>
> Then Brynhild answers: "Since you've asked me this, I can answer easily and there is no dishonor to me in it. The mighty king Gunnar came to my castle, and many mighty chieftains with him, and I took him as my man by consent of my kinsmen, and I was given to him with many signs of honor, and it was celebrated with the most splendid feast with many attending, and I came home with him here to Niflunga-land. And I do not mean to conceal this from you or from any other who asks about it, that he was my first man [*frumverr*]."
>
> Now Grimhild answers: "Now you lie about what I asked you about, as I expected. The man who took your virginity the first time, he is called Sigurd the warrior."
>
> Now Brynhild answers: "I was never Sigurd's woman and he was never my man."
>
> Then Grimhild said: "I refute that by this gold ring, which he took from you when he had taken your

> virginity. He took this same ring from your hand and gave it to me."
>
> And now when Brynhild sees this ring, she recognizes that she had owned it, and it comes into her mind what had happened, and she now regrets very much that she had pressed this talk so far that many people must have heard it, and these things have now come out before everyone which previously few people had known. And Brynhild thinks this matters so much that her body is now as red as newly-shed blood, and she is silent and says not a word, stands up and goes away out of the hall.
>
> (*Þiðreks saga*, ed. Guthni Jónsson 1984: 466-8)

This is actually the most sensible of the four versions we have, the arguments expressed with particular clarity. Brynhild says, "I was never Sigurd's woman," and Grimhild says, "I refute that by this gold ring, which he took from you when he had taken your virginity. He took this same ring from your hand and gave it to me." Brynhild has not seen Grimhild with the ring before, but she recognizes it as her own as soon as she does see it, and knows that it has been given, not stolen. The only weak point is that, once again, this ring is not The Ring, 'the Nibelung's ring,' the ring Andvaranaut. It does its job in this scene, but does not connect this scene with the dwarf Andvari's curse, the dragon Fafnir's curse, and the curse which will fall on Brynhild, Grimhild, Sigurd, and Sigurd's murderers.

One thing these four scenes do is exemplify something Tolkien said, or had one of his characters say, with particular emphasis. In 'The Notion Club Papers' Ramer – an obvious Tolkien-projection – says to his clubmates:

> "I don't think you realize, I don't think any of us realize, the force, the daimonic force that the great myths and legends have. From the profundity of the emotions and perceptions that begot them, and from the multiplication

of them in many minds – and each mind, mark you, an
engine of obscure but unmeasured energy."
(*Sauron Defeated*, 228)

"Daimonic force" seems a good term for what animates the passages above. Four widely separated authors all knew that 'the quarrel of the queens' was a vital scene. They were all sure that the taunt of woman B to woman A was the precipitating factor of an immense tragedy, not least for both women. They knew the taunt had to be an accusation of sexual impropriety. They were all convinced that the display of a ring was the clinching proof. But what did it prove? How did it prove it? Which was the ring? Or were there two rings? Which woman had the ring? Was the ring 'The Ring,' or just a ring? They all set themselves to answer these questions, and sometimes they changed other parts of the story round to fit, often unsuccessfully, but they were all sure the scene, and the ring, *had to be there*. And failure to establish a canonical version just provoked other authors into trying their hand: of whom the greatest in modern times was Wagner.

There is no point in criticizing Wagner for altering his source, or sources.[7] He had every right to do so, especially as the sources didn't agree with each other, or in this case even provide a satisfactory answer. Nevertheless, what Wagner did here, and the concomitant changes he was obliged to make, might well have been enough to provoke Tolkien's indifference or dislike. It is always a doubtful business for a later critic to pronounce on what a writer meant to do, or what his 'design' was. But in this case it seems clear that Wagner decided, first, that whatever else happened, the ring which provoked the tragedy had to be The Ring, the Ring of the Nibelung itself, the one with a curse on it, whether imposed by the dwarf Andvari or the dwarf Alberich. One can hardly argue with this decision, but it cuts out both the *Nibelungenlied* version and the version in *Þiðreks saga*. Furthermore Wagner wanted Brünnhilde to be the one to see and recognize

---

[7] As some have done, see Hatto (1965: 7), criticized by Cooke (1979: 83).

it, in the most dramatic form possible, and this cuts out the *Prose Edda* story. He was left, then, with the version from *Völsunga saga*. This, however, has real trouble over the issue of virginity, the morning-gift, and the *frumverr* accusation which causes such particular friction in all the other ancient versions, even the courtly *Nibelungenlied* having Kriemhild call Brunhild a *kebse*, of which 'paramour' is a very polite translation. In *Völsunga saga* Brynhild cannot possibly have been a virgin at the time Sigurd won her in his disguised shape as Gunnar, for she had already had a daughter by him, Aslaug, mother of Ragnar Lóthbrok and so grandmother of the historical Ragnarssons who so nearly conquered England in the ninth century. This explains how she had the Ring Andvaranaut – he gave it to her presumably as the traditional 'morning-gift' – but does not at all explain why, if he did not lie with her in Gunnar's shape but kept his sword between them, in the morning "He took from her the ring Andvaranaut, which he had given her, and gave her now another ring" (Byock 1990: 81).

Wagner deals with all this neatly and expeditiously. Siegfried gave Brünnhilde the Ring when he woke her from her enchanted sleep, and they declared undying love. Hagen, son of Alberich, gave Siegfried the potion of forgetfulness, so that he forgot his love for Brünnhilde. He won her for Gunther, and Brünnhilde gave the Ring to the man who conquered her, whom she thought to be Gunther, perhaps as a sign of submission. She is then, in Act II scene 3 of *Götterdämmerung*, amazed to see it on Siegfried's finger. This is a good scene in every way – except for one very serious loss. Wagner's version has eliminated the whole motif of 'the quarrel of the queens,' found in all the ancient versions above! With it has gone the vital role in the scene of Gudrun, or Kriemhild – the central figure of six or more of the lays of the *Poetic Edda*, the pre-eminent heroine of Old Norse literature, the pre-eminent villainess of the *Nibelungelied*, now reduced, in Wagner, to a pathetic and confused bystander.

Nor is she the only casualty of Wagner's re-organisation. With her goes the figure of Högni/Hagen, brother of Gunnar/Gunther. As remarked in the essay below on 'Heroes and Heroism,' if there is one characteristic most admired in heroes of the Northern tradition, it is self-possession; and the archetypal exemplars of that are, in the poem *Atlakviða* of the *Poetic Edda*, Gunnar and Högni. Högni laughs as they cut out his small, hard, untrembling heart, and Gunnar looks at it with approval as he sets up his own death by torture: a scene at once cruel and comic, the very touchstone of the heroic mentality. None of this appears in Wagner, whose Hagen is a cunning plotter, egged on by his dwarf-father Alberich, and whose Gunther is weak and indecisive. As for Siegfried, Tolkien might well have felt that he was no great advertisement for the Northern heroic tradition either. It is true that he is fearless, but then if you are much bigger and stronger than anyone else, and possessed of an invincible sword, it might be said that courage comes easy. A real hero – a Gunnar, a Högni, a Hamthir, an Egil – shows his quality when he is trapped, helpless, or defeated, and when he knows it. Siegfried, especially in the opening scenes of the opera named for him, comes over as a mere lout. Furthermore Tolkien, on one occasion somewhat supercilious about even his own debt to the Grimms' fairy-tales, would certainly have noted the debt in those scenes to the Grimms' tale of 'The Boy Who Set Out to Find Fear,' and observed its anachronism. Tolkien thought Shakespeare in *Macbeth* had botched the brilliant idea of the marching wood, and he must have thought that Wagner in *Götterdämmerung* had botched the very kernel of the whole Norse/German heroic tradition.

Did he, nevertheless, learn anything from Wagner as he did, surreptitiously, from Shakespeare? One of Wagner's major – and probably least welcome – changes to the Scandinavian consensus comes in Acts I and II of *Siegfried*. The poems of the *Poetic Edda* are in one area quite clear and in full agreement with both the *Prose Edda* and the *Völsunga saga*. All three sources say that Sigurd was taught smithcraft by Regin, the brother of Fafnir, who forged a sword for him, incited Sigurd to kill Fafnir with it, and plotted to murder him once he had won the treasure and the ring, only for

Sigurd to learn of the plot from the chattering of birds and kill Regin instead. Regin figures in the 'Lay of Regin' and the 'Lay of Fafnir,' and while he is treacherous and self-serving, he is in no way comic, pathetic, or ridiculous, and there is no indication that he is a dwarf – if anything, he seems to be of giant stock. Wagner altered this consensus version sharply by turning Regin into the figure of the dwarf Mime. He did have a basis for this in the *Þiðreks saga*, which alone of the Old Norse versions replaces Regin by a smith called Mime. But it was Wagner's idea to make him a dwarf, the brother of Alberich, and further to make him a figure of fun. In Acts I and II of *Siegfried*, the hero – as said above, displaying for the most part merely loutish qualities – bullies Mime, sets a bear on him, knocks food out of his hands, reduces him to tears, and eventually kills him. Mime is represented as not just a dwarf, but also – and to Tolkien these were very un-dwarvish qualities – cowardly, treacherous, self-pitying, and incompetent even as a smith: in a word, petty.

Was this perhaps remembered in the figure of Mîm, of the Noegyth Nibin, the 'Petty Dwarves'? In the tale of Túrin, as told in *The Silmarillion* and at more length in *Unfinished Tales*, Mîm betrays Túrin to the orcs, and is killed for it by Túrin's father Húrin. Mîm and his people, however, are pathetic rather than contemptible, and Túrin shows some sympathy for him. Mîm is caught by Túrin, and offers him a refuge as ransom for his life; but his son Khîm is shot and killed by one of Túrin's men, one has to say for no good reason. Túrin accordingly expresses regret and promises to pay compensation when he can; but this never happens, for Mîm and his remaining son Ibun betray Túrin to the orcs. Even then, sympathy is not entirely alienated, for it is made clear that Mîm and his people have an older grudge, against the elves and especially the Noldor, who have dispossessed them and hunted them down as casually as Túrin's man shoots them. Now they are all but extinct, forgotten even by the more powerful branches of their own people: one reason for Mîm's betrayal is the friendship of Túrin with the elf Beleg, whom Mîm sees as a representative of the usurpers. The

Noegyth Nibin, then, are treacherous, but provoked; pathetic, but not contemptible; above all they are weak, physically and morally, not at all like the dwarves met elsewhere in Tolkien. One could see Tolkien's creation of them as an attempt to integrate one conception of the dwarves, as presented by Wagner, and to explain away its inconsistency with his own conception and with more traditional sources. Just as (Tolkien implies) the perilous allure of Lothlórien gave rise to later fearful and hostile tales of the elves, so the sad and dispossessed figure of Mîm, passed on in tale and rumour, might have ended as Wagner's utterly degraded and un-dwarvish Mime.[8] Meanwhile and perhaps more pointedly, Tolkien has set up a further implied contrast between Siegfried and Túrin, not at all to the advantage of the former: Túrin is a real hero, capable of remorse, capable also of cruelty when provoked, but unlike Siegfried not at all interested in bullying the weak for his own amusement. One can see once more why Tolkien preferred to reject the connection with Wagner.

Yet there is another feature of the opera-cycle which may at least have given Tolkien a hint, and a most important hint: this is Wagner's concentration on, and original conception of, the Ring itself. None of the ancient sources gives the ring Andvaranaut the central place that Wagner does. Snorri's *Prose Edda* tells the story of the taking of the Ring from Andvari the dwarf, says there is a curse on it, and mentions it again with reference to the 'quarrel of the queens' scene cited above. Gunnar and Högni also inherit it after the deaths of Sigurd and Brynhild, but it then disappears from the story, and there is no mention of it with reference to Fafnir: it is a part only of the whole hoard. *Völsunga saga* follows the same pattern, with the Ring – as Byock notes (1990: 126) – "not explicitly mentioned" as part of Fafnir's treasure. *Þiðreks saga* and the *Nibelungenlied*, while still aware that rings have something to do with the Nibelung tragedy,

---

[8] In much the same way as Bilbo is preserved in hobbit-folklore only as "mad Baggins, who used to vanish with a bang and a flash and reappear with bags of jewels and gold" (*LotR*, 41).

see above, know nothing of Andvaranaut at all. It was Wagner who – one has to concede, in very Tolkienian fashion – noted the gaps of the ancient sources and wrote his version of the story determinedly into them. He follows the Ring from the Rhinemaidens to Alberich, to Loge and Wotan, to Fafner, to Siegfried, to Brünnhilde, and back to Siegfried, to Brünnhilde, to the Rhinemaidens. It is a continuing presence in the story. In much the same way, at some time between *The Hobbit* and *The Lord of the Rings*, Tolkien devised a chain of transmission from Sauron to Isildur, to Gollum, to Bilbo, to Frodo, with a final destruction by fire which parallels the return of Wagner's Ring to the Rhinemaidens and its drowning in the flood.

One more feature which Tolkien's Ring and Wagner's share (other than roundness) is their significance, their edging towards allegory. In the Old Norse sources, if one had to ascribe a meaning to Andvaranaut, one would have to say that it represents wealth: eagerly sought for, often disastrous. In Snorri's account, Andvari the dwarf begs to keep it after he has lost everything else because "he could multiply wealth for himself from the ring if he kept it" (Faulkes 1987: 100). In Wagner, it is quite clear that the Ring gives *maßlose Macht*, 'immeasurable power,' once the Rhinegold is fashioned into a Ring, it *gewinnt dem Manne die Welt*, 'wins for its owner the world' (Wagner, trans. Porter 1977: 14, 30).[9] One might perhaps quibble that Wagner is not absolutely consistent in his presentation of the Ring, in that Siegfried shows relatively little interest in power, even when he owns the Ring, and neither does Brünnhilde; but Alberich the dwarf does demonstrate the mingled power/corruption of the Ring, ordering the terrified Nibelungs to obey *des Ringes Herrn*, 'the lord of the Ring,' prophesying that the gods' desire for gold will end in enslavement to it, and that the lord of the Ring will also be *des Ringes Knecht*, 'the slave of the Ring' (Wagner, trans. Porter 1977: 45, 47, 58). While Wagner's Ring does not

---

[9] I have given my own more literal translations rather than Porter's singable ones.

give invisibility, it is strongly associated with the magic Tarnhelm, which does. All these points at least find an echo in Tolkien.

What very much does *not* is the sense that Wagner understands and sympathises with the desire for power, if it could be acquired without paying the price for it. There is no-one in his cycle who does *not* want the Ring, and there are no scenes of powerful characters refusing to take it, as there are repeatedly – Gandalf, Aragorn, Galadriel, Faramir – in Tolkien's story. Nor, one feels, could hobbits possibly ever find a place in Wagner's conception. Along with this there goes very strong political and military opposition. It might or might not be possible to excuse Wagner for the uses made of his work by the Nazis after he was dead, but from Tolkien's perspective, perhaps even more than from ours, the seeds of horror were there in Siegfried's casual and uncondemned brutality, in the picture of a divine/heroic world constantly threatened by cunning, sneaking dwarf-shapes, so easily converted ideologically into *Untermenschen*, sub-humans. The least one can say of this is that Wagner and Tolkien were on opposite sides of a great divide created by two world wars and all that went with them: of this divide Tolkien at least was fiercely conscious and deeply resentful (see *Letters*, 55-6). If Tolkien did take anything from Wagner, it was perhaps no more than the idea that something could be done with the idea of the Ring of Power, something more, and more laden with significance, than anything in an ancient source, but at the same time and very definitely *not* what Wagner had done with it.

There is one final thing that might be said, if tentatively. Tolkien perhaps had an ambiguous attitude to stories, especially traditional stories. He was certainly highly protective of his own creations, and felt (for instance) that people should at least ask his permission before using the names and settings which he himself had invented. At the same time he was well aware that some parts of Middle-earth were not his own invention, were the common property of the ages. On the Stairs of Cirith Ungol Sam realizes that he and Frodo are in a sense still in the same story which he has always regarded as over, belonging to the far past, the tale of the Silmarils and the Iron Crown and Beren and Eärendil. He asks, "Don't the great tales never end?", and the answer is 'No' (*LotR*, 697). Nor, one might say, do they ever reach a final shape: Tolkien's own repeated versions of the scene between Beren and Thingol, for instance, are similar in their variations to the different versions of 'the quarrel of the queens' as given above (see Shippey 2003a: 313-7). Tolkien was accordingly, and again I say 'perhaps,' prepared to accept that in a way the 'great tales' might speak through and even against their individual authors. He thought that both Shakespeare and Milton were seriously misguided artistically and politically, but they were great poets, and sometimes – in *Macbeth*, in *Comus* – it seemed as if the language spoke through them, their stories took them over. Possibly the same was true of Wagner. Whatever one thought of him and his individual creation, his mind too was "an engine of obscure but unmeasured energy," as Ramer says in 'The Notion Club Papers' (see above), and whatever he made of it, the tale he told, not all of it his own invention, was indeed one filled with "daimonic force." One could concede that without feeling any urge to like what Wagner made of it; and one could dislike what he made of it very much without expelling it from the tradition.

Goths and Huns:
The Rediscovery of the Northern Cultures
in the Nineteenth Century[1]

The paper which follows may be seen most readily as a response to E.G. Stanley's monograph, *The Search for Anglo-Saxon Paganism* (1975). In this work Professor Stanley studied the history of the reception of Old English literature and its effect on scholars during the nineteenth and much of the twentieth century; and came to the rueful conclusion that "for a long time Old English literature was much read in the hope of discovering in it a lost world of pre-Christian antiquity, *for the reconstruction of which the Old English writings themselves do not provide sufficient fragments*" (Stanley 1975: viii, my emphasis). The evidence amassed makes this conclusion incontestable. It remains possible, however, to feel doubt over the last words of the monograph, which point to the persistence of romantic attitudes in scholars, and declare that "[t]racing to its origins the error on which these attitudes are based may perhaps help to eradicate them" (Stanley 1975: 122). The origins of the search for the 'lost world' of Germanic prehistory should not be confused with the first manifestations of it; nor was its appeal confined only to scholars, though without scholarship the appeal would not have existed. The questions which this paper seeks in part to answer are how images of the past were created by nineteenth-century philology, and why there should be a particular charm for scholars and creative authors alike in 'the unknown,' even, as Professor Stanley (1975: 122) calls it, "the unknowable unknown."

A twentieth-century example makes several points with particular specificity. In J.R.R. Tolkien's fantasy *The Lord of the Rings* (1954-5), a

---

[1] This piece appeared first as a contribution to Andreas Haarder (ed.). 1982. *The Medieval Legacy: A Symposium*. Odense: Odense University Press, 51-69. I am very grateful to Prof. Haarder both for the initial invitation, and for much help and hospitality over the years; and to Odense UP, now Syddansk UP, for permission to reprint.

prominent part is played by a people known as 'the Riders of Rohan,' or of 'the Riddermark.' As has often been noticed, this race is Anglo-Saxon by language, nomenclature, and in most respects by behaviour: the fragments of their language quoted are in Old English, their names are usually Old English words capitalised, as with the king 'Théoden,' the hall 'Meduseld,' and the sword 'Herugrim,' while the whole sequence of the visitors' approach to their king in Volume 2, Book 1, chapter 6, is most closely modelled on lines 229-404 of *Beowulf*. As has less often been noticed, though, the 'Riders' are different from historical Anglo-Saxons in one vital respect, namely their fascination with horses. They call themselves 'Éotheod,' 'the horse-people,' use personal names such as 'Éowyn,' 'horse-joy,' and have as their main rank below the king that of 'Marshal,' a word derived, as *The Oxford English Dictionary* tells us, from Old French *mareschal* but before that from Old Teutonic **marho-skalko-z,* 'horse-servant.' By contrast the Anglo-Saxons seem determinedly pedestrian. There might have been a word **mearh-scealc* in Old English, but it is not recorded. Meanwhile the *Anglo-Saxon Chronicle* gloomily reports that at the battle of Hereford in 1055 "the English army fled before a spear was thrown, because they were on horseback"; perhaps coincidentally, the fragment of the poem on *The Battle of Maldon* opens with the English commander ordering his men to drive away their horses and go into battle on foot. This particular difference between the Anglo-Saxons of history and their fictional analogues is especially marked, and one may wonder whether it has any basis or motive.

Certainly it does not appear to be mere free invention. A very strong clue lies in the first word from the Riders' language quoted in the fantasy, the place-name 'Eastemnet' used by the narrator in near the start of *The Two Towers*: "the Horse-lords had formerly kept many herds and studs in the Eastemnet, this easterly region of their realm" (*LotR*, 417). A few pages later we hear of 'the Westemnet.' And if 'east' and 'west' are mere prefixes, one is left with the word 'emnet,' a word whose status is in several respects typical of the 'lost worlds' and fantasies of reconstruction derived by philologists from scanty material from the nineteenth century on. 'Emnet' is not listed in *The Oxford English Dictionary*. It is in Bosworth and Toller's *Anglo-Saxon Dictionary*, glossed as 'level ground' or 'plain.' However it can also be found in *The Concise Oxford Dictionary of English Place-Names*, under the heading *Emneth* (Norfolk), a name explained by the editor, Eilert Ekwall, as derived either from *Æmenan-gemýþe*, 'the mouth of the river *Æmene*,' or else (since the *Æmene* is totally conjectural) from Old English *mǽþ*, 'meadow,' prefixed by *efn* or *emn*, 'smooth.' What has this to do with the Riders and the Riddermark? In brief, one may well surmise that Professor Tolkien at some point asked himself why modern English has no native word for the concept 'steppe' or 'prairie,' no word corresponding to the German *Ebene, Grasebene*; concluded, reasonably enough, that it is because the thing itself is unknown in a small and densely-wooded island; but noted that a form of a native word had indeed survived, not by coincidence, in the flattest and most prairie-like of all the English counties, Norfolk. If, then, the Anglo-Saxons had been familiar with the plains of North-West Europe (instead of emigrating to England), they would have called them 'emnets'; and if they had had to use 'emnet' as an everyday word for a familiar landscape, it is only reasonable to assume that their attitude to horses would have been much more receptive!

Suppositions of this nature may appear to have no value; they are indeed ventures into the unknown and unknowable. However one may say that latent in the history of 'emnet' there lies a thesis about the effect of landscape on history and culture. That Tolkien brooded upon this thesis is confirmed, as it happens, by a further linguistic oddity embedded by him in his fictional account of the Riders' ancestry; in this (see *LotR*, 1021-2, Appendix A I/iv), several names, such as Vidugavia, Vidumavi, and Vinitharya, are not Old English at all, but Gothic, Latinized spellings of *Widugauja*, 'wood-dweller,' *Widumawi*, 'woodmaiden' and *Winithahar-*

jis, perhaps 'Wend-host.'[2] In his posthumously published *Unfinished Tales* we find also *Marhwini,* a word which could interestingly be either Gothic, 'horse-friend,' or Old English (in an Anglian dialect) with the same meaning. It is as if Tolkien had remembered, in his broodings on words, that 'horse-folk' *par excellence,* the *equitatus Gothorum,* 'the cavalry of the Goths,' and had noted furthermore the once close kinship, linguistic and presumably racial and behavioural, between ancient English and ancient Goths. One group had turned west, to lasting survival on their wooded island, and one east, to the steppes of Russia and the Ukraine, and to eventual oblivion. What would the English have been like had they turned the other way? And what image would the Goths present, if any of their literature had survived for us to form a judgement? An answer to both is given in Tolkien's picture of the Riders of Rohan, with their English names and Gothic history, their English word for Gothic landscape, their highly un-English adaptation to grasslands and horses.

The Riders, one may say, are a 'reconstructed' culture, just as 'emnet,' in modern English, is a 'reconstructed' word – one which does not exist and has not survived, but which *could* have survived (if English resistance to foreign imports had been greater), and which could be *said* to exist, as a name (leeched of all but particular meaning). The process of 'reconstruction' is of course to philologists a familiar one, marked by the universal use of the '*', for a word never recorded but which the philologist genuinely believes to have existed; and it is the genuineness of the belief on which one should concentrate. Professor Tolkien no doubt did not believe in the real prehistoric existence of his 'Riders.' However he may very well have believed in the existence of something very like them. It is true that the evidence for early Gothic culture (as it has been discussed in this paper so far) rests on no more than a handful of words, or non-words, a sense of

---

[2] The point is made by Christopher Tolkien in his edition of his father's *Unfinished Tales* (1981: 311). The first and third names are discussed in Mommsen (1882), part of the *Monumenta Germaniae Historica* series.

linguistic kinship, and a certain response to early texts such as *Beowulf*. However behind these scraps there lies a technique, developed with increasing confidence by Tolkien's professional predecessors; and even a tradition. Under the heading *philolog* in the *Deutsches Wörterbuch* originated by Jacob Grimm, one finds Grimm himself being cited:

> Man kann alle philologen, die es zu etwas gebracht haben, in solche theilen, welche die worte um der sachen, oder die sachen um der worte willen treiben [...] ich mich lieber zu den ersteren halte.
> [One can divide all philologists who have got anywhere with it into those who deal with words for the sake of things, or those who deal with things for the sake of words [...] I prefer to hold with the former]
> (Grimm 1999: XIII, col. 1829; and Grimm 1879-90: I, 150)

Others besides Tolkien started from words, but went beyond them.

To return to the nineteenth century, we can find very close analogues to Tolkien's fictional practice in two romances written by William Morris, *The House of the Wolfings* (1888) and *The Roots of the Mountains* (1889).[3] Reaction to these has always been mixed, but it is fair to say that such critical praise as they have had has been vague. They represent "the epic or Icelandic side of the author's imagination," writes one critic; Morris was trying "to reproduce the old sagas," declares another.[4] Morris's own daughter wrote that in these two romances "my father seems to have got back to the atmosphere of the sagas," adding by way of a further disclaimer that "after the Wolfings came out" a German professor "wrote and asked learned questions about the Mark, expecting, I fear, equally learned answers from our Poet who sometimes dreamed realities without having

---

[3] Volumes XIV and XV of *The Collected Works of William Morris* (1910-12).
[4] Respectively Mackail (1899: II, 214) and Thompson (1967: 161).

documentary evidence of them."[5] However, though his critics seem to use 'the sagas' as a generic description for anything pre-Norman, Morris may have had better evidence, if not 'documentary evidence,' than they realised, as also a more developed historical and geographical sense than they themselves show.

He took pains, admittedly, to avoid anachronistically direct datings and placings. The ordinary reader of 1889, opening *The Roots of the Mountains,* might well have assumed he was about to read a romance about early England. He would find on page 1 a description of a valley set among mountains, with in the valley "a town or thorp," and in the town a tower; the tower is called 'the burg,' and so the town is 'Burgstead,' and the valley 'the Dale' or 'Burgdale.' There is no 'Burgstead' in *The Oxford Dictionary of English Place-Names,* but there is a 'Burstead' in Essex, while thorps, dales, fells and tofts are all perfectly familiar (and strongly localised) in the north of England. The people of Burgdale might then be taken to be English, at least for a while: but before long it becomes clear that some other place and time must be intended. The mountains, for one thing, have glaciers on them, as English fells do not. Furthermore the pine-woods are full of enemies. The main action of *The Roots of the Mountains* is of war, between the Burgdalers, who are tall and fair, and a race of invaders, who are not. It is the description of these invaders – called throughout the romance 'the Dusky Men' – which indeed allows us first to guess at the kind of source from which Morris drew, and second at the precise historical (or philological) setting into which he placed his imaginary story.

The first description of 'the Dusky Men' says that they were:

> short of stature, crooked-legged, long-armed, very strong for their size: with small blue eyes, snubbed-nosed, wide-mouthed, thin-lipped, very swarthy of skin,

---

[5] 'Introduction' to Morris (1910-12: XIV, xxv).

> exceeding foul of favour.
> (Morris 1910-12: XIV, 88)

Most of the features listed there – short stature, strength, small eyes, darkness and ugliness – are also to be found in one passage of Jordanes's *Historia Getica*, which declares that the race which fell on Ermanaric the Goth inspired panic:

> because their swarthy aspect was fearful, and they had, if I may call it so, a sort of shapeless lump, not a head, with pin-holes rather than eyes [...] They are short in stature, quick in bodily movement, alert horsemen, broad shouldered, ready in the use of bow and arrow, and have firm-set necks which are ever erect in pride.
> (Mierow 1915: 86, translating Mommsen 1882)

Even the snub-noses are to be found later, in the description of Attila in Jordanes's *Historia Getica*. For Jordanes is describing the Huns, and there can be no doubt that Morris meant his invaders to be the same people. Furthermore, if the 'Dusky Men' are Huns, it seems very likely that the 'Burgdalers' are meant to be Goths. By failing to say so plainly, Morris was perhaps trying, not to give his story the air of a 'Never-Never Land,' but to suggest how events might seem to a people without maps or written history, and with very limited horizons. He may also have welcomed the possible confusion, for an ordinary reader of 1889, between the Burgdalers as Goths and the Burgdalers as Englishmen. Like Tolkien, Morris was prepared to promote the Goths to 'very-much-the-same-as-English' status; certainly he meant his readers to take their side. For all its lack of dates and places, then, and in spite of the fact that 'the roots of the mountains' themselves have no names, Morris's romance of 1889 could arguably be called a 'historical novel,' and even assigned to a century: not the "second or third," as Mackail guesses (1899: II, 213, changing his mind next page to not later than the seventh), but the fourth, when Goths and Huns first came into conflict somewhere in eastern Europe.

Jordanes had of course been known to Gibbon, and before. There is nothing distinctively novel, or philological, about drawing on him for a passage in a novel.[6] Narrower inferences may be drawn, more easily at least, from Morris's earlier story of *The House of the Wolfings*. In this he is unequivocal about labelling the 'Wolfings' as Goths, and in giving many more details about the war between Goths on one hand, and on the other Romans, with both Gothic and Burgundian allies. The date implied seems once again to be round the end of the fourth century, earlier if one stresses the defensive posture of the Goths, later if one pays heed to the hero Thiodolf's memory of having fought and beaten three kings of the Huns.[7] Further hints of datability, if not date, come from the vague memory repeated within the romance of an early expedition against the Romans, carried out in alliance with 'the Kymry' and recorded in 'the South-Welsh Lay'; possibly Morris is attempting to identify the 'Cimbri' and 'Teutones' who invaded Italy in the time of Marius, and to imagine how memory of their expedition might have been preserved in non-Roman tradition, in the tradition of the other side.

However, one comes closer to philology proper, as often, by considering single words: it is thus significant that Thiodolf recalls fighting his Hun-kings "in the *hazelled* field" (my italics), a verb not recorded in the *OED* at any date, and in all probability a borrowing from the 'Goths and Huns' section of the *Hervarar saga,* to be discussed below. More prominent is Morris's declaration, on page 2 of his story, that it was set in the clearings "amidst of the Mirkwood," and that the clearings were called the "Marks." As one can see from the *OED,* this latter word (in the sense of 'tract of

---

[6] Though the standard edition of Jordanes had come out only seven years before, as noted above.

[7] There is some slight difficulty in Morris's remark in *The Roots of the Mountains* (Morris 1910-12: XV, xi) that "the condition of the people [...] is later (whatever their date may be) than that of the Wolfings"; for Thiodolf, in the earlier work, can remember fighting the Huns who have just appeared in the later one. Morris may have thought of 'the Dale' as more secluded than 'the Mark.'

land') had no currency at all in England between the Anglo-Saxon period and its use in John Kemble's philological speculations of 1848. For Morris to use it, indeed to centre his story on it, is a clear case of scholarship affecting fiction. Indeed one may say that just as 'emnet' was a creative flashpoint for Tolkien's Riders, so the 'Mark' and the 'Mirkwood' (and the relationship between them) point clearly to the texts which generated Morris's Wolfings.

'Mirkwood' is now familiar enough as a name (largely from Tolkien's *The Lord of the Rings*); but it also causes modern scholars no difficulty. Hans Kuhn, in the glossary to his corrected version of Gustav Neckel's edition of the *Edda* (1968: 147), translates *myrcviðr* as *dunkelwald* [...] *auch name, u. von diesem schwer abzugrenzen*, 'dark forest [...] also a name, and hard to distinguish from the latter.' As a name it is encountered some seven times in the poems of the *Edda*, though in one or two cases, as Dronke (1969: 47-8) notes, it seems to have lost any precise meaning: when in the *Locasenna* Loki says to Freyr that he will miss his sword "when the sons of Muspell ride over Mirkwood," he means by 'Mirkwood' nothing more definite than 'the world, the edge of the world.' In the poem *Atlakviða*, however, there is at least a hint of actual location; the Hunnish messenger says to the Burgundian kings that Attila has sent him on his errand over *Myrcvið inn ókunna*, 'the pathless Mirkwood,' while later he offers them as an inducement 'the plain of broad Gnitaheithr':

> stórar meiðmar oc staði Danpar,
> hrís þat iþ mæra, er meðr Myrcvið kalla
> [vast treasures and homesteads on the Dnieper, the famous wood that men call Mirkwood][8]

---

[8] Quotations from the *Poetic Edda* are normally from Neckel and Kuhn (1962, 1968); translations are my own.

Mirkwood is accordingly – so Detter and Heinzel in their edition of 1903 – between Huns and Burgundians, but belonging to the Huns.

After more than a hundred and fifty years of scholarship, it is perhaps hard for modern readers to realise how troublesome some of these Eddic passages seemed to those pioneers who were obliged to edit and translate them first. A few stanzas after the two passages just quoted we come upon what is at least a perturbation in the clear line of the *Atlakviða*. The Burgundian kings ride on their journey to the Huns, and as one might expect, pass over the 'fells' or mountains, and also:

> [...] Myrcvið inn ókunna;
> hristiz öll Húnmörc, þar er harðmóðgir fóro.
> [through untracked Mirkwood. All Hunmark shuddered
> as the stern ones passed.]

The translation just given is that of Ursula Dronke (1969: 10) which makes no difficulty of *myrc* = 'dark,' *viðr* = 'wood,' and *mörc* = 'mark' or 'province.' To the first editors of the *Edda* as a whole, in 1818, matters did not seem so clear: they were obliged to render the lines above as *per opacam sylvam illam ignotam. Concussa est universa Hunnorum sylva*, 'through the dark and unknown wood. All the wood of the Huns trembled.' In so doing they gave one translation *(sylva)* for two words *(viðr, mörc)*, while offering no account at all of the relationship, if any, between the similar sounds of *mörc* and *myrc*. There is no attempt to make even limited sense out of the geography of *Atlakviða* and the realms of the Huns. As for Mirkwood, it is left for others to explore: *Germani horum locorum mystae rem melius decreverint* 'the Germans will have better perceived the status (?) of these places' (Thorkelin *et al.* 1818: II, 376, 365).

These passages attracted the eye of the indefatigable Jacob Grimm, on whose comments all later editions and translations are based, at however many removes. In his essay of 1843, on 'Deutsche Grenzalterthümer,' he addressed himself with typical boldness to questions of beauty and propriety as well as semantic change. He began, naturally, with words:

> Meine ganz folgende untersuchung hat von einer durchsicht der verschiednen wörter auszugehn, mit welchen der eben entwickelte begrif der grenze bezeichnet wird.
> [The whole of my subsequent investigation starts off from a survey of the different words by which the developed concept 'frontier' is indicated.]
> (Grimm 1879-90: II, 31)

Modern words, however, would not do. *Grenze*, he thought, was not:

> der echte ausdruck. Unser älteres schöneres wort lautete *marka* [...] ahd. Marcha, alts. marka, ags. mearc, und aus der bedeutung grenze sehen wir es allmälich vorschreiten in die des abgegrenzten landes oder dazu verwandten zeichens.
> [the correct expression. Our older and more beautiful word was *marka* […] OHG Marcha, OS marka, OE mearc, and we see it gradually extend from the meaning 'frontier' into that of 'the land by the frontier' or 'the landmark associated with it.']
> (Grimm 1879-90, loc.cit.)

Frontier, province, landmark: these meanings are all related to each other. However the existence of Old Norse *mörc* (feminine), 'a wood,' and Old Norse *mark* (neuter), 'a boundary,' lead Grimm back to consideration of the *Edda*, Mirkwood, and Hunmark. Perhaps 'wood' was the original meaning, he decides, with that of 'frontier' attached at a very early stage because of the fact that forests so often in reality indicated the limits of kingdoms and their power. The Eddic *Hunmörc* means no more than *Hunnenland*, and shows *wie frühe die vorstellung silva übertrat in die von limes und regio*, 'how soon the notion 'wood' became extended to 'frontier' and 'region'' (Grimm 1879-90: II, 33).

Something very like this discussion, one can see, lies behind Morris's *The House of the Wolfings.* In that romance Morris has taken the word 'mark,' and given it one of Grimm's meanings: it means 'land, our land.' However since the land is a clearing in an enormous wood, the word is associated also with what Grimm thought was the original meaning, of 'forest.' As for Mirkwood, which Grimm had allowed to stand as 'dark forest' simply because *in sprache und poesie der schwarze, dunkle wald sein gutes recht hat*, 'the dark, gloomy wood has its proper place in language and poetry' (loc. cit.), Morris gives no translation of it, but cuts the Gordian knot of interpretation by implying that if 'Mark' means 'land, our land,' then 'Mirkwood' is 'the wood our land is in, the wood we have cut our land out of.' A name known only from heroic poetry, and known as a puzzle even within heroic poetry, has been made by Morris both as simple and as homely as possible. At the same time the 'Markmen' have not been removed from the context of heroic poetry. Their wood is still a *Grenzwald*, a 'frontier forest,' in which armies and races clash; their milieu, it is implied, is the one from which such later songs as the *Atlakviða* could spring.

One can see, between 1818 and 1889, the tangled way in which 'lost worlds' of Germanic prehistory were 'reconstructed' from words and fragments: first a couple of names, then a handful of words, then an attempt to show under what circumstances the words could have come to mean different things, then increasingly positive statements about the historical and geographical implications of the names which made it inevitable that someone would eventually base a thesis on locating them[9] – and, before the process reached its climax, an attempt by Morris to 'feel his way back' from words and names to description of a country and a social condition. This last is romantic enough, and no doubt deeply erroneous. Yet one must repeat that however erroneous the conclusions and the 'lost worlds,' the process of philological reconstruction itself offered plausibility and claimed truth. The conclusion of Professor Stanley, quoted at the start of this paper,

---

[9] There is an extensive discussion of such theses in Christopher Tolkien 1953-7.

that in the end there was not enough to go on, is powerful only retrospectively. To Grimm, to Morris, to Tolkien and to many others, it must have seemed that there was very *nearly* enough to go on; in any case philologists excelled in wringing as much as possible out of fragmentary evidence. It has to be added that ponderings over Mirkwood did not end with *Atlakviða*, Grimm and the Wolfings. One may still wonder what took Morris from Mirkwood and the Wolfings to the Burgdalers and 'the roots of the mountains.' Which mountains? Once again, the answer seems to be in the *Edda*, or rather in the *Eddica Minora*, specifically in the poem known as 'The Battle of the Goths and Huns,' the *Hunnenschlachtlied*, or the *Hlöðskviða* and found in fragmentary and interpolated form only in the *Hervarar saga*, mentioned once already.

This poem, with its explanatory prose interpolations, completes the seven references to Mirkwood given by Neckel and Kuhn. The saga in which it is embedded tells the story of how King Heithrek of Hreithgotaland leaves two sons, one called Angantýr, a Goth on both sides of his family tree, and one called Hlöthr, son of Sitka, a Hunnish princess. On the death of Heithrek the half-Hunnish son asks for a share of his father's inheritance, but is refused; has an alternative offer made him, but in insulting fashion Angantýr's counsellor Gizurr says when he hears it, that it is 'A bountiful offer / for a bondmaid's child – / child of a bondmaid, / though born to a king!'[10] At this Hlöthr takes offence, returns to his grandfather the Hunnish king, and with him and a vast army marches on the Goths. They ride through *skóg þann er Myrkviðr heitir, er skilr Húnaland ok Gotaland*, 'the forest called Mirkwood, which divided the land of the Huns from the land of the Goths.' After a preliminary battle, a challenge and reply, the main battle is joined; and in this Hlöthr the half-Hun is defeated and killed by his Gothic brother.

---

[10] All quotations and translations from this work are from Christopher Tolkien 1960, here p. 51.

This sequence of prose and poetry attracted great attention during the nineteenth century and after, as its difficulties and tantalising hints of information became more apparent. One point that struck scholars was that in this context Mirkwood was quite definitely a frontier, and labelled as such by the saga-writer; the circumstance kept *Grenzwald*, 'frontier forest,' alive as a translation alternative to *Dunkelwald*, 'dark forest.' Another was that parts of the poem on 'The Battle of the Goths and Huns,' or *Hlöðskviða*, were very similar to the *Atlakviða*, though in a different context. Where the Hunnish messenger in the *Atlakviða* offered (see above):

> stórar meiðmar oc staði Danpar,
> hrís þat iþ mœra, er meðr Myrcvið kalla,

the Hunnish prince in the *Hlöðskviða* demanded:

> hrís þat it mæra, er Myrkviðr heitir,
> gröf þá ina helgu, er stendr á Gotþjóðu,
> stein þann inn fagra, er stendr á stöðum Danpar
> [the renowned forest that is named Mirkwood, the hallowed grave in Gothland standing, the fair-wrought stone beside the Dnieper]
> (Christopher Tolkien 1960: 49)

Each poem shared the same line, in close proximity to which was the rare place-name of the Dnieper, while also common was the assumption that Mirkwood was a 'debatable land.' However if one took a literal view of the two poems, Mirkwood must have changed hands. In *Atlakviða* it is a Hunnish possession, to be given away, in *Hlöðskviða* a Gothic one, to be claimed. The hints of a possible historicity in this discrepancy were tantalising, though they led no further.

However, the most striking place-name for scholars in this section of the *Hervarar saga* was not a wood, but a mountain – which takes us back to the question of William Morris. King Heithrek does not meet a natural death, but is murdered by his slaves, whom Angantýr accordingly seeks out for his revenge. Eventually he comes on them fishing, and one of them uses a sword – Tyrfing, taken from King Heithrek – to cut off a fish's head. As he does so, he says:

> þess galt hon gedda fyrir Grafár ósi,
> er Heiðrekr var veginn undir Harvaða fjöllum.
> [The pike has paid / by the pools of Grafa / for
> Heidrek's slaying under Harvad-fells.]
> (Christopher Tolkien 1960: 45)

Angantýr recognises the sword, and the men, and kills them. But it was not the story of vengeance which made this passage famous among philologists, but the place-name, *undir Harvaða fjöllum*. It should be noted that, as with *Hunmörc* and the 1818 edition of *Atlakviða*, to pre-philological editors the phrase was virtually intractable. In his 1785 edition of the saga Stefán Björnsson could only translate, *Hoc mali lucius passus est, ante ostium amnis Greiptice quod Heidrekus interfectus sit, sub Havaða fiöllis*, 'the pike endured this evil before the mouth of the river Greiptice, that Heidrek was killed,' adding then in parenthesis *(montibus strepitus)*, 'the mountains of tumult' (Björnsson 1785: 183). He took the name to be a form of the noun *hávaði*, 'tumult,' though there was no special reason for identifying a range of 'tumult-mountains.'

A hundred years later the phrase seemed very different: not as it stood, but as it was 'reconstructed.' If one assumes that *Harvað-* has over the centuries been affected in the same way as other Norse words by the First Consonant Shift, as tabulated in Grimm's Law, one can work back to an original **karpat-*, which suggests strongly that the mountains under which Heithrek was killed were the Carpathians. If he was killed there, he and his son presumably ruled there; the philologist has then come upon strong evidence for the location of the kingdom of the Goths, on whose boundary lay Mirkwood, with beyond that the kingdom of the Huns. *Undir Harvaða fjöllum* was in any case first translated as 'under the Carpathian hills' by Gudbrand Vigfusson and F. York Powell in their edition of the

Corpus Poeticum Boreale (1883), of which Morris certainly owned a copy.[11] It seems likely, then, that in Morris's mind as he wrote *The Roots of the Mountains* was not "the wonderful land about the foot of the Italian Alps" as his daughter rather enthusiastically wrote in the introduction already cited, but the valleys of the Carpathians: and not the real valleys (in the sense that he felt any obligation to know any details about them), but rather a 'lost world' tinged with the sense of age, of memory, and yet of buried truth which this one phrase and its reconstruction between them create so vividly.

The equation of *Harvað-* and **karpat-* appealed, indeed, to scholars in a way one can call aesthetic. It echoes *verlockend wie ein Sirenenlied*, 'enticing as a Siren's song,' declared H. Meyer in the sober pages of *Zeitschrift für deutsches Altertum*, 1901. It was philological, both corroborating and depending on Grimm's Law; it was excellent evidence, since the equation would have been impossible to the saga-author and he could not have been able to forge it; it hinted at an immense chain of transmission down the years, from the fourth- or fifth-century milieu of war between the Goths and the Huns to the fourteenth-century date of the earliest *Hervarar saga* manuscripts. Its existence tended very strongly to authenticate the other passages cited, about the 'renowned forest' of Mirkwood, the 'hallowed grave in Gothland,' the 'fair-wrought stone beside the Dnieper.' Opinion on the subject, finally, is crystallised in the remarks, at once romantic and severely scholarly, of Christopher Tolkien (1960: xxv):

> the matter of legend has roots, however much transformed by poets, and though no actual corresponding event has been found in the meagrely recorded history of

---

[11] It is recorded in a catalogue of books owned by Morris and sold by Hodgson and Co., July 6th 1939. It is odd that Vigfusson and Powell make so little of equation, merely translating without comment; perhaps it was not original to them, though I have found no earlier reference. Only Christopher Tolkien has spelled out its importance (1960: xxiii).

> those times, and surely never will be, in such things as the 'grave' and the 'stone' on the banks of the Dnieper one is probably being taken back a thousand years even beyond *Heiðreks Saga* to the burial-place of Gothic kings in south-eastern Europe and the high stone in their chief place, on which the king stepped to have homage done to him in the sight of all the people.

It is of course appropriate that the author of that passage should be the son of the author of *The Lord of the Rings*, with which this paper began: the dual point of the whole discussion so far of Grimm and the Tolkiens, of Morris and Mirkwood and the mountains of the Goths and Huns, has been that in the nineteenth century men who were not scholars could find inspiration, of a sophisticated kind, in the detailed discoveries of scholarship; while on the other the 'reconstructing' processes of philology, with their insidious capacity to stretch from single words to whole histories, could not themselves be anything but intensely romantic. It is true that philology has since failed to reach a wider audience (which is why Morris's critics seem so linguistically naive). However, for a time the 'lost worlds' were very nearly in focus, all but irresistibly appealing.

Many examples could be added, to show the penetration even of popular literature by learned reconstructions. One might note, for instance, the existence of a paraphrase of a *fornaldarsaga*, the *Hrólfs saga Kraka*, published in 1973 by a well-known science fiction author, Poul Anderson. Before the wave of imitations of *The Lord of the Rings* another heroic fantasy drawing on Old English and Old Norse made some reputation, namely *The Well of the Unicorn*, by Fletcher Pratt (1948). In 1971 a book by R.A. Lafferty, called *The Fall of Rome*, devoted itself to strange panegyric on the Goths. On the other side, the romanticism of scholarship has produced several works still readable, in a way, as entertainment, because of their determined attempts to create a setting or a world into which their philological constructs could plausibly fit. The line began with Wilhelm Grimm's *Die deutsche Heldensage* (1st edition Gütersloh, 1829). It continued with several books which tried, for instance, to explain how stories about the Goths of the fourth century, presumably composed in Gothic, could have made their way across Europe to Scandinavia and to Germany, and why what were presumably the same events and people should often have emerged in such different forms. R. Heinzel argued in his *Über die Hervararsaga* (1887: 475ff.) that the place of transit could have been the court of the Byzantine Emperor, where men of the Varangian Guard might have mixed with the descendants of the Ostrogoths still living in the Crimea. Caroline Brady's *The Legends of Ermanaric* (1943) preferred to lay a trail for Gothic stories through Italy, or along the amber-route to the Baltic, concerned as it did so to explain why the *Hamðismál* had managed to delete all mention of Huns. Between 1928 and 1934 Hermann Schneider's *Germanische Heldensage* (1928) – a book owned by Tolkien sr. – tried to fit all possible evidence together, noting among much else how in all echoes of the war with the Huns place-names like the Dnieper *ragen wie Gespenster [...] den Bereich der einstigen Gotenherrschaft kennzeichend* 'tower up like phantoms [...] indicating the extent of the former Gothic dominion.'

Enquiries of this kind are now, on the whole, discredited. Scholars like Schneider had to use too high a proportion of speculation, because the fragments they were working from – nearly all marginal to the historical centre of their interests – were simply not enough (as Professor Stanley concluded of the parallel quest for 'paganism' in the passage already cited). Nevertheless the attraction of these researches is still alive, can still be felt. One notes it, for instance, in Ursula Dronke's pages on '*Atlakviða* and History' in her Eddic edition of 1969. Why is the death of Atli in the late Norse poem so similar, in some respects, to the contemporary account of Priscus, and yet so different in being a tale of murder rather than of accident? There is a relatively early version in which Attila *was* murdered, she notes:

> What Attila's guard, catching sight of the body in the blood-stained bed, must have thought – 'the Khan has been murdered by the woman' – and then disproved by

examination of the corpse, has usurped the place of fact. It is as if some, on hearing the true account of his death, had said 'I do not believe he died like that: the woman killed him – was she not a German?' (1969: 32)

So Burgundian poets, seeking some salve for the destruction of their country by the Huns, could have made the tale one of revenge. 'Must have,' 'as if': the phrases mark the trail of the 'reconstructor'! On the other hand the 'reconstruction' is a good one; it takes in all the data; if 'asterisk-words' can be accepted, 'asterisk-cultures' and (as in this case) 'asterisk-lays' gain added plausibility. But the true strength, or charm, of such passages as Mrs Dronke's is that they offer us a history in a sense truer, even, than such contemporary Greek accounts as that of Priscus. *Her* hypothesis is history from a particular angle; history containing an old perspective, coloured by the feelings of the Burgundians; it tells us not about Attila as he was, or as he may have been, but as he *seemed.* One might add that perhaps the most romantic of all philological revisions of old data was the perception, at some time in the nineteenth century, that the name of the Hunnish king himself, Attila, was not Hunnish at all, but the Gothic diminutive of *atta,* 'father,' *atti-la,* 'little father'![12] Again one comes on new perspective, on history as it was felt: clearly the Scourge of God found some adherents, some defenders even in Germanic heroic tradition. The temptation to imagine what they said about him, to put this together with the mixed feelings of Angantýr in the *Hlöðskviða,* to start 'reconstructing,' may be improper, but remains alluring.

Between the time of the first (often baffled) editors of Edda and saga, and our own growing professionalised scepticism, Germanic philology

---

[12] I do not know who first suggested this explanation of the name. It is accepted by Maenchen-Helfen (1973: 386). The first reference given there is to F. Kluge in *Englische Studien* for 1895. By contrast the 1818 editors of the *Poetic Edda* derive 'Attila' from an old name for the river Volga (Thorkelin 1818: vi-vii). See also Tolkien, *Letters,* 264.

opened up something of a 'Wonderland' of hints, ghosts, echoes and sirens. Some aspects of these have been mentioned: many others – the relation between the 'Goths and Huns' and *Widsith,* the history of the Scyldings and *Beowulf,* the whole tangled web of theories as to the growth of the *Nibelungenlied* – have necessarily been omitted. However it should be clear that for many in the nineteenth century and after, apprehension of the past was made *qualitatively different* by philology. They did not read accounts of the Goths and Huns; they inferred them; but they thought (with some reason) that their methods of inference were reliable and sound. It remains to ask whether the re-creations of a William Morris (or a Tolkien, or a German professor asking scholarly questions about the Mark) appear actually better than those of less learned appreciators of the past. Was this legacy of the Middle Ages a fruitful one?

There are strong reasons for replying 'No.' One conclusion about medieval legacies – it is stimulated in part by the evidence of other papers at the 'Medieval Legacy Symposium' (Haarder 1982) – is that in the past we have a tendency to see ourselves as we are, but healed of contemporary traumas: so the German *Kleinadel* looked back at the *Nibelungenlied* and saw themselves given worthy employment, so Denmark and Sweden looked back at the Vikings and saw themselves victorious and dominant. William Morris, meanwhile, produced his fantasies of almost-Englishmen living in egalitarian communities where leaders were elected and even slaves were content with their lot, and saw, all too clearly, a past vision of *riches without industry, and so without guilt!* This was a powerful image, in its time; but we are now conscious mostly of its wish-fulfilment. A more ominous note comes from the way in which Morris leant on the linguistic connections and affiliations discovered during the nineteenth century to produce a scheme in which the Goths (who were nearly English because their language was 'Germanic') were totally different by race, almost by species, from their 'dusky' enemies. The phrase 'almost by species' is exact, for at one moment in *The Roots of the Mountains* Morris has his characters explain that though the Huns may rape their Germanic slaves, and have children by them, "all or most of the said children favoured the race of their begetters" (1912: XV, 203). There are, in short, no 'half-breeds' to complicate the issue. In this convenient thesis one may well see a reflection of theories developed during the spread of the British Empire to prevent infiltration of the rulers by the ruled. The contribution of Germanic philology to racism was unintentional, but still strong; in view of the results it is not surprising that no scholar has had the heart to assess it fully.[13]

Using the past to soothe or to validate the present remains a temptation, then, and mere knowledge of words or of languages can be no shield against it. Nevertheless it remains possible to feel that the philological view of the Dark Ages, whatever its mistakes, did mark a genuine step forward. There can be no doubt that the researches of the nineteenth century totally altered our view of the nature of language, and added a new element to estimates of what human beings can do.[14] In a similar way it increased our estimation of what human beings, even illiterate ones, can retain. Where Edward Gibbon, in the eighteenth century, had dismissed the possibility of Gothic histories with the lofty remark that "the memory of past events cannot long be preserved, in the frequent and remote emigrations of illiterate Barbarians" (*Decline and Fall of the Roman Empire,* ch. 26), no historian of the later nineteenth century could afford to forget the accounts of Jörmunrekkr and Eormenric, and their demonstration that Greek and Latin civilisations were not the only ones that mattered. Perhaps the true contribution of the new linguistic visions of the past, however, was one more imponderable. Much as one may disagree with the conclusions of Hermann Schneider, or Jacob Grimm, or indeed William Morris with his strings of strange words like 'motestead' or 'doomring' or 'sackless' or 'wainburg,' one is obliged to admit that all of them were men who could 'render a reason';

---

[13] Though there are some remarks on the subject in Stanley (1975: 18-21, 24, 26 *et passim*), and in Haarder (1975: 251-3).

[14] See further Shippey 2005a.

who gave not only their beliefs but also the evidence on which those beliefs were based. Disagreement was anticipated, if not courted. In this at least the philologists and their followers tried to look outwards at the past, and not merely to project the present backwards. Their art contained strong elements of imagination, or fantasy; but its enthusiasms were at least kindled by a rigorous and academic discipline.

Heartwood

Tolkien and Scholarship

Fighting the Long Defeat:
Philology in Tolkien's Life and Fiction[1]

Those who have read Professor Tolkien's works will be aware that they tell the story of a bitter war, "long and deadly, and fought for the most part in deep places," ending in catastrophic defeat. In his fiction, these words describe the War of the Dwarves and the Orcs, which ended in the Battle of Azanulbizar, or Nanduhirion, "at the memory of which the Orcs still shudder and the Dwarves weep" (*LotR*, 1048). In his life, however, these words better describe the war of the philologists and the critics, or to put it another way the war between 'language' and 'literature,' fought out with the utmost bitterness in university English departments all over the English-speaking world, and ending with the utter rout of Tolkien's side, the philologists.

To put this less fancifully: I am sure that if Tolkien had been asked for a one-word description of himself, he would have said, 'I am a philologist,' which he might have qualified by saying, as he did on at least one recorded occasion, "I am a *pure* philologist" (*Letters*, 264). His aim throughout his professional life was to establish a successful philological curriculum in British universities, and in this he failed; he failed even to maintain the curriculum in the state it was in when he joined the profession – and I say this without derision, for exactly the same could be said about me, as I know very well; the end result is that I believe it is now very difficult, even almost impossible, to follow a course of study of the sort Tolkien would have approved anywhere in the world, especially the English-speaking world, and especially in England itself. When Galadriel says of herself and her husband Celeborn that, "throughout the ages we have fought the long defeat" (*LotR*, 348), there is a sense that Tolkien could have said the

---

[1] This essay has not previously been published, but is based on on a lecture with the same title delivered at the University of Georgia, on 5 November 2002. My thanks go to my host, Dr Jonathan Evans, for the invitation, and for many interesting conversations over the years.

same of himself, and his professional predecessors and successors: we all fought the long defeat together. Though it is not the least of ironies that outside that small academic world the defeat has been very markedly reversed, by Tolkien's fiction, and in a way which not even Gandalf could have predicted.

That sense of defeat may be demonstrated by looking at three documents from Tolkien's own life. The first comes from Tolkien's application for the Oxford Chair of Anglo-Saxon vacated by W.A. Craigie, dated 27th June 1925. Its literary genre is obvious: the application for a future job which is also an extended boast about how well you have done in the current one. Tolkien says that at Leeds University, where he had been Reader since 1920 and Professor since 1924:

> I began with five hesitant pioneers out of a School [...] of about sixty members. The proportion today is 43 literary to 20 linguistic students. The linguists are in no way isolated or cut off from the general life and work of the department, and share in many of the literary courses and activities of the School, but since 1922 their purely linguistic work has been conducted in special classes, and examined in distinct papers of special standard and attitude [...] Courses are given on Old English heroic verse, the history of English, various Old and Middle English texts, Old and Middle English philology, introductory Germanic philology, Gothic, Old Icelandic [...] and Medieval Welsh. [...] Philology, indeed, appears to have lost for these students its connotations of terror if not of mystery. An active discussion-class has been conducted [...] which has borne fruit in friendly rivalry and open debate with the corresponding literary assembly [...] [If elected] I should endeavour to advance, to the best of my ability, the growing neighbourliness of linguistic and literary studies, which can never be enemies except by misunderstanding or without loss to both; and

to continue in a wider and more fertile field the encouragement of philological enthusiasm among the young. (*Letters*, 12-13)

The sub-text of this is again obvious. Note the remarks, "in no way isolated […] friendly rivalry […] growing neighbourliness," and of course no more "connotations of terror." Other evidence suggests that this was by no means completely true, and that the philologists and the critics at Leeds were as usual at daggers drawn – the *Songs for the Philologists* published in 1936 contains at least one poem by Tolkien cruelly mocking the literary students and the literary faculty.[2] But Tolkien knew that the selection committee at Oxford would be looking for someone who was not going to cause trouble, who would co-operate with his modernist colleagues, and he made out that he was just the right person (as one does in such circumstances). He really could not have expected to be appointed to the Oxford Chair. He had only been in the business for five years, he had published little except the edition of *Sir Gawain and the Green Knight*, co-edited with E.V. Gordon, and Kenneth Sisam had also applied: Sisam was older than Tolkien, had been his tutor, and already had an Oxford job. It is a mystery why Tolkien won, by a single vote.[3]

A few years later Tolkien, by now securely in place, wrote a rather franker piece in *The Oxford Magazine* for 29th May 1930, a proposal for reforming 'The Oxford English School.' You will see that Tolkien here wastes no time on "friendly rivalry" or "neighbourliness," but admits that the opposite is true:

In the English School, owing to the accidents of its history, the distinction between philology and literature is

---

[2] This collection was privately printed at the University of London by a former student of Tolkien's who had retained copies from his time at Leeds. The poem is titled 'Two Little Schemes' on the Contents Page, but 'Lit. and Lang.' in the main text.

[3] For a brief account of the proceedings, see Carpenter (1977: 108).

> notoriously marked [...] its branches are customarily but loosely dubbed the 'language' and 'literature' side – titles which never were accurate, fortunately for both. History may explain their arising, but provides no defence for their retention. Their banishment is probably the first need of reform in the Oxford School, even A and B would be preferable [...]
>
> There is also 'philology' – the special burden of Northern tongues, even of classical Icelandic, yet in fact the special advantage they possess as a discipline. From their study philology cannot be eliminated. It is essential to the critical apparatus of student and scholar. The poems and prose they study – the senses of their words, their syntax, their idiom, metre, and allusion – were rescued from oblivion by philologists.[4]

The sub-text of this – noticed I should think by no-one at the time, and few later – is that Tolkien wanted to replace the Oxford syllabus by the one he was used to at Leeds, where the 'Two Little Schemes' of his poem mentioned above were in fact called 'the A-scheme' and 'the B-scheme.' (By 1979, when I arrived at Leeds from Oxford to take up the Chair of English Language and Medieval English Literature held more than fifty years before by Tolkien, they had mutated into A-, B-, C-, and D-schemes, and there was a plan for an E-scheme. I was largely responsible for abolishing the whole bureaucratic edifice in 1983.) Opinions differ as to how far Tolkien's 1930 plan was successful: by the time I arrived to teach at Oxford in 1972 the philological option within the School of English (which is what Tolkien seems to mean by the scheme he wished to label 'B') was effectively moribund, taken by fewer than ten students a year out of around 250. On the other hand, it is assumed by Gross (1999: 440) that the Tolkien/Lewis plan of reform was in fact accepted, though I do not know on what evidence. It is

---

[4] Tolkien, 'The Oxford English School,' *The Oxford Magazine*, 29 May 1930, 778-82 (778).

also by no means clear what Tolkien meant by his talk of "special burden" and "special advantage": there is a sense that the whole piece is as it were 'coded,' with particular meaning only to insiders.

By the end of his career, however, Tolkien was in a position to speak even more frankly, and this he did in his 'Valedictory Address to the University of Oxford' – characteristically he had never got round to an Inaugural – delivered after he had retired on 5th June 1959. By this time he was apparently in rather a bad temper with many of his Oxford faculty colleagues, and he coined a word to describe them: they were 'misologists,' the exact opposite of 'philologists,' not 'lovers of the word' but 'haters of the word.' Such people should not be in a university at all, as students or as teachers:

> I do not think that [Philology] should be thrust down throats as a pill, because I think that if such a process seems needed, the sufferers should not be here, at least not studying or teaching English letters. Philology is the foundation of humane letters; 'misology' is a disqualifying defect, or disease.
>
> It is not, in my experience, a defect or disease found in those whose literary learning, wisdom, and critical acumen place them in the highest rank […] But there are other voices […] I must confess that at times in the last thirty odd years I have been aggrieved by them; by those, afflicted in some degree by misology, who have decried what they usually call *language* […] Dullness is to be pitied. Or so I hope, being myself dull at many points. But dullness should be confessed with humility; and I have therefore felt it a grievance that certain professional persons should suppose their dullness and ignorance to be a human norm, the measure of what is good; and anger when they have sought to impose the limitation of their minds upon younger minds, dissuading those with philological curiosity from

> their bent, encouraging those without this interest to believe that their lack marked them as minds of a superior order.
> (*Essays*, 225-6)

Of course, he says (on this public occasion), he does not mean *everyone*, just "certain professional persons," and those "not of the highest rank." But I am sure they knew who they were. No doubt several of them were present, which accounts for Tolkien's not very convincing display of tact.

Behind these documents, and extending over the forty years of Tolkien's academic career, lay the steady pressure, in British and American university Departments of English, to get rid of compulsory Anglo-Saxon, compulsory History of the Language papers, compulsory medieval papers, all to be replaced by more modern, more literary, and more critical studies. This has continued for a further fifty years, and as said above has been almost completely successful in the English-speaking world. One cannot help thinking that things need not have gone that way. Tolkien's Middle-earth, after all, has been unmistakably 'saleable' to an enormous audience, and curiosity as to the sources of his world and his ideas and his languages is passionate and widespread – proof, as Tolkien could have said, that an instinct for philology was normal and natural in the minds of the young, whatever their teachers may have thought. So what went wrong?

One root cause of "the long defeat" was a failure to define the subject, and the word. 'Philology' is indeed a hard word, with several meanings, as I have tried to explain at some length elsewhere (Shippey 2003a: 6-13). Here I will only say that *The Oxford English Dictionary*, itself a characteristically philological enterprise, fails to give much help. The definitions it offers are:

1. Love of learning and literature; the study of literature, in a wide sense […] polite learning
2. Love of talk, speech, or argument, as opposed to love of wisdom, philosophy

3. The study of the structure and development of language; the study of language; linguistics (really a branch of sense 1)[5]

None of this has much bearing on Tolkien. Whatever the "polite learning" of sense 1 may be, he had no interest in it. The strange confusions of sense 3, in which philology is "the study of language" but "really" a branch of sense 1, which is "the study of literature," do not account for the evident hostility between the two fields which you can see becoming more apparent in the three documents quoted above. Sense 2, meanwhile, philology is logic-chopping, love of talk as opposed to love of wisdom, does not account for the fact that we have so many academic journals with names like *Studies in Philology, Modern Philology, Philological Quarterly, Journal of English and Germanic Philology*. Who would found a journal called, as these appear to be, if you believe the *OED*, 'Quibbling Studies,' or 'Modern Casuistry'? Finally, none of the definitions in the *OED* explains Jacob Grimm's characterization of *Philologie* in the older German counterpart of the *OED*, the Grimm brothers' *Deutsches Wörterbuch*: "keine unter allen den wissenschaften ist stolzer, edler, streitsüchtiger als die philologie, oder gegen fehler unbarmherziger," 'none among all the sciences is prouder, nobler, more disputatious than philology, or less merciful to error' (Grimm 1999: XIII, col. 1829). Grimm did not think philology was "polite learning" at all. He thought it was a hard science.[6]

The word the *OED* does not use is 'comparative.' Philology was all the things the *OED* says until it became 'comparative philology,' *vergleichende Philologie*, an event signaled by the publication of Jacob Grimm's *Deutsche Grammatik* between 1819 and 1837. I have again discussed the importance of the book and the intellectual breakthrough it rep-

---

[5] *OED*, 1st edition of 1933, VII: 778, repeated with slight amplification of definition 3 in the 1989 2nd edition, XI: 684.

[6] Henry Gee, a real scientist, points out that the new science of 'cladistics' is in essence identical with the old philological practice of 'stemmatics.' Both are about drawing order from 'degraded information' (see Gee 2004: 36-9, and further 147, 152-3).

resented elsewhere, and more than once, and again will not repeat myself here.[7] But in brief, comparative philology was an entirely new discipline, unknown to the ancient and medieval worlds; it laid bare the relationships between languages, as also the history of those languages, and of the people who spoke them; it enabled the decoding of extinct languages, the reading of many ancient and forgotten texts, the recovery of lost literary traditions. At a very basic level it explained why there are two words with the same meaning in modern English, 'break' and 'fracture,' and how the difference arose; it cast light indeed on scores if not hundreds of thousands of words; it made it possible for Tolkien to consider the significance of his Aunt Jane's name, 'Neave,' and invent names with deep roots and suggestions, like 'Frodo' and 'Baggins'; it helped him to create, or recreate, words, names and concepts like 'wood-wose' and 'hobbit' and 'dwimmerlaik' and 'Saruman,' all discussed elsewhere in these pages.[8] Even more significantly, comparative philology opened up a whole new continent of imaginative space, of which Tolkien's 'Middle-earth' and William Morris's 'Mark of the Wolfings' are only two examples. And it did so with a mixture of rigour and romance. I will try to exemplify this through just one example.

There is a notorious problem in *Beowulf*: is the dragon's treasure cursed, does Beowulf himself succumb to it, how does the curse work, has it been lifted? This comes up first in lines 3051-7, which say fairly clearly that there was a curse, but God could lift it – though it does not say that He did. Tolkien used line 3052, "iumonna gold galdre bewunden", 'gold of ancient men, wound round with spell,' as the title of a poem published in 1923, which he rewrote again in 1962 and again in 1970. Meanwhile lines 3069-75 read in part that those who buried the treasure put a curse on it. I print part of these here exactly as found in the manuscript, i.e. without ac-

---

[7] See the essays on 'Grimm, Grundtvig, Tolkien,' and 'History in Words' in this volume, and at greater length Shippey 2005a.
[8] See the essays on 'Tolkien and the *Gawain*-Poet,' 'Heroes and Heroism,' and 'History in Words' in this volume.

cents, without corrected word divisions, with manuscript line endings marked by a double slash (//), and written out like prose. The curse said:

> þæt se secg wære synnum scildig [...] seðone // wong strade næshe goldhwæte gearwor // hæfde agendes est ær gesceawod

There are all kinds of questions here. The lines say 'the man would be guilty of sin,' for the verb is in the subjunctive, *wære*, not *wæs*. A few words later it appears to say, this time in the indicative, *næs*, that 'he was not eager for gold,' 'he' being presumably the same as 'the man' just before. Furthermore, one might think that *agend*, singular, is 'the owner,' the person who buried the treasure, but a few lines earlier it has been 'the people,' plural, who buried the treasure. *Agend* with a capital letter (not used in this way by writers of Old English) might possibly mean 'the Owner,' i.e. 'God.' Meanwhile, the word *strade* is not recognizable as Old English. It must be a verb. There is an Old English verb, *strúdan*, 'to plunder,' which fits the context, but *strade* is not one of its possible forms. Before Grimm, no-one would have bothered about this last point, since no-one knew how to decline Old English verbs, and there was a general view among scholars that the poor barbarians simply couldn't spell, so odd variations were to be expected (which led the old scholars into strange errors).[9] But post-Grimm one could say that the verb was a Class 2 strong verb (and if you didn't know what a class 2 strong verb was, then your opinion on this crux was of no value);[10] so the form must either be *stread*, 3rd person singular past

---

[9] The first editor of *Beowulf*, Grímur Thorkelin, failed to realize that the poem started with a funeral, partly because he read the name Scyld as the common Old English verb *sceolde*, or 'should.' He assumed the difference in spelling was just random variation.

[10] Smaug is a class 2 strong verb as well, his name being the past tense of Old Norse *smjuga*, 'to creep, to penetrate,' so 'he crept.' If he had been an Old English dragon, his name would have been Sméah, from the OE verb *smúgan*. Gollum's real name Sméagol is from the same root, but may derive from the related weak verb *sméagan*, 'to enquire': so either 'Slinker' (Sam Gamgee's view) or 'Snooper.' See also *Letters*, 31, where

indicative, or *strude*, 3rd person singular past subjunctive. One can see already that there are many variables in this equation, and between them they determine the meaning of a highly significant passage, even the final meaning of the whole complex poem. Are we to think that the curse fell on Beowulf, and caused his death? Was he or wasn't he 'eager for gold'? Are we supposed to see him as 'guilty of sin'? We do not know what Tolkien thought about the passage, or whether he ever reached it in his many lectures commenting on the poem,[11] and his translation has not been published, but I would translate, without great conviction: '[the curse said] that he who might plunder [*strude*] the burial-place [*wong*] would be [*wære*] guilty of sin, unless [*nefne*, changed from *næs*] in his desire for gold he had previously looked on the favour of its [ultimate] Owner [i.e. God].' It seems to me that a further issue, unresolved by my translation, is whether the curse was something put *on* the treasure, as on Andvari's ring, 'the Ring of the Nibelung,' and so something external, or whether it was connected with the sin of greed, something *in* the treasure, something psychological, something internal. I suspect also that Tolkien concluded, as he often did, that it must mean both: the curse and the sin of greed are the same thing. That is the "dragon-sickness" which afflicts Smaug, and Thorin Oakenshield in *The Hobbit*, and the Master of Laketown who steals the gold and dies starving in the wilderness, and the repeated characters of the poem 'Iumonna Gold [...],' alias 'The Hoard,' which traces the always-disastrous progress of a hoard from elf to dwarf to dragon to young hero, the latter dying as an old miser, his treasure buried and lost for ever.[12] The climax of *The Hobbit*, one may say, depends on a crux in *Beowulf*. But one may note that it is not an inevitable curse. Bilbo Baggins is quite immune to it, and so may Beowulf have been.

---

[11] Tolkien gives the verb in its 'Common Germanic' form, i.e. in the form ancestral to both OE and ON.
Oral evidence from those who attended suggests that he rarely if ever got that far.
[12] See the essay on 'The Versions of 'The Hoard'' in this volume.

The real point of the preceding paragraph, however, is not to solve a notoriously irresolvable crux, but to say that is how philologists worked: subjunctives and the classes of strong verbs were bound up in their heads with (in Bilbo's phrase, *Hobbit*, 7) "dragons and goblins and giants and the rescue of princesses and the unexpected luck of widows' sons." *And they (or some of them) saw no discrepancy between the two*. But this is what they failed to make clear. In the end, and in the hands of duller scholars than Tolkien, the strong verbs and the sound-shifts and the pedantic (but vital) details lost contact with the poems and the romances and the myths and the stories, to the detriment of both sides of the subject. This was the start of "the long defeat," the exile of the subject (comparative philology, and especially comparative Germanic philology) from all but a very few university departments of English, which the early philologists themselves had been instrumental in founding.[13] Yet one of the great advantages of comparative philology was that it could wake romance from almost anything, even from a single word – as said very clearly by Tolkien himself. In a letter to his son Christopher, praising Christopher for a paper he had read on Attila the Hun, he wrote:

> All the same, I suddenly realized that I am a *pure* philologist. I like history, and am moved by it, but its finest moments for me are those in which it throws light on words and names! Several people (and I agree) spoke to me of the art with which you made the beady-eyed Attila on his couch almost vividly present. Yet oddly, I find the thing that thrills my nerves is the one you mentioned casually: *atta, attila.* Without those syllables the whole great drama both of history and legend loses savour for me. (*Letters*, 264)

---

[13] As Tolkien appears to indicate, in allegorical form, through Alf's rebuke to Nokes in *Smith of Wootton Major*, 57; see the essay 'Allegory versus Bounce' in this volume.

Tolkien's point, which he did not need to explain to his son, is that while Attila has become a byword for savagery, and famous also in both Roman and Northern tradition as the oppressor of the Goths, the name he is known by is in fact not Hunnish but Gothic, and it is an affectionate nickname, from a dimunitive form of Gothic *atta*, 'father,' so 'Little Father, Daddy.' So *somebody* among the Goths must have liked him! There must have been a pro-Hunnish faction among the Goths, and the interaction between the factions perhaps accounts for poems like the Old Norse 'Battle of the Goths and Huns,' eventually edited by Christopher Tolkien two years after giving the paper mentioned above (1960). One word, then, can open up a whole vista of historical possibilities, and trigger thoughts about a whole range of poems and chronicles. *And that would be true of many hundreds, if not thousands, of words, names, allusions, and in the modern world just as much as in the ancient one.* Tolkien's Aunt Jane's married name, and the address of his office at Leeds University, were as potentially filled with romance, for Tolkien, as the name of Attila;[14] and he thought that was potentially true for everyone else as well. The subject was literally inexhaustible, and one may well feel that it has been a disaster for the humanities that it has been allowed to drift into oblivion. But to open up the treasure-chest, you needed the philological key. And all too often, by the time a scholar had painfully forged the key through years of study, he had forgotten about the treasure.

Is there any possibility of reversing this intellectual tide, which in the academic world has been flowing for a hundred years in the wrong direction? One attempt was made, in the 1990s, by a group of scholars mostly from departments of French – this of course would have raised Tolkien's hackles immediately – who proclaimed the advent of 'the New

---

[14] See the essays on 'Heroes and Heroism' and 'Tolkien and the *Gawain*-Poet' in this volume.

Philology' (see Nichols 1990, Bloch and Nichols 1996).[15] The argument of the New Philologists (characteristically rather hard to understand unless one can follow modern academic jargon) is that "medieval philology has been marginalized by contemporary cognitive methodologies [...] while within the discipline itself, a very limited and by now grossly anachronistic conception of it remains far too current" (Nichols 1990: 1). In this view, what philologists used to do was:

- to establish a standardising view of language, especially early language
- to edit medieval texts to fit that view
- to eliminate everything that didn't fit
- and in the process (a) to destroy the variations and variants characteristic of manuscript culture, and
- (b) to create an entirely false, and probably phallocentric image of the Great Men and Great Poets who wrote the texts which we don't have any more, until these have been reconstructed by the editors.

The catch-phrase of this movement is "l'écriture mediévale ne produit pas de variantes, elle est variance," 'medieval literature does not produce variants, it is variation.'

There is a certain truth in some of this. Old Philologists like Tolkien certainly *did* emend texts to fit their views of good grammar and good sense;[16] but their views were based very often on a rejection of modern standardized languages, and a positive fascination (strongly shared by Tolkien) with non-standard forms like dialects.[17] They were *comparative* philologists, and comparing language forms was what they did. In the New Philol-

---

[15] It is only fair to say that there was prompt resistance from other French scholars, see Busby 1993.
[16] See 'A Look at *Exodus* and *Finn and Hengest*' in this volume.
[17] As shown by Tolkien's appreciative 'Foreword' to Haigh 1928; see further the item on *A New Glossary of the Dialect of the Huddersfield District* in Drout 2007.

ogy there is furthermore a good deal of academic politics: the scholars concerned are afraid of being marginalized in their departments, they want to stake a claim to being in on "contemporary cognitive methodologies," or theory, and they offer a repeated image of the boring old fuddy-duddy being brushed aside by the exciting young modernist. They do not, in other words, want to share in "the long defeat," and hope to change sides. It seems to me, however, that the New Philologists, passionately concerned to differentiate themselves from the failures of the twentieth century (the academic losers like Tolkien), have actually forgotten the successes of the nineteenth century (the academic winners like Grimm). They have also forgotten what it was like before the real 'New Philology' came on the scene with Jacob Grimm, when variation really did rule the editorial scene, and scholars tacitly assumed that you could not expect very much sense, or grammar, from the poor barbarians who wrote poems like *Beowulf*. It is probably not coincidental that built into the New Philology is an old élitism: the manuscripts are important, and study should be left to scholars at major research universities who alone have access to them, as was the case at Oxford and Cambridge and London in the eighteenth century. This offers a way forward only to selected academics.[18] Nothing could be more alien to natural and committed popularisers like Tolkien, or the Grimms, or Tolkien's friend Lewis.

Are there, then, any signs of a better way forward? In conclusion, I shall attempt to do three things. First, I shall sum up on Tolkien's life and fiction. Second, I shall, like Milton, "by occasion, foretell the ruin of our corrupted clergy now in its height," and pronounce the Curse of Philology on Critical Studies. And finally I shall switch from the role of Cassandra to that of Merlin and imagine, without foretelling, a brighter future.

First, then, one has to admit that Tolkien's professional life was a "long defeat," which continued after his death. His beloved B scheme at

---

[18] For further strictures, and further ironies, see Shippey 1997b.

Leeds, the philological scheme, lasted till 1983 when it graduated its last eight students (out of an intake of a hundred and fifty) and was then, as said above, closed down by me. If my ghost meets the ghost of Tolkien, he will say, I hope, "I know you had to do it," and I will say, "But I made them pay a price for it." I was carrying out a rearguard action, and that's what you do in rearguard actions, to save what can be saved. But as Churchill so wisely said, Dunkirk-style retreats may be very admirable, but they don't win wars. In the longer term, in Tolkien's lifetime and my own, literature, and modernism, and then postmodernism, and theory, rolled over poor Dame Philology and squashed her flat.

The obverse of that, however, is that outside the academic world Tolkien's life was a triumphant success, and this has continued even more strongly after his death. I say nothing here of his own popularity, or that of the Jackson movies, stunning though the figures are. I do not even point to the scores of fantasy novels now published every year, few of which escape the imprint of Tolkien, as one can tell from the titles alone: *The Fellowship of the Talisman*; *The Halfling's Gem*; *The Weirdstone of Brisingamen*; *The Malloreon*; *The Defenders of the West*; *Halflings, Hobbits, Warrows and Wee Folk*, and so on. One motive, of course, has been pure commercial opportunism, but that on the whole comes from the publishers, not the writers: the writers often clearly just want to submerge themselves in Middle-earth. And while there are others who have been at pains to distance themselves from Tolkien, they must know that their chances of publication depended very much on an audience already sensitized to fantasy. The real point I would wish to make, though, is what authors have learned from Tolkien, which can be expressed in one word, and though it is not 'philology,' in Tolkien's case it was a product of philology. All fantasy authors know now that what a work has to have is 'depth.' You must have a map, like Ursula Le Guin's map of Earthsea. You must have a way of generating strings of names which are both strange and consistent, as Stephen Donaldson does, and even more than Donaldson, the great Jack Vance.[19] You can base whole works on etymology, as was done by Avram Davidson – the only author I have ever come across who actually quotes chunks of ancient Oscan (or possibly Umbrian) in a work designed for popular composition, his novel *Peregrine: Secundus* (1981). With competitive strangeness, Philip José Farmer uses Middle Yiddish in his science fiction/fantasy *The Maker of Universes* (1965). Furthermore, you should always go back, where you can, to the original sources of folktale. I suspect Michael Swanwick, author of *The Iron Dragon's Daughter* (1993) – a brilliant work – of having gone back beyond Tolkien to read the nineteenth-century work which first uses the word 'hobbits,' *The Denham Tracts*: Swanwick gets his lists of strange elf- and goblin-species from the same list as 'hobbit.' It is well understood now, among writers if not among 'misologists,' that philology gives depth, and depth sells books.

So we cannot help seeing a great gap between professional defeat and popular triumph. Turning now to the academic triumph of modernism, postmodernism, etc., one can see that for all its academic success this has been marked by corresponding popular failure. In the USA, the number of students majoring in humanities has fallen precipitously, to little more than a third of what it might have been expected to be if the humanities had held on to the same proportion of students they attracted in the year of Tolkien's death.[20] The fall is just as great in English Studies, and here there is a potential for even greater future disaster. University departments of English in the USA depend for their budgets on large numbers of students taking 'core courses' on how to write, usually called 'Rhetoric and Composition.' But the weak point of almost all courses on 'Rhetoric and Composition' is that the graduate students who teach it – all of them products of undergraduate

---

[19] I point with particular admiration to his 'Lyonesse' trilogy, *Suldrun's Garden* (1983), *The Green Pearl* (1985), *Madouc* (1989).

[20] See Menand 2001 for figures. Delbanco 1999 considers the situation for PhDs in English.

courses in English – know nothing useful about language, whether historical language or modern language. They spend much time on inculcating essentially eighteenth-century notions of 'proper English,' with rules about not beginning sentences with a conjunction and not ending them with a preposition, and so on.[21] Their only analytic method, all too often, is the archaic notion of 'diagramming sentences,' at which both Grimm and Tolkien would have stared incredulously, and which most of the students furthermore cannot do. One day a college president is going to say, in effect: "there's no 'value-added' here, I've looked at the 'outcomes assessments,' I'm going to switch the core teaching to someone who can do it better" – such as the department of Communications Studies. If that switch is successful, and followed, then English Studies, or as Tolkien would have called it, 'literature,' will revert to the diminished status now held by, for instance, Classical Studies.[22] It will pay the penalty for having exiled from its curriculum all forms of serious language study. The dying curse of Dame Philology, or perhaps of the great dragon Comparative Philology, will then have taken effect.

Turning now to the future, I would say that if we were to start again in English Studies, the first requirement would be to include within elementary Rhetoric and Composition an up-to-date structuralist grammar of modern English: that would be really useful to the students in their lives and careers. This would provide the necessary grounding for a philological history of English (and related languages) at all periods: that would be really interesting. And who knows, if the profession got so far it might then be able to approach the study of literature with a theory which was able to take in works of fantasy – even works popular with the general public! But by this time I fear that I am looking in the Mirror of Galadriel, or possibly the

---

[21] I heard much about this in a discussion among English teachers the day before this piece was written, in October 2006. The discussion was vitiated, however, by the fact that none of the speakers could tell a preposition from a conjunction.

[22] A diminished status well discussed, and explained, in Hanson *et al.* 2001.

mirror of Macbeth's witches. And this shows many things, as we know, including those that never come to be.

History in Words:
Tolkien's Ruling Passion[1]

Tolkien remarked that one form of fantasy, which he called Chestertonian Fantasy, comes from seeing familiar things (like an ordinary word suddenly seen backwards) from an entirely new angle. It was a "wholesome enough" type of fantasy, he argued, and readily available, but of "limited power" (*Essays*, 146). I quite agree with Tolkien's general proposition, but I would add that if you want to see words and the meaning of words from a new angle, an excellent way of doing so is to look them up in a dictionary, or in a thesaurus like Richard Blackwelder's invaluable *Tolkien Thesaurus* (1990), which I shall discuss shortly: because such works have their words organized not according to sense or habit or ordinary collocation, but alphabetically, which in terms of semantics is as good as to say, at random.

But when I say 'dictionaries,' I do not mean mere foreign-language dictionaries, full of dubious equations between words and an overpowering smell of homework; nor yet ordinary reference dictionaries, full of the meanings of words which you know perfectly well already and recommendations about pronunciation which made excellent sense fifty years ago: no, I mean *etymological* dictionaries, and these spell wisdom. A very good example of such a dictionary is *The Oxford Dictionary of English Etymology*, edited by C.T. Onions (Onions 1969). There is something surprising about this, for the first edition of this was not published till 1966, but Charles Onions was already well established at *The Oxford English Dictionary* in 1920, before Tolkien began to work there, and had indeed been there since 1905. He was born in 1873, almost twenty years before Tolkien, and died in 1965. His *Dictionary of English Etymology*, then, was very much a

---

[1] This piece was delivered first at the Marquette University conference in honour of Richard E. Blackwelder, 21-23 October 2004, and subsequently published in Hammond and Scull (2006: 25-39). I am grateful to Marquette University and to the organisers, in particular Matt Blessing, for the initial invitation and for permission to reprint here.

lifetime's work, and a long lifetime's at that. Onions was also the fourth of the Four Wise Clerks of Oxenford, whom Tolkien guys affectionately in *Farmer Giles of Ham*,[2] and there were other connections between the two men. Like Tolkien, Onions was a Birmingham man, and also in a way an Old Edwardian, though he did not go to the main branch of King Edward's Birmingham but to one of the outer campuses, King Edward's Camp Hill. I am also told (though this is pure oral tradition) that he did not like to be called Onions, but insisted on 'On-aye-ons,' and that unlike Tolkien he retained a Birmingham accent through his life, and also some specialized local terms. I dare say he would have recognized the term 'gamgee,' though it is not to be found in his dictionary, and I was told long ago that he never used the term 'pavement,' still less 'sidewalk,' but always said 'horse-road' – or in his speech, 'orse-rowd.' Be these matters as they may, his *Dictionary of English Etymology* (like its many predecessors) is a mine of pregnant suggestion, about words and about history.

Take for instance the word *fiction*, on page 353 of the *Dictionary* (abbreviated from now on as *ODEE*). Like *fictile*, the word which precedes it in *ODEE* – a word I have never till now used or heard used – it comes from the past participle stem of Latin *fingere* 'to fashion,' *fingo fingere finxi fictum*, with no medial -n- in the past participle form, from which is derived the noun *fictio*, accusative form *fictionem*, hence French *fiction* and our word 'fiction,' all clear and predictable. Less apparently predictable – but just as predictable to those who know their etymology – is the native English cognate of it. Some may well ask, at this point, what a 'cognate' is, and like Tolkien in *Farmer Giles*, I shall give the answer of the Four Wise Clerks (in other words the appropriate definition from the main *Oxford*

---

[2] See *Reader*, 131: Tolkien asks what a 'blunderbuss' is, says that the question was put to "the Four Wise Clerks of Oxenford," who replied – and Tolkien then cites the *OED* definition of the word, only to prove it wrong. The "Four Wise Clerks" are clearly the four editors of *The Oxford English Dictionary* up to the date of *Farmer Giles*, Onions being one of them.

English Dictionary, abbreviated from now on as *OED*). Cognate words are those "coming naturally from the same root, or representing the same original word, with differences due to subsequent separate phonetic development; thus, Eng[lish] *five*, L[atin] *quinque*, Gr[eek] *pente*, are cognate words, representing a primitive **penke*" (*OED*, III: 445). What is the English cognate of 'fiction,' the word which has descended from the remote and unrecorded common ancestor of many European and Asian languages in one line to Latin *fictio*, and in another line to English? The native English word we are looking for is 'dough.' 'Dough' is the English word for 'fiction' (see *ODEE*, 286).

This seems instantly implausible, because the two words do not look or sound like each other at all, in fact they hardly share a single letter. The first rule of etymology, you might say, is that words which look like each other cannot possibly be related in reality, while words which are so related certainly will not look like each other. But this does tell you something about the unexpected nature of reality, as it does about otherwise unrecorded history. In brief – and I take this explanation from Walter Skeat's *Principles of English Etymology*, published in Oxford the year Tolkien was born (Skeat 1892) – Sanskrit *dh*- corresponds regularly to Greek *th*- and to Latin *f*-, but even more regularly to English *d*- and German *t*-. On the one hand we have Sanskrit *dhughiter*, Greek *thugatyr*, English 'daughter,' German *Tochter* – the word is related to Hindi *dudh*, which means 'milk,' and according to Max Müller had as its original meaning 'little milker' (Müller 1880, II: 26) which shows what daughters were once mainly useful for. On the other we have Sanskrit *dhigh* 'to smear,' Greek *thigganein* 'to handle,' Latin *fingere* 'to mould,' and Old English *digan* 'to knead.' This word, by the way, survives as the second element in modern English 'lady,' Old English *hlæfdige*, 'she who kneads the loaf,' which tells us what ladies were once mainly useful for. But disregarding all phonetic complexities, the equation thus set up between 'dough' and 'fiction' still makes a certain sense. 'Fiction' is rather like 'dough.' Neither of them is natural. They both take a good deal of work, and shaping, and kneading, and you also have to allow them to rise, and you have to put yeast into them – another interesting word, related to Sanskrit *yasyati* 'to seethe or boil.'

All such information, so readily available now through the work of scholars like Mr. Onions, comes as a result of one of the great intellectual breakthroughs of world history, which I associate in particular with the work of Tolkien's mighty predecessor in philology and fairy-tale, two things which are quite clearly connected, Jacob Grimm. I would put it like this and very briefly: Grimm's *Deutsche Grammatik* of 1819 was the humanities equivalent of Darwin's *Origin of Species* in 1859, and in its way just as influential. Both works solved a problem which had been obvious since remote antiquity: why are languages different, why are species different? To these questions the only answers had been a kind of folk-tale, in the case of Darwin the story of Noah's Flood, in the case of Grimm the Tower of Babel. In both cases there was a very great deal of evidence available for solving the problem, but it existed either in far parts of the world like the Galápagos Islands or North India, or else at levels of society beneath those of the educated classes: as Darwin said, among dog-breeders and pigeon-fanciers, as Grimm said among *ammen und spinnerinnen*, 'old grannies and poor spinstresses' (Grimm 1875-8, I: v-vi), of whom no educated male previously had taken any notice. Both great works were essentially evolutionary, both had an immediate impact, and both triggered enormous amounts of follow-up work. The real difference is that people have remembered Darwin, but almost completely forgotten Grimm, except as regards his spin-off collection of fairy-tales.

Tolkien did not forget Grimm, and the question of etymologies, and what can be learned from them, was on his mind, I would assert, literally every day of his life. Let me say again that you can start this process from anywhere. I took *fiction*, which lead me to *fingere*, so let's consider English 'finger' – in the Birmingham pronunciation, 'feenger.' Are these two words connected? No, of course not, see the first rule of etymology as given above! Onions suggests (*ODEE*, 357) that 'finger' derives from the ancestral word for 'five,' which he gives as **pengqe*, diverging rather from his colleagues' solution given just above.³ This also gave us 'fist.' One of the simpler bits of Grimm's Law tells us that English *f-* corresponds to Latin *p-*, as in 'fish' and *piscis*, or *pellis* and the word for skin which Tolkien uses only once in this sense, 'fell,' "unclean beast-fell" (*LotR*, 913). 'Finger,' then, finds a parallel in Latin *pugnare* 'to fight,' which perhaps also tells us something about ancient culture, or maybe about human nature.

It is very tempting to go on like this, but I will summarize a truly prodigious amount of data as follows:

> The nineteenth century succeeded in recovering the underlying logic of sound-change.
>
> It would very much have liked to extend this to the underlying logic of semantic change, change of meaning, but in fact got stuck at the level of many individual flashes of insight, which could not be reduced to invariable law.

Tolkien, by temperament and by professional training, was aware of the history of words at an almost visceral level: I would say that he never stopped thinking about it, because once you are aware of it, the data never stops flowing in, every time, for instance, you hear a new name.

And this helps to explain what he meant when he said things like "the invention of languages is the foundation. The 'stories' were made rather to provide a world for the languages than the reverse" (*Letters*, 219).

Indeed I would suggest that just as Tolkien expended truly enormous effort in writing version after version of, say, 'The Tale of Beren and Lúthien,' in different languages, from different perspectives, because he thought that a real traditional tale gained much of its power from being

---

[3] Comparative philology had continued to develop throughout Onions's and Tolkien's lifetimes. Early volumes of the *OED*, which first began to appear in 1884, often contain outdated etymologies and reconstructions: one of the strengths of the work as a whole has been its capacity for revision and improvement.

filtered down to us through many minds, many disagreements, many rejections – just so did he expend further enormous effort in providing not only samples of many languages, human and non-human, but also in making those samples relate to each other through complex and rigorous processes of change. What good was a language without a history? It would be like a day without sunshine.

There was, of course, an element of 'pedantry' in much of the effort so expended – 'pedantry,' a word "of obscure origin," so Mr Onions informs me (*ODEE*, 661), but probably a popular or half-educated formation from Latin *paedagogus*, the slave who accompanies a child to school, so a schoolteacher of relatively low rank. This is pretty much the status which language teachers have continued to occupy. Tolkien was well aware of this, perhaps even painfully aware of the low and sinking status of his branch of the profession, and consoled himself now and then by making little jokes about it. One self-image is the parson of *Farmer Giles of Ham*, remarkable for his book-learning and ability to read "epigraphical signs." But does it do him any good? Should he not have guessed that the oaths of Chrysophylax the dragon were not to be relied on? "Maybe he did," notes Tolkien. "He was a grammarian, and could doubtless see further into the future than others" (*Reader*, 146, 160). In our world grammarians are not notable for their ability to see into the future or for their practical abilities, indeed our modern grammarians – those who teach Rhet. and Comp. 101, who show freshmen how to use their spell-checkers and where to put apostrophes and semi-colons – these are I will not say the lowest of the low, but I can say often graduate students going through a phase of their career which they do not wish to prolong. So the joke in Tolkien's "doubtless" remains as pointed as ever: though the parson-grammarian is in the end proved right, by reminding Giles to take some rope with him on his second expedition.

Less successful is the philological herb-master of the Houses of Healing, who knows all the names for *athelas* and indeed a rhyme from Middle-earth's equivalent of Grimm's *ammen und spinnerinnen*, but does not actually have the herb or feel any need for it. He shows, in a rather prophetic way, how genuine knowledge can dwindle down to ancient lore, which is remembered but no longer felt to have any practical value. That is what happened, in the end, to etymology and to Tolkien's own speciality, no longer taught anywhere within the English-speaking world of learning.

Finally, I cannot help thinking of Gollum as a kind of Tolkienian self-image. The constant cross-checking of one language against another, of which I have given some fleeting examples above, led the etymologists into an obsessive concern, not with the forms of any one particular language but with the unrecorded forms of whatever it was they had all descended from. If you look, not at Onions's *Dictionary of English Etymology*, but at successive 'comparative dictionaries of the Indo-Germanic languages,' such as Fick 1874 or Walde 1930, you will see that they are in a way all but unreadable, and almost unusable, because they are organized by roots, a *root* being, according to the *OED* (sense 15a), "one of those ultimate elements of a language, that cannot be further analysed, and form the basis of its vocabulary" (*OED* XIV: 88). Gollum too, you will remember, back when he was still Sméagol, lived in a family "ruled by a grandmother of the folk, stern and wise in old lore, such as they had." And he followed in her footsteps in a way, being "inquisitive and curious-minded [...] He was interested in roots and beginnings." But this potentially admirable interest leads to him no longer looking upward, and in the end he goes underground, thinking: "The roots of those mountains must be roots indeed; there must be great secrets there which have not been discovered since the beginning." But Gollum is mistaken. As Gandalf says, "there was nothing more to find out, nothing worth doing" (*LotR*, 51, 53, 54). It is a hard thing to say of one's own subject, but this reminds me strongly of the sense which Tolkien must often have felt of an intellectual revolution being forgotten, slipping away, turning into a low-grade series of tests you had to bully the students through, and which most of the students – alienated by poor teaching and poor teachers – could not give up fast enough. Throughout his professional life Tolkien "fought the long defeat," in Galadriel's phrase (*LotR*, 348), sensed the danger of becoming a Gollum, too interested in roots, as we say, to stop and smell the roses.

How could the history of words be made to live again? Now I turn at last to Richard Blackwelder's *Tolkien Thesaurus*. When I first encountered this, I must say that I thought, 'Well, what is the point of that? It is a typical hobbit-work, full of things we knew already, set out fair and square with no contradictions.' In this I misjudged it, because I failed to see how useful it is to have lists of words taken out of their immediate contexts and set down where they can be cross-referred in a different way. And I should not have misjudged it, because I should have remembered how much of Tolkien's work, especially his early academic work, was in fact taken up with doing very much this sort of activity.[4] He began by making the Glossary (1922) to Kenneth Sisam's *Fourteenth-Century Verse and Prose*, and while this was in a way a classic graduate-student job, designed only to be useful, there is a great deal of work and thought in it. As there is in the ground-breaking and unprecedented glossary to his and E.V. Gordon's edition of *Sir Gawain and the Green Knight* (1925), which, NB, does not just give the meaning of words so you can translate them but also carefully gives the etymology of each one as well. Tolkien also clearly read with attention and applause W.E. Haigh's *A New Glossary of the Dialect of the Huddersfield District* (1928), and this indeed did show one way forward out of the Gollum-like obsession with roots and beginnings – which was, to see how those roots had flowered, to observe closely the connection between ancient words and entirely contemporary ones, contemporary ones, NB again, which tended to be ignored by the educated because they were now recorded at a lower social level than they wished to consider, by dog-breeders and pigeon-fanciers, *ammen und spinnerinnen* once more. Perhaps the real achievement

---

[4] See further on this topic, as on Tolkien and dictionaries in general, Gilliver *et al.* 2006.

would be, not only to work from root to flower, but also to work back again, from flower to root, and further, from dead leaf to living plant. And this would have particular force if one applied it not just to words and to philology, but to beliefs and to mythology.

Tolkien's very earliest academic works, which have, I regret to say, mostly sunk without leaving a trace in scholarship, are usually of this nature. He was trying to feel his way back along the language to the beliefs from which words must have sprung, though those beliefs were often, indeed usually, misunderstood even by the very people who first set them down. The author, or scribe, of *Sir Gawain* misunderstood the word *woses*.[5] A succession of Anglo-Saxon scribes (and modern scholars right up to the dictionary-makers of the present day) failed to understand the word *hearwan*, cognate with *carbo* 'soot' (see Tolkien 1932, 1934). The word *eaueres* in Middle English had been misread, so losing the point of an image of the underworld and the demons who live in it (Tolkien 1925). The word 'dwarf' had lost its proper and authentic plural until Tolkien re-introduced it, and words like 'elvish' and 'etten' had either lost their proper meaning or dwindled into remote dialects. But from such lost meanings and remote dialects one could regenerate the original concepts, as was the case with almost all of Tolkien's imagined species, from hobbits to Balrogs.

Turning again to Richard Blackwelder's *Thesaurus*, I have found it repeatedly useful in locating and tracing both words and concepts. One thing it helps you to do is check your own suspicions. It struck me as both odd and significant that Tolkien rarely but occasionally uses the word 'heathen' in *The Lord of the Rings*, an anachronism in Middle-earth because, you would think, only Christians use it. Looking at Blackwelder enabled me to check that he does indeed use it twice in that work, both times in connection with Denethor, which suggests that it is not an acci-

---

[5] See *SGGK*, entry under *wodwos*, 208. The editors tactfully make no comment on the scribe's error, but it can be deduced from the etymology they give for the word. See also further explanation on p. 70 in my paper on 'Tolkien and the *Gawain*-Poet'.

dental anachronism, but a deliberate pointer. I felt fairly sure that Tolkien's important word 'wraith' was derived from the Anglo-Saxon *wríthan* 'to bend,' and that this was an important word to the Inklings, creating besides the Ringwraiths Lewis's parallel notion of the 'bent eldil,' who is Satan. The verb *wríthan* has become, in modern English, 'to writhe,' and a glance at the *Thesaurus* shows that Tolkien uses that verb in perfectly normal modern style, past tense 'writhed,' present participle 'writhing.' But if the verb had been allowed to develop normally, we would say, not 'writhe-writhed-writhed,' but 'writhe-wrothe-writhen'; and Tolkien does indeed use that now irregular and very uncommon past participle twice, "writhen hills, writhen with age." But I would never have found that confirmation, except by chance, without the *Thesaurus*. I used to say that Tolkien dropped the word 'goblin' after he introduced the word 'orc,' because he was not satisfied with its etymology – and I add that he hung on to the word 'gnome' long after anyone would have told him he had to drop it, because he felt sure that sensible people would recognize its etymology (see *BLT 1*, 43-44). I was wrong about 'goblin,' as the *Thesaurus* again revealed to me, with nine uses of the word in *The Lord of the Rings*. The *Thesaurus* also reveals, however, that the word tends to be used, in *The Lord of the Rings*, not by the wise and the long-lived, like Gandalf or Elrond, but by the hobbits:[6] and hobbits, like modern English-speakers, are not good at etymology. The word is perhaps part of their low-style speech-mode, which attracts particular attention in Gondor and indeed in the Riddermark. Tolkien's use of language, in short, is deep and consistent, and the *Thesaurus* helps you to trace it.

---

[6] Five times out of nine the word is either used by a hobbit or in an entirely hobbitic context. Gimli and Gamling the Rider also use the word once, the latter perhaps showing the connection between the Riders' language and the ancestral speech of the hobbits. Twice it is used in general narration.

I will conclude, though, by looking at some of Tolkien's strikingly odd words, and time allows me to deal with only a couple.[7] I have chosen them from extreme ends of the literary and social scale, elevated Rohirric and vulgar hobbitic. To start with the latter, Sam Gamgee twice uses the word 'ninnyhammer' (*LotR*, 594, 596). At the top of the cliff in the Emyn Muil, when he suddenly remembers they've got a rope, he says, "you're nowt but a ninnyhammer, Sam Gamgee," and adds that that is what his father Hamfast used to call him. At the bottom of the cliff, when he thinks that he can't get the rope down again, he adds: "Ninnyhammers! Noodles! My beautiful rope!" Now what, we may ask, is a 'ninnyhammer'? This question, too, was put to the Four Wise Clerks of Oxenford, by which I mean once again *The Oxford English Dictionary*, and I have to report that they replied evasively, saying only "(app[arently] f[rom] *ninny*, but the force of the second element is not clear.) A simpleton" (*OED*, X: 430). But Charles Onions must have thought again, for in the later *Oxford Dictionary of Etymology* he gives rather more detail (see *ODEE*, 611). It is characteristic of English, for no known reason, to 'nunnate': that is, to add an *n-* to the start of words, especially names, and especially the short form of names. Tolkien seems to have been amused by this, for in *Smith of Wootton Major*, the names of all the minor human characters are nunnated, Nokes, Ned – from Edward, Nan – from Ann, Nell – from Eleanor. *Ninny* is one of these words, and it is so to speak a familiar form of the name *Innocent*. It is as if people had once said, of someone, 'he is an innocent,' then, mishearing or mispronouncing, 'he is a ninnocent,' and then, abbreviating, 'he is a ninny.' The word further becomes more pejorative with each alteration, so that in the end a 'ninny' is someone who is unfit for practical purposes. 'Hammer,' as the Four Wise Clerks concede above, is a little harder, but I would begin

---

[7] Since this piece was published, both words have been discussed along with a number of others in Gilliver *et al.* 2006. 'Dwimmerlaik' is discussed on pp. 108-10, 'ninnyhammer' on pp. 170-1. The authors stick fairly closely to the *OED* definitions, which Tolkien often challenged.

by observing – and Tolkien was punctilious about this too, though in a way which people rarely notice[8] – that over most of England, certainly including Tolkien's own West Midlands, there is a tendency not to pronounce initial h-, and conversely to put it on words, in writing, where it has no business to be. So I suggest that the word would actually be 'ninny-ammer,' and that this is what Sam and Ham Gamgee would actually have said. Now there is an Anglo-Saxon word *amore*, recorded only once, in a glossary, where it glosses Latin *scorellus*. We know the meaning of neither word, but the former survives also in the bird-name 'yellow-hammer,' or 'yellow-ammer,' and is no doubt cognate with modern German *Ammer*, 'a bunting.' What Sam's word is intended to convey, then, is first someone impractical, and then perhaps someone 'bird-brained' – which is pretty much exactly what Sam at that moment feels about himself. I would add that neither I, nor the Four Wise Clerks of Oxenford, nor Onions in later life, could do anything with Sam's "Noodles!," though it certainly has nothing to do with the things you eat in Chinese restaurants.[9] Tolkien was, however, not the only one to put the two words together, as one can see from a 1723 citation in the *OED*, under *noodle*, "the words ninnyhammer, noodle, and numskull, are frequently bandied to and fro betwixt them"; while there is also a certain point in a 1622 citation under *ninnyhammer*, which has some unknown person lamenting: "I might haue beene a scholler, learn'd my Grammar, But I haue

---

[8] As noted on p. 71 in my paper on 'Tolkien and the *Gawain*-Poet,' in the medieval poem *Sir Gawain and the Green Knight*, a number of lines (such as 5, 136, 140) become metrically irregular unless one fails to pronounce written initial *h*-. In his translation of the poem, Tolkien carefully reproduced this peculiarity: a number of his lines also become metrically regular only with the 'vulgar' or native pronunciation.

[9] Other meanings of this word, as far as I can see all entirely unhelpful, include: "A trill or improvisation on an instrument [...] To search for opals (in opal dumps or 'mullock') [...] to improvise or play casually on a musical instrument," (see *OED*, X: 506–507). [After writing and indeed publishing these words, however, I discovered – from Haigh 1928 – that the Yorkshire term *nuidl* was a diminutive form of *noddy*, 'one who is half-asleep.' Haigh also records, as a word of equivalent meaning, *sæmmi*, which he derives from OE *sámwís*, so Sam's self-accusation is entirely appropriate to him. See further entry on *New Glossary* in Drout 2007.]

lost all, like a Ninnie-hammer" (*OED*, X: 506, 430). The unknown's high valuation of grammar rather contrasts with Gaffer Gamgee's doubts about the wisdom of Sam learning his letters, but they both seem to inhabit the low end of the social scale.

At the other end of the social scale, meanwhile, we have the royal family of the Mark, just as much native English speakers as Gaffer Gamgee, but in a much more archaic and aristocratic mode. When she faces the Nazgûl, Éowyn shouts at it: "Begone, foul dwimmerlaik, lord of carrion!" Now what in the world is a 'dwimmerlaik'? The last element offers no problem. It is Old English *lác*, which means 'sport' or 'play,' and is used in names like *Guthlac* and *Hygelac*. The pronunciation, though, shows the influence of the cognate Old Norse term *leikr*, with the same meaning, which survives in northern England as the usual word for 'to play,' and is found both in the fourteenth-century poem *Sir Gawain* and in Haigh's twentieth-century *New Glossary* of 1928.

How about 'dwimmer'? According to the *OED*, the word is recorded in English, outside Tolkien, some five times only, and only in the two compounds *dweomercræft* (once) and *demerlayk* (four times). The word *dweomercræft* is recorded only from Layamon's *Brut*, a work written in Tolkien's home county of Worcestershire, close in both time and space to the *Ancrene Wisse* on which Tolkien worked for so many years, and like the *Ancrene Wisse* preserving many scraps of the native traditions of belief whose loss Tolkien so much regretted. The *OED* suggests (V: 3) that the word means 'jugglery, magic art,' and derives from Old English *gedwimer* 'illusion,' or *gedwimere*, 'juggler, sorcerer.' I do not think that Tolkien would have appreciated the use of the word 'jugglery' for 'magic art' – like the definition of 'blunderbuss' in *Farmer Giles* it smacks of the haughty rationalizing of the Victorian nineteenth century. His doubts would have been increased by the *OED*'s attempt to deal with *demerlayk* itself (IV: 435–36). Once again this is defined as "magic, practice of occult art, jugglery," but the four citations given do not substantiate this particularly well.

Two are again from Layamon, one of them referring to ways of being killed, "mid drenche oðer wid dweomerlace oðer mid steles bite." Here *dweomerlace* could possibly mean 'sorcery,' and this is true also of one of the other citations, from a medieval Alexander poem in alliterative verse, which says: "All þis demerlayke he did bot be þe deuyllis craftis." However the second Layamon quotation refers to "dweomerlakes song;" this could mean 'song of sorcery,' but leaves open the possibility that a 'dwimmer-laik' might be a thing or a person, not an abstraction. Meanwhile the last citation, also from a medieval alliterative poem, talks of "Deuinores of de-morlaykes þat dremes cowþe rede," where a 'demorlayke' must be some kind of dream or nightmare. The intended meanings cluster in the area of the supernatural, but are not easily shepherded together in the way the *OED* suggests. Faced with apparent contradictions like this, Tolkien was all his life reluctant to dismiss any of the evidence (since he felt we had all too little of it), and even more reluctant to assume that the ancient authors had no clear idea of what they meant – a solution he thought too frequently seized on by arrogant modern critics. Though he was always very ready to accept that the ancient authors' clear and sensible statements had been miscopied, misread, or misunderstood with the passing of the centuries.

His response to this problem of language history can be pieced together with the invaluable help of Richard Blackwelder's *Thesaurus*. If you consult this under *dwimmer* and *dwimor*, you will see that Tolkien uses the word seven times in *The Lord of the Rings*. Éowyn's use of it to the Nazgûl has already been mentioned, but this is the last of the seven. We hear the word first from Éomer, who says of Saruman, "he is a wizard both cunning and dwimmer-crafty, having many guises" (426). At this point the word seems strange, and helps to characterize Éomer's mode of speech as archaic but not entirely unfamiliar. Tolkien also has Éomer gloss his own word, so that "dwimmer-crafty" must mean something like 'skilled in magic,' though with a particular implication of being able to change shape, or change appearance. The next time the word is used, though, it comes from Gríma

Wormtongue, who says that it is not surprising that they came through Lothlórien with the aid of Galadriel, "Sorceress of the Golden Wood," for "webs of deceit were ever woven in Dwimordene" (502). 'Dwimordene' is clearly the Riders' word for Lothlórien, a place they all fear and distrust, Éomer included, if only through ignorance. The name could mean 'valley of magic,' but one should note the association with 'webs' and 'deceit,' which once again suggest veiling, illusion, shape-shifting. Gandalf picks the word up and repeats it twice, as if he is prepared to accept it, though not the interpretation placed on it. But the ominous nature of 'dwimor' is confirmed by the place-name Dwimorberg, which Tolkien translates twice as "the Haunted Mountain" (768, 777). By the time Éowyn comes to use the word 'dwimmerlaik,' then, we have had a number of hints as to its meaning, though I would add one more piece to the jigsaw: the *OED* also cites a word *dwalm, dwam*, and glosses it as 'a swoon, a fainting fit,' though I have also encountered it with the meaning of 'deep abstraction, a brown study.'

I think that Tolkien's train of thought was something like this. The word comes from Old English *gedwimer*, etc., and if it had survived into modern English it would appear as 'dwimmer'; the *OED*'s preference for *demer* in one of its entries is wrong, as one can see from its own citations. 'Magic art' is, however, only one aspect of its meaning. It is in fact a word rather like 'shimmer' or 'glimmer,' with a root meaning of 'being hard to make out, being on the edge of sight.' People then associate this with ghosts, as in 'Dwimorberg,' with deceit, as in 'Dwimordene,' with shape-shifting, as in 'dwimmer-crafty,' all of which have something to do with blurred or warped vision; and with dreams, in which people see things that are not there. The word implies a belief that the magic arts themselves depend on casting spells of illusion, which was famously the native belief of the North, as in the well-known account of Thor's visit to Útgartha-Loki's hall of deceptions in Snorri Sturluson's *Prose Edda*. What does Éowyn then mean, finally, by calling the Nazgûl 'dwimmerlaik'? She may mean 'creature of sorcery,' which is true. Remembering the force of *-laik*, she may mean 'sport of nightmare.' The word hints also at the Nazgûl's doubtful reality, seeming non-existence, as if he too is a creature of deceit and altered vision. It is in fact a dwimmery sort of a word, defined only, within *The Lord of the Rings*, by triangulation from a number of quite different perspectives, Gríma's, Gandalf's, Éomer's, Éowyn's, and outside it by a similar process of guessing from a number of themselves doubtful or poorly-recorded uses. Tolkien's various uses and compound terms do, however, several times remind us that the Riders as a whole inhabit an intellectual world quite different from ours, though at the same time, Tolkien would have insisted, quite literally cognate with it.

There is of course a further and most extensive history of words in Tolkien's Elvish languages, designed as they are to frame and corroborate the narrative history which is the many versions of 'The Silmarillion.' It would take a great deal of work to decode, and I can only look on admiringly at the efforts and the results of scholars like Carl Hostetter. But there is an even more extensive history of words in the whole body of human languages, and it would take an effort at least of the proportions of that dedicated to plotting the human genome to decode this – though there is not the slightest chance, of course, of attracting anything like similar funding.

As regards *The Lord of the Rings* itself, I would close by saying that it seems to me that one of the major sources of its continuing appeal, fifty years on, is the enormous range of its vocabulary – I think I would back Tolkien against Shakespeare any day, and certainly against any modern author – and along with that the extreme versatility of its narrative styles. Tolkien is often rebuked for being archaic, and he is, of course, with a whole range of odd or barely comprehensible words coming from the Riders, from Gandalf, from Elrond, from Treebeard. But he is also frequently highly colloquial, with the voices of Hamfast and Samwise Gamgee, and the other hobbits too, and this is very much part of philological tradition – philology, I may as well say, has always been a highly democratic tradition, quite unlike the increasingly haughty and confessedly élitist tradition of modernist literature (let alone post-modernist literature). Going back to Tolkien's range of styles, one of the amusing things in his work is to hear the hobbits trying to change their speech, with Merry in particular trying to talk to Théoden King in a way which Théoden will accept and understand, and Pippin more awkwardly trying to talk in Gondorian fashion to Denethor.

If I may end with a personal reflection, we often hear these days of the importance of getting rid of the literary canon, and of listening for the silenced voices of the past. But it is strange that the more we hear about 'firing the canon,' the less variety there is in what is actually read in departments of humanities; and the more we listen for the silenced voices, the more we seem to hear only echoes of our own. Modern literature becomes a weary trawl for victim-groups to patronize (without the slightest intention, of course, of giving up élite privileges), while even medieval English literature is redefined as overwhelmingly metropolitan, literary, middle-class, bureaucratic – as if it had all been written by paid-up members of the Modern Language Association, something which no literary tradition could survive. As Tolkien pointed out in his 'Valedictory Address' of 1959 (see *Essays*, 225-6), the 'misologists,' those who see no point in the study of words as words, they are in the ascendant: but only in the academic world and only in the humanities. Their views cut no ice with Tolkien, they cut no ice with working scientists like Dr. Blackwelder, and they have gained no credit with the general public. It is indeed a pity that the English-speaking academic world has seen it as a duty to extinguish philological study, marginalize linguistic study, and sharply restrict literary study. Nevertheless, all the efforts of the misologists very obviously failed to quench Tolkien himself, and his associates, devotees, and followers. Possibly, then, from the ashes a fire may be woken, and from the shadows a light may spring, as has happened with the unexpected and welcome benefactions of Dr. Blackwelder. I will not complete Bilbo's rhyme, but I will offer it here as a good omen for the future.

A Look at *Exodus* and *Finn and Hengest*[1]

The Old English Exodus: Text, Translation and Commentary, by J.R.R. Tolkien, edited by Joan Turville-Petre (Oxford: Clarendon Press, 1981).

Finn and Hengest: The Fragment and the Episode, by J.R.R. Tolkien, edited by Alan Bliss (London: George Allen & Unwin, 1982).

Both these editions are, in a double sense, works of reconstruction. In the first place both are based on notes for lecture sequences, delivered in the 1930s and 1940s in the case of *Exodus*, in the case of *Finn and Hengest* between 1928 and 1937, again in 1963, and in intention (though not in fact, as a result of the outbreak of war) in 1939. Anyone with experience of professors can imagine what a set of lecture notes looks like: it says a great deal for Tolkien's conscientiousness that anything is recoverable at all. When one adds to this the fact that the lectures were worked over again and again, and furthermore remembers Tolkien's notorious inability to revise without extensively rewriting, it becomes apparent that Professors Bliss and Turville-Petre must have been studying what were in effect palimpsests. Bliss indeed remarks that: "The task facing the editor of this material resembles the task facing Tolkien himself when in his last years he envisaged revising *The Silmarillion* for publication: 'the manuscripts themselves had proliferated, so that he was no longer certain which of them represented his latest thoughts on any particular passage.'" (*Finn*, vii, quoting Carpenter 1977: 251). Working out Tolkien's intentions for both the *Exodus* and *Finn and Hengest*, then, is trying to arrive at something never in fact recorded, and perhaps never in final shape even in the deepest recesses of Tolkien's

---

[1] This piece appeared first in the journal of the Swedish Tolkien Society, *Arda* 1982-3 (published 1986): 72-80. I am grateful to the editor, Anders Stenström, for allowing me to reprint it here.

mind; both volumes ought to have an asterisk on the front, to indicate their provisional/inferential status.

There is however another sense in which these editions are works of reconstruction, a rather more contentious one, and one which Tolkien certainly intended. Almost all Old English poetry exists in one manuscript alone. An editor of these poems (as is not the case with Chaucer, say, or Shakespeare) hardly ever has to choose between readings, accepting one and rejecting another. The custom has accordingly grown steadily stronger over the decades of changing in a text as little as possible. The man who wrote the manuscript, it is argued, may not have been the poet, and may not have understood the poem, but he *was* a native speaker of Old English, and his guesses are therefore more likely to be correct than ours. 'Leave well alone' is the motto of most modern editors; some have become quite slavish in their reluctance to meddle, refusing (for instance) to do so much as expand an Anglo-Saxon '&'-sign into *and* – for, they fear, it might after all in some dialects have been really *ond*.

With this pusillanimity Tolkien had little patience. He did not think much of the scribe of *Exodus*, who, he felt, had misrepresented the original poet "grievously" (*Exodus*, 33). He had a higher opinion of the man who copied our version of *Beowulf* (in which the 'Finnsburg Episode' is to be found) but even so he thought the copier had made too many mistakes to be trusted: he could not for instance recognise the heroic name *Éomer,* and substituted the adjective *geomor,* which is the Old English word for 'sad' and in context meaningless. As for the *Finnsburg Fragment*, Tolkien was on much stronger ground: the manuscript no longer exists, and the scrap of poetry is preserved only in what could well be a very inaccurate copy from the early eighteenth century, as likely to be wrong as right.

Tolkien's commentary on these poems accordingly abounds in such remarks as "is nonsense," or "impossible form." He felt, and this is enough to arouse the ire of many modern scholars, that he knew better what Anglo-Saxon poets intended than even native Anglo-Saxon speaking scribes did.

Weredon wælnet, reads *Exodus* line 202, in an extremely difficult passage: *wæl-net* seems to mean 'death-nets,' but *weredon* could mean 'wore' or possibly 'defended,' and neither translation makes much sense as the poem stands. P.J. Lucas, the most recent editor (who incidentally had Tolkien's notes available to him and seems to have used them as much as he dared) comes down for the translation "corslets hindered [the Israelites in their desire to run away]" (Lucas 1977: 106). This is philologically safe, but unheroic in the highest degree: also unpoetic to the point of utter banality. Tolkien, by contrast, cuts the knot by suggesting that *weredon* is a mistake; the verb should be *wyrgdon,* from *wyrgan,* 'to choke or strangle,' a word incidentally related to the 'Wargs' of *The Hobbit.* As for *wælnet,* he rejects the idea that this means 'metal nets for warriors,' so 'shirts of mail'; he thinks it is a case of the poet using a concrete image for an abstract idea: the Israelites were choked, caught in "deadly toils" of indecision or paralysis (*Exodus*, 53).

'But that is not what the poem says!' cries the orthodox scholar. 'We don't know what the poem said,' replies Tolkien, 'only what the scribe says, and he is not to be trusted. Furthermore *my* interpretation is much more attractive' – as indeed it is, reminding us for instance of the curious beliefs which in some Germanic texts make the heroes seem to go to their deaths like sleepwalkers, with their eyes open, but unswervingly, and also, if only by hindsight, of the 'web' of doom, the 'deadly net' of coincidences in which Túrin Turambar perishes enmeshed.

Still, many readers may wonder, what does all this matter to me? Are these editions not just rumours from the past, echoes from forgotten scholarly battlefields? To these questions there are perhaps two main answers. In the first place one may say, quickly enough, that the battlefields are not forgotten, but still being fought over: much of the hostile learned reaction to Tolkien's fiction (as I have argued in successive editions of *The Road to Middle-earth*) stems from just this disgust at and suspicion of the traditional methods of philology, especially 'reconstruction.' However, and more positively, it is also possible, in these poems and in the notes on them, to make out something of Tolkien's lifelong inspirations: the things he read the poems for, the things in them that stirred his imagination, the appeal they made to him for the recovery of forgotten (but not discredited) truths. His editions of the poems may have seemed to him like Meriadoc Brandybuck's use of the sword taken from the wight's barrow on the Black Captain: "glad would he have been to know its fate who wrought it slowly long ago" (*LotR*, 844). He was rescuing these poems from the un-dead hands of editors, scholars, critics and philologists; and he did it because he felt himself to be a kindred spirit of the poets,[2] not only cleaning and restoring what they had written, but going on to use it in the way they had intended – in the creation of more poems, more fictions, more truths.

The place of *Exodus* in Tolkien's thought is the easier to explain. Tolkien thought this was an early poem, earlier even than *Beowulf*. He does not quite say so in the edition we have here, though he hints at the opinion on pp. 34-5. However I feel sure that in his famous allegory of the tower in '*Beowulf*: The Monsters and the Critics' (see *Essays*, 7-8), we are meant to assume that the tower is *Beowulf*, the "old stone" of which the tower is made is the accumulation of early pre-Christian poems and legends known to the *Beowulf*-poet but not to us – but "the house in which *the poet* actually lived, not far from the old house of his fathers" (and, n.b., made from the same "old stone" as *Beowulf*) is the early Christian civilisation now best represented by the poem *Exodus*. The allegory may be confirmed in three ways. First, the "house in which [the poet] actually lived" ought to be older than "the tower": and there are good philological grounds for thinking *Exodus* is older than *Beowulf*, though Tolkien does not rehearse them. Second, the "house" ought not to be far removed (in spirit) from "the old house" of the ancestors: and Tolkien spends much time in his commentary here in

---

[2] See further the essays on 'Tolkien and the *Beowulf*-Poet' and 'Tolkien and the *Gawain*-Poet' in this volume.

showing how the military ideas of Anglo-Saxon pagandom remained in *Exodus* largely unchanged by Christianity. Third, and most revealingly, the "house" ought to be made of "old stone": and the distinguishing mark of Tolkien's *Exodus* notes is the care he spends on old words and old ideas.

Of these the most famous is *Sigelwara land*, 'the land of the Ethiopians.' Tolkien was sure this was wrong. It ought to be *Sigel-warena* (better grammar and metre) or *Sigelhearwena* (better mythology and better sense as well). *Sigelwara* in fact was a clear case of the scribe not understanding an old word of the poet's, like *Éomer* in *Beowulf* or *wodwos* in *Sir Gawain*; and indeed *Sigelhearwa* (nominative singular form of genitive plural *Sigelhearwena*) would, as a word, be exactly parallel to *wod-wos,* or indeed to *hol-bytla.* In each case:

a) the first element in the word is absolutely familiar, meaning respectively 'sun,' 'wood,' and 'hole'
b) the second element is completely unknown, leaving only the faintest, or no, traces in modern English
c) the whole refers to a being or class of beings once believed in but now forgotten, 'fire-spirit,' 'wild man of the woods,' and 'hobbit,' and
d) traces of this belief (except in the case of the hobbits) can nevertheless be discovered so widely as to suggest that it was once all but universal.

Sigelwara in fact is a mistake which nevertheless gives us a glimpse through the mists of time into a very old world of belief: and a world by no means fantastic, but organised, plausible, almost matter-of-fact. Tolkien prized these glimpses above everything. For them he scoured the poems. What others can one trace in this edition of *Exodus*?

All Tolkien's notes take a good deal of digesting, but I would suggest that there were three main areas of interest for him in this poem. One is simple and literal: he felt that the poet had a good eye for military detail and custom, and therefore showed us how the ancient English actually did their soldiering (the relevance to the Riders of Rohan being obvious). In lines 247-50, for instance, other modern editors normally see a description of the Pillar of Cloud appearing at daybreak to guide the Israelites on their way (P.J. Lucas further 'abstracting' this so that it becomes a giant image of the Cross). Tolkien thought this was unheroic and devious. Making several changes to the text (all rejected by Lucas) he says that we should really see the scene "in terms of contemporary military custom." First we have a display of "marshalling" (I comment on the significance of this word to the Riders in Shippey 2003a: 123); then "the banner is raised" (not the Pillar of Cloud) "to indicate that the host is ready for battle." In the background we have a sequence of horn-calls, elaborated in the note to line 191, for "reveille [...] tent-pitching [...] striking tents" (*Exodus*, 53). This last idea is likely enough. It would be characteristic of modern scholars (often sedentary, disorganized and unmilitary by disposition) to miss it. It would furthermore provide that element of continuity in English life which Tolkien so much prized – for even this reviewer remembers with horror the notes of the bugle dragging him from his blankets, and Tolkien must have heard the same bugle-call far more often.[3]

The detail is remembered at least once in *The Lord of the Rings*, in 'The Muster of Rohan': there too the Riders setting off for Gondor are "marshalled." When they are ready "a single trumpet" sounds. Théoden King raises his hand, and the host of the Mark moves off – silently, however, as befits the grim mood of the passage (*LotR*, 785). It would be possible, I suspect, to analyse and find significance in the military signals of Tolkien's fiction – and to relate them back to *Exodus*.

Other warlike details are noted, like the clasping of vizor to chinguard at lines 174-5, an unusually precise reference to armour; or the shak-

---

[3] A stray, but interesting fact is that Tolkien's regiment, the Lancashire Fusiliers, won more Victoria Crosses during the First World War than any other. See Garth 2003 for a detailed study of Tolkien's World War I experience.

ing down of ruckled mailshirts at line 176, another detail no doubt once utterly familiar (like the habitual stamping of British infantrymen climbing out of lorries, to settle trouser-legs over gaiters) but as utterly forgotten. However Tolkien saw other things than literalism in the poem: menace, and a paganism rejected but still present in the background.

In lines 162-6, for instance, he comments on a cluster of ominous words. *Drihtneas*, he notes, is an archaic word for corpses; in *Beowulf* the second element is compounded with *orc* (which raises the interesting question of whether the *Beowulf*-poet knew what 'orcs' were, and whether he thought of them as being in some sense or other, like wights or wraiths, dead). The raven that comes to eat the corpses is called *wælceasega*, a word quite like 'valkyrie' but not the same. It means, suggests Tolkien, not only that the old gods sent their messengers to 'pick' the dead, but also that the raven was one that "habitually picks over" battle-corpses (*Exodus*, 50) – eyes for choice, as other Old English poets remark. The Riders, one notes, are quick to bury their casualties. Finally *cwyldrof*, says Tolkien, is "an echo of a dark pagan word" (*Exodus*, 50). It does not mean "brave in scavenging" (Lucas) but "grown bold at the dying of day"; with the night, one remembers from *Beowulf*, the "shapes from the shadow-helms" emerge.

And what are 'shadow-helms'? Helm can mean just 'covering' and so one gets the monsters emerging simply from the cover of darkness, from their caves no doubt. Yet the idea of a real 'shadow-helm(et)' seems to have affected Tolkien profoundly: Mordor, like the mountain-tops in *Sir Gawain* with their 'mist hackles,' seems to wear a helm of smoke and shadow permanently. Furthermore the Ringwraiths' helms of shadow are prominent – see for instance a passage in 'The Stairs of Cirith Ungol' (*LotR*, 691). This remark takes us to the last area of stimulus in *Exodus* for Tolkien, which is quite simply its vocabulary, and the poised balance of that vocabulary between literal and allegorical meanings. Is a raven a bird or a divine emissary? Is a helm a helmet of metal or a covering of darkness? In modern English one expects to know. In ancient English, though, both notions can exist simultaneously, giving dragons for instance a violent, cruel, animal life of their own, and yet making them in a faint but perceptible way images of human vice, greed and avarice. Tolkien disliked pure allegory; but he disliked mere meaningless history as well (and mere meaningless fiction). He wanted an area in between, and he found one example of it in *Exodus*, "at once" (he said) "a historical poem about events of extreme importance [...] and [...] an allegory of the soul, or of the Church of militant souls" (*Exodus*, 53). Modern critics have swerved very heavily to the allegorical pole (with the exception of this reviewer, see Shippey 1972: 136-43). Tolkien would have expected them to. In reaction it is very tempting (especially for this reviewer) to hurl allegory out of the window altogether and to concentrate on *things* – ravens, horn-calls, chin-guards, and all the other details so often ignored. From this abyss, however, Tolkien calls us back: not allegory, but not mere literalism either. A just balance. A large symbolism. An applicability controlled by the reader.

The *Finnsburg* poem tells a different story. This may be summed up (as so often in Old English) by pondering one philological detail. In Old English there were two words. One was *eoten,* a giant. The other (never recorded in the singular) was *Eota*, a Jute, a man from Jutland. These two words would normally be distinct, *except in the genitive plural form*, when both became *eotena* (one is *eoten-a,* the other is *eot-ena,* but this distinction of course is unmarked in speech or writing). *Beowulf* is the only work in Old English which ever mentions *eotenas*, or giants (how nearly this once common word vanished!). Alas, it is also a work which at one point, the 'Finnsburg Episode,' has much to say of *Eotena bearn,* the Jutes, the children of the Jutes – or is it of the giants? Are we talking about history, in other words, or about myth?

History, replied Tolkien firmly. His edition of *Finn and Hengest* is dedicated to the belief that not only do these two Old English fragments reflect a real event, not just a story, they also and in unexpected ways reflect a critical event – the beginning, indeed, of the founding of England.

Both the *Finnsburg Fragment* (now lost) and the 'Finnsburg Episode' in *Beowulf* appear to centre on a fight. This takes place in Finnsburg. On one side is Finn, king of the Frisians (a well-known people). On the other is Hnæf, a prince of the Danes (also still on the map). On Hnæf's side, and avenging him once he is dead, is Hengest, a character prominent in both poems. Hengest is also the name (though neither poem says this) of the first invader of England. The historian Bede appears to say he was a Jute, like his followers, who later settled in Kent and some other areas. But in the 'Finnsburg Episode' it appears that the *enemies* of Hnæf and Hengest are Jutes; it is Frisians and Jutes against Danes and Hengest. Can this discrepancy (Tolkien seems to have asked himself) be reconciled, made sense of? Other, of course, than by saying there were *two* Hengests living at much the same time, but not connected with each other; or alternatively by saying that Bede got it wrong, and that Hengest the invader was not a Jute at all.

Tolkien's answer is, in essence, a 'Jutes-on-both-sides' theory, developed in great detail. Behind that, though, there lies a theory which says that the fate of the Jutes was in fact critical for the ancient North as a whole. They were a people slowly being dispossessed and crushed by the Danes, in their advance from Skaane to Sjælland and beyond. On the other side they faced a resolute front from the Frisians, Franks and peoples of the more civilised South. The fight at Finnsburg is then, in a way, their last stand, their last attempted vengeance. Dispossessed Jutes, Tolkien suggests, entered the service of Finn. Finn, however, was anxious to stay on terms with the Danes, marrying a Danish princess. When, however, that princess's brother came to visit, the anger of the dispossessed Jutes was too great to control; they attempted to murder Hnæf in a night-attack in Finn's own hall but unsuccessfully, for sentries had been posted. The sight of weapons flashing in the moonlight is indeed the start of the *Finnsburg Fragment*.

But what of Hengest? Tolkien will not call him this, but the suggestion is that he was a renegade, even a quisling, though indeed a Jute – one *who took service with the Danish side*. Once Hnæf was dead, his position was especially delicate: he should avenge his lord, he could however change sides; he may have been the worst-hated hero of all (by his own countrymen). In the end he arranges terms for his own Jutish followers, and for his Danish allies; but then breaks out, kills Finn (the politician) and escapes to Denmark – but then, in Tolkien's view, has no option but to leave this whole tangled scene entirely and embark on a new series of conquests, in England, with a following of masterless, tribeless and broken men, who may have been Jutes, or Danes, or Saxons, or English (or Swedes or Swabians), as long as they would fight, and not fight each other.

This view creates, within these poems, several moments of added excitement. In the *Fragment* a young man, Garulf son of Guthlaf, rushes to the fight, to be restrained by an older one who does not want him to risk his "precious life." Why is *his* life precious? Because, says Tolkien, he was the last prince of the Jutish royal stock, centre of the hopes of the scattered Jutish nation. His name, thinks Tolkien – quick as ever to emend a text – was really *Gefwulf*, mentioned in another Old English poem. His father should not have been *Guthlaf* (there is a Guthlaf on the other side, among the Danes, but Tolkien thinks that is another mistake) but perhaps *Guthulf*. The fall of Garulf/Gefwulf, in any case, at the hands of another exile or broken man, extinguishes the hopes of Jutland and ironically creates yet more masterless men to find a home in England.

And find a home in England they did. It has been argued (see Joe Houghton's review in *Amon Hen* 61, p. 4) that *Finn and Hengest* is an "unreadable" list of names. A list of names it is, but names have a real fascination. As Stenström rightly says (in his review in *Amon Hen* 66, pp. 5-7), even the heroic name of Hnæf survived – very very quietly (like hobbits) and yet very securely. Just as 'wood-woses' survive in the common modern English surname 'Woodhouse,' so Hnæf lives on, in a way, in the common modern English surname 'Neave,' the name of course of Tolkien's own Aunt Jane. To this I can add that Hengest does too. Tolkien does not say this in the book reviewed here, but at some time in the winter of 1972-3 I exchanged a few words with him on this very subject, and he did two things. One was to correct my pronunciation of 'Hengest': I gave it the modern English spelling pronunciation with medial hard /g/. He said this should be medial /j/, as in (for instance) 'Stonehenge,' from the word 'hang,' 'hinge,' also from 'hang,' or 'stingy,' from the word 'sting.' We bickered about this slightly, but he then remarked that Hengest was still there, so to speak, in the landscape. The village of Hinksey, just outside Oxford, he remarked, goes back to an older form *Hengestes-ig*, or 'Hengest's Island.'

There may have been an eyot (Tolkien's word, see 'The Great River,' *LotR*, 373) in the river once. Was it called after the famous leader? It seems unlikely, but then everything in history seems unlikely. Tolkien clearly thought that the connection was anyway appropriate. He himself had rubbed shoulders with heroes (see my note on the Lancashire Fusiliers above). Many of them no doubt came from places like Hinksey. Just because a place like Hinksey, or Oxfordshire, or the Shire itself, seems boring and flat and everyday, one should not write it off. It may have been a scene of daring and passion, where heroes walked; it may become so yet again. Beneath some dull village in the dunes of Holland there lie, no doubt, even yet the bones and ashes of the combatants at Finnsburg.

Tolkien believed (as I have remarked repeatedly in *The Road to Middle-earth*) in three things, at least: which I call 'the reality of history,' 'the reality of language,' 'the reality of human nature.' All three are exemplified in these two editions. There is a kind of enduring continuity in the horn-calls of *Exodus*, which stretch much altered but no doubt in unbroken line from the manoeuvres of Dark Age battlefields to the bugles of any modern barracks: human nature changes in many ways, but some things remain the same because they are natural, easy or sensible. In the same way names shift and change, like 'Neave' or 'Woodhouse' or 'Hinksey,' but their connection with the past remains unbroken – and they remain good evidence, too, because people do not feel any need to lie about them, or distort them wilfully, but let them change in their own regular and recoverable way. As for the 'reality of history,' no nation in Europe is less aware of that than the English – a nation, one may note, without a state, a language or a monarchy it does not share with aliens (like the Scots and the Welsh), without a national anthem or a national dress, and with no apparent wish for any of them. The English seem indeed to have no self-awareness and the history they have been taught about themselves is mostly rubbish. Yet a true history, Tolkien thought, was still there, in the *Finnsburg Fragment* if nowhere else. Even an old national mythology lurked behind the error of *Sigelwara land*. Could all these old truths be once more brought to light?

The obvious answer is 'No' – and one may doubt, indeed, whether *Finn and Hengest* will find many readers. Yet *The Lord of the Rings* found readers, against all the probabilities. And between the two works there is some slight connection. In both one feels that Tolkien had a hidden resource. If ideas failed him, he did not have to *invent*. He could turn instead to the map, to the telephone directory, to his memory of his own family and his own experiences, and *find out* what could or should have happened. Professor Bliss remarks that Tolkien represented a "unique blend of philological erudition and poetic imagination." In that blend, though, I would recognise a very strong element of close observation and plain prose sense.

Tolkien and Iceland:
The Philology of Envy[1]

One of the things most often said about J.R.R. Tolkien is that it was his intention, in his fiction, to create 'a mythology for England.' It seems that he never in fact used this particular phrase (see Stenström 1995); but just the same, on more than one occasion he said something quite similar. Thus, in one letter written after the publication of *The Lord of the Rings*, or *Hringadróttins saga*, he says that he had set himself a task in life, which was "to restore to the English an epic tradition and present them with a mythology of their own" (*Letters*, 231). In another letter he says in more detail, "once upon a time [...] I had in mind to make a body of more or less connected legend, ranging from the large and cosmogonic, to the level of romantic fairy-story [...] which I could dedicate simply: to England; to my country" (*Letters*, 144). This second letter was written in 1951, when *The Lord of the Rings* was still not published, and not accepted by any publisher, while *The Silmarillion* had been shown once to a publisher and firmly rejected. We know now that in 1951 Tolkien had already written a body of legend ranging from the cosmogonic (the early parts of *The Silmarillion*) to an epic romance (*The Lord of the Rings*). He abandoned the attempt to dedicate these works "to England; to my country," but it is very likely that a major initial motive for him was both nationalist and mythological.

In this, of course, he was by no means alone, though he was a hundred years late. In 1835 Jacob Grimm had produced his *Deutsche Mythologie*, and even earlier Nikolai Grundtvig had produced his two different versions of *Nordens Mytologi* (1808 and 1832), both of them with similarly

---

[1] This paper was first given at a conference on 'Tolkien, Undset, Laxness,' at the Norroena Hus in the Icelandic National University in Reykjavik, and has been available since on http://www.nordals.hi.is/shippey.html. I am much indebted to the organisers, especially Ulfar Bragason, for the initial invitation, for permission to reprint here, and for much hospitality. I have added some references, and some explanations not needed by the original Icelandic audience.

nationalist motives. Tolkien, however, had a problem, or rather two problems, which were not so acute for his two predecessors. One is that almost nothing survives of Old English pre-Christian tradition, or myth: there is no Old English Edda. There is no English equivalent to Jón Árnason's collection of Icelandic folktales either,[2] not even to the Grimms' *Haus- und Kindermärchen*. By the time folk-tale collectors got to work in England, there was almost nothing left to collect. This was not true in other areas of the British Isles – so, for instance, the Grimms could bring out in 1826 their translation of Thomas Croker's *Irische Elfenmärchen* – but Tolkien was never a British or Celtic nationalist, he was an English nationalist, so this was no help to him. In the second letter already quoted he says indeed, "I was from early days grieved by the poverty of my own beloved country; it had no stories of its own" (*Letters*, 144). An element of jealousy, or envy, is added in a note he wrote maybe as early as 1917, in which he declares, speaking of very early versions of *The Silmarillion*, "Thus it is that [...] the *Engle* [the English] have the true tradition of the fairies, of which the *Iras* and the *Wéalas* [the Irish and the Welsh] tell garbled things" (*BLT 2*, 290). Tolkien wanted English myths, and English legends, and English fairy-stories, and these did not exist. He refused to borrow from Celtic tradition, which he regarded as alien. What was he going to do? The answer is, of course, that he was going to borrow from Old Norse, which, for philological reasons, he did NOT regard as alien.

Tolkien, however, had another problem, which is that he was his life a believing Christian and (unlike Grimm and Grundtvig) a Roman Catholic. It could well be said that a believing Christian has no business reviving heathen myths and constructing alternative mythologies. There is only one true myth, which is the Christian one, and it tolerates no competitors, as we all know from the First Commandment, 'Thou shalt have no other gods but

---

[2] A good introduction to these (probably the finest collection ever made in any European country) is Simpson 2005.

me.' If the first question I have raised, then, is 'How could Tolkien create a mythology for England?,' my second must be 'Why would he want to create a mythology for anyone?' I shall give my detailed answer to this second question first.

It is very easy now for us to forget or to underestimate the impact which Old Norse literature had on the learned world as it was rediscovered, from Icelandic sources, between the seventeenth and the nineteenth centuries. The history of this impact has been written in part, for instance by Dr Wawn in his book *The Vikings and the Victorians* (2002), but of course it began before the Victorians. I cannot give a complete account any more than anyone else, but major turning points include Ole Worm's *Runer, seu Danica Literatura Antiquissima vulgo Gothica dicta hic reddita opera* (1636), based on manuscripts supplied by Magnús Óláfsson of Laufás, Bishop Brynjófr Sveinsson's delivery of the Codex Regius manuscript of the *Poetic Edda* to Copenhagen in 1662, Thomas Bartholinus's *Antiquitatum Danicarum de Causis Contempt & Mortis a Danis adhuc gentilibus libri tres ex vetustis codicis & monumentis hactenus ineditis congesti* (1689), Mallet's *Monumens de la mythologie et de la poésie des Celtes et particulierement des anciens Scandinaves* (1755-56), Thomas Percy's translation of Mallet as *Northern Antiquities* (1770), and Percy's own *Five Pieces of Runic Poetry, translated from the Islandic Language* (1763). Furthermore, even the partial accounts of this impact which I know about do not answer the question, what made the *Poetic Edda*, and Snorri Sturluson's *Prose Edda*, and the *Krakumál*, and indeed the *fornaldarsögur*, so irresistibly attractive. I will give here, very briefly, three reasons, which I think apply to Tolkien's urge to recreate England's missing mythology, and perhaps to other recreators as well.

The first is that Old Norse myth is strangely funny. I don't mean 'comic,' exactly, I mean amusing. Thórr is often a figure of fun, in a way which is not true of Zeus or Jupiter. Think of him disguised as Freyja when he tries to recover his hammer in *Þrymskviða*, with the giant asking:

> Hví eru öndótt augo Freyio?
> þicci mér ór augum eldr of brenna
> [Why is there such a terrible look in Freya's eyes?
> It seems to me as if fire burns from them.]

and Loki craftily replying:

> Svaf vætr Freyia átta nóttum,
> svá var hon óðfús í iötunheima.
> [Freya has not slept for eight nights,
> so eager was she to come to Giant-land.]
> (Neckel/Kuhn 1962: 115, my translation)

Think of him struggling to drain the drinking-horn in the house of Útgarða-Loki, which is connected to the sea, or to pick up the cat, which is really the Miðgarðsormr. This is not the kind of story we are told about Hercules. But there are plenty of other examples. The *Krakumál* ends with Ragnarr Loðbrók saying *hlæjandi skal ek deyja*, and in another of the versions of his death in the *ormgarðr* his last words are *gnyðja munu grísir ef galtar hag vissi* – 'if they knew how the old boar died, the little pigs would grunt.' But *gnyðja* is surely a vulgar word, and 'the little pigs' is a funny way to refer to Ívarr hinn beinlaussi and Sigurðr orm-i-auga. They do not say things like this in Virgil's *Aeneid*.

Nevertheless these vulgar or amusing ways of telling mythic or heroic story are not intended in any way to diminish the status of Norse gods or heroes, just the opposite. And Norse saga and Edda is perfectly capable of reaching out to the sublime and the magnificent, as we see from the *Völuspá* or the *Sólarljóð*. You will find the funny, and the heroic, and the sublime, all very close together in the pages of the *Introduction to Old Norse* brought out by E.V. Gordon in 1927, a book which announces its special debt to Tolkien in the 'Preface,' and which was clearly prepared at a time when Tolkien and Gordon were close colleagues and collaborators, at Leeds University in the mid-1920s. I would suggest, in fact, that this book shows very well a second reason for the attraction of Old Norse literature in the learned world, which is that as well as being funny, it rejects the classical notion of decorum: of keeping the styles separate, high style, middle style, low style. This is notoriously a native English trait as well – it is what made Shakespeare unacceptable to Voltaire – but Old Norse literature gave this English failing a distinguished ancestry. (Let me note, *en passant*, that in this *Introduction* Gordon gives a strangely composite account of the Battle of Stiklastaðir, which is highly 'indecorous,' and reminds me in a way of the end of Halldór Laxness's novel *Gerpla*.)[3]

However, the third reason I would indicate for the powerful impact of Old Norse on European scholars, and on Tolkien, is the rationale it gives for heroism. The most surprising image of Old Norse mythology, for Christians, is perhaps the idea of Ragnarök, an Armageddon which the wrong side wins. Tolkien was very impressed by this, but – writing just before the outbreak of World War II – also rather disturbed by it: he saw that the ethos it represented could be used by either side, as indeed it was in the deliberate cultivation of *Götterdämmerung* by the Nazi leadership a few years later. Nevertheless it did provide an image of heroic virtue which could exist, and could be admired, outside the Christian framework. In some respects (as you can see from Tolkien's comments in his 1936 *Beowulf* lecture, see *Essays*, 24-25) the Old Norse 'theory of courage' might even be regarded as ethically superior to the Classical if not to the Christian world-view, in that it demanded commitment to virtue without any offer of lasting reward. Men must fight monsters because it was their duty, not because they thought the monsters would lose, or the gods would win. In the deep disillusionment which overtook the Western world, and England especially, after 1918, the Old Norse mythology seemed immune to self-doubt, precisely because it had no self-belief.

In answer to my question, 'Why did Tolkien want to invent a new mythology?,' then, I would say that, like Grimm or Grundtvig, he very

---

[3] Translated into English as *The Happy Warriors* by Katherine John 1958.

much wanted a mythology which seemed native, which was not identifiably Judaeo-Classical. He also felt that Old Norse mythology provided a model for what one might call 'virtuous paganism,' which was heathen; conscious of its own inadequacy, and so ripe for conversion; but not yet sunk into despair and disillusionment like so much of 20th-century post-Christian literature; a mythology which was in its way light-hearted. He defended his right to create mythology in a long poem called 'Mythopoeia,' printed only in later editions of *Tree and Leaf*. But I would just add that one final attraction which Icelandic literature had for Tolkien was the fact that so much of it is lost. All his life, Tolkien enjoyed filling gaps in what survives. There is, for instance, a well-known gap in the Codex Regius manuscript of the *Poetic Edda*, where some eight pages of the Sigurðr cycle are missing. But Tolkien wrote a poem to fill this gap, in Old Norse, in the appropriate meter, called *Volsungakviða en nyja* (see *Letters*, 379, 452). Unfortunately the Tolkien Estate has not allowed anyone to print it.

I should turn now to my other question, how Tolkien created his new 'mythology for England' with nothing English to work from, and the answer is in essence quite simple. He practised what we shall call 'the Leeds University Evasion,' still in perfect working order,[4] which is to say that Norse literature is really English: first, because the two languages, and cultural traditions, are philologically cognate, and second because once upon a time, in parts of England, including Leeds, the natives spoke Norse as well as English. The poems of the *Elder Edda* may not be written in English but they could have been written in England. In any case, perhaps they *are* written in English – there is certainly an old academic tradition of saying so, though of course that does not make it true. However, Grímur Jónsson Thorkelín said that *Beowulf* was written in Old English, but, like Old

---

[4] At Leeds University Old Norse, or Old Icelandic, was allowed to be part of the English department's course offerings, and during my tenure as Chair of English Language and Medieval Literature was an extremely popular option at all levels, as it has since remained.

Icelandic, this is just a dialect of Old Danish, *poema danicum dialecto anglosaxonica*. Grundtvig agreed with him, saying that all these languages are just dialects of *Old-Nordisk*. Grimm of course did not agree, insisting that English was a German language, a form of *Plattdeutsch*, but then what do you expect from a German nationalist like Grimm? He was answered by Gísli Brynjólfsson in the 1850s, who argued that English was really South-Scandinavian, not West-Germanic. The last work of George Stephens, the Copenhagen professor, was titled *Er Engelsk en tysk sprog?*, and his answer was 'No'! The issue remains (just about) debatable to this day, though I fear that on this occasion the partisans of West-Germanic have the best of the argument. But let us just say that it is easy, and philologically justifiable, to translate Old Norse into Old English, and to tell yourself that what you have created really did once exist: and that is what Tolkien repeatedly did.

We can see this from the very dawn of his fiction, written perhaps as early as 1917, though not published till almost seventy years later. In these early drafts of *The Silmarillion* Tolkien creates a pantheon of Valar, who are so to speak demigods, or demiurges, subordinate to Eru, the One, who is God, of whom they are well aware, but with supernatural powers far above the human. The Valar, you might say, are the Æsir fitted in to a Christian framework. One in particular, the warlike Vala Tulkas, seems to be a rewriting of Snorri's account of the god Týr (compare *Silm*, 28-9 with Faulkes 1987: 25), while his name looks very like the hypothetical Primitive Germanic form of the Norse word *tulkr*, 'spokesman,' which came to mean 'warrior' in Middle English: so, you see, the word is English, 'tolke,' but derived from Norse, *tulkr*, but both are derived from the same root **tulkas*, so Norse and English are really the same thing.[5] In the same way Tolkien rather doubtfully incorporates a version of Snorri's description of Valhöll into his early mythology (later dropped as too warlike, see *BLT 1*, 77-8); while the very seed of all his mythological writings seems to be the idea of

---

[5] Please note that this, and similar remarks later, are meant to be gently ironic.

the elves, or *álfar*. I shall say nothing about this on this occasion, except that once again the very thin and flimsy accounts in Old English of the *ylfe* – just enough to show that the early English knew the word and the concept – are very much expanded to take in the accounts of Snorri Sturluson, and I suspect of Danish and Norwegian medieval ballads.[6]

However, perhaps the most revealing aspect of Tolkien's early mythology is his attempt to explain how it came to him. As a philologist, it was never enough for him to have a story: he also had to have a chain of transmission. How was it that the English alone had "the true tradition of the fairies, of which the Irish and the Welsh tell garbled things." Tolkien's answer (see *BLT 1*, 23-4) was that the mythology of the elves had been told by them to an early Englishman, whose name was Ottor (not Ohthere, which would be definitely English, not Ottarr, which would be definitely Norse, but Ottor, which could be either). This Ottor was the father of Hengest and Horsa, the legendary founders of England, so he must have been English. But no, for Hengest is known to have been a Jute, from Jutland, and so Danish. But no, because in Tolkien's view the Jutes of that time were deeply hostile to the Danes, and *Beowulf* is in part about that Jutish-Danish-English confrontation. So what was Hengest – or Henjest, as Tolkien always called him, insisting on the palatalisation? Never mind. His father Ottor, the bearer of the true tradition, was the ancestor of the English, but himself Norse. And the first man in Tolkien's mythology was not called Askr, as he is in *Völuspá*, but Æsc – the same name, but with English palatalisation (see *BLT 1*, 245). The English got the story right, the Celts got the story wrong, but the Norse are the ones who happened to remember it. Translate Old Norse, or Old Icelandic, back into Old English – they are after all the same language, see above – and everything will be OK.

---

[6] See further the essay on 'Light-elves, Dark-elves and Others: Tolkien's Elvish Problem' in this volume.

This was Tolkien's procedure not only in *The Silmarillion* but also to some extent in the more famous and more popular works, *The Hobbit* and *The Lord of the Rings*. The most inarguable case must be the names of the dwarves in *The Hobbit*: in order of appearance, on Bilbo Baggins's doorstep, Dwalin, Balin, Kili, Fili, Dori, Nori, Ori, Oin, Gloin, Bifur, Bofur, Bombur, Thorin Oakenshield son of Thrain son of Thror, descendant of Durin and relative of Dain, eighteen names in all including one nickname, and the nineteenth name of course being Gandalf. Well, there can be no doubt where these come from. They come from the 'Dvergatal' section of *Völuspá*, which I give in Snorri's version:

> Nýi, Niði, Norðri, Suðri,
> Austri, Vestri, Alþjólfr, Dvalinn,
> Nár, Náinn, Nípingr, Dáinn,
> Bífurr, Báfurr, Bömbörr, Nori,
> Óri, Ónarr, Óinn, Möðvitnir,
> Vigr og Gandálfr, Vindálfr, þorinn,
> Fíli, Kíli, Fundinn, Váli,
> þrór, þróinn, þettr, Litr, Vitr [...]
> Hörr, Hugstari, Hléþjólfr, Glóinn,
> Dóri, Óri, Dúfr, Andvari [...]
> Álfr, Ingi, Eikinskjaldi.
> (Faulkes 1982: 16-17)

Seventeen of the nineteen names are there, and Dúrinn is just a few lines away as the ancestor of the dwarves, just as he is in Tolkien. However Tolkien did not just copy the 'Tally of the Dwarves,' or quarry it for names. He must rather have looked at it, refused to see it, as most scholars do, as a meaningless or no longer comprehensible rigmarole, and instead asked himself a string of questions about it. What, for instance, is 'Gandálfr' doing in the list, when the second element is quite clearly *álfr*, 'elf,' a creature in all tradition quite distinct from a dwarf? And why is 'Eikinskjaldi' there, when unlike the others it does not seem to be a possible name, but looks like a nickname, 'Oakenshield'? In Tolkien of course it *is* a nickname, the origin of which is eventually given in Appendix A (III) of *The Lord of the Rings*. As for Gandálfr, or Gandalf, Tolkien seems to have worked out a more complex explanation. In early drafts of *The Hobbit* Gandalf was the name given to the chief dwarf, but Tolkien soon abandoned this: if someone is called *álfr* he cannot be a dwarf. *Gand*, however, must mean 'staff,' and a staff or magic wand is what magicians carry; and a magician might be called an *álfr* by people who associated the elves with magic. So Gandalf is a wizard, but the first thing that Bilbo sees is "an old man *with a staff*" (*Hobbit*, 5). The name creates the staff, and the staff creates the idea of a wizard. What Tolkien did, in other words, was to take the 'Dvergatal' seriously; to assume that it was a record of something that had had a story attached to it, an Odyssey of the dwarves; and that it had got garbled, so that nicknames got mixed up with names, and a magician, or elvish creature, with a magician's staff, had been listed wrongly but understandably, as a dwarf, when he was really a companion of the dwarves.

None of this explains Mr Baggins, or hobbits, but hobbits are easily overlooked. The creatures that he meets, however, very often come from Tolkien's imaginary world where Norse names and Norse concepts were appropriated as English. There are, for instance, the Wargs, the intelligent wolves who seem a cross between Old English *wearh* and Old Norse *vargr*; or Bard the bowman, son of Brand, who could easily be Barðr son of Brandr; or Beorn the were-bear, who is like both Böðvarr Bjarki in the *Hrólfs saga Kraka* and Beowulf in the English epic, and whose name could just as easily be Bjarni; or of course the dragon Smaug. If he were an English dragon, his name would come from the verb *sméogan, and would be *smeah, and there is a reference in Old English to the *smeogan wyrme*, the 'creeping worm.' But this time Tolkien has translated the Old English into Old Norse, the verb *smjúga*, whose past tense is *smaug*, 'he crept.' So if Beorn is an English hero, and Gollum, or Sméagol as he once was (with the same etymology), is an English villain, Smaug is a Norse dragon, perhaps because his enemies are Norse dwarves. But they all move in the same world. To Tolkien it was the same world: Middan-geard, Mið-garðr, Middle-earth. (Really, if Icelanders would just learn to palatalise their consonants like sensible people, we would all be speaking the same language.)

But Icelandic literature, and here I do mean Icelandic specifically, not the more neutral term Norse, had one more and more significant utility for Tolkien: which is that it gave him a behaviour-pattern. The dwarves in *The Hobbit* are rather attractive people, but no-one could call them 'nice.' They are surly, vengeful, tight-fisted. They keep their word, but only to the letter, not to the spirit. They are loyal to their fellows, and English 'fellow' is borrowed from Old Norse *félagi*, but they may decide you aren't a fellow at all. When the dwarves have escaped from the goblins in the Misty Mountains, without Bilbo, and are debating what to do, one of them says, "If we have got to go back into those abominable tunnels to look for him, then drat him, I say" (*Hobbit*, 85). Vengeful, tight-fisted, literal-minded, sometimes loyal and sometimes not – they are characters from Icelandic saga, and as the story goes on this element becomes more and more prominent. The whole story, I would suggest, really develops a contrast between two modes of heroic behaviour: the ancient one of Icelandic saga, exemplified by the dwarves, and by Beorn, and by Smaug, and the modern one of Tolkien's own life, of twentieth-century warfare, exemplified by Bilbo, and to some extent by Bard. The contrast between these provides much of the story's amusement: but the final point is that – just like modern English and Old Norse, or modern English and modern Icelandic – to the philologist they are different only superficially. (See for instance the final words of Balin the dwarf to Bilbo, and Bilbo's reply, *Hobbit*, 262.) The way they talk is very different. But what they are saying is the same thing.

What I have been saying is that Tolkien's response to Old Norse literature was philological in exactly the sense that he thought proper to that word. It was founded on a very acute sense of linguistic correspondences, which we must credit originally to Jacob Grimm. These correspondences, these details of comparative philology, were real and immediate to Tolkien.

They made him insist on the pronunciation 'Henjest' for Hengest. They made him insist that the plural of 'dwarf' was 'dwarves,' not 'dwarfs' – so much so that he made the printers change every single example in *The Hobbit*, hundreds of them, back to what he had written. He saw philology in every detail of daily life, including the surnames of modern people, like Neave and Woodhouse, or the names of modern places, like Hinksey – *Hengestes ieg* – or Brill, the model for the hobbits' Bree.

But to Tolkien philology was not just about linguistic correspondences, it was also about the criticism of literary works, which in his opinion could not and should not be separated from the language in which those works were written. That was why he disliked literary critics so much: because they characteristically ignored language when they talked about literature. But thought and word went together. There were some thoughts, Tolkien pointed out, again in his *Letters* (see pp. 225-6), which could not be said in modern words without sounding false. If you wanted to say them you must find a way of saying them which was modern enough to be understood, but old-fashioned enough to sound true. I would say that this was the problem of *The Lord of the Rings*: in that work Tolkien wanted to express a heroic ethic, set in a pre-Christian world, which he derived from Old English epic and Old Norse edda and saga. But he also wanted to make it sayable in a contemporary idiom, understandable to contemporary readers, and not in contradiction of Christian belief.

Let me take first the lesser issue of linguistic correspondences in *The Lord of the Rings*. We know now that Tolkien had great difficulty in getting his story going. In my opinion, he did not break through until, on February 9th 1942, he settled the issue of languages. Think about the dwarves, with their Old Norse names. Clearly it was not possible for the dwarves really to have had Old Norse names, they lived long long ago, long before Old Norse was a language. So the names Tolkien had given them, in a work written in modern English, must be there just to show that the dwarves, for convenience, spoke a language which related to the hobbits' language in the same sort of way as Old Norse to modern English, or modern Icelandic to modern English – these things do happen in reality. But if that was the case, then it was possible to imagine, in Middle-earth, a place where people were still speaking Old English, or even Gothic, a place where the poem *Beowulf* was still alive. Once Tolkien allowed himself to think this – and we can see him doing so on page 424 of *The Treason of Isengard* – then he could immediately, and with great ease, imagine the society of the Riders of Rohan, or the Riddermark, contrast them with the post-Imperial society of Gondor, and allow his story suddenly to expand in entirely new and to Tolkien quite unexpected directions. The linguistic correspondences freed Tolkien's imagination. They made the book three times as long as it was supposed to be. That's the first half of what I have to say about philology.

For the second half one has to remember the facts of Tolkien's life. An orphan from the age of 12, he graduated from Oxford University in 1915, and immediately joined the army like everyone else he knew. He fought as an infantry officer in the Battle of the Somme, in which his two closest friends were killed. The Battle of the Somme has become, in popular British history, a byword for disaster and futility. But I do not think Tolkien saw it like that. For one thing, his battalion, the 11th Lancashire Fusiliers, was an unusually successful one, congratulated by Field Marshal Haig in person for its attack on Regina Trench (see Garth 2003: 196-201). For another, he remembered an important fact that people forget nowadays, which was that the battle and the war were both won, when they could easily have been lost. Nevertheless, by the time Tolkien became an Oxford Professor in 1925, popular opinion had changed drastically. These were the years of the ascendancy of modernism; of T.S. Eliot and 'The Waste Land'; of Evelyn Waugh and his satirical novels; of E.M. Forster, Virginia Woolf and the Bloomsbury Group. The connecting factor was disillusionment and irony, especially against anything associated with military virtues. Heroes were out of fashion. It was impossible to take epic, or saga, seriously in the modern world.

Or at least in the modern literary world. Because the military virtues, it turned out, were just as vital as they had ever been. The Oxford Union, we remember, voted in 1936 in favour of the motion, 'This House will under no circumstances fight for King and country.' But it turned out they didn't mean it. In 1939 the British Government appealed for volunteers to fight the Nazis and got 250,000 men on the first day, and a million in the first week. Evelyn Waugh joined the army, to fight in the Battle of Crete, and Virginia Woolf committed suicide because no-one was paying any attention to her any more. It was under these circumstances that Tolkien began to write his heroic, and pre-Christian, romance: reviving ancient literary modes, which it turned out were vitally contemporary once again.

I will point only to one fact which connects *The Lord of the Rings* to Old Norse heroic and mythical literature. It is deeply sad, almost without hope. The story is not a quest, about finding something, it is an anti-quest, about throwing it away. The price of throwing it away is extinction. The elves will disappear. So will the ents, and the hobbits. Frodo, the hero, is incurably wounded. He is taken away across the sea, but only to die. The dominating word of the last page of the story is 'grey,' as the other characters ride back unspeaking on "the long grey road" from the "grey firth," and the "grey sea," and the "grey rain-curtains," and the Grey Havens. Something has gone out of the world, and it will not come back. And that is how things have always been. Much earlier in the story Elrond the Half-elf looks back over his life and says "I have seen […] many defeats, and many fruitless victories." Galadriel says of herself, "through ages of the world we have fought the long defeat" (*LotR*, 1007-8, 237, 348). There is a victory in *The Lord of the Rings*, but it is made as clear as ever it could be that this is local, and temporary, and dear-bought. The characters have only a dim idea – an inkling, one might say, but then Tolkien's literary group was called the Inklings – of any final victory over evil. And this is because they are pre-Christians.

Tolkien in a way is re-imagining characters like those so common in Icelandic saga, who are pre-Christians, but only because they know nothing else – men and women like Njáll, or Víga-Glúmr, or Guðrún, who are not Christians, but not exactly heathens either, and who will accept a better hope if someone will offer it to them. Such people, Tolkien believed, kept going because of the 'theory of courage,' which meant that you kept on even if you knew you were just fighting a 'long defeat,' with no ultimate hope at all. Gandalf in fact repeatedly makes statements about the 'theory of courage.' He does not expect to win, he knows there is a risk even for Frodo of becoming a wraith. "'Still,' he said, standing suddenly up and sticking out his chin, while his beard went stiff and straight like bristling wire, 'we must keep up our courage'" (*LotR*, 217).

But this was also, for Tolkien, the state of mind of many of his countrymen in the 1940s. Christianity was no longer the universally-accepted belief it had been. Evil seemed to be unconquerable, to rise again from every defeat. There was a strong impulse to give up, to make terms, to do the kind of deal with Sauron, or with Saruman, which is suggested several times in *The Lord of the Rings*. But they must not do it. They must learn to go on without assurance of victory, without trust in God, if necessary to go on fighting a long defeat. If the spirit of the godless Viking could be revived in modern times, as it had been in the Nazi ideology of heathenism and Odin-worship – Hitler too composed a work based on Old Norse themes, though I do not think it has survived – then the spirit of the virtuous pagan could also be revived: another aspect of saga-tradition, men like Njáll or Gunnarr, wise, brave, doing the best they could under difficult circumstances, going down in the end to defeat, but not allowing this to change their hearts.

And I believe that is why Tolkien has remained so strangely popular. I would put it this way. The standard accusation made by my critical colleagues about Tolkien is that his work is 'escapist.' I think this is the exact reverse of the truth. Like Orwell's *1984*, or Golding's *Lord of the Flies*, or

Halldór Laxness's *Gerpla*, Tolkien's fantastic or antiquarian works confront the major problems of the twentieth century, which have been war, despair, failure, disillusionment. And they provide answers which seem strangely old-fashioned, but which have come alive again. They are serious answers to serious questions, which in my opinion it is escapist to ignore. But the works also owe much of their charm to the mixture of gravity and amusement, and the extreme stylistic indecorum, which the world first learned to appreciate from the literature of Iceland. It has been well said that the true hero of Tolkien's work is Middle-earth itself. In it he recreated his version of the lost world of pre-Christian English myth; but he could do this only by working from the much more impressive and fortunately-preserved world of Icelandic tradition.

Tolkien's Academic Reputation Now[1]

It is common, in these degenerate days, for academics to have to write reports justifying their own existence in terms of research productivity.[2] The idea was around, I would expect, even in the 1930s and 1940s, and lies behind the veiled threats made to Niggle (in 'Leaf by Niggle') that he might expect a "visit from an Inspector" (see *Reader*, 102). But hints about getting on with one's research are one thing; having to quantify the whole of one's career is another. How, one may wonder, would Professor Tolkien fare under modern systems?

There is quite a simple way of answering this question, which is to use the method of the 'Humanities Citations Index.' This expensive and rather dismal volume scores academics under two headings: Primary and Secondary Citations. Under 'Primary' it lists things you have yourself written. Under 'Secondary' it counts the number of times people refer to you in a range of standard periodicals. It is in many ways a crude system: it's not clear what counts as a unit under Primary – books, articles, short reviews, could all be one (or none, if the reviews aren't counted as 'review articles'); it doesn't count citations in other people's *books*, under Secondary (too much trouble to collect them); and it has been noticed that even a citation remarking that the work of Professor X is totally valueless counts under Secondary just the same as deep and heartfelt acknowledgement. Just the same, the Index is used, and it tells its readers something. How, to repeat the question above, would Professor Tolkien fare in this scoring system?

---

[1] This piece appeared first in *Amon Hen* 100 (1989): 18-22. I thank the Tolkien Society for permission to reprint here in slightly expanded form.

[2] Nowadays, in the UK, there is a five-yearly Research Assessment Exercise, on the results of which departmental budgets depend. Some say it has had a good effect overall, though others say it tends to reward the predictable and discourage long-term or high-risk projects. Tolkien would certainly not have done well on it, during most of the five-year periods of his career.

Under Primary, one can see that there would be at best a lowish score viewed as a lifetime's accumulation. It would, in fact, add up to something like 25 Primary Citations. These would be – I number them for future reference, but give only short titles – (1) *Middle English Vocabulary* (2) chapter in *Year's Work*, 1923 (3) 'M.E. Lexicography' (4) 'The Devil's Coach-Horses' (5) edition of *Sir Gawain*, with E.V. Gordon (6) chapter in *Year's Work*, 1924 (7) ditto, 1925 (8) 'Foreword' to Haigh's *Huddersfield Glossary* (9) article on *Ancrene Wisse* in *Essays and Studies* (10) short appendix on 'the name Nodens' (11) and (12) two articles on *Sigelwara Land* (13) 'Chaucer as a Philologist' in *Transactions of the Philological Society* (14) '*Beowulf*: The Monsters and the Critics' in *Proceedings of the British Academy* (15) 'Preface' to *Beowulf* translation by Clark Hall and Wrenn (16) and (17) two articles in collaboration with Simone D'Ardenne (18) 'On Fairy-Stories' (19) 'The Homecoming of Beorhtnoth' in *Essays and Studies* once again (20) article on 'M.E. Losenger' (21) the Early English Text Society edition of one manuscript of *Ancrene Riwle* (22) the piece on 'English and Welsh.' To this list, all items of which can be found with full details in Humphrey Carpenter's biography, one has to add three posthumous works: (23) the *Finn and Hengest* edition, ed. A.J. Bliss (24) the *Exodus* edition, ed. Joan Turville-Petre (25) the *Monsters and Critics* collection of 1983, which reprints (14), (15), (18) and (22) above, adds two other pieces which might or might not have been regarded as fully academic – 'A Secret Vice' and 'Valedictory Address' – and the important W.P. Ker lecture on *Sir Gawain*. Twenty-five, or twenty-seven if one counts the three new items in *Monsters and Critics* separately: a fair score, but not, over forty years, a high one. (One may note, *en passant*, that Tolkien hardly ever wrote reviews: I wonder why not?)

Never mind the quantity, look at the quality – a remark often made these days by the desperate, under-published and not-promoted. What about the Secondary Citations? What effect did Tolkien have on his whole subject? The results here would, I am sure, be extremely odd. For one thing, a high proportion of the pieces above are basically *never* referred to – some of them of course being very hard to find, or having been intended purely for immediate use, and not long-term record. Under this heading of 'never cited' one could put (2)-(4), (6)-(8), (10)-(13), (16), (17) and (20), and probably (21)-(22) – fifteen of the works published during Tolkien's life. The reason for the neglect of (2), (6) and (7) is obvious: they were intended to be useful only for a few years, as round-ups of recent writing. (16), (17) and (20) are all in a way extended footnotes (and (20) is very hard to come by). What might be regarded as more disappointing is the very near total neglect of (11), (12) and (13). One reason for this will be considered later, when I get on also to the two posthumous editions.

That leaves, however, some seven pieces, which have had different fortunes, but include some of the most widely-cited pieces of all time. (1), the *Middle English Vocabulary*, has been part of a standard student workbook, Kenneth Sisam's reader of *Fourteenth-Century Verse and Prose* for more than sixty years. I suppose it could be said that it is not often deliberately cited, just used; just the same, I was using it to teach classes at the University of Texas in 1988, and drawing people's attention firmly to the variant forms carefully listed by Tolkien before the students' parents, or maybe grandparents, were born.[3] The text and the vocabulary have not been superseded – Tolkien probably would have felt they should be. In rather similar style, (5), the collaborative *Gawain* edition remained a textbook classic till 1967, when it was replaced – and this is a compliment in itself – by a second edition, updated (but not fundamentally altered) by Norman Davis. This must have attracted *thousands* of citations on its own, in the last 60 odd years. It could be said that an early edition which stays in print is bound to get that sort of score; and one could note the relatively near-total neglect of (21), the edition of the most important manuscript of *Ancrene*

---

[3] Gilliver *et al.* (2006: 32-7) discuss the growth of the *Glossary*, and remark (37) that it remains "unparalleled for its concision, informativeness, and accuracy."

Wisse, awaited throughout Tolkien's career. Awaited, though, because of the immense effect created by study number (9). To put it briefly, while one can explain away much of Tolkien's Secondary Citation score by other factors – being a textbook, having a bearing on Tolkien's fictional success (so especially (18), 'On Fairy-Stories') – there is no doubt that three of Tolkien's articles rocked the collective jaw of academe right back on its spine, and would have done so if he had never published a line of fiction. These are (9), (14) and (19).

What was the reason for their success, and has that success remained? The answers here are interesting and curiously different. In order, I would say that (9) convinced everyone immediately it appeared, and in a way had the effect of stopping large possibilities for research dead in their tracks; only very recently has anyone dared to argue (I think correctly) that the wrong conclusions might have been drawn from Tolkien's still fundamentally correct and detailed observations. As for (14), for decades it held the field, inaugurating to everyone's agreement the new age of *Beowulf* studies. Challenges and disagreements began to spread, however, rather after the author's death, and now the modern consensus (this time I think wrongly) is that Tolkien was again wrong, at least in his view of the poem's origin. (19), meanwhile, totally reversed previous opinion of *The Battle of Maldon*, especially that of Tolkien's earlier collaborator E.V. Gordon, and has been swallowed absolutely whole – see, for instance, the edition of *Maldon* by D.G. Scragg (1981), printed to supersede Gordon's, where the Tolkien view is utterly dominant. But once again I think Tolkien was wrong.[4]

The result of the above – for those who have failed to follow my doubts and parentheses – looks like this:

---

[4] I comment further on the works involved in these three pieces, and Tolkien's attitude to them, in the pieces on (respectively) 'Tolkien and the West Midlands,' 'Tolkien and the *Beowulf*-Poet,' and 'The Homecoming of Beorhtnoth' elsewhere in this volume.

Tolkien on *Ancrene W*:   Tolkien on B*eowulf*:   Tolkien on *Maldon:*

GENERAL ACADEMIC VIEW

RIGHT (or maybe, er)   WRONG   RIGHT
WRONG

MY PERSONAL VIEW (T.A.S.)

WRONG   RIGHT   WRONG

There is one consistent element in the above, which we can ignore, but what about the inconsistent elements? What about the substantial articles that got ignored, like (11), (12) and (13)? And what about the reception of (23) and (24)? There are, I think, two threads running through this labyrinth.

One is that Tolkien was a *philologist*. There really are very few of these left, at any rate in the English-speaking world. They have been replaced by modern linguists – who are good on language, but have little interest in literature and usually none at all in historical language – or by literary critics, who may take an interest in early literature, but, as they often say, often citing Tolkien (14) in support, only as literature, not as language. Most people don't know what philology is, and wouldn't trust it if they did. That alone accounts for the neglect of (11), (12) and (13): for in them Tolkien tried in each case to draw very far-reaching conclusions from the minutiae of words, phrases, or – see the *Vocabulary* again – the particular *forms* of words and phrases. The piece on 'Chaucer as a Philologist' is fascinating in its detail, and still completely convincing in its demonstration that Chaucer was trying to make a joke by close, careful imitation of the dialect of Durham: but it's a joke about language, and that now has no market.[5]

'Tolkien's blocker,' as we might call it, on *Ancrene Wisse* and *Hali Meiðhad* is likewise philological. His point was this:

(a) Old English distinguished carefully, if pointlessly, between two types of weak verb: you said *he leornaþ*, 'he learns,' but *he læreþ*, 'he teaches,' for example, -ath or -eth. There are other differences in declension, but these lead only to the conclusion that declining Old English was too hard to be much fun. So,

(b) the post-Conquest speakers of sub-Old English dropped that whole distinction. They said *leorneþ*, *læreþ*, both the same, and we, their degenerate descendants, simply tag on an -s in the same circumstance (which is what Chaucer's Durham students would have said all along). But – and this is Tolkien's discovery –

(c) in the Far-West shire of Hereford, not only did they keep their -*eths* and -*aths* apart, they separated out the -*aths* into two *new and separate* sub-classes, and,

(d) they did it so carefully that even people with different handwriting wrote exactly the same way.

There's a standard English now; and there was one before the Conquest; but in between, if you wanted standard English, you had to go to Hereford. Tolkien substantiated this point by counting the thousands of instances of the appropriate verbs in his texts, and remarking that there were only three mistakes – and (characteristic touch) that if you called the scribes from the grave and silently indicated the passages, they would as silently scratch out the mistakes, and write in the 'correct' forms instead.

---

[5] It is only fair to say that Tolkien's view of Chaucer has now been challenged in Horobin 2001. In my opinion Chaucer made another joke about language which has never been noticed, see Shippey 2003b. I wish I had been able to show this to Tolkien. It is in a way a coda to (13) above.

How did this block research? Because Tolkien demonstrated the special, accurate, philological qualities of his texts so powerfully that all other Middle English texts got downrated! Professor Tolkien's scribes were reliable, accurate, punctilious. The rest – well (so it seemed), they wrote the way they felt, and every time some new copier came along, he copied what was in front of him, imitated a bit, spelt a few words his own way, produced a garble, and then handed it on to the next garbler. If you had a Hereford text copied by a Londoner copied by a chap who came from Norwich, what had you got? Forget it. Everyone did. The study of Middle English dialects paused for a generation.

But what happened if the chap from Norwich decided to translate the whole thing into his own dialect? Haven't you then got a Norwich text? 'Normalisers' produce just as good evidence as 'originals.' And if there are enough 'normalisers' around, sooner or later every text is going to meet one, and get 'normalised'! And then you have evidence about dialect again. This point has only very recently been insisted on, by Angus McIntosh and his collaborators, in their four-volume *Linguistic Atlas of Late Medieval English* (1986); but that insistence has in a way restored the morale of Middle English Dialectology.

Tolkien was, one has to say, silver-tongued. Even when he was wrong he could put matters so powerfully that no-one would challenge him. This is what happened with his *Essays and Studies* piece on *Maldon*, which I think has directed later critics down a largely bogus 'ironic/Christianising' approach to the poem, the doubtful nature of which is evident enough from the poetic half of the piece, which never gets cited in academic contexts. In the same way, his insistence on *Beowulf* as a poem compelled immediate and lasting assent; now questioned, really, on one point alone – the date of the poem. Tolkien said that he accepted without debate the view that it came from the "age of Bede" (ie. approximately 670-735 – see *Essays*, 20). He didn't say why he thought that, but by inference one can say that he thought it was post-Christian, but not too much so (because it was still interested in the pre-Christian). Recent research would like to put the poem three centuries later, by pointing out that there were *two* conversions in the North, one of the pagan Angles (seventh century) and one of the pagan Danes (tenth century); and the poem is largely about Danes. Why not, then, pick the latter not the former?

If Tolkien were still professing, he would, I think, be the best man to make out the philological case for not believing that, and for believing that the poem (in spite of never mentioning England) is English and not (in spite of talking about them all the time) Danish. But he has gone, and the overall view of the poem which he promoted is being superseded, largely by default and the pressure of organised academic consensus. This is at least partly his own fault. He did *not* express himself clearly on the reasons for early dating. He was even vaguer in his remarks on *Sigelwara Land*, at least when it came to the date and provenance of the poem *Exodus*, to which he thought *Beowulf* was related. By the time his edition of *Exodus* came out, it was so far away from the academic centre-ground as to be virtually ignored. If he had 'fought his corner' philologically in the 1940s and 1950s, one may say, the study of *Exodus*, of *Beowulf*, and of Old English generally, could quite easily look very different!

You can collect thousands of Secondary Citations and still not make your point. But if you don't make your point, in the end, in the long run, *geara hwyrftum*, with the rolling years, the obvious – as Tolkien did not say – may well slide out of sight altogether, in a way that explains the neglect of Tolkien's two posthumously-edited editions, of *Finn and Hengest* and *Exodus*. I have said what I think of these elsewhere (see my article on these two works in this volume) and will not repeat myself. But the fact is that these editions, with their assumptions (a) that Old English poems are basically historically true, even in minor details, and (b) that they have been copied so much that a sensitive modern editor should feel free to recreate 'correct' forms and readings, have not made and will not make much impact. They might have done so thirty years before – when the lectures they were based on were given. In the same way a real edition, by Tolkien, of *Ancrene Wisse* Corpus Christi 402, with an introduction, notes and philological appendices, would have been eagerly read. But what appeared in the end was only a sort of printed transcript, with no opinions in it at all.[6] All these things left philology, and scholarship, the poorer.

Verdict on Professor Tolkien, purely as an academic? Primary Citations: low. Secondary Citations: amazingly high. Was that caused by his fictional success? No. It was purely on academic merit. If, then, some modern 'Inspector' were looking at Professor Tolkien to see if he should be asked to take early retirement at the age of 55 (50? 45?), as is now the custom, he would certainly have to lick his chops, slink off snarling, and look for easier prey. Tolkien certainly had a lot of influence.

Was it a good influence? There matters are more doubtful.[7] I would myself put it this way: Tolkien was the most talented philologist of his generation, but like other talented philologists, he did not bother to establish the security of his profession in educational institutions, as a result of which it is now all but dead – not defeated in argument, but bypassed and allowed to wither on the vine. It is true that on other occasions he put forward powerful arguments, which should have had powerful rejoinders, so that scholarship could be advanced by debate. He hardly ever got them. That at least was not his fault, but it was not fortunate either.

---

[6] It could be said, though, in Tolkien's defence, that he allowed his graduate student Simone D'Ardenne to develop some of his ideas in her very detailed and influential account of 'AB language' – the language of the Herefordshire school – in her edition of *Seinte Iuliene* (D'Ardenne 1961). See further Zettersten 2006.

[7] For one informed estimate, see Mitchell 1995.

'Two lords talk, one speaks': the Welsh proverb means that you can only get a conversation going among equals. Tolkien had few equals, for philological range or for persuasiveness in argument. As a result, even his most widely-cited pieces tend to be looked up to, rather than answered. But most of his pieces were barely understood, or not understood at all.

The Trunk

The Lord of the Rings
The Silmarillion

Light-elves, Dark-elves, and Others: Tolkien's Elvish Problem[1]

In chapter 15 of C.S. Lewis's 1938 novel, *Out of the Silent Planet*, Elwin Ransom the philologist for the first time encounters a *sorn*, one of the tall, intellectual species that inhabits the highlands of Mars. They fall into a discussion of Oyarsa, the spiritual being who rules the planet, and Augray the *sorn* tells him that Oyarsa is an *eldil*. The *eldila* seem insubstantial to humans and Martians, Augray explains, but this is a mistake. The *eldila* can go through walls and doors not because they themselves are insubstantial but because to them our material world is insubstantial. "These things are not strange," says Augray, "though they are beyond our senses. But it is strange that the *eldila* never visit Thulcandra" – Thulcandra being 'the silent planet' itself, Earth:

> 'Of that I am not certain,' said Ransom. It had dawned on him that the recurrent human tradition of bright, elusive people appearing on the earth – *albs, devas*, and the like – might after all have another explanation than the anthropologists had yet given.
> (Lewis 1938, ch. 15)

What, one may well ask, are 'albs' and 'devas'? The second word presents no difficulties. If one looks it up in *The Oxford English Dictionary*, the sense given for 'deva,' entirely appropriately for the context above, is "'a bright, shining one' [...] a god, a divinity; one of the good spirits of Hindu mythology" (IV: 561). All the *OED* has to offer for 'alb,' however, is that it is a tunic or ecclesiastical vestment, while 'albs' does not occur at all.

---

[1] This piece is reprinted from *Tolkien Studies* 1 (2004), 1-15. Thanks are due to the editors, Douglas Anderson, Michael Drout, and Verlyn Flieger, and to the publishers, West Virginia University Press, for permission to republish.

Tolkien's connections with this passage are multiple. In the first place it is generally agreed that Elwin Ransom is an affectionate portrait of Tolkien himself. In the second place, the whole novel is now known to have grown out of the famous agreement by Tolkien and Lewis, in 1936, to write separate fictions, Lewis taking the theme of space-travel and Tolkien that of time-travel.[2] Tolkien's contribution was never finished or published in his lifetime, seeing print eventually first as 'The Lost Road' and then as 'The Notion Club Papers,' in volumes V and VIII respectively of 'The History of Middle-earth.'[3] In both the name Elwin, or forms of it such as Alwyn or Alboin, are significant.[4] However, the immediate connection with the passage above is that 'albs' is surely a word borrowed by Lewis from Tolkien, perhaps in conversation. *albs is in fact the unrecorded and hypothetical, or 'reconstructed' Proto-Germanic form of the word which descends into English as 'elf,' into Old English as *ælf*, into Old Norse as *álfr*, into Middle High German as *alp*, and so on. It then makes an entirely suitable match with 'deva,' being mythological, widespread, and bearing witness to a human attempt to label some phenomenon outside their normal comprehension. Only Tolkien is likely to have told Lewis such a thing. It would be entirely typical of Lewis, whose recorded remarks show several errors in Old English morphology, though he taught the subject at Magdalen College,[5] to mis-hear it, and to assume the -s was a plural ending, so making 'alb-s' (wrongly) parallel with 'deva-s.'

---

[2] The best account of this remains Rateliff 2000.
[3] There is a full-length study of them, see Flieger 1997.
[4] I discuss the origin and significance of the name in its variant forms in Shippey (2003a: 295-7).
[5] Lewis for instance wrote a piece in praise of Tolkien, the title of which began "*Hwæt we holbytlan* [...]," clearly echoing the opening words of *Beowulf*, *Hwæt we Gar-Dena* [...] But *Gar-Dena* is genitive plural. The genitive plural of *holbytla* would be, not *holbytlan*, but *holbytlena*. Lewis was extremely learned and an excellent Classicist, but he could not be called a philologist in Tolkien's sense of the word.

What the word and the passage show is that Tolkien had considered the whole problem of the variant forms of 'elf' in Germanic languages, and presumably talked about it. It must have been a topic of Inkling conversation, one of several we can infer from cross-comparison of Lewis's, Tolkien's, Williams's and Barfield's works (and possibly others as well). If Tolkien had considered the problem, we may again well ask what conclusions he had come to, and what further problems in the conflicting traditions of North-West Europe he would have encountered. The purpose of this essay is to suggest that it was indeed in these problems – even more than in the traditions – that Tolkien found inspiration for his fiction in the various versions of 'the Silmarillion,' and eventually in sections of *The Lord of the Rings*.

The problems take a certain amount of explanation. One may begin with the thought, fundamental to the early investigators of comparative philology and mythology, that if a word existed in several 'cognate,' i.e. clearly related but nevertheless independent forms in different languages, then the word and presumably the concept behind it must go back to a time before the languages separated from each other: the word and idea of 'elf,' then, is quite literally immemorially old.[6] But how does one then cope with the fact that the different linguistic and cultural traditions often seem to have quite different ideas of what the word means? Does this just mean that the word never did have any clear, agreed, stable referent (probably because the whole thing was pure fantasy, 'just mythical,' made-up from nothing)?

---

[6] This point is made explicitly by Max Müller in his 1856 essay 'Comparative Mythology' (see Müller 1880). The essay is best-known now for Müller's attempt to relate all myth to celestial phenomena, for his argument that myth is 'a disease of language,' and for the parody of the whole theory by R.F. Littledale, 'The Oxford Solar Myth,' in which the Rev. Littledale proved by Müller's own methods that Müller was himself a solar myth. Most of the essay, however, is a reasoned statement of the methods of comparative philology, before the proposal is made that a similar technique could be used to create comparative mythology. Both Müller's and Littledale's pieces can be found reprinted in Smythe Palmer 1909/1977. Tolkien refers to Müller, while inverting the 'disease of language' thesis, in 'On Fairy-Stories' (see *Reader*, 48).

Such an answer makes good sense, but was entirely unacceptable to Tolkien. This is the opinion of 'the anthropologists' which Lewis's Ransom suddenly finds himself doubting.[7] Or is it the case that we have not understood the data? That we need to think differently, as Augray the *sorn* tells Ransom he must rethink the idea of *eldila*? This was the view of Tolkien and the Inklings.

The data as regards elves had been known to investigators, at least in great part, since well before Tolkien's time.[8] There are some ten words for 'elf' in Old English, the male and female forms *ælf* and *ælfen*, and the compound words *land-, dún-, feld-, munt-, sæ-, wæter-, wudu-* and possibly *berg-ælfen*, or, more rarely, *-ælf*, i.e. 'hill-, land-, field-, mountain-, sea-, water-, wood-' and once again 'mountain-elf.' These look promisingly precise and varied, but are in fact almost always glosses, words written in over a Latin text to translate a hard word in Latin, in this case and respectively to items four to nine in the list above *castalides, moides, oreades, naiades, nymphae,* and *dryades*. The simplest explanation is that an Anglo-Saxon translator long ago, stumped for an equivalent to 'naiad, nymph, dryad,' decided not unreasonably to solve all his problems at once and create 'sea-elf, water-elf, wood-elf' etc. Meanwhile Anglo-Saxon medical or magic texts throw up another run of more interesting if more threatening compounds, such as *ælfadl, wæterælfadl, ælfsiden, ælfsogoða*, the names of 'elf-diseases' like (it has been suggested) chicken-pox, dropsy, lunacy, epilepsy,

---

[7] It is not absolutely clear which anthropologists Lewis meant here, but probably not American structural or cultural anthropologists. He was probably thinking of post-Müllerian schools of thought like the followers of J.G. Frazer, or the 'ritual' school of Jane Harrison. Lewis's essay 'The Anthropological Approach,' in his *Selected Essays* (ed. Hooper, 1969: 301-11), attacks later and minor members of these groups, and they appear in disguised form in his 1956 novel *Till We Have Faces*, see further Shippey 2007 (forthcoming).

[8] I discuss the data at much greater length in Shippey 2005b. The essays in this collection discuss the accounts of various groups of Germanic non-humans, including elves, dwarves, trolls, dragons, etc., but all contributors were warned *not* to discuss Tolkien. The problem now is to imagine any solutions *other* than Tolkien's: a measure of his success.

anaemia.[9] The last is a guess from *ælfsogoða*, 'elf-sucking,' and indicates that one way elves were thought to work their damage was by a kind of vampirism; while we also hear several times of 'elf-shot' or *ylfa gescot*, which implies a belief (perhaps illustrated in one of these texts) in invisible disease-bearing darts. Elves also appear to have been associated with sexual temptation. Several charms associate the elves with *nihtgengan*, 'night-walkers,' with 'temptations of the fiend' and with *þam mannum þe deofol mid hæmð*, 'the people the devil has sex with.' It is not surprising that Anglo-Saxon elves are commonly called 'malignant' by modern scholars.[10] And yet it is a compliment for a woman to be called *ælfsciene*, 'elf-beautiful,' and Anglo-Saxons stubbornly continued to give their children names like Ælf-wine, Ælf-red, Ælf-stan and so on, 'Elf-friend, Elf-counsel, Elf-stone.' Some of the names, like the common Alfred and the rare Elwin (as in Elwin Ransom), have remained in use to this day, though no longer with any sense of their meaning, and some of the beliefs about sexually alluring elves, elf-hills and elf-changelings also lasted into the modern period.

The Scandinavian tradition is even more well-attested, though not as old, and on the face of it rather different. The *álfar* are mentioned thirty times in the poems of the *Elder Edda*, though in a rather restricted list of uses: usually they occur in association with either the *Æsir*, the pagan gods, or with the *iötnar*, the giants, as if to imply universality: 'everyone knows it, elves and gods,' 'tell me its name among the elves, tell me its name among the giants,' and so on. There are hints of meaning in the poems of the *Elder Edda*, as there are here and there in sagas. But the work which attracted most attention from the beginning of modern investigation, and which seemed closest to giving answers of the thoroughness and complexity which philologists demanded, was the *Prose Edda* of Snorri

---

[9] As is discussed in the valuable book, *Anglo-Saxon Medicine*, by M.L. Cameron 1993. Professor Cameron is a professor of biology, and so able to talk about the recipes and their possible efficacy in a pragmatic way.

[10] See for instance Thun 1969 and Stuart 1976.

Sturluson, the nearest thing we have to a mythical handbook of pre-Christian belief.

It should be said straight away (for it is often forgotten) that Snorri was not writing a pagan text. He wrote his work in the 1230s, by which time Iceland had been Christian for more than two centuries, and Snorri's own family had been Christian for six generations. He knew no more about what pagans really did, or really thought, than we would about the folk-beliefs of the 18th century. His work was in essence an attempt to explain poetic diction, the phrases used and allusions made in traditional poetry, but to do this he had to tell stories, often about the gods, giants, elves, dwarves and other supernatural creatures of the pre-Christian world. The connected nature (and the literary power) of what Snorri wrote perhaps aroused unreal expectations in his first modern admirers: for what Snorri says about elves is hard to make out. He invariably uses the word as a compound, one of these being *Álfheim* or 'Elf-home.' But every other time he uses the word *álfr*, he prefixes it with a word of colour, *ljós-*, *dökk-*, or *svart-*, i.e. 'light-elves,' 'dark-elves,' 'black-elves.' A critical passage is this one:

> Sá er einn staðr þar er kallaðr er Álfheimr. Þar byggvir fólk þat er ljósálfar heita, en dökkálfar búa niðri í jörðu, ok eru þeir ólíkir þeim sýnum en myklu ólíkari reyndum. Ljósálfar eru fegri en sól sýnum, en dökkálfar eru svartari en bik.
> [There is one place that is called Alfheim. There live the folk called light-elves, but dark-elves live down in the ground, and they are unlike them in appearance, and even more unlike them in nature. Light-elves are fairer than the sun to look at, but dark-elves are blacker than pitch.]
> (Faulkes 1982: 19, and 1987: 19-20)

What Snorri says is clear and unequivocal, but it raises an immediate problem. 'Dark-elves,' he says, (*dökkálfar*) are 'black' (*svart*). Surely that means that they are 'black-elves' (*svartálfar*)? But everywhere else in

Snorri's work, it is clear that when he says 'black-elves' (*svartálfar*), he means 'dwarves': Odin sends Skirnir *í Svartálfaheim til dverga nokkurra*, 'to the home of the black-elves to certain dwarfs,' and Loki too goes into *Svartálfaheim* where he too 'comes across a dwarf.' There is a simple explanation here, which is that while Snorri identifies four groups, light-elves, dark-elves, black-elves and dwarves, there are really only two: the last three are just different names for the same group. The first group, meanwhile, are very like angels, or for that matter *eldila* – these are Lewis's 'albs' – while the last group has been made to seem faintly diabolic, quite like the Anglo-Saxon elves of the medical textbooks, indeed. This line of thought has the blessing of being clear, and of not multiplying entities, but it was once again quite unacceptable to early investigators, including Tolkien: it meant, in effect, throwing away their best text, just as my suggestion about a baffled Anglo-Saxon translator above meant saying that *dún-ælf* and the rest were just 'ghost-words,' with no real meaning in Anglo-Saxon culture. Neither proposal has been popular, and Tolkien devoted considerable fictional energy to providing more face-saving refutations to both.

It is not absolutely clear when Tolkien focused for the first time on what we may call the 'elf-problem.' When he did do so, though, it would be natural for him to look at what 'the authorities' said, and entirely characteristic of him (as happens so often with Tolkien and the *OED*) then to found a theory on profound disagreement with scholarly opinion, and to make a determined attempt to protect the original sources, if necessary by explaining how they could have been mistaken. The author of *Sir Gawain*, after all, or perhaps the scribe who copied him, had made the same mistake as C.S. Lewis, taking a singular ending in -s to be a plural, writing *wodwos* for what should have been *wodwosen. It was the job of the true scholar, Tolkien thought – he exemplifies it frequently in his edition of the Old English *Exodus* and the 'Finnsburg' poems – to rescue poems and myths from their careless or uncomprehending scribes and annotators. And this is what he tried to do, in my opinion, with the elves.

The original sources mentioned above had been known to scholars for centuries, if with very little original circulation. Snorri's *Prose Edda*, for instance, had been edited by the Dane Peter Resen (Resenius) as early as 1665, while the Old English medical texts and glosses had been discovered at various times up to the 1830s. The 'elf-problem,' however, did not surface until scholars began to ask themselves not just about the words, but about what they represented. And here two famous scholars, in particular, are likely to have attracted Tolkien's attention.

The first was the Dane, N.F.S. Grundtvig (1783-1872). There are several reasons why Tolkien might have paid careful attention to him. Nikolai Grundtvig was, for one thing, the first person in modern times to read *Beowulf* intelligently. (It was he, for instance, alone of the first seven reviewers of the first modern edition of the poem, Grímur Thorkelin's of 1815, who realized that the poem began with a funeral, not a Viking raid as the editor had thought.) He continued to be an active scholar for nearly sixty years after that, with particular interest in *Beowulf*, in Old English, and in Northern mythology. But even more importantly, Grundtvig did for Denmark what Tolkien would have liked to do for England: he gave it a history and a mythology founded on ancient sources, but released again into national life and national politics by Grundtvig's popular writings, his many songs and hymns, and his creation of the Grundtvig High Schools with their avowed aim of protecting national culture, primarily from German encroachment.[11] Grundtvig in Denmark, Lönnrot of the *Kalevala* in Finland: if Tolkien ever had 'role-models,' they would be these.

Grundtvig's first book on mythology, *Nordens Mytologi*, was published in 1808, at which point works like *Beowulf* were still unpublished. Grundtvig rewrote the work as (different spelling) *Nordens Mythologi* in 1832, and in this he turned his attention to 'Vætter, Alfer, og Dværge,'

---

[11] For an account in English of Grundtvig's life and works, see the essays in Allchin *et al.* 1994.

'Wights, Elves, and Dwarves'; and was (I believe) the first to note and be concerned about Snorri's inconsistencies in the *Prose Edda*, as noted above. His solution was to go part of the way towards the reductionist four-groups-down-to-two model outlined above, with one significant compromise. Light-elves were obviously angelic, and black-elves were evidently dwarves, but perhaps dark-elves were different from both:

> Alfer var det gamle Nordens Engle, og Dværgene kun et Mellem-Slags af dem: hverken Lys-Alfer eller Mörk-Alfer, men saa at sige Skumrings-Alfer.
> [Elves were the angels of the ancient North, and dwarves only a middle grade of them: neither light-elves nor dark-elves, but so to speak elves of the twilight.]
> (Grundtvig 1832: 263, my translation)

The trouble with this otherwise neat solution, one might say, is that it puts black-elves in between the other two groups, where one might expect them to be a limiting term. But it does introduce the rather attractive idea of *Skumrings-Alfer*, 'elves of the twilight.'

Jacob Grimm's *Deutsche Mythologie*, the first edition of which was published in 1835, may have owed more to Grundtvig's pioneering work than Grimm was prepared to admit. The philological battle-lines were already drawn up – they were to become real battle-lines in the two Prusso-Danish wars over Schleswig-Holstein, or Slesvig-Holsten, in 1850-51 and 1864 – with the Germans, and Grimm in particular, claiming that Scandinavian languages were really just a branch of 'Germanic,' with the Eddas and sagas as in effect common intellectual property, and Scandinavian scholars replying furiously that Scandinavia had a right to cultural as well as political autonomy. It was a problem and an annoyance for Grimm that the Middle High German word for 'elf' seemed to have been lost, to be replaced in modern German by a borrowing from English, *Elfe, Elfen*. Grimm dealt with this by deleting the latter from his *Deutsches Wörterbuch* or 'German Dictionary' and inserting a modernized version of the former: *Elb, Elbe*.

But he too was bothered by Snorri, though his solution was significantly worse than Grundtvig's, vague and indecisive. I give it below, in sections, in Grimm's German and in the translation of J.S. Stallybrass, with my own attempts to explain what he meant interpolated:[12]

> Man findet in dem Gegensatz der lichten und schwarzen elbe den dualismus, der auch in anderen mythologien zwischen guten und bösen, freundlichen und feindlichen, himlischen und höllischen geistern, zwischen engel des lichts und der finsternis aufgestellt wird.
> [Some have seen, in this antithesis of light and black elves, the same Dualism that other mythologies have set up between spirits good and bad, friendly and hostile, heavenly and hellish, between angels of light and of darkness.]

Grimm is here, I think, contradicting Grundtvig without mentioning him. He feels that Grundtvig has abandoned Snorri's tripartite division too readily:

> Sollten aber nicht drei arten nordischer genien anzunehmen sein: *liosálfar, döckálfar, svartálfar*?
> [But ought we not rather to assume three kinds of Norse genii, *liosálfar, döckálfar, svartálfar*?]

The trouble with this is Snorri's statement above that dark-elves are black, which would lead to the first reduction, dark-elves = black-elves. But Grimm cannot accept this because he knows it would lead on to black-elves = dwarves. He therefore continues:

> ich erkläre damit freilich Snorris satz 'döckálfar eru svartari en bik' für irreleitend.

---

[12] See Grimm (1875-78, I: 368), trans. Stallybrass (1882-88, II: 444-5).

[No doubt I am thereby pronouncing Snorri's statement
fallacious: 'dark-elves are blacker than pitch.']

The easiest way out at this stage is to say, rather unconvincingly, that maybe Snorri was half-right, did not choose his words carefully, at any rate has to be overruled:

> *döckr* scheint mir weniger das entschieden schwarze, als das trübe, finstere; nicht niger, sondern obscurus, fuscus, aquilus.
> [*Döckr* seems to me not so much downright black as dim, dingy; not niger but obscurus, fuscus, aquilus.]

Grimm backs this up with a sentence about a reference to dwarves and a dwarf name that contain or resemble the word *iarpr*, 'dark,' which actually does not seem to help his case that dark-elves are different from black-elves and dwarves, but concludes that rejecting Snorri's one-off statement on the whole saves more trouble than it creates:

> dann bliebe die gleichstellung der zwerge und schwarzelbe gültig, aber auch jener alteddische unterschied zwischen zwergen und dunkelelben gerechtfertigt.
> [In that case the identity of dwarfs and *black* elves would still hold good, and at the same time the Old Eddic distinction between dwarfs and *dark* elves be justified.]

Grimm then embarks on a lengthy search for other references in German story to tripartite colour-systems, but ends abruptly, perhaps aware of his own inconclusiveness:

> Festgehalten werden muss die identität der *svartálfar* und *dvergar*.
> [One thing we must not let go: the identity of *svartálfar* and *dvergar*.]

Snorri can be trusted, then, when he says something Grimm is prepared to accept, but has to be ruled out when his statement is unwelcome.

I cannot believe either that Tolkien had not read this passage in the most familiar account of Northern mythology, or that he would have been anything but annoyed by it. All that can be said for it is that, along with Snorri and Grundtvig and the other Old English texts mentioned above, it does raise a whole sequence of problems which cry out for some better solution. I would list them as follows:

1) what are light-elves and dark-elves, and what is the difference between them if it is not a matter of colour?
2) if it is not a matter of colour, why does Snorri say that dark-elves are black?
3) if dwarves are different from elves, as almost all early evidence agrees, then why call them black-elves?
4) what are all these Old English groups, like wood-elves and sea-elves, and where do they fit in?
5) is there anything to be said for Grundtvig's idea that there may have been 'elves of the twilight'?

Anyone familiar with *The Silmarillion* can see how clearly and incisively, if imaginatively, Tolkien was in the end to answer these questions. Did he have the questions, if not the answers, in mind from the beginning? He was to say of himself at one point, with reference to ents, "As usually with me, they grew rather out of their name, than the other way about" (*Letters*, 313), and I would suggest that the same may be true of Tolkien's elves. One of the starting points of his whole developed mythology was this problem in nomenclature, this apparent contradiction in ancient texts and in one ancient text in particular, a problem made only more challenging by the groping attempts of earlier scholars to solve it. However, as the twelve volumes of 'The History of Middle-earth' have made abundantly clear, it was also characteristic of Tolkien to edge up on the solution to a problem through several or many stages of dissatisfaction.

The Book of Lost Tales thus does not, as far as I can see, contain the basic distinction later to be made between Light-elves and Dark-elves: such references as are indexed are to later stages of Tolkien's conception. There is however an interesting passage in *BLT 1* which suggests that Tolkien was already considering the terms, and was perhaps aware of Grundtvig's compromise solution quoted above. In 'Gilfanon's Tale,' just after the first mention of 'Dark Elves,' we are told of "a certain fay [...] Tu the wizard":

> wandering about the world he found the [...] Elves and drew them to him and taught them many deep things, and he became as a mighty king among them, and their tales name him the Lord of Gloaming and all the fairies of his realm Hisildi or the twilight people.
> (*BLT 1*, 232)

The missing word in the phrase "the [...] Elves" above, Christopher Tolkien reports, could be either 'dim' or 'dun' (244). 'Dun' would correspond to one of the Anglo-Saxon glossary words noted above, but 'dim' is one of Grimm's suggestions, at least as translated by Stallybrass.[13] Meanwhile "Gloaming" is a good translation of the first word in Grundtvig's phrase *Skumrings-Alfer*, but "twilight people" is used as well. Perhaps Tolkien had already rejected the concept 'black-elves,' looking on this as an uninformed variant on 'dwarves,' as it seems to be, but at this point had no explanation of 'dark-elves' other than to say that they were only to be glimpsed at twilight. The index of *BLT 2* supports the suggestion that Tolkien was groping, for there one finds ten different groups of elves, but not yet 'Light-elves.' The tale of 'The Fall of Gondolin' already has the character of Meglin (later

---

[13] In context 'dun-elves' sounds better, but in that case one wonders whether Tolkien could be playing on the two senses of the word, Old English *dūn-ælf*, 'mountain-elf,' and modern English 'dun,' i.e. 'dark.'

Maeglin), son of Eöl, but very little is said of the latter other than (165), "that tale of Isfin and Eöl may not here be told." 'The Lay of the Fall of Gondolin,' included among the 'Poems Early Abandoned' in *The Lays of Beleriand*, goes a little further in describing the capture of Isfin by Eöl:

> [...] that she ever since hath been
> his mate in Doriath's forest, where she weepeth in the gloam;
> for the Dark Elves were his kindred that wander without home.
> (146)

But though the idea of a White Lady glimpsed in the half-light was to remain through to *The Silmarillion*, there is no further advance on the dark/light distinction. Tolkien seems to have no clear idea of what a 'dark-elf' is, in which, of course, he is in agreement with his predecessors; and the term 'light-elves' is not used at all.

This last was to change with the writing of 'The Earliest Silmarillion,' in the late 1920s, where we find (*Shaping*, 13) the division of the Eldar into three groups, 'Light-elves,' 'Deep-elves,' and 'Sea-elves,' corresponding closely though not exactly to the Vanyar, Noldor and Teleri of *The Silmarillion*. The real breakthrough comes, however, in the 'Quenta' of 1930. Here, on page 85 of *Shaping*, we find that the Quendi, led by Ingwë, are "the Light-elves," the Noldoli, led by Finwë, are "the Deep-elves," and the Teleri, led by Elwë, are "the Sea-elves." A vital addition, though, is that "many of the elfin race were lost upon the long dark roads [...] and never came to Valinor, nor saw the light of the Two Trees [...] The Dark-elves are they [...]." One might note at this time the use of the invented Anglo-Saxon terms *léohtelfe, deorc-elf[e]*,[14] in 'The Earliest Annals of Valinor,' (*Shaping*, 286, 288), words which correspond exactly to Snorri's *ljósálfar, dökkálfar*. This decision to make the light/dark distinction not a matter of colour, as Grimm had tacitly assumed, was a brilliant stroke, rather like

---

[14] The form *deorc-elfa* (*Shaping*, 288) is another genitive plural.

Augray the *sorn* explaining the *eldila*. But one result was that it left Eöl, identified already as a Dark Elf, see above, without any clear mark of distinction. He is mentioned in both 'The Earliest Silmarillion' and the 'Quenta' as "the Dark-elf Eöl" (*Shaping*, 34, 136, with variant spellings), but in both cases this could just mean that he is *a* Dark-elf, *one* of the Dark-elves: there is nothing particular to mark him out. His son Meglin, though, is picked out as "swart" (*Shaping*, 141), a word that goes back to *BLT 1* (165), as if Tolkien had not yet quite abandoned hope of reconciling Snorri's *dökkálfar* and *svartálfar* – could Eöl be seen as 'a' Dark-elf, but also 'the' Swart-elf? This hint was never taken up, and indeed may never have been in Tolkien's mind, but as so often with Tolkien, it seems that for him to solve one problem was to generate another.

Tolkien was to develop his basic distinction between those who had and those who had not seen the Light of the Two Trees in 'The Lhammas' and 'The Quenta Silmarillion' (see *The Lost Road*, 197, 215), while some of his terminology became canonical in the familiar passage from chapter 8 of *The Hobbit*, published in 1937, about the Wood-elves: "more dangerous and less wise" than "the High Elves of the West," these latter further particularized as "the Light-elves and the Deep-elves and the Sea-elves." As for the Wood-elves, they:

> lingered in the twilight of our Sun and Moon, but loved best the stars; and they wandered in the great forests that grew tall in lands that are now lost. They dwelt most often by the edges of the woods, from which they would escape at times to hunt, or to ride and run over the open lands by moonlight or starlight, and after the coming of Men they took more and more to the gloaming and the dusk. (*Hobbit*, 151-2)[15]

---

[15] The text given appeared first in the revised edition of 1966. Earlier versions have slightly different wording, and the "twilight" is "the twilight before the raising of the Sun and Moon," see Hammond and Anderson (1993: 32).

They are, in other words, very much *Skumrings-Alfer*, twilight-elves.

At this stage, one might say, Tolkien had settled the first and fifth of the questions outlined above, and made space for a solution to the fourth. The other two, however, remained quite obscure: why dark-elves might be black, as Snorri reported, and what if anything they had to do with dwarves. Both are nevertheless settled firmly and even convincingly by the re-organization of the story of Eöl, Dark Elf *par excellence*, in chapter 16 of *The Silmarillion*. It is astonishing how much of previous speculation is taken up and dealt with on pages 132-3 of that work.

We learn first that Eöl "was named the Dark Elf," and here it is his personal appellation, not just a generic description. The reason he is "*the Dark Elf*" is that he has left Doriath for Nan Elmoth, and "there he lived in deep shadow, loving the night and the twilight under the stars." He resents in particular the Noldor among the Light-elves, as usurpers, "but for the Dwarves he had more liking than any other of the Elvenfolk of old." From them he learns metalwork, and devises a metal of his own. "He named it *galvorn*, for it was black and shining like jet, and he was clad in it whenever he went abroad." His son Maeglin is called (by his mother) Lómion, "Child of the Twilight." From these few sentences one could construct a story which would explain all that Snorri says, without corroborating it. It would not be true that there were three kinds of elf, for there were no 'black-elves,' no *svartálfar* at all. Just the same, in later story someone might well think there were, for while there were no 'black-elves,' there was an elf always dressed in black, whom someone might have labeled 'the Black Elf.' Similarly, this *svartálfr* was certainly not a dwarf, but was associated with them and shared some of their characteristics, like the fascination with metalwork. Again, in careless repetition 'like' could become 'the same as.' Finally, there may be no such generic term as a *Skumrings-Alf* or 'twilight elf,' but if Maeglin is "Child of the Twilight," then his father might again, mistakenly, be heard as 'the twilight,' especially as that is the time he goes abroad. One may at this point see the force of Christopher Tolkien's repeated statements that *The Silmarillion* was seen all along by his father as a "compendium," which needs to be read from the point of view of someone looking back at events from a much later period.[16] A text, to Tolkien sr., was not just the words on the page one happened to be reading, it was also the whole history of how the words got there – a history, in many of the works he devoted his professional life to studying, of misunderstanding and downright error. One might paraphrase by saying that Tolkien (like Grimm) was prepared to say that Snorri Sturluson had just got it wrong. But unlike Grimm he insisted on providing a story to explain *how* Snorri got it wrong, and to make that explanation plausible and even natural.

The same went also for the Anglo-Saxons, with their oddly contradictory accounts of malignant elves, and seeming deep-rooted respect for them. In *The Lord of the Rings* Tolkien confronts this problem at least three times. The feeling that elves are dangerous is expressed first by Boromir, who does not want to enter the Golden Wood of Lothlórien, because "of that perilous land we have heard in Gondor, and it is said that few come out who once go in; and of that few none have escaped unscathed" (*LotR*, 329). Aragorn corrects Boromir, but does not entirely deny what he says. Boromir's feelings are then echoed by Éomer (*LotR*, 422), who uses 'elvish' to mean 'uncanny,' and also believes the Lady of the Golden Wood to be some kind of sorceress. This time Gimli corrects him. Just the same, though both men are misinformed, there is a basis for their fear and suspicion, as Sam Gamgee points out. When Faramir, wiser than his brother, nevertheless hints that Galadriel must be "perilously fair," Sam picks up the implied criticism and half-agrees with it:

> I don't know about *perilous* [...] It strikes me that folk takes their peril with them into Lórien, and finds it there

---

[16] Christopher Tolkien makes the point in *BLT 1*, 4: "To read *The Silmarillion* one must place oneself imaginatively at the time of the ending of the Third Age – within Middle-earth, looking back." This is good advice, but the exercise becomes much easier if one has prior experience of the way texts and stories change over time.

> because they've brought it. But perhaps you could call her perilous, because she's so strong in herself. You, you could dash yourself to pieces on her, like a ship on a rock; or drown yourself, like a hobbit in a river. But neither rock nor river would be to blame. (*LotR*, 664-5)

At the end of a long chain of transmission it might be agreed that to be *ælfsciene* like Galadriel would be an immense compliment, but at the same time that any association with elves might well be disastrous for ordinary people; the end of this chain is line 112 of *Beowulf*, *eotenas ond ylfe ond orcneas*, in which elves and orcs have become much the same thing.[17] Tolkien put a very high value on his ancient texts, like *Beowulf* and the *Prose Edda*, but he knew they were the work of fallible mortals, and probably several generations away from what he would have regarded as authentic tradition.

What he meant to do, then, was to recover the authentic tradition which lay further back than any account we possess, the tradition which gave rise to Snorri and *Beowulf* and the Eddic poems and the Anglo-Saxon charms and all the other scraps of evidence, which however integrated them, resolved their contradictions, and explained the nature of their misunderstandings. The idea that there *was* some such authentic tradition is the thought that strikes Ransom/Tolkien in Lewis's story quoted at the start of this essay. It is possible, of course, that the whole idea is mistaken,[18] and highly probable that even if there were to have been some original single integrated conception of "elves" or "devas," then it is now beyond recall.

---

[17] The line is part of the introduction of the monster Grendel. The poet says that all the monster-species derive from the first murderer, Cain, and exemplifies them as "ettins and elves and (?) demon-corpses, and the giants, who fought against God for a long time." This is the most 'hard-line' hostile statement made about elves in any ancient source, and must have caused Tolkien some thought, as it comes from a text he respected and valued greatly: it was often identified by early scholars as an interpolation, not the work of the original poet.

[18] As asserted in Stanley 1975; see further the essay on 'Goths and Huns' in this volume.

Nevertheless, Tolkien's reconstructions are not only imaginative, they are also rigorous, controlled both by respect for evidence and awareness of the nature of the evidence. Philology was a hard science, not a soft science. This is one of the qualities which makes Tolkien's work inimitable.

Indexing and Poetry in *The Lord of the Rings*[1]

Anyone who has had to prepare an index, either the old-fashioned way with index cards, or the modern way with an indexing program, will find it easy to forgive errors – though some kinds of error are easier to forgive than others. Working through the index of the third US edition of my own *Road to Middle-earth* (prepared without my input by a professional indexer using a computer program and without much in the way of what used to be called 'general knowledge' – John Milton, William Wordsworth, who cares, both dead white guys) has left me feeling rather unforgiving. On the other hand, looking at the Indices of *The Lord of the Rings* throws up errors of a more interesting kind, errors which deserve to be called issues.

The first edition, of course, had no Indices, but carried instead a little 'Publisher's Note' at the end of Appendix F which said "We regret that it has not been possible to include as an appendix to this edition the index of names announced in the Preface of *The Fellowship of the Ring*." When the second edition came out there were, however, four indices, for 'Songs and Verses,' 'Persons, Beasts and Monsters,' 'Places,' and 'Things.' 'Songs and Verses' were furthermore dealt with two ways, under 'Titles' and 'First Lines.' One of the titles listed is 'Old Walking Song, The,' with four page references following – as well as the usual page references, I give Book and chapter references here, since these do not change with different editions. What the indexer means to indicate as 'The Old Walking Song' are: (1) the eight lines of 'The Road goes ever on and on' sung by Bilbo as he leaves Bag End in I/1, p. 35 (2) the same lines said by Frodo in I/3, p. 72, with one significant change, "weary" for "eager" in line 5 (3) eight lines said by Bilbo in VI/6, p. 965, which start in the same way as the others but alter sharply in words and meaning from line 3, to fit Bilbo's again "weary" but

---

[1] This piece appeared first in *Lembas Extra* 2004, edited by Ron Pirson. Leiden: De Tolkienwinkel, pp. 66-74, and I am once again grateful to the editor and members of Unquendor for permission to reprint.

now resigned and contented state of mind in Rivendell, seemingly near the end of his life (4) six lines sung by Frodo in the last chapter, VI/9, p. 1005.

But these last six lines are not at all the same as the other three cases indexed. They in fact are a variant on the poem indexed in the second edition as 'Walking Song, A.' Of this we have three ten-line stanzas sung by Frodo and his three companions collectively in I/3, p. 76, a few pages after (2) above; and the six-line excerpt from it just mentioned, sung much later by Frodo alone on p. 1005, almost at the end of the work. But as was the case with (2) and (3) above, in Frodo's six lines "the words were not quite the same," in fact are sharply altered in meaning, almost inverted from the sense they carry when first sung: in these later lines Frodo signals his intention to "take the hidden paths that run," which he and his companions years earlier imagined themselves *not* taking, leaving for another day.

The error with the index is easily remedied, of course. All one needs to do is shift the fourth entry under 'Old Walking Song, The' to become the second entry under 'Walking Song, A.' But one can sympathise with the indexer's difficulty, because hobbit-poetry seems intrinsically fluid; and indeed, in the new 'Index of Poems and Songs' carefully compiled by Christina Scull and Wayne G. Hammond for the 2002 edition, the three versions of "The Road goes ever on and on" are listed together, but the two versions of, or excerpts from 'A Walking Song' are now listed separately under first lines, respectively "Upon the hearth the fire is red" and "Still round the corner there may wait," though they are clearly the same poem, and referred to as such in the text, on p. 1005 once more. My point here, to anticipate myself, is not that indexers get things wrong, but that hobbit-poetry does not lend itself well to tidy listings.

The issue is complicated by a further question: where does 'The Old Walking Song' come from? Pippin asks, when Frodo gives his version of it in I/3, whether it was made by Bilbo or is one of Frodo's imitations, and Frodo says he does not know (72). In fact an attentive reader knows that Bilbo has already sung it, so it presumably *is* "a bit of old Bilbo's rhyming." Or at least it *was*, because as already said Frodo has adapted it to suit his own situation. Meanwhile the other 'Walking Song' definitely does come from Bilbo, who "had made the words [...] and taught it to Frodo" (76). But he sets it to a tune "as old as the hills," and Frodo once again has no difficulty in altering it till it says what he wants it to say. It seems that there is no 'intellectual property' in hobbit-poetry. Anyone can take words or tunes and use them any way they like. It is not particularly surprising, then, that the 2nd edition indexer, no doubt seeing the words "old walking song" in the text at VI/9, and having already decided to give the 'Road' song that title, could not remember which was which.

One thing this does show is that Tolkien, unlike almost all of his contemporaries, had a strong sense of the difference between a literary tradition and a living oral tradition. Only vestiges of the latter survive in the Western world, as for instance in proverbs, riddles, nursery-rhymes, folktales – all genres, or sub-genres, in which Tolkien took lifelong interest.[2] But widespread literacy has meant that even the vestiges are significantly changed. They become fossilised, fixed in form. There is only one way to say a proverb like 'Where there's a will there's a way.' In Tolkien, though, there are several ways: Dernhelm/Éowyn says, "where will wants not, a way opens," in V/3 (787). The orc slave-driver in VI/2 takes a different view with his "Where there's a whip there's a will" (910). No-one in Tolkien ever says, 'where there's no will there's no way,' but this is not an unreasonable translation – one with significant applicability in the modern bureaucratic world – of a Norse proverb Tolkien would certainly have encountered in the Eddic poem *Hamðismál*, '*Illt er blauðom hal brautir kenna*,' 'it's no good showing a faint-heart the way.' One sees even more fossilisation in nursery-rhymes, still learned almost entirely orally, and so fixed in form that they are repeated from generation to generation even though some of them no

---

[2] 'Survivor-genres,' as I call them in the essay on 'A Fund of Wise Sayings: Proverbiality in Tolkien' in this volume.

longer make sense. What would their originals have been like centuries ago, before they became fossilised? Tolkien wondered about it, and of course wrote or rewrote his 'Man in the Moon' poems to answer the question; as he also wrote riddles in Anglo-Saxon to serve as 'ancestors' of riddles now found among schoolchildren. It hardly needs saying that fairy-tales underwent a similar post-medieval downgrading in status from adult and aristocratic to childish and lower-class, and that Tolkien set himself once more to reverse this centuries-old trend.

And the same is true of folk-poetry as opposed to literary poetry. The one is at once old and new, ancient in source but continuously rehandled, accordingly anonymous, not the property of the poet or singer except in the moment of performance, simple on the surface but capable of expressing powerful feeling through personal adaptations. By contrast literary poetry, and especially 'modernist' poetry, is defiantly original, to the point of eccentricity or incomprehensibility, always provided with name and title, heavily protected by copyright – and, many would say, heartless, artificial, unmemorable. It is not surprising that Tolkien's poetry has been dismissed by literary anthologists; while the literary anthologies in their turn have become texts to read in school, without appeal outside the educational system. Tolkien's view would no doubt be that the 'literary critics' whom he taunted and opposed all his life had forgotten something deeply important about poetry, which he tried to convey by example rather than by argument.

Turning back to the 'Songs and Verses' index to the 2nd edition of *The Lord of the Rings*, one might note for instance the entry "Elbereth Gilthoniel, Elven hymns to," which once again raises an issue, this time perhaps insoluble. The index offers four entries, which refer to (1) the four four-line stanzas given in English, but sung in an elvish language by one of the elves met by Frodo and his companions in the woods of the Shire in I/3 (78) (2) seven lines in an elvish language (not translated), beginning *A Elbereth Gilthoniel*, near the end of II/1 (231) (3) four lines, also in an elvish language but not translated, also beginning *A Elbereth Gilthoniel* but from then on almost completely different, which Sam cries out as he faces Shelob in IV/10 (712), and finally (4) four lines in VI/9 (1005), again in an elvish language, the first three lines identical with the first three lines of (2) above, but this time and for the first time translated into three lines of English – these latter identical with the last three lines of (1) above. It is probably best for readers to look at these four examples one after the other to see how they shift, for the wording is never exactly the same, though there are always recognisable overlaps. Briefly, though, item (4) is critical, for only then is the connection made between three lines of (2) and three lines of (1). Otherwise – since the elvish lines in (2) and (3) are not translated[3] – there is no way to tell that they are parts of the same poem as (1). If indeed they *are*, because it is carefully pointed out with regard to (1) that even if it is quoted in English, it was sung in an elvish language which Frodo does not well understand, so that we have only "the song as Frodo heard it" (78).

And what was the language? In the first and second editions of *The Road to Middle-earth* (1982: 143 and 1992: 171 respectively), I identified the language of (1) unhesitatingly as Quenya, contrasting it with the Sindarin song of (2), (3) and (4), and taking no notice of the indexer's opinion. On reading the proofs of the third edition, however, Carl Hostetter pointed out that it must have been in Sindarin too, and it is perhaps worth setting out the argument for either view. In favour of Carl one may say that (4) above clearly brings together three lines of (1) and three lines of (2), which suggests strongly that the one translates the other; and since both (2) and (3) are in Sindarin, presumably (1) was too. Against that, Frodo identifies the singers of (1) as "High Elves" (78), and when he greets Gildor Inglorion a page later he does so "in the high-elven speech," also identified as "the

---

[3] They were eventually translated in Donald Swann's song-cycle *The Road Goes Ever On* (London: George Allen and Unwin, 1968), p. 64. However, even there a problem remains: in the 'plain English' translation of item (2), Tolkien missed out the Sindarin phrase *o galadhremmin ennorath*, which he had translated in the line-by-line literal version just above as "from tree-tangled middle-lands."

Ancient Tongue," while his four words of greeting are definitely in Quenya. If "high-elven" is Quenya (which it is), and Frodo can tell the singers are High Elves (which he can), then presumably the song which he and the rest "only partly understood" is in Quenya too. But there is no doubt that something very similar is sung in Rivendell, and this time in Sindarin; and there is also a certain lack of logic in Frodo saying that the singers must be High Elves because they use the name Elbereth, for 'Elbereth' is the Sindarin form of Quenya 'Varda.' Carl points out further that the song is one of exile, and so appropriately sung by the elves in the language of exile, Sindarin. But one could reply that a song of exile from Valimar might just as appropriately be sung in the language of Valimar, Quenya, as is the case with Galadriel's Quenya song at the end of II/8 (368).

Can this issue be resolved? One way to do so would be to argue, rather unsatisfyingly, that Tolkien might not have made his mind up how to deal with elvish languages near the start of *The Lord of the Rings*. Faced with the enormous corpus of *Widersprüchen* or contradictions which German ingenuity had discovered in *Beowulf*, and which had been used to 'prove' that the poem was the work of several authors, Tolkien pointed out that even nowadays, with copy-editors and proof-readers and every literate advantage, it was hard to make all items of a long narrative completely consistent: a good example is the tangle over Durin's Day, which continued to have two different definitions in *The Hobbit* (end of chapter 3, start of chapter 4) for sixty years after publication.[4]

But a better way to resolve the issue, I would suggest, is to say that elvish poetry is like hobbit poetry in being fluid, adaptable, continually remade. Gildor and his companions are High Elves, elves of the light, native speakers of Quenya. For ages, however, they have spoken Sindarin along with the Moriquendi, the elves of the darkness. Why should they not know the same poem in two different languages – as we, for instance, may

---

[4] On this issue of unnoticed contradictions see further Drout (2002: xviii).

well know English and Latin versions of familiar carols like 'O come, all ye faithful'/'Adeste fideles'? Furthermore there is a repeated sense, in Tolkien, that poetry can overleap the boundaries of language. Frodo understands the sense of Gildor's song, even though he has only a smattering of the language it is sung in. Later on in Rivendell (II/1) he finds the words of elvish song almost taking shape, though once again "he understood them little" (227). Sam remembers both these scenes as he confronts Shelob, and they help him to call out lines of poetry "in a language which he did not know" (712). And one should note that Tolkien suited his own practice to his theory in repeatedly not translating elvish words and songs, assuming that they would have the same effect on his modern readers as he claimed for his characters. Perhaps this too is a part of the nature of living poetry. The place for it is in the memory, even the unconscious memory, rather than on the page; and in the memory it can take another shape, be adapted to a different circumstance, so that it becomes entirely personal, though the tradition from which it springs is anonymous and impersonal.

To all this the work of the indexer remains alien, even opposed. Indices, like dictionaries and databases, have the habits of literacy built into them: organisation which is alphabetical and so random with regard to sense; assumption that there is a place for everything and everything in its place; information broken down into single discrete items; all leading insidiously to an educational system along the lines of that proposed by Councillor Tompkins in 'Leaf by Niggle,' hard facts, no fancies, social engineering at work. Perhaps it is just as well that there should be doubts and discrepancies in the Indices of *The Lord of the Rings*, and no final or assured text of several of Tolkien's poems, as there is no one text of many traditional ballads. In these ways a living poetry escapes from the embalming fluid of the indexer and the literary historian.

Orcs, Wraiths, Wights: Tolkien's Images of Evil[1]

One of Tolkien's least-noted, but most significant ironies in *The Lord of the Rings* occurs almost at the end of *The Two Towers*, in 'The Choices of Master Samwise.' Sam here, wearing the Ring which he has taken from Frodo's apparently dead body, overhears the conversation between the two orc-captains, Shagrat of Cirith Ungol and Gorbag from the Tower of Minas Morgul – one of six occasions in *The Lord of the Rings* where we hear orcs talking. Gorbag tries to convince Shagrat that Frodo cannot be the only interloper in the area: someone else must have cut the cords on the body, and stabbed Shelob. "I'd say there's a large warrior loose, Elf most likely [...]" This someone else, this "large warrior" (actually Sam himself) is the real danger, and the "little fellow," Frodo, may be relatively insignificant. "The big fellow with the sharp sword doesn't seem to have thought him worth much anyhow – just left him lying: regular elvish trick" (722).

There is no mistaking the disapproval in Gorbag's last three words. Like to other characters in *The Lord of the Rings* (not all of them on the side of Sauron), 'elvish' to him is pejorative. It is clear that he regards abandoning one's comrades as contemptible, and also characteristic of the other side. And yet only a page later it is exactly what characterises his own side. Shagrat responds to Gorbag's argument by pointing out "there's a lot you don't know," and one of the things the Morgul-captain does not know is that a sting from Shelob is not necessarily fatal (723):

> "She's got more than one poison. When she's hunting, she just gives 'em a dab in the neck and they go as limp

---

[1] This article appeared first in George Clark and Daniel Timmons (eds.). 2000. *J.R.R. Tolkien and his Literary Resonances: Views of Middle-earth*. Westport, CT: Greenwood Press, pp. 183-98. I thank Greenwood Press and George Clark (Dan Timmons has, sadly, died) for permission to reprint. Much of the argument of this article was subsumed into Shippey (2000a: 121-34), but I hope the cross-references here to Lewis, in particular, add something to what is there.

> as boned fish, and then she has her way with them. D'you remember old Ufthak? We lost him for days. Then we found him in a corner; hanging up he was, but he was wide awake and glaring. How we laughed! She'd forgotten him, maybe, but we didn't touch him – no good interfering with Her."

Regular orcish trick, one might say, to abandon one's comrade to a particularly horrible and fully conscious death, and furthermore to laugh about it, and expect the laughter to be shared. It might be argued that it is one orc who condemns desertion, and the other who practices it, but in this respect at least Shagrat and Gorbag seem to be of one mind. Shagrat sees nothing wrong with Gorbag's use of 'elvish,' and Gorbag has no quarrel with Shagrat's sense of humour.

The minor irony furthermore makes a point which is repeated again and again in the orcish conversations we hear, and which was in its wider implications also important enough for Tolkien to stress again and again. It can be stated very simply, though its implications then take a good deal of drawing out (and cost Tolkien a good deal of later concern). Briefly, what the episode with Shagrat and Gorbag reveals is that orcs are moral beings, with an underlying morality much the same as ours. But if that is true, it seems that an underlying morality has no effect at all on actual behaviour. How, then, is an essentially correct theory of good and evil corrupted? If one starts from a sound moral basis, how can things go so disastrously wrong? It should require no demonstration to show that this is one of the vital questions raised with particular force during the twentieth century, in which the worst atrocities have often been committed by the most civilised people. Tolkien deserves credit for noting the problem, and refusing to turn his back on it as so many of his more canonical literary contemporaries did.

Tolkien's general attitude to the problem of the orcs is in *The Lord of the Rings* both clear and orthodox. He insists in several places that evil has no creative power.² It 'mocks,' it does not 'make.' Treebeard says this to Merry and Pippin as the ents march on Isengard (474), and Frodo repeats it to Sam as they prepare to leave the Tower of Cirith Ungol (893):

> "I don't think it [the Shadow] gave life to the orcs, it only ruined them and twisted them; and if they are to live at all, they have to live like other living creatures. Foul waters and foul meats they'll take, if they can get no better, but not poison [...] There must be food and water somewhere in this place."

The orcs cannot live on poison, and they cannot live on a basis of total amorality: though of course neither their food nor their moral sense may be what one would wish to share. The importance of these very clear statements is moreover drawn out in several places by C.S. Lewis, a more discursive writer than Tolkien, in a way with which his friend would probably have had no fundamental disagreement. In his many defences of Christianity Lewis was several times concerned to repeat the argument against Dualism, or Manichaeanism, an old heresy with which he evidently had some sympathy (he saw it as reappearing in the heroic mythology of Scandinavia), but which he also regarded, rather surprisingly, as dangerous because all too capable of revival.³ But, he insists in *Mere Christianity* (1955: 45-6), the old heresy does not ultimately make sense. No-one "likes badness for its own sake [...] just because it is bad." They like it because it gives them something, whether that is sensual gratification (in the case of sadists), or something else, "money, or power, or safety." But these latter are all good things in themselves. Wickedness is always, according to

---

[2] For more extended comment on this point, see Shippey (2003a: 140-6).

[3] Besides the passage cited below, see for instance the short article, 'Evil and God,' in *God in the Dock: Essays on Theology and Ethics* (1970: 21-4). The reviving relevance of a kind of Manichaeanism was another point where Tolkien and Lewis were in agreement, see Tolkien, '*Beowulf*: The Monsters and the Critics,' *Essays*, 26.

Lewis, "the pursuit of some good in the wrong way." But since "Goodness is, so to speak, itself" while "badness is only spoiled goodness," then it follows that the two equal and opposite powers of the Dualist world-view cannot exist. The evil power, the Dark Power in which Lewis seriously believed, must be a mistake, a corruption, not an independent and autonomous force.

This opinion is of course very firmly built into Tolkien's whole mythology.[4] But the critical element, for practical purposes and indeed for understanding of Tolkien's and Lewis's contemporary world, must have been (and must remain) the question of how this ancient and mythological corruption would show itself in daily life. Much of Lewis's reputation, for instance in *The Screwtape Letters* (a work dedicated to Tolkien), derives from the acuteness with which he connects theological speculation to what one might call 'the psychopathology of everyday life.'[5] Tolkien made no attempt to compete with him here. But one can see certain parallels with Lewis, and a certain shared Inkling attitude to the problem of evil, even evil in daily life, if one looks at Tolkien's highly original and provocative images of evil: not just evil characters like Sauron and Saruman, but generic evil, in the shape of the orcs, the wraiths, the wight(s).

To repeat, there are six orcish conversations in *The Lord of the Rings*, and all make very similar and consistent points. Orcs are marked above all by a strong sense of humour. Almost the first thing Pippin notices as he comes round in 'The Uruk-hai' (longest of the orcish conversation-pieces) is an orc laughing at his struggles. The orcs laugh again when Uglúk picks him up by his hair, and "hoot" with mirth when Merry struggles against

---

[4] The most perceptive statements of the differences between the good and evil sides in *The Lord of the Rings*, and the most convincing refutation of complaints about their similarities, come in W.H. Auden's 1956 review and 1968 article.

[5] I take the phrase from Sigmund Freud's *Zur Psychopathologie des Alltagslebens* (1929). As a guide to events in everyday life the book is almost comically disappointing. Lewis repeatedly drew attention to the inadequacies of Freud's views of human evil (and everyday life) throughout his works.

Uglúk's medicine. In speech they make jokes continually, from the yellow-fanged guard's "Lie quiet, or I'll *tickle* you with this" (my emphasis), to the orcish spectators' "Can't take his medicine," or Uglúk's sarcastic reply to the Northern orcs' question, "Go on running [...] What do you think? Sit on the grass and wait for the Whiteskins to join the picnic" (438, 435, 439). Common words in orcish mouths are 'sport,' 'play,' 'fun.' There is a characteristic orcish joke in the slavedriver-uruk's proverb-adaptation near the end of 'The Land of Shadow': "'There now!' he laughed, flicking at their legs. 'Where there's a whip there's a will, my slugs'" (910). Of course orcish 'fun' usually derives from torture, their jokes are aggressively sarcastic, and their mirth comes from seeing others (including their own comrades, like "old Ufthak") suffering or helpless. But these are all components of human humour too, loath as one may be to admit it. Even hobbits understand it enough to join in, as Merry does with his defiant "Where do we get bed and breakfast?" (438). The orcs may be well down, or even off, the scale of humorous acceptability, but it is the same scale as our own: and humour is, in conformity with Lewis's opinion above, a good quality in itself, though like all good qualities it can be perverted.

Orcs indeed are quite ready to use the word 'good,' as the slavedriver-uruk does. He follows up his proverb with the threat, "you'll get as much lash as your skins will carry when you come in late to your camp. *Do you good.* Don't you know we're at war?" (910, my emphasis again). When Grishnákh the Mordor-orc rejoins Uglúk's company in the chapter 'The Uruk-hai,' he too says that while he could not care less about Uglúk, "there were some stout fellows with him that are too good to lose. I knew you'd lead them into a mess. I've come to help them" (441). Grishnákh is lying, of course – he has come back in search of the Ring – but it is the kind of thing orcs say, and they are not always lying. Orcs in fact put a high theoretical value on mutual trust and loyalty. 'Rebel' is another of their pejorative words, used both by Shagrat (of Gorbag in 'The Tower of Cirith Ungol') and by the soldier-orc to the tracker-orc in 'The Land of Shadow.' Snaga says to Shagrat, "I've fought for the Tower against those stinking Morgul-rats," which shows a kind of limited loyalty (885); and another favourite word among the orcs is 'lads,' a word which implies male bonding and good fellowship. Gorbag proposes to Shagrat that "you and me'll slip off and set up somewhere on our own with a few trusty lads" (721); "let the lads play!" says Shagrat just a little earlier (719); surrounded by the Riders of Rohan, Uglúk says to his followers that there is one thing the Riders do not know, "Mauhúr and his lads are in the forest, and they should turn up any time now" (444). It should be pointed out that while Gorbag and Shagrat soon fall out, and their ideal of being 'trusty' is immediately ironised by the fact that (as Shagrat says), "I don't trust all my lads, and none of yours; nor you neither, when you're mad for fun" (724), nevertheless, Mauhúr and his lads *do* turn up and do make an attempt at a rescue. The orcs furthermore – to say the best one can of them – understand the concept of a parley, in the chapter 'Helm's Deep,' and even obey the rules of war with their warning, "Get down or we will shoot you from the wall" (527). Saruman's orcs show group pride in their boast, many times repeated, "We are the fighting Uruk-hai." While all orcs appear to be man-eaters, they do not regard this as cannibalistic, but reserve that accusation for orcs who eat other orcs, hence Grishnákh's accusation, "How do you folk [the Northerners] like being called *swine* by the muck-rakers of a dirty little wizard? It's orc-flesh they eat, I'll warrant" (436).

It would be tedious to point out the ways in which all these claims are systematically disproved or ironised, as by the Ufthak-vignette mentioned above. But the point remains: the orcs recognise the idea of goodness, appreciate humour, value loyalty, trust, group cohesion and the ideal of a higher cause than themselves, and condemn failings from these ideals in others. So, if they know what is right, how does it happen that they persist in wrong? The question becomes more pressing in that orcish behaviour is also perfectly clearly human behaviour. The point could be argued from *The Lord of the Rings* itself, but it is confirmed by Tolkien's "very finished essay on the origin of the Orcs" to be found in *Morgoth's Ring* (415), which Christopher Tolkien sums up (*Morgoth*, 421) as "my father's final view of the question: Orcs were bred from Men." Well before that, however (in *The Hobbit*, 59), Tolkien had suggested a connection between the goblins of that work and the agents of technological 'advancement' in human history; and though he became increasingly concerned over the implications of the orcs in his story, and tried out several explanations for them, their analogousness to humanity always remained clear.[6] The slavedriver-uruk's cry, "Don't you know we're at war?" is also one which almost all Europeans of the earlier twentieth century must have heard in daily life, in whatever language, too many times. But if orcs represent only an exaggerated form of recognisably human behaviour, the question returns: in all reality, how do people get like that?

The issue of the process of corruption in what was originally good seems to have been a topic among the Inklings, considered both theologically and mythologically (as in *Mere Christianity* or *The Lord of the Rings*), but also in straightforwardly human terms, the latter especially by Lewis. The third volume of his 'Space' trilogy, *That Hideous Strength*, often seems, indeed, to be a translation into a more realistic setting of the kind of thing that Tolkien was describing in fantasy: one might say, simultaneously describing, for though *That Hideous Strength* came out nine years before *The Lord of the Rings*, in 1945, Lewis was always much quicker to publish than his friend, and both works were in gestation during the same period – a

---

[6] Tolkien's shifting views over the origin of the orcs can be seen in several places, notably *Letters* (187-95, 355), and *Morgoth's Ring* (123-4, 408-24). Were they bred from elves or from humans? Could they interbreed with humans? How did they reproduce? Were they of 'mixed origin'? Were some of them perhaps in origin Maiar? The horns of the dilemma which Tolkien found all but impossible to resolve were these: on the one horn, the inability of the evil powers (Melkor, Sauron) to create, forced on Tolkien by Lewis's orthodox argument summarised above, meant that they must be a corruption of something pre-existing; but if this were so, then on the other horn they must in theory be not 'irredeemable,' unlikely as this seemed, and impossible as it might be for elves or men to carry out, see *Morgoth's Ring*, 419. For further comment see Shippey (2003a: 233-4).

period in which the two authors were moreover in constant contact.[7] Be that as it may, one can see in the death of Frost the arch-materialist at the end of chapter 16 of Lewis's book an attempt to write an account of something, in a human, which might be seen as the analogue of being turned to stone, in a troll. At the start of chapter 6 the language of Wither, the unbelievably dreary Deputy Director of N.I.C.E. (the National Institute for Co-ordinated Experiments) has strong overlaps with that of Saruman. And if one reverts to orcs, there is a classically orcish conversation in Lewis's novel between two humans, Len and Sid, who come upon Mr Bultitude the bear in chapter 14. They are in fact looking for animals for N.I.C.E.'s experiments, they know that this one cannot be theirs, nor have they been sent to catch it, but they drug it and steal it anyway. Their conversation follows exactly the same lines as the orcs' rhetoric of co-operation covering mutual distrust and fear, along with their heavy use of sarcastic humour (though rendered less realistic, as was also the case with Tolkien, by Lewis's refusal to allow obscenity):

> "You're a bucking good mate to have," said Len, groping in a greasy parcel [for something to put dope on, Sid having refused to let his dinner be used]. "It's a good thing for you I'm not the sort of chap to split on you."
> "You done it already," said the driver [Sid]. "I know all your little games." (382)

The two men talk about being 'mates,' refer to each other's 'little games,' just like orcs, but their motivation is naturally easier to understand. Sid at least does not like what he is doing – "Get out? [...] I wish to hell I knew how to" – and Len's silent expectoration may well indicate agreement along with resignation. They have got into their state as willing co-operators with

---

[7] The first volume of the 'Space' trilogy, *Out of the Silent Planet*, was published in 1938, the third volume, *That Hideous Strength*, in 1945. Lewis published an abridged edition of the latter in 1955, which omits some of the passages cited here.

evil through initial weakness or necessity, reinforced by fear, and as one can see made to seem palatable or even admirable by the steady, dulling use of a rhetoric of smartness and shrewdness. The process is traced in much more detail throughout Lewis's book in the career of the ambitious, feeble, superficially clever university don Mark Studdock (though Studdock ultimately saves himself, in chapter 15, in a scene which also has Tolkienian connections).

A further slant on the process of corruption comes moreover from another work by Lewis of almost exactly the same period, his *The Great Divorce*, first published in 1946. In this work Lewis takes up the question of the nature of Hell, something which forms a natural challenge, as Lewis saw, to the whole thesis of 'badness' being only 'spoiled goodness.' After all, if all evil creatures were good in the beginning, as even Sauron was according to Elrond, what justice is there in condemning them irrevocably to perdition? Could there not be some way of saving them? Tolkien never took up the challenge of finding some way of educating or 'rehabilitating' orcs, though he was aware of it (see note 6), and though he did spend considerable time on the possibility of rehabilitating Gollum, not to mention Saruman and even Gríma Wormtongue. But Lewis tackled the issue of justice straightforwardly in *The Great Divorce*, with a succession of easily recognisable human types, all marked however by intense self-absorption and refusal to admit an initial error: the Spoiled Poet, the Atheist Bishop, the Dwarf Tragedian, and others. Lewis's point is simply that these people are not condemned to Hell by some outside power, but by their own selfishness. The doors to Hell are locked indeed, but only on the inside.

This was a theme of some importance to Lewis, to be returned to in several works and re-imaged in several ways, and one need not assume that Tolkien always agreed with him, or approved what may have been Lewisian borrowings. However, the overlap between the works of the two men in the 1940s and 1950s is enough to suggest that they shared some views. Orcish behaviour, whether in orcs or in humans, has its root not in an inverted morality which sees bad as good and vice versa, but in a kind of self-centredness which sees indeed what is good – like standing by one's comrades or being loyal to one's mates – but is unable to set one's own behaviour in the right place on this accepted scale. It has another root in a ready tolerance of evil as long as it is made into a kind of joke (*Screwtape Letter* no. XI has a good deal to say about this). And there is a third root in the effect of the steady corruption of language. Lewis returned to this theme also again and again, in his comments on the work of 'the Philological Arm' in *Screwtape*, in the scene in which Haldanian arguments about the inevitability of progress prove untranslatable into a sensible tongue in *Out of the Silent Planet* ch. 20, in the reworking of the Tower of Babel myth at the climax of *That Hideous Strength*, 435 – "*Qui Verbum Dei contempserunt, eis auferetur autem Verbum hominis*" ('They that have despised the Word of God, from them shall the word of man also be taken away').[8] Tolkien did not present similar images of negative language, but he spent enormous amounts of effort in trying to create language which was aesthetically and morally more pleasing than that of everyday. He would surely have agreed entirely with Lewis (and with their other contemporary Orwell) that while foolish thoughts give rise to foolish language, a feeble or perverted language, or rhetoric within that language, makes it difficult if not impossible not to have foolish and perverted thoughts. The orcs' constant sarcasm is in this view a major and not just a superficial problem.

To summarise: there is in Tolkien's presentation of the orcs (as much more obviously in Lewis's gallery of the dupes and the self-deluded) a quite deliberate realism. Orcish behaviour is human behaviour, and their inability to judge their own actions by their own moral criteria is a problem all too sadly familiar. The orcs and their human counterparts are, however, an ancient problem and an ancient type. Just as the word 'orc' is in origin Anglo-

---

[8] Merlin's Latin curse is one of the passages cut out of the abridged version of *That Hideous Strength*. The novel's title-phrase is taken from a Middle Scots retelling of the Babel story, as Lewis notes in his epigraph.

Saxon (see *Morgoth*, 124, 422), so the creatures themselves would fit or could find counterparts in old epic or fairy-tale. Yet in Tolkien's lifetime it must have seemed to many that an entirely new species of evil had come upon the world, one which also had its origin in perversion or corruption of the good, but one which was even more insidious, familiar and threatening, not least to academic minds. For this too Tolkien found an image and a word, and in this too he was echoed and glossed by his friend Lewis. Tolkien's second major generic image of evil is the 'wraith,' or 'Ringwraith.'

The image itself is strikingly original: there is nothing like it in any early epic, not even *Beowulf*. Yet as with so many of Tolkien's creations, light is shed on the 'wraiths' by the exercise of looking the meaning of the word up in *The Oxford English Dictionary* [*OED*], on which Tolkien worked in his youth and with which he so often openly or tacitly disagreed. The entry on 'wraith' in the *OED* shows a rather characteristic self-contradiction. Under meaning 1 it offers the definition, "An apparition or spectre of a dead person; a phantom or ghost," giving Gavin Douglas's 1513 translation of the *Aeneid* as its first citation. As sense b, however, and once again citing Douglas's *Aeneid* in support, the *OED* offers "An immaterial or spectral appearance of a living being." Are wraiths, then, alive or dead? The *OED* editors accept both solutions, for which (since the contradiction occurs in their source-text) they cannot be blamed. On the other hand the *OED* has nothing at all to say about the word's etymology, commenting only "Of obscure origin" – just the kind of puzzle which repeatedly caught Tolkien's attention (see Shippey 2003a: 55-70 and *passim*). Both the contradiction as to meaning and the uncertainty about derivation seem in fact to have had some bearing on Tolkien's creation of the 'wraiths': he integrated the former and solved the latter.

To take the issue of etymology first, an obvious suggestion to anyone with Tolkien's background would be to take 'wraith' as a Scottish form derived from Anglo-Saxon *wríðan*, to twist or to writhe. If this verb had survived in full into modern English, it would have had the same conjugational pattern as, for instance, the common verbs 'ride' or 'write,' giving 'writhe – wrothe – writhen' as its principal parts, parallel to 'ride – rode – ridden,' 'write – wrote – written.' This has not happened. Verbs of this kind, however, commonly create nouns associated in meaning but differentiated by vowel change, as with 'road' from 'ride', or 'writ' from 'write.' The *OED* cites both 'wreath' and 'wrath' as deriving from 'writhe,' the first rather obviously (a twisted thing), the second less obviously, but paralleling for instance Old English *gebolgen*, 'angry, swollen with rage,' from a verb deriving from the same root as 'belly' – wrath, then, a twisted emotion as anger is a swollen one. Could 'wraith' not be from the same root as 'writhe'?[9] That Tolkien thought so is suggested by a word that Legolas uses in 'The Ring Goes South.' There the Company's attempted crossing of Caradhras is frustrated by snow and the malice of the elements, and Legolas goes forward to scout out their retreat. He returns to say that the snow does not reach far, though he has not brought the sun with him: "She is walking in the blue fields of the South, and a little wreath of snow on this Redhorn hillock troubles her not at all" (*LotR*, 285). By 'wreath' here, Legolas clearly means something like 'wisp,' something barely substantial, and though the *OED* does not record it, that is also a meaning of 'wraith' – a wraith of mist, a wraith of smoke, a wreath of snow.

Wraiths then are not exactly 'immaterial,' rather something defined by their shape (a twist, a coil, a ring) more than by their substance. In this they are like shadows, and indeed the 1b citation from Gavin Douglas offers the two words as alternatives, a "wrath or schaddo" of Aeneas. And just as

---

[9] In view of the early Scottish provenance, the obvious derivation would be from the past tense of the verb, *wráð* in Old English. This would give *wrothe in standard modern English, but Scots and Northern English dialects did not round Old English long *-á*, creating doublets like home (standard) vs. hame (Northern), or stone (standard) vs. stane (Northern). Gavin Douglas's 'wraith,' from *wríðan*, would then be an exact parallel to 'raid,' from *rídan*, the latter introduced into standard English from Scottish by Walter Scott. Its etymology is exactly parallel to standard 'road,' and both derive from Old English *rád*, as (in my view) 'wraith' does from *wráð*.

they are ambiguous as regards substance, if you see one, you cannot be sure (according to the *OED*) whether it is alive or dead. All these points are taken up by Tolkien; and, indeed, not very much is added, for though the Ringwraiths appear some thirty or forty times during *The Lord of the Rings*, we are in fact told very little about them. They were once Men, says Gandalf early on, who were given rings by Sauron, and so "ensnared [...] Long ago they fell under the dominion of the One [Ring], and they became Ringwraiths, shadows under his great Shadow, his most terrible servants" (*LotR*, 50). The Lord of the Nazgûl, we learn very much later, in 'The Battle of the Pelennor Fields,' was once the sorcerer-king of Angmar, a realm overthrown more than a thousand years in the past. He should, therefore, be dead, but is clearly alive in some way or other, and so positioned neatly between the two meanings given by the *OED*. He is also in a sense insubstantial, like a shadow, for when he throws back his hood at the end of 'The Siege of Gondor,' there is nothing there. Yet there must be something there, for "he had a kingly crown; and yet upon no head visible was it set" (*LotR*, 811). He and his fellows can act physically, carrying steel swords, riding horses or winged reptiles, the Lord of the Nazgûl wielding a mace. But they cannot be harmed physically, by flood or weapon – except, coincidentally, by Merry's blade of Westernesse, wound round with spells for the defeat of Angmar: it is the spells that work, not the blade itself. The Ringwraiths share something, then, with mist and smoke, also physical, even dangerous or choking, but at the same time effectively intangible.

None of these etymological points, however, helps with the most important questions about the Ringwraith-concept: how do you become one, and how persuasive, or suggestive, is the process implied? Probably Tolkien himself developed answers to these questions only slowly. The Ringwraiths, or Black Riders, appear many times in the first book of *The Lord of the Rings*, and in the first chapter of the second book, but seem relatively undeveloped, having little tangible impact except in the attack on Weathertop. Three times they encounter hobbits or men – Gaffer Gamgee,

Farmer Maggot, Barliman Butterbur – and try in a rather straightforward way to get information from them. Several times they are seen as shadows or shapes, sniffing or crawling. They raid the house in Buckland and the inn in Bree, again in straightforwardly human ways. In *The Fellowship of the Ring* (apart from Weathertop and the account given of the Morgul-knife by Gandalf in 'Many Meetings'), it is really only in the brief account of them given by Boromir in 'The Council of Elrond' that there is much sign of the meanings and the impact that they develop later.

What Boromir says is that Gondor was defeated in Ithilien not by numbers but by "A power [...] that we have not felt before." Boromir describes this (as usual) as "a great black horseman, a dark shadow under the moon," but adds that "Wherever he came, a madness filled our foes, but fear fell on our boldest" (*LotR*, 239). This is to be the leading characteristic of the wraiths from the moment they begin to reappear (now on winged steeds in the sky) after the Fellowship has emerged from Lothlórien. After that there are perhaps a dozen occasions in *The Lord of the Rings* when a Nazgûl passes overhead, over Sam and Frodo, or over Gondor, or over the Riders, and the description is usually a combination of the same elements: shadow, cry, freezing of the blood, fear. Typical is the moment when Pippin and Beregond hear the Black Riders and see them swoop on Faramir in 'The Siege of Gondor' (*LotR*, 790-1):

> Suddenly as they talked they were stricken dumb, frozen as it were to listening stones. Pippin cowered down with his hands pressed to his ears; but Beregond [...] remained there, stiffened, staring out with starting eyes. Pippin knew the shuddering cry that he had heard: it was the same that he had heard long ago in the Marish of the Shire, but now it was grown in power and hatred, piercing the heart with a poisonous despair.

The last word is a critical one. As *The Lord of the Rings* develops, it becomes clear that though the Ringwraiths do have physical capacities, their real weapon is psychological: they disarm their victims by striking them with fear and despair.

This at least is a suggestive concept. Many people during the course of the twentieth century, and authors as different from Tolkien and from each other as Alexander Solzhenitsyn and William Golding, have been surprised, even baffled, by the strange passivity of the Western world (a phrase Tolkien would have accepted) in the face of deadly dangers coming out of the East. Whole communities seem again and again to have gone to their deaths in a sleepwalking state, abandoning thoughts of resistance when it would have been entirely feasible.[10] In contests between the strong and the weak, the weak (the wraiths) have often won. This thought is not entirely unconnected with suspicions about how one becomes a wraith. It can happen as a result of a blow from outside, as Gandalf points out: if the splinter of the Morgul-knife had not been cut out of Frodo, "You would have become a wraith under the dominion of the Dark Lord" (*LotR*, 216). But more usually the suspicion is that people make themselves into wraiths. They start off with good intentions; they accept rings from Sauron (as Lewis would have said) not with any commitment to 'badness,' but with the intention of using them for some purpose which is in essence good, for power or security or knowledge. But then they start to cut corners, to eliminate opponents, to believe (as has so often happened during the twentieth century in literature and in life) in a 'cause' which justifies anything they do. The spectacle of the person eaten up by the cause is familiar enough to give the wraith-idea plausibility.

Once again, Lewis seems to have developed the wraith-concept in a more realistic mode in *That Hideous Strength* (almost certainly under the

---

[10] Solzhenitsyn muses on the failure to resist extermination squads in *The Gulag Archipelago* (1974: 11-15); Golding's hero Ralph in *The Lord of the Flies* is marked not by lack of courage, but lack of aggression: his passivity leads to the death of Piggy. Parallels might easily be drawn in the post-War period (*The Lord of the Flies* came out in the same year as the first volume of *The Lord of the Rings*, 1954) with the failure of the League of Nations twenty years before.

influence of Tolkien: the concept, like so much mentioned in this essay, must have been a topic of Inkling conversation). The obvious wraith in Lewis's book is Wither, the Deputy Director of N.I.C.E. On one level he is an obvious example of the bureaucrat, that characteristic twentieth-century figure. His language is elaborate, polished, utterly evasive. He is a master of getting his own way, and forcing weak people like Mark Studdock into disastrous situations, without committing himself to any statement at all. It is impossible to argue with him since he never says anything which contains any substance; nor does he appear to remember anything he has said before. All this is familiar enough to those who work in large organisations. But Wither turns out to be something very like a wraith on a non-realistic level as well. At a critical moment in chapter 9, when Mark Studdock has made his mind up to resign from N.I.C.E. and leave, he walks into the Deputy Director's office without an appointment. He thinks for a moment that he has found a corpse, but Wither is breathing, and even awake and conscious. He seems however to be in another world: "What looked out of those pale, watery eyes was, in a sense, infinity – the shapeless and the interminable. The room was still and cold: there was no clock and the fire had gone out. It was impossible to speak to a face like that" (230). Wither tells Studdock to go away, his nerve breaks, and he runs out. But fast as he runs, as he reaches the edge of N.I.C.E.'s grounds, he sees a figure before him: "a tall, very tall, slightly stooping figure, sauntering and humming a little dreary tune; the Deputy Director himself" (231). Studdock loses courage and turns back to slavery and self-betrayal. What he has seen must be a wraith in the second sense given by the *OED*, a 'sending' or an 'eidolon' of a living person. But Wither is a wraith in all the senses so far accumulated: he hovers between life and death, he can be both real and insubstantial, if you see him you cannot be sure it is him, he creates a kind of existential despair, he has been eaten up by his job and his professional bureaucrat's idiolect.

We do not meet anyone quite like Wither in *The Lord of the Rings*, and anyone like him would be an anomaly in Middle-earth. Nevertheless the Withers of this world and the Ringwraiths have a certain 'applicability' to each other, to use Tolkien's word from the 'Foreword' to the second edition (*LotR*, xvii). Saruman approaches the bureaucratic style and idiom, and can be imagined as a Ringwraith in the making. When he dies, at the end of 'The Scouring of the Shire,' his near-wraith status is revealed, as a "grey mist" gathers round his body, rises "like smoke," is "dissolved into nothing," and leaves behind a corpse shrunken by "long years of death" (*LotR*, 996-7). Like a wraith, he has been effectively dead for many years, but without realising it. Something similar might be said about the fleshless Gollum, but many of the characters in *The Lord of the Rings* show the first signs, or are aware of the first risks, of becoming a wraith: Bilbo (with his petulant anger at Gandalf), Frodo (starting to become transparent), Gandalf himself (refusing to touch the Ring). The image is a fantastic one in Tolkien, and hovers between fantasy and realism in Lewis, but most people with much experience of 'the psychopathology of everyday life' will find it easy to translate into a non-fantastic mode. Screwtape makes the transition neatly at the end of 'Letter XII,' when he remarks that Christians describe God as the One "without whom Nothing is strong." They speak truer than they know, he goes on, for (Lewis 1961: 64):

> Nothing is very strong: strong enough to steal away a man's best years not in sweet sins but in a dreary flickering of the mind over it knows not what and knows not why, in the gratification of curiosities so feeble that the man is only half aware of them [...] or in the long, dim labyrinth of reveries that have not even lust or ambition to give them a relish.

Or, he might have added, in watching daytime television. When Frodo says just before Weathertop that if the "short commons" and the "thinning process" continues, "I shall become a wraith," he expresses a fear which extends outside Middle-earth, and it is no wonder that Strider rebukes him "with surprising earnestness" (*LotR*, 180). (If one should want to read the autobiography of a wraith, set in a world somewhere between medieval allegory and working in a modern office, a classic example is (or should be) Gene Wolfe's novella 'Forlesen,' a work written in ironic celebration of Labour Day, see Wolfe 1981). Tolkien, Lewis and Wolfe demonstrate between them that one of the major advantages of fantasy in the modern world is that it effectively addresses the major threats of the modern world, like work, tedium, despair and bureaucracy, so often a closed book to modern mainstream authors without real-life work experience.

Orcs and wraiths do, finally, share one quality. In both one can see, if faintly, an element of goodness perverted, of evil as a mistake, something insidious. Neither image contradicts the orthodox, anti-Manichaean, Lewisite/Boethian view that evil is an absence, not an independent force or 'mighty opposite.' Yet Tolkien's imagination was in some respects wider than Lewis's, and less controlled by abstract reasoning. There is one generic image in *The Lord of the Rings* which raises a doubt about the whole thesis outlined above, which is that of the 'Barrow-wight.' The wight appears only once, and it is in any case a hangover from a period before Tolkien conceived *The Lord of the Rings* (see Shippey 2003a: 105-10); it could be left aside as merely an anomaly. Still, it is a disturbing anomaly, if one considers all the details given.

In 'Fog on the Barrow-downs' the four hobbits are caught by the Barrow-wight, dressed in white, and laid out in the barrow with "many treasures" about them; there is a sword across the necks of all but Frodo; the wight's arm then comes in and reaches for the sword, evidently intending to sacrifice its victims; Frodo cuts the arm off and calls on Tom Bombadil, who appears, banishes the wight, and revives the other three hobbits. As Merry wakes up, he says, "The men of Carn Dûm came on us at night, and we were worsted. Ah! the spear in my heart!" (*LotR*, 137, 140). Tom distributes some of the treasures, piles most of them on the grass to break the spell, and keeps one for himself and Goldberry, "Fair was she who long ago wore this on her shoulder. Goldberry shall wear it now, and we will not forget her!" (*LotR*, 142).

Some puzzles emerge even from the paraphrase above. The easiest explanation of a 'Barrow-wight' is to say that it is a *draugr*, in Old Norse, a 'drow' in later Orkney dialect, that is to say a ghost or an animated corpse which haunts the barrow in which it has been buried, and especially the treasure in the barrow. But this cannot be the case with the wight. The treasure clearly belonged to the "Men of Westernesse," as Tom calls them, and he remembers them benevolently. That is why he takes the brooch for Goldberry. The men of Westernesse, meanwhile, are the enemies of Carn Dûm, the country ruled by the sorceror-king who would in time become Lord of the Nazgûl. While Merry is asleep he seems to have been possessed by the spirit of a man of Westernesse, and he relives the latter's death-agony when he wakes. The wight, then, does not come from the people buried in the barrow; and what it seems to be doing, in some way or other, is trying to relive an earlier triumph, by turning the hobbits once again into the people buried in the barrow (through the influence of the clothes and the treasure), and then once again killing them. But this does not explain where the wight itself comes from.

There is as so often in Tolkien a rather similar problem in *Beowulf*, in lines 2233-77, in which we are told that long ago the survivor of a noble race hid treasure in the ground, in a barrow (*beorh*). He then died, 'the surge of death ran to his heart,' and – the poem follows on without a break – a dragon found the hoard 'standing open' (*opene standan*). This does not make much sense in *Beowulf*, for the main point about burying a treasure is of course to conceal it, not leave it standing open: many have thought that the Last Survivor and the dragon are one and the same creature. Like several heroes of Norse saga, and like Eustace Scrubb in Lewis's children's book *The Voyage of the Dawn Treader*, the Last Survivor 'lay down on his gold' and turned into a dragon. If this latter idea were to be accepted for *The Lord of the Rings*, the wight would indeed have to be the spirit or the undead body of one of those interred in the barrow, the "Men of Westernesse." But the unwelcome corollary of that solution is that in death a foe of the Dark Lord had been turned into one of his allies, if not servants – perhaps embittered and corrupted by ages of greed and loneliness. Alternatively, the *Beowulf*-poet could have the story right after all. The treasure was deposited, but the barrow left open. Then something came in from outside, from the place to which Tom returns it, *"Where gates stand for ever shut, till the world is mended"* (*LotR*, 139). But even this view contains a certain inner contradiction, for Tom also calls back the sleeping hobbits, on the same page, with the words *"Dark door is standing wide [...] and the Gate is open."* The gate could be open for the hobbits and shut for the wight, but not then "for ever shut." The two disturbing suggestions here are, first, that the wight really is a 'drow' or a dragon, the spirit of a buried person; but in that case good can be turned to evil even after death, as in some branches of Classical mythology, which suggest that the dead all hate the living, even their own dearest relations, simply out of jealousy of life.[11] Alternatively, the wight is just an alien power, perhaps created by the spells of Angmar, which has made its way into the barrow; in that case it seems that persecution can be carried beyond the grave, to be visited on the person whose spirit is briefly reanimated in Merry. Neither view is entirely satisfactory, but both of them suggest that there are some things not accountable by Lewisite or Boethian philosophy. Goodness may be omnipotent, but it has its own reasons for not intervening.

---

[11] Lewis puts this belief into the mouth of the Un-man in chapter 13 of the second volume of the 'Space' trilogy, *Perelandra*. The Un-man here could also be cited as a kind of 'wraith.' The body of the scientist Weston is clearly possessed by the Devil, but sometimes (as in chapter 13) reverts to being itself; unless this is a trick, or only a 'dying psychic energy' like the one which animates Merry for a moment.

And in the meantime (which may be millennia) humans and hobbits are in effect in a Manichaean world in which one does not have to have the seeds of evil in one's heart to become a victim, and in which "Nothing is strong" in ways which Screwtape did not envisage. This world, alas, is the real world of the twentieth century and of Tolkien's own lifetime, a lifetime in which many things which had been rendered apparently impossible by 'the progress of civilisation' returned to confound optimists: state-authorised torture, death camps, genocide, 'ethnic cleansing.' Such actions must have been carried out, one might think, by 'orcs,' but there is every evidence that they were planned by 'wraiths' – and Tolkien's point, which he repeats again and again, that no-one is secure from the prospect of becoming a 'wraith,' is one that no-one, not even the most *bien pensant* of his critics, can afford to ignore. It could be argued with some logic that if these were the real-life points which Tolkien (and Lewis) wanted to make, then they should have set them in real-life contexts without the veil or, for some, the distraction of fantasy. To this one can only reply that the topic of the origins of evil is one which several of their contemporaries, including the most distinguished (Orwell, Golding, Vonnegut, Le Guin, T.H. White), were able to handle only through media in one way or another non-realistic.[12] We do not know why this should be so, but the pattern is consistent enough to suggest that the fantastic element is not a whimsy but a necessity.

Furthermore there can be little doubt that the reason for the massive appeal of Tolkien in particular does not lie merely in an appetite for whimsy, but in a feeling that his work addresses serious issues which demand a response not forthcoming from the official spokesmen of his and our culture. During most of Tolkien's professional and creative life the literary environment of England was dominated by groups such as the 'Bloomsberries' centered on Virginia Woolf, E.M. Forster and Bertrand

---

[12] I discuss the relationship between some of the members of this group in Shippey (2000a: 158, 311-12).

Russell, or the *Sonnenkinder* of Evelyn Waugh. These had their own themes and their own merits, but if one asks what a reader was likely to learn from any of them about the origins of evil, say, or the balance between freedom and responsibility in political power, then the answer must be, 'very little.'[13] One of the most apparent features of all those writers mentioned is their severe concentration on private morality. Those inhabitants of the twentieth century, however, who did not have the luxury of a private income, 'a room of one's own,' freedom from conscription, or the ability to avoid political choices like service (or the refusal of service) in Vietnam, have consistently found in Tolkien an integration of private with public morality which commands their attention, and often their imitation. It is not an accident that Tolkien has in effect created a new mass-genre, the epic fantasy trilogy; nor that his works are consistently to be found on barricades and among protesters in England, the South Seas, Russia, and across the world.[14] His and his friends' theorisings about the nature and sources of evil may have seemed recondite or atavistic at the time, but they combined fantastic speculation with a wide and painful experience, and a certain hard realism, notably absent from the works of more professional and more sheltered philosophers, not to mention psychologists. Middle-earth certainly has an appeal based on its landscape, its characters, its revival of romance; but this would be purely superficial (as it is in the works of some but not all of its imitators) without its animating themes of power, evil, and corruption. Sauron and the Ringwraiths, Big Brother and the Party, the pig's head and the choirboys: these have been the defining images of evil – wholly

---

[13] One can, for instance, read the much-praised and ambitiously-titled work *Principia Ethica* (1903) by G.E. Moore, a leading 'Bloomsberry,' from beginning to end without finding anything which has any practical bearing on the issues which were to dominate the century. I take the term *Sonnenkinder*, meanwhile, from Martin Green's account of the Waugh circle, *Children of the Sun* (1977). The relationship between the Inklings and the Bloomsbury group has yet to be studied, but it seems clear that Lewis at least was responding to some of the latter (Forster, Russell) in several of his works.

[14] A point made with great force in Curry (1997: 54-6).

original, highly varied, oddly consistent – for a culture and a century which have had too close a contact with evil for more traditional images of it to seem any longer entirely adequate.

Heroes and Heroism:
Tolkien's Problems, Tolkien's Solutions [1]

It has been pointed out that an area of human life strangely neglected in modern fiction is that of work. Novels show people exploring human relationships *in their spare time*; or having adventures *when they're not at work*. If work does come into a novel it will usually be of some relatively glamorous variety, or else the focus of interest will once again be human relationships in the work place ('office politics,' as this is often called). Many major English novelists – Dickens, Scott, Jane Austen, Henry James – have got through lengthy and productive careers without ever seriously showing anyone engaged in working for a living, perhaps because many professional novelists after all do not know much at first hand about it. The science fiction author Greg Benford, who is also a professor of astrophysics, once remarked on this to me, and said that chapter 20 of his award-winning novel *Timescape* (1980) was an attempt to correct this imbalance, and show a scene familiar to all professional academics, the contested or uncertain PhD thesis interview. The trouble with doing this, Benford said, was that while such interviews – as he and I both knew from experience – were in reality extremely interesting, the chance of conveying this to someone who was not involved with them was almost zero: such scenes to outsiders look intensely boring. That is the trouble with work in fiction, and in fact. It is at one and the same time extremely tedious – I have never encountered a job which was interesting all, or even most of the time – and also totally absorbing. Nearly everyone likes to talk about their work. Hardly anyone wants to listen.

My point as regards Tolkien is not that he too should have included the world of work in his fiction – there are obvious reasons why he

---

[1] This piece was first published in *Lembas Extra* (1991): 5-17. I am grateful to the editors and the Dutch Tolkien Society Unquendor for the initial invitation to deliver it, and for permission to reprint.

shouldn't! – but that his work affected him at least as much as it affects everyone else, and that criticism of him has, as usual, consistently underrated the effect of it on him. It is clear now that Tolkien was one of the world's most determined writers and rewriters, a man who spent enormous amounts of time working on his fiction, both what he published and what he did not. Yet I would hazard the guess that for every hour he spent on his fiction he spent four working for Leeds or for Oxford University. This immense amount of time, spent on teaching, marking, reading, preparing, arguing, sitting on committees, wondering about the future of his subject (etc.), cannot have failed to mark him deeply. If what I say subsequently in this essay seems exaggerated or farfetched, I ask its readers once again to reflect on work: it is the Great Unsaid of fiction, and of criticism.

Tolkien himself clearly was sensitive on the subject of his professional duties, for evident reasons. He became a Professor at Leeds in 1924, and at Oxford in 1925, holding one Chair or another till his retirement in 1959. During these thirty-five years he never actually wrote a book on his subject. He edited the poem *Sir Gawain and the Green Knight*, in collaboration with E.V. Gordon. He did not, however, go on from there to the projected edition of *Pearl* (see Ida Gordon's 'Preface' to that edition when it finally came out in 1953). His edition of the Corpus Christi 402 MS of *Ancrene Wisse* came out in 1962, more than thirty years after his extremely important and suggestive article on that work in *Essays and Studies*; it is however no more than a transcript of the manuscript, without the extensive introduction and notes which must surely have been hoped for.[2] Two or three of Tolkien's learned articles – including the one on *Ancrene Wisse* and above all the one on '*Beowulf*: The Monsters and the Critics' – have been immensely influential (see further the essay on 'Tolkien's Academic Reputation Now' in this volume). But almost all of his publications to do with

---

[2] Though as noted in my paper 'Tolkien's Academic Reputation Now' in this volume, much of Tolkien's thinking on the subject may have been subsumed into the publication of his student, Simone D'Ardenne (see D'Ardenne 1961).

work had come out by 1940, twenty years before he retired. I persist in regarding 'Leaf by Niggle' as a personal allegory, with Niggle's painting as Tolkien's fiction and Niggle's garden as Tolkien's work, and it is clear from this that *some people*, at least, thought that Niggle was not doing his proper job: "Some of his visitors hinted that his garden was rather neglected, and that he might get a visit from an Inspector" (*Reader*, 102). When they realise he will soon have to go on his journey, "They wondered who would take his house, and if the garden would be better kept" (*Reader*, 103). Speculation about who will take over which Chair is of course a major feature of academic 'office politics,' not least in Oxford.

Yet in my opinion Tolkien, however defensive he may (occasionally) have felt, or been made to feel, *was* doing his job all the time, often in a highly inspirational way. Since his death we have seen his edition of *The Old English Exodus*, brought out by Joan Turville-Petre, and of *Finn and Hengest*, edited by Alan Bliss (for which, again, see the essay 'A Look at *Exodus* and *Finn and Hengest*' in this volume). Both these represent a great deal of thought, passed on in lecture form to many generations of students. They prove what we should have guessed anyway, that even as he was writing *The Lord of the Rings*, and rewriting *The Silmarillion* and so much else, Tolkien never ceased thinking about his work and grappling with its problems. My argument here is simply that one way for him to solve these problems was to put them into his fiction.

What was Tolkien's everyday work-problem? It was, I would say, to explain ancient texts and ancient stories: to consider and solve the crux. If I seem to be spending too much time on cruxes (or cruces), I repeat, it is a great deal less than the time Tolkien spent on them: because they were his job. I offer, then, three difficult places from old Germanic story – they could easily be thirty-three – not as special cases but as mere samples of the kind of thing Tolkien always had to think about.

The first of these is the story of Alboin son of Audoin and the Gepid king Thurisind (as well as the latter's son and daughter Cunimund and

Rosamunda). This story, recorded from the eighth century, clearly meant something to Tolkien, perhaps just because Alboin is so clearly the Lombard form of Old English Ælfwine, 'Elf-friend,' a name which always caught Tolkien's attention. The name and the story are both reused in his unfinished tale 'The Lost Road,' now brought out by Christopher Tolkien in the volume of that name, on pages 53-5 of which its editor also paraphrases the original story and adds a significant footnote. Paraphrasing the story rather more briefly than is done there, one can say that in it Alboin, prince of the Lombards, fails to be 'promoted' by his father because he has not yet been 'knighted,' so to speak; and this honour can only be granted (to avoid favouritism, one supposes) by the king of some *other* tribe. Alboin then goes to ask for this honour from the neighbouring king of the Gepids, Thurisind, whose son he has himself just killed. Thurisind does as he is asked and sends Alboin back safely to his father. In two sequels to the story we learn first that Alboin later repaid this generosity by killing Thurisind's other son, Cunimund, making a goblet out of his skull, and inviting Cunimund's daughter Rosamunda, whom he had since married, to drink a toast out of it. For this Rosamunda later murdered him. The problem for Tolkien – and I repeat that this was work for him, not mere idle curiosity – is how to make sense of the story. Specifically, what made Alboin into a hero of Germanic song, as he is – famous for his open-handedness – not only in the perhaps biased history of Paul the Deacon (a Lombard), but also in the Old English poem *Widsith*? Alboin after all comes over as cruel and graceless in the extreme, as Christopher Tolkien indeed remarks in his significant footnote, quoting a quite different and not hero-worshipping view of Alboin as a remorseless slayer. The answer might be, I would suggest, that what made Alboin admirable to some early bard was the way he was prepared to risk his life on a point of honour, and on that point of honour being recognised not only by himself but by his enemies. He trusted to Thurisind's magnanimity. He invited Thurisind to recognise that a code of honour was more important than Thurisind's own feelings, and than Alboin's own life. To use a modern and anachronistic term, both Alboin and Thurisind showed themselves capable of 'decentring,' seeing themselves respectively not as rejected son or grieved father but in the roles of aspirant warrior or fair-minded king. This admirable lack of self-centring coexists, though, with the custom of head-hunting and with an evident and almost Orcish cruel humour – for Alboin invited Rosamunda 'to drink merrily with her father,' i.e. out of her father's skull.

A second scene Tolkien must have reflected on, though I do not think it is drawn on directly in his fiction, comes from *The Saga of Egil Skalla-Grimsson*, which one can read now in the Penguin translation by Hermann Pálsson and Paul Edwards (1976). One scene in this which may well have attracted Tolkien's particular attention takes place after the battle of Vinheith, in which – the saga says – the English king Æthelstan, supported by Egil and his brother Thorolf, defeated a coalition of Northern kings. The battle is generally identified with the historical battle which the English called Brunanburh, commemorated in a long English poem in the *Anglo-Saxon Chronicle* – though no English account mentions anyone like Egil the Icelander at all. Tolkien was professionally interested in events which showed up (like the story of Alboin) in more than one Germanic tradition, and he also showed particular interest in events which 'crossed' Norse and English tradition. He did that kind of thing himself: Christopher Tolkien again notes (*BLT 1*, 245) that at one point in a manuscript his father had written over an Elvish name the Old English word *Aesc*. He remarks: "It seems conceivable that this is an anglicization of Old Norse *Askr* ('ash'), in the northern mythology the name of the first man." If this is so, then one can see Tolkien attempting to anglicise, to put into (Old) English, a fragment of Norse mythology – all too obviously because 'the northern mythology' had survived well in Norse, but hardly at all in English. He wanted to reclaim bits of Norse for English, and Egil's saga provided considerable material for reclaiming, with several events set in England, and a strong case made inside the work for Egil's famous poem *Höfuðlausn* being actually composed at York, and so in a sense 'English' even if written in Norse.

Be that as it may, the scene I have in mind shows Egil's behaviour after the battle has been fought and won – but also, regrettably for everyone, after his brother Thorolf has been killed. Egil sat, the saga-writer says, at the seat of honour at the banquet, with his head down. He kept his sword across his knees, and every now and then half drew it, then thrust it back in the sheath. He was an unusually ugly man, the writer comments at this point, prematurely bald, with a short, thick nose, broad lips, unusually broad chin, harsh and fierce in his expression. As he sat, slamming his sword in and out and refusing to drink, he "did nothing but pull his eyebrows up and down, now this one, now the other" (Pálsson and Edwards 1976: 129). This alarming behaviour is eventually dealt with by the king Æthelstan, who silently takes a big gold ring from his arm, puts it on his sword-point, and reaches it over to Egil, who accepts it in the same style. Egil then levels his brows, puts down his sword, and accepts a drink, cheering up even more as the king presents him with further gifts. But what is the point of this scene, where once again we have a Germanic hero behaving churlishly, but this time almost childishly, like a five-year old in a temper?

Behind the scene, I would say, lies the awareness of the saga audience that Egil is not entirely human. He takes after his father, Skalla-Grim (= 'Bald-Grim'). He in turn takes after *his* father, Kveld-Ulf (= 'Evening-Wolf'). Why the name 'evening-wolf'? Because Ulf takes after his uncle Hallbjörn Halftroll. There is in fact monstrous blood in the family as well as human, a cross which throws up a tendency to go werewolf, or to go berserk (= 'bear-shirt'), and to produce in each generation one handsome, able, socially well-adjusted brother, from the human side of the family – in this case Thorolf – who has to act as a sort of 'minder' for the ugly, bald, talented but psychopathic brother from the other side of the family. Tolkien, I think, very much liked the idea of the monstrous genes lurking in a family, and kept flirting with it: people whisper of Meglin the Dark-elf (*BLT 2*, 165) "that he had Orc's blood in his veins," though how this could possibly be under any of the conditions of Tolkien's developed cosmology one could not imagine. But also striking in the scene are, once again, the element of satirical humour directed this time against Egil; and the strangely unabashed materialism by which the only way to console someone's grief for the death of a beloved brother is simply to give him money for it. It is a strain in Egil's character that he is extremely mean. A part of his grief may stem from the fact that he has (driven by emotion, and social convention) buried two gold rings with his brother in the grave.

There is no doubt, in short, that Egil is a hero of Germanic story. But he adds strange notes of greed and childishness to the conception of the hero. Finally, and briefly, one might think of the famous tale of Gunnar and his brother Högni in the Old Norse poem *Atlakviða*. Both are captured by the Huns, whose king, Attila, demands of Gunnar where the famous treasure of his family lies. Gunnar refuses to reply till they bring him the heart of his brother Högni. First the Huns bring him another heart, which he rejects for its flabbiness. Then they bring him the heart of Högni, immediately recognised with approval by Gunnar for its small size and its hardness. "That is the heart of Högni the brave," he says, "not like the heart of Hjalli the coward. It trembles little as it lies on the plate. It trembled not so much when it lay in his breast" (my translation, from Dronke 1969: 8). But now his brother is dead, he says, he will not tell where the treasure is, but will die under torture instead. He could never be sure of the secret as long as another person was alive who knew it. But now he has seen the heart, he can do what he likes. In this scene, what is striking is the strange cruelty of Gunnar's behaviour, and also the totally unsentimental way in which he combines admiration for his brother with lack of trust in anyone except himself. He loves Högni, but he wants to see his heart cut out. He knows him to be totally fearless, but feels there is no point in taking risks. Also prominent in the scene is Gunnar's utter self-confidence, his sense of relief when matters come down to him alone. This too is a part of the definition of a hero.

As I have said before, all these scenes – and many more – were part of Tolkien's daily fare as Professor of Anglo-Saxon, then Professor of English Language (a wider brief), as teacher of heroic poetry and of Germanic legend. He had to confront them. He had to explain them. He had to explore fully their extremely distinctive and yet consistent behavioural style, or, one might say, 'flavour.' I think one of his goals was to re-introduce this heroic style into a literature and a language which had forgotten it entirely. Yet there were evident problems in making such a re-introduction:

1) this style – Alboin, Egil, Gunnar – is extremely cruel
2) all the characters concerned were heathens, though their stories were written down and copied by admiring Christians.

Tolkien, I think, was extremely concerned about both points, though perhaps especially about the latter.

I have suggested at some length in my paper on 'The Homecoming of Beorhtnoth' in this volume that Tolkien's essay/poem of 1953, 'The Homecoming of Beorhtnoth Beorhthelm's Son,' is a meditation on the problem of Christian heroism, and I have suggested there also that the sign of Tolkien's difficulty is the way that he was obliged (in my view) to distort the Old English poem on *The Battle of Maldon* quite seriously to make it fit what he wanted to say. It is only fair to add that my view is not that of the academic consensus, which has been almost totally persuaded on this matter to agree with Tolkien – who was, one has to say, a most persuasive writer. People interested in a relatively full analysis of *Maldon* and 'The Homecoming' should look at my essay in this volume. But in the context of what I have said already in *this* essay, let me remark that yet one more difficult case for Tolkien in the history of Germanic concepts of the hero was the speech near the end of the poem of *Maldon*, where the old retainer Beorhtwold says that he has no intention of surviving the death of his leader Beorhtnoth, even though – as Tolkien pointed out, but as Beorthwold definitely did not – Beorhtnoth had made a tactical error of disastrous proportions in inviting the Viking army to cross the river Blackwater unopposed and fight it out on level ground. Beorhtwold's speech goes, in my rough but line-by-line translation:

> "Thought shall be the harder, heart the keener
> Courage the greater, as our strength lessens.
> Here lies our leader, all hewn down,
> The good man on the ground. He can mourn for ever
> Who means to turn now from this warplay.
> I am old in years. I will not go,
> But by the side of my lord,
> The man who was so dear to me, I mean to lie."

There is nothing cruel in this passage, unlike the scenes we have had with Alboin, Egil and Gunnar. But it does share something with them in, for instance, its *sang froid* – Beorhtwold talks about himself as if his own life or death were really very trivial matters – and also in what I have called above its 'decentring' quality. Line 6 for instance is a very good example of what Anglo-Saxon scholars would call 'causal parataxis' (common in Old English poetry). Beorhtwold seems to mean 'I am old. *So* I haven't long to go anyway. *So* it doesn't matter much whether I live or die. *So*, since it doesn't matter much I might as well stay. *So*, I will not go [...]' All this is very much diminishing his own heroic gesture, but of course also and by converse implying that heroic behaviour is simply the right, natural and logical thing to do.

Tolkien certainly worried about this speech and this scene a good deal. I venture to say that he did not like it. He thought it was too traditional, too heroic, and too evidently un-Christian for the year 991 (when the battle was fought), almost four centuries after the coming of Christianity to England. Early Lombards and still-unconverted Vikings might behave like that. Cradle-Christian Englishmen like Beorhtwold should not, and the *Maldon*-poet had no business admiring such sentiments. In 'The Homecoming of Beorhtnoth' Tolkien accordingly, as I have suggested in the essay already cited, remodelled the Old English poem to express more acceptable sentiments. And – and this is the striking thing – he took Beorhtwold's speech out and *transferred it to the other side*, the heathen side, quoting the first two lines of it only as part of a dream experienced by the addle-headed Torhthelm and immediately disapproved of as "heathenish" by the sensible Tidwald; and furthermore adding a couple of lines, of Tolkien's own invention, just to make sure the whole thing did indeed sound 'heathenish'! Torhthelm's chanted words, as he wakes up, are:

> "Heart shall be bolder, harder be purpose,
> more proud the spirit as our power lessens!
> Mind shall not falter nor mood waver,
> though doom shall come and dark conquer."

The last two lines, to take us back to a Tolkien context, sound more suitable to Túrin Turambar, say, than to a wiser figure such as Gandalf or Aragorn.

Quite how 'The Homecoming of Beorhtnoth' (published 1953) relates to *The Lord of the Rings* (completed in essence by 1949), I am not sure. If the dates above are not misleading – and Tolkien often wrote things many years before he finally published them[3] – then the essay/poem might appear as a kind of apology for having created a new heroic work without evident debt or reference to Christianity. Or it might be seen as a sort of 'authorisation' for creating a Christian/heroic dialogue. However one takes it, though, 'The Homecoming' does show just the sort of interest in and

---

[3] We now know that a version of Tolkien's 'Homecoming' poem did indeed exist years before *The Lord of the Rings* was even started, see Hammond and Anderson (1993: 303), and *Treason*, 106-7. Other fragments have been found among Tolkien's papers deposited in the Bodleian Library, and are considered in Honegger 2007 (forthcoming).

uneasiness with scenes and attitudes from early poetry which I think Tolkien's job forced upon him. How did this affect his fiction?

At this point it would be possible – and perhaps another day or for another person it would be a good idea – to work through a list of Tolkien's major heroes (Théoden and Éomer; Boromir, Faramir and Denethor; Aragorn; Frodo; Thorin Oakenshield; Beren and Túrin) and put them into some sort of order or ranking between the two poles represented in their different ways by Tídwald (Christian, long-suffering) and by Egil Skalla-Grímsson (heathen, monstrous, vengeful, dauntless). Denethor for instance would be very close to the 'heathen' end of the order, and is in fact – as I have often remarked – the only character in *The Lord of the Rings* to whom this word is quite anachronistically and even improperly applied. He has gone too far, as has Túrin Turambar, another suicide-committer (obviously a heathen trait). Yet Tolkien's view of Túrin was a good deal more forgiving than his view of Denethor: in *The Book of Lost Tales 2*, 116, and again in *The Shaping of Middle-earth*, 73, Túrin is even given a sort of forgiveness beyond the grave, with more than a hint of the heathen Norse myth of Ragnarök, when we are told that in some ultimate battle it is the black sword of Túrin that will be the final death of Melko.

By contrast to both these, Aragorn shows some of the qualities of a Christian hero, in his mildness, ability to put up with provocation, and self-effacement – though again one might note that these qualities were less prominent in the first edition of *The Lord of the Rings* than they became later (see my comments in Shippey 2003a: 232, 374).[4] Each of the other characters mentioned would, I think, benefit from this sort of comparative study. But my main point is only this: that in all the heroic characters of

---

[4] In the first edition Aragorn loses his temper with Gimli and snaps at him for querying the decision to look in the Stone of Orthanc. This was cut out of later editions (the scene, in its abbreviated form, is on p. 763 of the 2005 edition used for this volume). It is not often noticed, however, how consistently negative Gimli has been to Aragorn's decisions from the start of *The Two Towers*: one might think that Tolkien had been building towards a clash of personalities.

Tolkien's fiction one can see at least some trace of this tension between two different heroic styles (archaic/heathen and modern/Christian), or perhaps one might say between a principled disapproval and a reluctant admiration of the good qualities of the former, on which Tolkien's attention was so firmly focused as a result of his profession. Was the 'decentring' and the admirable self-control of the Alboins and Beorhtwolds of story inseparable from the cruelty of the Egils and the Gunnars? Could humour be presented without hearts on plates? Could you have the delicate point of honour without the custom of head-hunting? Just saying 'yes, of course' to all these questions goes against the evidence of the literature Tolkien knew so well. But saying 'no, the one is a necessary part of the other' amounts to a defeat for civilisation. In between these doubts Tolkien's fiction oscillates: and from that oscillation, I would say, it gains a strength and vitality which is one of the major things missing from its host of imitators, all of which (I would say from my reading) have a much flatter and less authentic view of the heroic world and the heroic mentality.

But a second point I would make is this: that though there is a lot to be gained by looking at Tolkien's major characters in this way, one device Tolkien often used was to project the tension I have been describing in its most extreme forms off on to *minor* characters, and even to Appendices – as if he delighted in creating scenes analogous to the ones I have discussed, but did not want them disturbing the major thrust of his story. A highly Egil-like character in *The Lord of the Rings*, for instance, is Helm Hammerhand, from Appendix A, II, 'The House of Eorl.' Helm is a very clear 'decentrer.' The point of the first story told about him and his quarrel with Freca is that Helm refuses to take offence at Freca's insulting accusation of age *while he is in council*, while he is being the king. But once the council is over he forces Freca outside the hall (and so outside the area of the 'king's peace,' an important element in Anglo-Saxon law), to kill him not as king to subject, but man to man. In a way what he does is the opposite of the magnanimous action of the Gepid king Thurisind, who insisted on act-ing as a king, not as a father: but Helm, in his highly characteristic twisting of the proverb said to him, shows also the cruel, amused word-play of Alboin offering the skull to Rosamunda his wife (see *LotR*, 1040). Meanwhile in the second story told of Helm, about his grief and vengeance for his own son, one can only say that he turns into a sort of monster – he is "like a snow-troll" – just like the ancestors of Egil (*LotR*, 1041). Helm in fact is less like Beowulf at this point than he is like Grendel: it is believed of both of them that weapons cannot bite on them, and neither uses weapons himself, preferring to kill people with his bare hands (though this last is true of Beowulf too, and it is only alleged of Helm that he is a cannibal like Grendel, not proven). Just the same, the grim and ruthless streak of ancient Northern heroism is much clearer in Helm Hammerhand than in any central character of *The Lord of the Rings*. Tolkien liked it, I would suggest, as a literary taste, but he could not tolerate it. He presents Helm as a 'wraith,' but allows the *simbelmynë* to grow on his grave.

Or consider Dáin Ironfoot, who appears (but only by report) within *The Lord of the Rings* itself, in 'The Council of Elrond,' and again in Appendix A, III, 'Durin's Folk.' At the council, Dáin stands out by the way he talks (reported by Glóin, but still given in the form of direct speech). The messenger of Sauron tells him to find and recover the Ring known to have been taken by a hobbit, and Dáin replies: "I say neither yea nor nay. I must consider this message and what it means under its fair cloak." "Consider well, but not too long," says the messenger. "The time of my thought is my own to spend," answers Dáin. "For the present," says the messenger, and rides into the darkness (*LotR*, 235). What is going on in this passage is evidently a process of escalation, as the messenger gets closer and closer to naked threat – which would probably provoke complete break-off – while Dáin stubbornly indicates distrust and independence, without reaching absolute defiance, which would in its turn probably provoke direct attack. I can only say, first, that this is an archaic mode of speech derived above all from Norse (though Anglo-Saxon heroes value a similar obliqueness), and second, that the qualities it appreciates are qualities we in the modern world have often been taught not to value: lack of openness, deep insincerity, an attitude which finds non-co-operation easy and natural. The positive side of that attitude, of course, is refusal to give in to threats or to force. Dáin shows the former – says Glóin – in his later refusals to bargain with the messenger, and the latter in his death, reported by Gandalf in Appendix A. Gandalf refuses to call that death a loss: it was redeemed, he says, by the way Dáin in old age wielded his axe till he was killed, "standing over the body of King Brand before the Gate of Erebor until the darkness fell" (*LotR*, 1053). What is this darkness? Just night? Or death? Or, perhaps, considering the circumstances, death and defeat with as far as Dáin knew no prospect of ultimate victory – all considerations which affected Dáin, like Beorhtwold at the battle of Maldon, not at all. The true heroic spirit, Tolkien knew, was founded on "the creed of unyielding will" (*Essays*, 21) and on a fundamental lack of hope,[5] and was unavailable, at least in theory, to the Christian, who is not allowed to lose hope. Gandalf goes straight on from the report I have just quoted to make remarks strongly suggestive of his ultimate belief in the Valar; but that more optimistic attitude only makes the contrast with the death of Dáin. One could say that Dáin, like Beorhtwold and like Théoden, is a striking image of the spirit unaffected by age, of the dauntless old man (or dwarf).[6] But Dáin goes a little further than

---

[5] The point is surprisingly often missed. Edwin Muir's imperceptive remarks of long ago (Muir 1955), accusing Tolkien of producing a bland and happy ending to *The Lord of the Rings*, were repeated – one might even say parroted – by Professor Jasper Griffin of the University of Oxford, in the *New York Review of Books* (Griffin 2006). I replied to them in the same journal (Shippey 2006), ending with the remark which is said to have been addressed to Queen Elizabeth I by a loyal English farmer, *à propos* of her dealings with King Philip of Spain and the Spanish Armada: "he got the wrong sow by the ear that time!"

[6] Such figures are, once again, characteristic of the Old English/Old Norse literary tradition, which seems to have taken pleasure in the idea of the heart which only grows harder with increasing age and weakness. Besides figures already mentioned, one might think of the hero of *Víga-Glúms saga*, of the legendary Starkath, of the *eald æscwiga* of *Beowulf*. But such figures exemplify a harsh and cruel ideal, whose major quality – to-

Théoden, further even than Húrin, but not as far as Beorhtwold (whose words, remember, Tolkien could not approve), along the road that leads from resistance into suicidal despair. If he had been in the main story, this might have been harder to handle.

My third and final case of archaic feeling relegated to an Appendix is the death of Aragorn and of Arwen Undómiel, at the very end of Appendix A, I (v) (*LotR*, 1037-8). Aragorn, one has to say, dies very like a Christian saint: he has foreknowledge of his death, he can even choose the time of it, he dies peacefully talking and giving consolation to other people in confidence of a sort of resurrection ("We are not bound for ever to the circles of the world, and beyond them is more than memory," *LotR*, 1038). But all the consolation and instruction that he offers to Arwen appears valueless. She dies, one has to say, much more like a heathen of old: trying to persuade Aragorn to live on, saying that at last she understands the error of the Numenóreans (with their sacrifices for long life and their embalmings), speaking movingly of the bitterness of death, refusing consolation and in the end dying alone. Yet there is no hint of criticism for her, only sorrow and sympathy. She represents an attitude Tolkien (and Aragorn) thought was wholly wrong, but also wholly natural. In her special position, as an immortal who has forfeited immortality, she feels the nature of death more than anyone else in *The Lord of the Rings* – but only as much as mortals in the real world of Anglo-Saxon history, before they were offered even hope of a life beyond the grave.

I cannot help thinking – though this is now pure speculation – that when Tolkien thought of early Germanic paganism he did not think of the faintly glamorous notions we now have of Valhallas and warrior-burials and burning ships with chieftains on them, but of things like the grave found not far from where I write, and where he used to work, in Yorkshire.

---

tally opposed to the Christian ideal – is desire for vengeance, refusal to forgive or even to negotiate.

In this archaeologists have found an old lady, from the early period of English settlement, laid out decently with her arms crossed and her jewellery on. But on top of her is the skeleton of a young woman, still all too obviously trying to push herself up out of the grave into which she had been thrown, on her elbows. The reason she failed is that her back was broken. The reason her back was broken is that a millstone had been thrown in on top of her. She was still alive when they filled the grave in.[7]

Well, there, Tolkien might have said, but for the grace of God (and he would have meant that literally) go we. That is what ancient Germanic heathenism was really like. That is what his and my ancestors used to do. There is nothing admirable about it at all.[8] Yet it co-existed with the fierce, cruel, humorous, fearless culture which both he and I have studied and respected all our lives. Tolkien's problem as regards the heroic literature of antiquity was, I would say, on the one hand great professional liking, and on the other extreme ideological aversion. What was the solution? Simply, to try again and again to reconcile them. One definition of a myth is that it is an attempt by a particular culture to reconcile or to mediate between irreconcilables. In that case Tolkien was producing a twentieth-century myth in more ways than he may have known, or than have readily been seen. He was asking, fictionally, whether in a post-Christian age you could have a noble world which was not Christian; whether you could have a developed sense of ethics without the back-ups of revelation and faith; whether the virtues of noble pagans could be detached from their vices. These questions seem to me to have become more and more relevant with time, and more

---

[7] See Laing and Laing (1979: 81-2) and further Hirst 1985.

[8] There is a sense of the horror from which Christianity delivered the pagan North in Tolkien's poem on 'King Sheave,' in *Lost Road*, 87-91, and especially on p. 89. See also the quotation from his father's lectures on *Beowulf* given by Christopher Tolkien on pp. 95-6. It is true that in that poem and the narrative associated with it, relief (if not salvation) comes from the figure of Sheaf or Sheave: what Tolkien thought of the tangle of legends associated with him is not easy to make out. The problem deserves further study.

and more urgent, as Western Europe at least enters into a post-Christian era. In Tolkien, though, the questions are expressed above all through contrasting heroic styles.

Noblesse Oblige: Images of Class in Tolkien[1]

Thoughts for this paper began when a journalist from the *Times* – once upon a time the phrase was 'a gentleman from the *Times*' – rang me and asked what I had to say to Michael Moorcock's allegation that Tolkien stood only for 'the values of a morally bankrupt middle class.' The answer I gave to that was too rude to be repeated here, but it did make me think about the issue of class in Tolkien.

It may not seem a very important or relevant question. One feature of several English fantasy-lands – in William Morris and in T.H. White's *The Sword in the Stone* as well as in Tolkien – is that they appear to be set in a sort of Utopia which is not without social class but is free of the pressures of class-competition, as if the authors' main aim was just to enable people to forget for a while about the English class-system (or, some would say, to give them a sanitized version of it to make them accept it more dutifully in real life). In this view the fantasy authors have basically nothing original to say about class. In the case of William Morris particularly the notion that he might have had has been determinedly rejected by his heirs and critics. Speaking of Morris's *The House of the Wolfings* (1888), his daughter May Morris told a story about how, after the book came out, a German professor "wrote and asked learned questions about the Mark, expecting, I fear, equally learned answers from our Poet who sometimes dreamed realities without having documentary evidence of them."[2] The joke, she feels, is on the German professor, who should have known better than to expect Morris to have a clear opinion about the Mark he had invented. In almost exactly the same way E.P. Thompson, the most formidable of Morris's biographers, passes on a story to the effect that when "a German archaeologist wrote to

---

[1] This essay appeared first in *Lembas Extra* 93/94 (1994: 27-43), having been first read at an Unquendor meeting in Rotterdam. I am as always grateful to René van Rossenberg and the Dutch Tolkien Society for the invitation to speak and for their hospitality.

[2] In her 'Introduction' to Morris (1910-12, XIV: xxv).

Morris asking him what sources of information he had used in writing *The House of the Wolfings*, Morris exclaimed: 'Doesn't the fool realize [...] that it's a romance, a work of fiction – that it's all LIES!'"[3] I do not know if May Morris's 'German professor' and E.P. Thompson's 'German archaeologist' were the same person,[4] but both stories have the same point. The English commentators on Morris want to deny that his fiction could have been anything other than a 'romance,' could have had any serious social point or understanding to offer. The thought that maybe he did know what he was writing about is shuffled off on to stupid comic German pedants – Germans having a reputation in England for being over-serious about things.

Morris was actually an extremely learned person with an extensive library, whose imagination had furthermore been powerfully stimulated by exactly that (largely German) tradition of philological musing on the recently rediscovered Northern literary past in which I would locate Tolkien's own inspiration. The very use of words like 'the Mark' in *The House of the Wolfings* shows that Morris had been reading scholarly editions and philological commentaries.[5] It seems to me quite likely that Morris was in fact trying to say something about class in his fictions, even if it was something his daughter and his left-wing *bien-pensant* critics didn't want to hear. I think the same is even more strongly true of Tolkien. But, as the reactions from May Morris to Michael Moorcock show, the problem (especially for someone English) is to be able to consider this issue of class without becoming entangled in it. The best way to do this is linguistically.

---

[3] See Thompson (1955: 784). The story was told first by H.H. Sparling 1924.

[4] My own suspicion is that both are an invention of the idle and linguistically-challenged, which excuses them from thinking or enquiring any further. May Morris, incidentally, knew the Tolkiens, and sent a young Icelandic lady to stay with them in Oxford (and be appropriately chaperoned): I am told that she complained that Professor Tolkien 'always wanted to talk about Icelandic.'

[5] See further my article on 'Goths and Huns' in this volume.

What is the situation as regards social class in the Shire? It is clear that there is a class-system: but the system has gaps. There is no-one at the top of it. The Shire-hobbits still verbally recognise the authority of the king, but they have not had one for nearly a thousand years. Instead they have a Thain, "to hold the authority of the king that was gone" (*LotR*, 5). The word Thain (like Morris's word Mark) makes a point in itself, for it is clearly the Anglo-Saxon word *Þegn*, 'servant,' but re-spelled to make it look familiar and easy to pronounce. Tolkien however deliberately rejects the Shakespearean spelling 'thane,' probably because that form shows the malign influence of the Great Vowel Shift. In the Shire, 'Thain' is a hereditary title held by the Took family.

The Tooks however are not unqualifiedly top of the hobbit social ladder. Their position in relation to the Baggins family is made clear at the very start of *The Hobbit*, where we are told in a slightly apologetic way that "the fact remained that the Tooks were not as respectable as the Bagginses, though they were undoubtedly richer" (*Hobbit*, 4). But is being 'respectable' a good thing? In *The Hobbit* being respectable is equated with never having any adventures or doing anything unexpected. The Bagginses are as respectable as they are because "you could tell what a Baggins would say on any question without the bother of asking him" (*Hobbit*, 3). At the end of the story Bilbo "was no longer quite respectable" (*Hobbit*, 271), though he has gained credit in the wide world outside, and among the younger Tooks.

All this makes good sense within the rather complex social terminology of England. Defining the word 'respectable,' *The Oxford English Dictionary* [*OED*] – Tolkien's long-term inspiration – says predictably enough that it means "Worthy of notice" etc., but then gets down to an important point under heading 4, where it moves from "social standing" to "moral qualities," and ends up by saying "Hence, in later use, honest and decent in character or conduct, without reference to social position, or in spite of being in humble circumstances." You can in short aspire to being respectable even if you are poor, though it is probably easier to reach that status if you are not poor. It is certainly not a qualification to be rich, like the Tooks, or Bilbo at the end of *The Hobbit*. But it is perfectly all right to be 'well-to-do,' like Bilbo at the start.

What all this shows is that the Shire has a vestigial upper class, in families like the Tooks and the Brandybucks, which has title, authority, and long descent, but only nominal or emergency powers, like being captain of "the Shire-muster and the Hobbitry-in-arms" (*LotR*, 9, not called out, one notes, by the Thain against Saruman). Meanwhile it puts a high value on 'respectability,' a quality which can be possessed, in theory, by people from any class. The Bagginses have only limited reason to feel inferior to the upper-class Tooks, with whom they have of course intermarried. But does the Shire have class distinctions lower down the scale than the Took/Baggins line? The answer here is much more clearly 'yes.' In the *Ivy Bush*, in chapter 1 of *LotR*, the first thing Gaffer Gamgee says is that 'Mr. Bilbo' (as the Gaffer calls him, careful to give both title and forename, so being both familiar and respectful), is "A very nice well-spoken gentlehobbit" (*LotR*, 22). 'Gentlehobbit' is *not* in the *OED*. It is obviously a formation from 'gentleman' (for which see further below). And it has caused translators of Tolkien at least to stop and think. The Dutch translation reads "een heel aardige en beleefde hobbit-heer" (Schuchart 1956, I: 30); the older German translation "Ein sehr liebenswürdiger und feiner Edelhobbit" (Carroux 1972, I: 36);[6] the Norwegian, "riktig en fin hobbitherre" (Høverstad 1980, I: 34). None of these versions gets very close to the English 'well-spoken,' an adjective of special importance within the English class and educational systems, though the Icelandic version has "einstaklega orðprúður og göfuglyndur Höfðings-Hobbiti" (Thorarensen

---

[6] A later one reads "Ein sehr feiner und vornehmer Hobbit" (Krege 2000: 37). This avoids the issues of both "well-spoken" and "gentle."

2001, I: 32).[7] More significant perhaps is the fact that none of these closely-related Germanic languages has an exact parallel to 'gentle.'

How do you define a gentleman (or a gentlehobbit)? Within *The Lord of the Rings* it is pretty clear what Gaffer Gamgee means. He, the Gaffer, may be 'respectable' (though I don't think he ever claims to be), but he is not 'gentle.' He calls Bilbo 'Mister,' but Bilbo calls him 'Master' (in my youth this was the form used for boys, like 'Miss' for girls, only boys graduated to being 'Misters' automatically on growing-up, not having to wait till they got married like girls: this asymmetry is what caused the rise of the female title 'Miz' or 'Ms.'). Gaffer is not really 'well-spoken,' in that his English betrays determined errors of grammar like 'drownded' for 'drowned,' while he pronounces some words in a colloquial way without concern for their etymology, like 'vittles' for 'victuals': as far as I can see these errors are not imitated by the three translations above, but in English they are significant.[8] He is not rich, he has no ambition to get rich, and he is on the whole hostile to the idea of education. When he mentions that Bilbo has "learned [Sam] his letters" – 'learned' being another error for 'taught' – he adds quickly "meaning no harm, mark you, and I hope none will come of it." His advice to Sam is not to get mixed up in "the business of your betters," the last phrase translated literally in the Norwegian version, and quite closely in the Icelandic one, "meiri háttar Hobbitum" (Thorarensen 2001, I: 34), 'hobbits of greater status,' but rejected in both German and Dutch translations, which say respectively "die Angelegenheiten deiner Herrschaft" (Carroux 1972, I: 38) or "de zaken van je merderen" (Schuchart

---

[7] Ármann Jakobsson kindly tells me that the Icelandic phrase is "a bit further removed from normal vocabulary than its English counterpart, 'Höfðings-Hobbiti' does not echo any particular Icelandic phrase and 'orðprúður' is one of those words that make you recognize the phrase as a translation." For the problems of translating Tolkien generally, see the volume edited by Honegger 2003, and Turner 2005.

[8] See Johannesson 1997 for an in-depth discussion of the hobbits' dialect-features.

1956, I: 33). In German and Dutch 'business' may be too big for Sam, but that does not mean that he has 'betters.'[9]

Gaffer Gamgee in fact shows that the Shire is not totally democratic, or at least not democratic enough for modern German and Dutch readers. It has only a vestigial upper class in the Tooks, but a very clear lower class in the Gamgees. This lower class is well aware of its place and does not want to move out of it. Real moral authority, along with real respectability, is centred in the middle class families like the Bagginses. The Bagginses are at once well-to-do financially and respectable morally, and this is what makes them 'gentlehobbits.' So far one might say that some at least of Michael Moorcock's accusation at the start of this paper is proved: the values of the Shire may or may not be 'morally bankrupt,' but they are strongly 'middle-class.'

How far, one might ask, is the Shire's class system mirrored in the other societies of Middle-earth? Gondor, one could say, is a little like the Shire in that it has no king, with a hereditary Steward replacing the hereditary Thain. Gondor also has a lower class, represented most clearly by Ioreth, the old wife of the Houses of Healing. She is an interestingly mixed figure. The herbmaster of the Houses of Healing patronises her, obviously thinking that her rhyme about the herb *athelas* is of no value, a "doggrel [...] garbled in the memory of old wives," which old wives like her repeat "without understanding" (*LotR*, 847). He is half-right, for Ioreth does in fact betray surprising lack of understanding just over a hundred pages later, in the chapter 'The Steward and the King,' where the account she gives to her cousin of the halflings and the destruction of the Ring is extremely 'garbled,' and where we can see her also expanding her own part in events at the Houses of Healing well beyond the truth (Gandalf did not say "Ioreth, men will long remember your words" to her at all). Yet in spite of her lack

---

[9] Krege again diplomatically sidesteps the issue, with "Angelegenheiten, von denen du nichts verstehst," 'affairs of which you understand nothing' (Krege 2000: 39).

of education and of sense, Ioreth is the first to say "The hands of the king are the hands of a healer," and the first to recognise Aragorn as king. In class terms one might say that both in Gondor and in the Shire, true tradition of ancient days lingers on longest at the two extremes of upper and lower class, while the middle classes, like the herbmaster or Bilbo Baggins before he forfeited his respectability, have turned their back on it.

Yet having said so much, one has to concede that in other respects Gondor is not very like the Shire at all. Its upper class is much more powerful and evident than the Shire's, if it has no king it still has the Prince of Dol Amroth, and it also has the notion, not of class, but of status: Beregond declares that he has neither "office nor rank nor lordship," but in being a man-at-arms of the Guard of the Tower of Gondor he does have "honour in the land" (*LotR*, 750). It is doubtful that the Shire would recognise 'honour' in this way. The Gondorians call Peregrin *Ernil i Pheriannath*, "Prince of the Halflings," but anyone who knew the Shire would recognise how impossible such a title would be. In the last chapter Merry and Pippin are called 'lordly' even in the Shire, but it is hinted that normally in the Shire (as in England) the adjective would be critical, not approving. It is a peculiarity of the Common Speech as spoken by hobbits that they use the same second person pronoun to everybody, careless of rank.[10] All round one has to say that while the Shire may not be very democratic as compared with modern Holland or Germany, it is much more so than Gondor. The difference between the two societies is put forward insistently and by use of many significant details.

---

[10] In this the hobbit form of Westron compared with other forms of the language is like English as compared with most other European languages. English also has only one second person pronoun, and English speakers have difficulty understanding when to use *du, Sie, Ihr; u, jij, jullie* and the rest. One significant difference is that English has kept only the formal or plural form, while Hobbitic kept only the familiar form (as it were, saying 'thou' to everybody, not 'you' to everybody). When Tolkien remarks in Appendix F/II (*LotR*, 1107) that deferential forms lingered on as endearments among the villagers of the Shire and in the Westfarthing, he no doubt knew that the same is true of English familiar forms: 'thou' is still used in the West Riding as a sign of intimacy. As often, the 'calquing' of the Shire on England is very close.

I think it would be possible to express the distinction just drawn linguistically, by contrasting two English adjectives, but before doing that I would just like to draw a third society into our system of contrasts: that of the Riddermark. This is easy to describe, but far-removed from modern experience. The Riders have a king, Théoden. The word *Þéoden* itself, in Old English, does not exactly mean 'king' – it means something like 'head of the *Þéod*, or people' – but it is a word used of kings. The names of Théoden's father, grandfather, great-grandfather and remoter ancestors listed in Appendix A are mostly words of the same type, synonyms for 'king.' The name of the founder of Théoden's dynasty, however, Eorl, is not one of these. It means 'earl,' a word signifying rank, but rank below that of king. What this means is that Eorl was not born a king; he made himself one. But all his descendants are kings. Below this rank the Riders seem undifferentiated. We hear several times in 'The Battle of the Pelennor Fields' of the "knights of Théoden's house," but this seems only to indicate the close relation of these Riders to Théoden himself: in England for centuries a knight has been called 'Sir,' as in 'Sir Gawain' or nowadays 'Sir Richard' or 'Sir William,' but no-one calls any of Théoden's knights Sir Háma or Sir Éomer. I note that in all five of the Germanic-language translations I have, this distinction of 'rider' and 'knight' is not marked. The phrase used above is translated as "die Ritter seines Hauses," (both German translations agree), "de ridders van zijn huis," "Rytterne av hans eget hus," "riddarar af húshaldi hans."[11] I think this is essentially correct. Tolkien had a habit of trying to pre-date the Norman Conquest by introducing the term for 'mounted warrior' (i.e. 'knight') rather before mounted warriors became familiar.[12] Here 'knight,' though militarily correct, seems socially anachronistic. The Riders are a society of theoretical equals, without

---

[11] Respectively Carroux III: 127, Krege 886, Schuchart III: 1100, Høverstad III: 123, Thorarensen III: 106.

[12] See my remarks in 'Tolkien and *The Homecoming of Beorhtnoth*' in this volume.

Gondorian ranks or hobbitic notions about class and respectability. They recognise positions of responsibility, like 'marshal,' but I take it that these are in the king's gift: Háma, returning Éomer his sword without orders in 'The King of the Golden Hall,' seems to think that you can be under arrest without forfeiting your position as marshal, but that may be because Théoden had not yet made up his mind in that case. The only other sign of class that I can see in the Mark is the name of the man Théoden meets near the start of 'Helm's Deep,' Ceorl. In modern English this word has become 'churl,' an abusive term for a coarse or low-class person. But in Old English *ceorl* is much closer to modern German *Kerl*, and means either 'man' or 'husband.' Significantly the Eddic poem *Rígsþula* recognises only three ranks in society, with a fourth about to be added. They are 'thrall' or 'slave,' 'karl' or 'freeman,' 'jarl' or 'warrior.' The son of Jarl is Konr Ungr, Kon the Young, or 'king' (*konungr* in Old Norse). The Riders have no thralls. Their ancestor is Eorl (= Jarl). Ceorl (= Karl) is still a perfectly respectable name to bear. They are all (if male) both freemen and warriors, with a king over them, and such military officers as he chooses to appoint. In the Riddermark (as in William Morris's Mark so carefully denied logic by Morris's critics) we see a 'reconstructed' image drawn from Germanic antiquity: how true it ever was we may doubt, and Tolkien has 'purified' it by removing its slave-class. But it is clear that one of its charms is that it comes from a period before social class (and education, and wealth, and being well-spoken) were invented.

I would sum up what has been said so far by saying that in the history of English, and to some extent in its neighbour languages, there are or were three terms for superior status. These belong to the semantic families of 'gentle,' 'noble' and 'athel,' and they are exemplified by the Shire, Gondor, and the Mark respectively. Working backwards through these, the words derived from Old English *æþel* have almost vanished from modern English: 'atheling,' a prince, remains dimly familiar to historians. It is a native term, surviving in modern German *Adel, edel*, and note *Edelhobbit* above. This is the term – archaic, native, unfamiliar, Germanic – which seems to me to be exemplified by the Riders. The Gondorians meanwhile are 'noble,' an adjective which *The Oxford English Dictionary* [*OED*] tries to define with words like "titular pre-eminence," "magnificence" or "stateliness," all of them very appropriate to Gondor the City and to its inhabitants. The hobbits finally have no trace of the concept of *Adel*, and do not even aspire to 'nobility.' What they would like to be called, as Gaffer Gamgee said at the start, is 'gentlehobbits.' But how do you define a 'gentlehobbit,' or a 'gentleman'?

Some would say that the attempt to answer this question is much the same as the history of the English novel, in which case Tolkien is not so far away from the centre of his nation's literature as is usually thought. In brief – and remembering that there are about as many opinions on true gentility as there are English people – it is an old opinion (Chaucer's, in fact)[13] that there are three components of the gentleman, gentleperson, or lady. These are: birth, wealth, and virtue. To these I would now add a fourth: accent, or being 'well-spoken.' There is no doubt that if you have all four you will be accepted as a lady or gentleman. The problem arises if one or more is missing; and which ones? In practice one might think that wealth is the real determining factor. One definition which the *OED* quotes for a 'gentleman' is a person who has "no occupation" or "no work to do" – by which it means, clearly, not someone unemployed but someone rich enough not to need to work. Even at the start of *The Hobbit* Bilbo Baggins falls under this definition, while it is a status Gaffer Gamgee cannot aspire to. Nevertheless wealth on its own has never been accepted as the qualification for 'gentlemanliness,' as one can see again and again from the English novel. In Dick-

---

[13] See his short poem 'Gentilesse,' in which he discusses 'vertu,' 'richesse' and inheritance, without actually giving a ruling on which is most or more important. His poem 'The Franklin's Tale' is a narrative demonstration of 'gentilesse,' rather along the lines of R.L. Stevenson's essay five centuries later, as discussed below – one sign of English social conservatism. See also Chance 2006.

ens's *Great Expectations* Magwitch the returned convict is the one with the fortune; but no-one, not even Magwitch, thinks there is any chance of him setting up as a gentleman. Instead Magwitch gets his pleasure from thinking he can make or buy himself a gentleman, in Pip. Is Pip a gentleman? He has wealth, but is definitely not 'of gentle birth' (the first criterion the *OED* cites). On the other hand he does have a standard English accent (he is 'well-spoken'), and Dickens lays great stress on the fact that he has been taught it. One point that pleases Magwitch especially is that Pip can read foreign languages: in practice, for many centuries in Europe, you could say that being literate in Latin gave you a good claim to gentle status. There is an analogy to this in the fact that Bilbo and Frodo know Elvish. One wonders whether this might be included along with the 'letters' Sam's father is so suspicious of.

Finally there is the issue of moral virtue. Practically all commentators insist that this is essential for the 'true gentleman'; the problem is that all commentators have seen that moral virtue on its own (for instance in Chaucer's Ploughman) gets you absolutely nowhere. One way of solving the problem is to say that gentlemanliness involves a particular *kind* of moral virtue, which includes not only goodness but grace, or social dexterity. A traditional definition of a gentleman is that he is a man who never gives offence *accidentally*. Robert Louis Stevenson, in a long and interesting discussion,[14] finally argues for a "quality of exquisite aptitude" as the defining feature, shown in his view by General Grant accepting the surrender of Robert E. Lee in 1865. Even gentlehobbits, to be honest, show very little sign of this: and none at all of another traditional definition (very clear for instance to Sir Walter Scott) that a gentleman is someone who is *satisfaktionsfähig*, that is, capable of giving satisfaction for his behaviour by engaging in a duel without thereby dishonouring the other combatant. They

---

[14] See his essay, 'Gentlemen,' in Stevenson 1924. The essay came out first in *Scribner's Magazine* in 1888, four years before Tolkien was born.

are also not particularly gallant (in the sense of showing extreme devotion to ladies), though Tolkien was aware of the power of this notion in poems like *Sir Gawain and the Green Knight*, and gives an unexpected glimpse of it later on in Gimli's selfless devotion to Galadriel.

One could sum up by saying that the image of the 'gentlehobbit' in the Shire is indeed a middle-class one, being based on wealth (not having to work), accent and education (being 'well-spoken' and widely literate), birth in a limited sort of way (in coming from a well-known family capable of remembering all its cousins), and a certain steady politeness even to social inferiors: but no 'exquisite aptitude,' *Frauendienst*, or dueling, all of them rather aristocratic notions. As in so much else the Shire represents in idealised form the middle-class England of Tolkien's youth. Yet parts of what it leaves out ('nobility,' royalty, *Adel*) are placed in contrast with it in the characters from Gondor and the Mark.

My overall suggestion is this: in many classic English novels the debate over 'gentility' – how people should behave, and how far individual merit can be brought into line with social recognition – is acted out within one setting or even within one character. Is Dickens's Pip a gentleman? He has wealth but not birth, accent but (perhaps?) not strength of character. Is Hardy's Tess Turbeyfield a lady? She has no wealth and a doubtful accent – but she does happen to have birth. She is not a virgin – but then it was rape. And she was raped by someone who had wealth and accent, but obviously a poor moral character – and as it happens his appearance of good birth has been bought, as Tess's was not. Agonising indecisions like this make the classic English novel. Tolkien has none of them. But what he has in exchange is a very much clearer historical, linguistic and cultural awareness of how relative all these ideas of honour and rank are; how much they have changed over the centuries, and what alternatives English society has at one time or another possessed. It is these oppositions that are dramatised by the cultural contrasts within *The Lord of the Rings*. It is at least surprising that (in spite of the problems over *hobbit-heer* and *Edelhobbit*, over knights and

Riders and *ridders*) there seems to have been very little difficulty for readers over most of Europe and America in grasping the social tensions and complexities Tolkien demonstrates. It suggests that a good deal of knowledge about attitudes to social class still underlies our overt and official democracies.

There is another point I would add, which is that Tolkien was quite capable, outside *The Lord of the Rings*, of dramatising social tensions inside a single character. He does it in particular with Beren and Túrin. The world of *The Silmarillion*, in which they figure, contains far less in the way of cultural contrasts than the world of *The Lord of the Rings*: in the context of this argument I would say that its characters aim consistently at 'nobility,' not 'gentility,' still less 'respectability' – both of them much too tame and modern in their appeal – nor even at the Germanic virtue of *Adel*, a virtue appropriate to what Faramir would call Middle People, people of a simpler culture than the Édain. Nevertheless, even without culture contrasts, one can see that in the tales of Beren and Túrin Tolkien still showed an interest in class or rank or status, and in particular the demands imposed on characters by their own sense of worth: the demands in short of *noblesse oblige*.

In the case of Beren this shows up at one particular point, which I have discussed in *Lembas* before, the scene before Thingol in which Beren is provoked into uttering his ambiguous vow. A guiding motif in this whole sequence is the absolute necessity of keeping one's word, by tradition one of the most aristocratic of virtues. Within the 'Tale of Beren,' Beren, Thingol, Felagund and the sons of Fëanor are all bound by oath to their own misfortune, which in every case they enter consciously rather than go back on their word. Especially tense is the scene before Thingol, in which consciousness of status is at least a major factor in the "doom of Doriath." To begin with Thingol's anger against Beren is caused only by his appearance in Doriath, and Thingol's own fear for Lúthien. But when Beren asserts equality with Thingol by saying that nothing shall keep him from Lúthien, Thingol uses the offensive words "baseborn mortal [...] spies and thralls"

(*Silm.*, 167). 'Baseborn' and 'thrall' are especially offensive in class terms – one remembers how the idea of 'thralldom' was censored from the otherwise closely Eddic world of the Riddermark. In both cases it could be argued that Thingol does not actually mean the words in class terms: it could be that he regards "mortal" and "baseborn" as much the same thing, focusing on Beren's presumption in seeking to mate with an immortal, while in calling Beren a thrall he means a thrall (= servant) of Morgoth. Beren reacts to them, though, as if they were insults to his family not himself: "my house has not earned such names from any Elf" (*Silm*, 167) In the archaic world of 'nobility,' status depends very heavily on ancestry, and in a sense can never be earned, only inherited. Thingol seems to realise this and to play on it in his reply: "a father's deeds […] avail not to win the daughter of Thingol and Melian" (*Silm*, 167). One might note that Thingol in a way has started to talk like Beren. He does not say 'my daughter,' but "the daughter of Thingol," in the third person, as if his status were more important than himself. Is this really the way Thingol talks, or is it a further attempt to entrap Beren by making him prove his status, get into a nobility-contest? Melian, I think significantly, speaks very much more plainly when she eventually does speak, saying "my eyes […] your daughter […] yourself" (*Silm*, 168). Overall, in that scene I think one sees *noblesse* exercising a malign influence and creating a hollow rhetoric. At the same time a major attraction of *The Silmarillion* is the sense that its characters follow an ethical code more demanding than our own.

The case of Túrin is similar in several respects – both he and Beren are from great houses, are of high status, but effectively fatherless. A major difference is that Túrin is self-doubting, because in his youth his status is ambiguous or unrecognised. His first crime, the killing of Saeros, is provoked largely by his inner fear for his mother and sister, but combined with reaction to an attack on his table-manners (appearing at table "unkempt," an error which incidentally may seem trivial to us, but which to medieval authors like the *Gawain*-poet was the gravest discourtesy).[15] Thereafter it is noticeable that Túrin will always respond to any challenge to his status, or recognition of it. On page 203 of *The Silmarillion* the dwarf Mîm (a Petty-dwarf) recognises Túrin's lordliness – "You speak like a dwarf-lord of old" – and Túrin pities and befriends him. On page 204 Beleg gives him the Dragon-helm, hoping it will "lift [his] thought again" above his life "as the leader of a petty company": Túrin, disastrously, puts it on. One should note the repetition of the word 'petty,' which though a straight borrowing from French *petit* has strong connotations in modern English of the mean, small-minded or sneaking, accusations Túrin cannot bear. On pages 213-4 Glaurung again uses the word 'thrall' to Túrin, and accuses him of being a disgrace to his father and his blood: Túrin's response is disastrous again. Part of his tragedy is that he is consistently attempting to do the honourable thing.

It is accordingly a good sign when (*Silm*, 217) Túrin lays aside the aristocratic weapon of the sword, and relies on "the bow and the spear" instead; a bad one when (once more verbally provoked) he goes back to it. His ultimate crime, though, is the killing of Brandir, provoked yet again by the accusation – made by Glaurung but repeated by Brandir – that he is "a curse unto his kin" (*Silm*, 223, 224). The most significant thing about that killing, though, to my eye, is that Brandir when he first appears is described as "a man of gentle mood" (*Silm*, 216). What does 'gentle' mean here? No doubt it carries its modern English meaning, given in the *OED* as "Mild [...] kind, tender," also unwarlike, reluctant to cause pain. All those are true of Brandir. Nevertheless Tolkien was more aware than virtually anyone alive of the ways in which words changed their meaning, ways which he did not

---

[15] See lines 133-92 of the poem *Cleanness* (Anderson 1977) in the same manuscript and almost certainly by the same poet as *Sir Gawain and the Green Knight*. The poet there uses coming to dinner in your working clothes as an image for sexual impurity in priests: in both cases one appears before one's lord, or God, with dirty hands, a terrible breach of good manners.

think were accidents. In this particular case, also, the meaning of true *gentilesse* has been a subject of debate in English at least from Chaucer to R.L. Stevenson. I suggest that in the fatal clash of Brandir and Túrin we see both a tragic foreshadowing of the more comic opposition between Bilbo the gentlehobbit and the dwarves in *The Hobbit*, and a clash between the virtues of *gentilesse*, which Túrin lacks in every sense, and *noblesse*, which he feels called upon to practice to excess.

Summing up I would say three things in reply to the Michael Moorcock accusation at the beginning of this paper. First, I can see that Tolkien's values were on the whole middle-class, though this applies to virtually all English authors even now; but I do not think the class or the values are morally bankrupt.[16] If they were, I doubt the fictions that contain them would have proved so easy to understand or so capable of translation for most of the languages and cultures of Europe and America, if not the world. Second, while his values may have been middle-class, it would be quite wrong to see them as existing unchallenged; indeed, middle-class values in Tolkien's work have to work hard to prove themselves against powerful upper-class competitors, and even lower-class competitors in the unwavering self-confidence of the Gamgees. There is often a sense of social strain in Tolkien which one could relate, incidentally, to the sometimes difficult position in Tolkien's Oxford of being officially a member of the *noblesse de robe*, but usually without the financial means to uphold that status: it is a difficulty which Oxford professors have talked seriously to me about in the very recent past. Finally, I think I would say that on the issue of class as in many other respects Middle-earth seems to me to reflect specifically English states and traditions. A member of Unquendor remarked to me that he

---

[16] It is interesting that C.S. Lewis discusses the changing meanings of the word 'bourgeois' at some length in Lewis (1990: 21-2). It has remained a contemptuous word, but in his youth the bourgeoisie was despised for not being aristocratic, while later it was despised for not being proletarian. Lewis does not say so, but of course most of those doing the despising were – like Michael Moorcock – irretrievably bourgeois in origins and behaviour themselves. Snobbery takes many forms.

enjoyed going to England because it was like stepping back in time; English social structures are indeed still extraordinarily archaic, from the House of Lords to the chance professors still have of being formally knighted (for good behaviour). Yet it would be a mistake to think that that archaism and cultural conservatism cannot co-exist with deep self-questioning and a readiness to examine the inner meaning of words and ethical systems: as, I believe, Tolkien did as a continuing thread within the web of his fiction.

'A Fund of Wise Sayings': Proverbiality in Tolkien[1]

It should come as no surprise if I remark that Tolkien was from an early age interested in rather unexpected genres. One was nursery-rhyme: he rewrote 'The Cat and the Fiddle' and 'The Man in the Moon' as independently-published poems, and reworked the latter for us in the *Prancing Pony* scene in *The Lord of the Rings*. Another was the riddle: he wrote 'Enigmata Anglo-Saxonica Nuper Inventa Duo,' or 'Two Recently Discovered Anglo-Saxon Riddles' in the 1920s, and once again reworked and expanded some of this material in *The Hobbit* a few years later. A third was fairy-tale: there is no need to dilate on Tolkien's scholarly and creative interest in these. And a fourth was names, both place-names and personal names. I would go so far as to say that Tolkien never *stopped* thinking about the latter. He could not see a signpost, or pick up a telephone directory, without pondering the etymology of what he saw, and his own readiness to invent onomastically is evident in *Farmer Giles*, in *The Lord of the Rings*, in *The Silmarillion*, and elsewhere – though not, as it happens, in *The Hobbit*.

The first question I ask is what connects these very different genres? And I answer, they are all what I call 'survivor-genres.' They exist in perfectly familiar, indeed everyday form, in the modern period. But there is every indication that they are also very old. They point, then, to a kind of continuity between the ancient and the modern world which Tolkien valued very highly, though it is a completely unscholarly one (which scholars actually rarely notice or study). In fact all these genres have become *déclassé*. They have sunk down, like fairy-tales and nursery-rhymes, to being the possession of children, or old wives – Jacob Grimm called the latter *ammen und spinnerinnen*, 'nannies and spinstresses'[2] – or like names are felt to have lost any meaning they once had. But to some, this makes them

---

[1] This paper was first delivered on August 12th 2005 at the 50th Anniversary Conference organised by the Tolkien Society and held at Aston, Birmingham.

[2] Grimm (1875-78, I: v-vi).

especially valuable. Things which are known to have no value, or no meaning, are not interfered with. They are like the immensely valuable Anglo-Saxon poetry texts surviving, which were left behind in badly-run, inefficient libraries, used as bread-boards and beer-stands, and accordingly not rewritten to make them up-to-date, or thrown out by smart librarians to make room for government-authorised publications. Tolkien, like other philologists, had a keen eye for survivor-genres, and valued the information about the past which they contained, and which they continued to make relevant (one way or another) into the present.

What I want to say is that there is another survivor-genre which Tolkien valued highly, and that is the proverb, or maxim, or wise saying. These also are common knowledge – very common knowledge. They are also often as old as our knowledge of English, or older. One of the most familiar, but oldest, proverbs still in common use is – and I like to think it is characteristically English in its scorn for rhetoric – 'actions speak louder than words,' or in Anglo-Saxon *weorc sprecað swiþor þonne þa nacodan word, þe nabbað nane fremminge* 'works say more than naked words, which go no further.'[3] (It perhaps has more punch in its Anglo-Saxon form because in that language 'works' and 'words' sound like each other, and are grammatically similar, both neuter nouns uninflected in the plural.)

Now, scholars do not study Old and Middle English proverbs much, for reasons I could explain but do not sympathise with, and this is a pity.[4] There are in fact two extensive collections of Old English proverbs extant, the *Durham Proverbs* and the *Distichs of Cato*, and several Middle English ones, of which the most important are the *Proverbs of Alfred*, the *Proverbs of Hendyng*, and the *Middle English Cato*. There are two Old Norse ones as

---

[3] This is from Ælfric's letter to the thane Sigwerd, entitled 'On the Old and New Testament' in Crawford (1922: 74).

[4] Louis 1993 has loyally compiled some ninety pages of scholarly references, but the results are deeply disappointing. The scholarship is largely nineteenth-century, often from Continental Europe, and almost entirely editorial, concerned with determining texts or arguing definitions.

well, the famous *Hávamál* from the *Poetic Edda*, and the *Hugsvinnsmál*, another work indebted to Cato. And there are early poems which consist entirely of proverbs, like the Middle English *Poema Morale* and the Old Norse *Málshattakvæði*. There is plenty there to study, the material is very enigmatic, but potentially very illuminating – and almost no interest has been shown in it at all. Proverbs, like the other 'survivor-genres' mentioned, are *déclassé*, and have been for hundreds of years. "A man of fashion never has recourse to proverbs," said Lord Chesterfield, arbiter of eighteenth-century fashion. A modern scholar adds with exactly the same supercilious tone, "Proverbs, because they apply to most situations, really apply to none."[5] Proverbs are trite, obvious, known to everyone, general not particular, show no interest in the *mot juste*, banal, sub-literary – and they are low-class. Ever since Don Quixote and Sancho Panza, it has been the low-class sidekick who uses proverbs, the Tonto rather than the Lone Ranger. As I said, they are just like fairy-tales.

I could readily refute the pseudo-learned opinion, and in fact I will. Here are two Anglo-Saxon proverbs, translated as near as I can word for word from the original.[6] The words are perfectly familiar: but can you tell me what they mean?

> He that wishes to run down the hart
> must not mourn for the horse.

It is not too difficult to decode the metaphor here. The proverb means something like, if you want to achieve a result, you must not scruple to pay the cost: in effect, 'you can't make an omelette without breaking eggs.' But try this one, noting that Old English *fæt* means 'vat,' or 'container,' or 'cup.'

---

[5] The modern scholar is Gabriel Josipovici: note the thoroughly Saruman-style use of "really." For references to these (and other) remarks, see Shippey 1977.

[6] They are, respectively, numbers 41, 42 and 6, in Arngart 1981.

The fuller the 'fat', the fairer you must bear it.

You may understand the image, but what is it telling you? Be more careful with what is more valuable? I would prefer to say that it goes: a full cup is hard to carry without it spilling; but not impossible; so don't complain about a difficult task, work harder at it. I would like to see it over the main entrance of every university. One more sample of the wisdom of our ancestors, and by no means the most enigmatic:

It's a good year when the hound gives to the raven.

I think – though it would take too long to spell out my reasoning – that this is the opposite of our standard 'never look a gift-horse in the mouth.' It means, '*always* look a gift-horse in the mouth, and count its teeth as well'! It perhaps takes a certain kind of mind to appreciate both the sense and the humour of proverbs – and they can be funny but grim at the same time. It is particularly true of good proverbs (and this is what Lord Chesterfield and his fashionable successors have failed to recognise) that they have an absolutely obvious, trite, banal meaning on the surface, but another one, often a harsh or unwelcome one, buried underneath it. If I could cite one which I learned from my father:

A bit of pain never hurt anyone.

I still wonder whether he realised this was totally paradoxical – for on the surface it is complete nonsense, pain *always* hurts *everyone*. But he meant it just the same, and the way he meant it, it isn't nonsense.

What did Tolkien think about proverbs? He clearly also thought they were funny, as one can tell from Sunny Sam the blacksmith in *Farmer Giles of Ham*, with his fund of gloomy remarks, "No news is bad news," or "A worm won't return" (*Reader*, 167, 159). There is a joke in both of these, based on the way familiar sayings have been inverted, or altered in meaning to fit a new context, but I will not stop to explain it. I would prefer to recall Bilbo, lost in the goblin tunnels – but not quite as without resource as we might be, for "hobbits are not quite like ordinary people [...] they have a fund of wisdom and wise sayings that men have mostly never heard or have forgotten long ago" (*Hobbit*, 65). I wish we had heard more of these in *The Hobbit*. On the other hand we do have a scene in which a proverb is created. Bilbo, scorched by the blast from Smaug, says to himself, "'Never laugh at live dragons' [...] and it became a favourite saying of his later, and passed into a proverb" (*Hobbit*, 204). To put this in scholarly style, what Bilbo says is in origin a *Denkspruch*, made up by one person, relevant to one context, and literally obvious. But it becomes a *Sprichwort*, a familiar saying, common property, with its literal meaning turned into metaphor and so made widely applicable – just like, perhaps, 'It's no use crying over spilled milk,' or 'let sleeping dogs lie.' Sometimes you may still catch a proverb coalescing, like one I heard from the golfer Lee Trevino:

You gotta dance with who you brung.

This surely needs no explanation.[7]

If proverbs are rather rare in *The Hobbit*, though, they are very common, and very varied, in *The Lord of the Rings*. I have made a list of some seventy of them, but you cannot always tell what is a proverb and what is not, something which applies both to Tolkien and to the ancient texts from which he picked up this habit. Someone else counting might well get a higher figure. If we should ever see an *Annotated Lord of the Rings* along the lines of Douglas Anderson's *Annotated Hobbit*, it seems to me that we might well hope for marginal comments on each one of the sort that Doug-

---

[7] Some may think it needs a great deal. I would say that on the surface, and literally, it expresses a maxim about etiquette: if you invite a lady to a dance, it is your duty to dance with her. What Trevino *meant*, though, was that you have to play a golf tournament with the skills you have already acquired: you can't practice something once the competition has started.

las gives to all the riddles in chapter 5 of *The Hobbit*, and who knows? – we might get a conclusion like the one which can be drawn from Douglas's annotations in that chapter: namely, that all Gollum's riddles have ancient sources, while all Bilbo's riddles are to be found now in places like the Opies' *Language and Lore of Schoolchildren*[8] – because riddles have become *déclassé*, as I have said already. But that's not the fault of the riddles. The fact that Bilbo and Gollum understand each other, as Gandalf later says in *The Lord of the Rings* – "There was a great deal in the background of their minds and memories that was very similar […] Think of the riddles they both knew, for one thing" (53) – points to exactly the kind of continuity between ancient and modern which Tolkien thought was literally true, in England, and very valuable. Hobbits, one might say, are a survivor-species, as proverbs are a survivor-genre.

The seventy or so proverbs in *The Lord of the Rings* tell us a lot about the different societies, and people, who produce them; though in the end, I shall suggest, there remains a core of proverbial wisdom, shared out among different characters, which seems to me designed to *sound* traditional, though in fact it is original to Tolkien. Because these sayings are shared out among different characters, who nevertheless agree with each other, it seems to me also that this is meant to be not just illuminating, but actually true: the proverbial core is close to the work's structural core, and expresses in very condensed form what might be seen (though Tolkien would have disliked the adjective) its 'ideological' core. But at the same time this proverbial core, as I call it, is not very like a core, being dispersed through the whole three volumes, and disguised by the very similar sayings which come from all directions. This seems to me to be very characteristic of Tolkien's way of working when it comes to conveying an 'ideology,' or a world-view: it becomes like magic in Lothlórien – you cannot put your finger on it, but "you can see and feel it everywhere" (*LotR*, 351).

---

[8] See Anderson (2002: 121-28).

At the bottom of the proverbial ladder, there is a comic character whose sayings are all the things that learned scholars say about them, banal, trite, obvious etc. The character is Barliman Butterbur, who comes out with a string of utter clichés: "It never rains but it pours," he says (a quite strikingly untrue proverb on the literal level, in England anyway, the land of the steady drizzle, but not that this stops people saying it). Another Butterbur gem is, "one thing drives out another," followed soon by "What's done can't be undone" (which for a change is strikingly true on the literal level, but of course no help at all). Butterbur's especially annoying quality is bringing these completely familiar sayings out with an air of one who reveals esoteric knowledge, "as we say in Bree." The other characters start to parody him. Strider says, shortly afterwards, "every little helps," and Pippin joins in with "handsome is as handsome does, as we say in the Shire." Sam later says that too (see *LotR* 150, 153, 163-4 for Butterbur, 165 for Strider, 167 for Pippin, 665 for Sam).

Shire wisdom is in fact not all that different from Bree wisdom, as you might expect. Sam says "Live and learn," and a bit later, "It's the job that's never started as takes longest to finish" (*LotR*, 338, 352) – though this last one has the slightly paradoxical quality of 'don't cross your bridges till you come to them.' Sam has also learned something from his father, Gaffer Gamgee, who fits one of my criteria for a 'proverbious' person – he is confident enough in proverbial wisdom to alter the words and the meaning.[9] So Gaffer says near the end, not only the standard "it's an ill wind that blows nobody any good," but also the non-standard, "All's well as ends Better"; while Sam also quotes him as saying, "where there's life there's hope [...] and, as he mostways used to add, and need of vittles" – the upbeat standard

---

[9] In my view, in a living oral culture proverbs are not just repeated mechanically, always in the same form of words, as nowadays – a habit which has contributed to modern downgrading of them – but can be varied to suit different situations: though only by people with the wisdom and authority to do so. Such people are 'proverbious' rather than 'proverbial,' as is their language. See further Shippey 1977.

saying is sardonically varied by a downbeat and personal addition (999, 685). I also like Pippin's novel, but in form entirely traditional four-beat "Short cuts make long delays" (*LotR*, 86). But Shire wisdom is best expressed by Bilbo: he varies 'don't get too big for your boots' with the equally alliterative "Don't let your heads get too big for your hats!," given we are told "in Shire fashion" (*LotR*, 965). Most significant is the little poem he makes up, titled in the index 'The Riddle of Strider.' It's eight lines long and strikingly paratactic – i.e., every line is a separate sentence, so it appears to be extremely simple. But how you fit the sentences together is more difficult. The rhyme goes (*LotR*, 167):

> All that is gold does not glitter,
> Not all those who wander are lost,
> The old that is strong does not wither,
> Deep roots are not reached by the frost.
> From the ashes a fire shall be woken,
> A light from the shadows shall spring,
> Renewed shall be blade that was broken,
> The crownless again shall be king.

I would say, of this, that the first four lines are proverbial, but the next four are not, although, as often when one is dealing with proverbs, it is not easy to give strict definitions or make clear distinctions. Briefly, the first line is a 'proverbious' alteration of a very familiar proverb, 'All that glitters is not gold,' but it does not reverse the familiar saying, as Sunny Sam's "No news is bad news" reverses the normal 'No news is good news': rather it gives the *obverse* of it, the standard saying's commonly disregarded complement. The next three lines are all different in surface shape and grammar, but all have the same deeper structure, which one might sum up as: 'While it is accepted that generally X (being gold, wandering, being old, being roots) is likely to entail Y (glittering, being lost, withering, being susceptible to frost), nevertheless, in particular cases this is not so.' One might even go so far as to describe them as 'anti-gnomic,' for if a 'gnomic saying' (as some have argued) is one which indicates essential qualities, like the Anglo-Saxon 'hawk shall be on glove [...] wolf shall be in forest [...] dragon shall be in barrow' etc.,[10] then an 'anti-gnomic' one is one which indicates exceptions. But Bilbo's rhyme is the only example I know of this theoretically possible but rarely-encountered genre.

Meanwhile the last four lines of Bilbo's poem are different from the first four. They all have the word 'shall' in them, and arguably they are not proverbs, but come from another survivor-genre, which is prophecies. Furthermore, they approach more and more closely to having, not general meaning, but specific meaning, with reference in the last two lines to Andúril and to Aragorn, and to nothing else. Yet there is a kind of general meta-statement behind them, which one could again laboriously paraphrase as 'Though in general certain things (ash, darkness, etc.) indicate extinction (of fire, light, etc.), in certain circumstances including the ones I, Bilbo, am thinking of, this not only need not but will not be true.' And the word *sceal* (pronounced 'shall') is very common in Old English maxims and wise sayings, though it does not mean quite what it does in modern English. One could sum up by saying that Bilbo's poem moves from the general and the proverbial to the specific and the prophetic, but it does so by stages, and one meaning never quite excludes the other: line one, after all, is definitely proverbial, and equally definitely could well apply to Strider, though to much else as well. As people still say about the particular reference of proverbial judgements, 'If the cap fits, wear it!' Note finally that the poem is labelled also as a 'riddle.' Hobbit-poetry, one may conclude, like hobbits, is trickier than it looks: *sciolto volto, pensieri stretti*, might be their motto ['open face, closed thoughts']. Gandalf himself pays tribute to this quality in them.[11]

---

[10] Treebeard's 'Long List of the Ents' is a gnomic poem, clearly modelled on the Old English poem *Maxims II*, for which see Shippey (1976: 12-15, 76-79).

[11] All of which makes Mr Josipovici's remark quoted in paragraph four above even sillier than it seemed at first sight. Tolkien was often to conclude that critics, trained in what

The other cultures of Middle-earth of course have their own proverbial styles, though here they can only be treated cursorily. The dwarves go for a rather grim and archaic style, which fits their well-marked habit of not saying much – in the Council of Elrond the only character present who never says anything is Gimli. But on leaving Rivendell Gimli says, in response to a long speech by Elrond, "Faithless is he that says farewell when the road darkens." Elrond replies within the same metaphor, "let him not vow to walk in the dark who has not seen the nightfall." Gimli plays back with the fairly straightforward, "sworn word may strengthen quaking heart," capped by Elrond with, "or break it" (*LotR*, 274). I know of no ancient model for these, but their shape and most of their vocabulary is Old English.

The Riders, too, are very Old English. Háma the doorward, faced with a difficult decision, comes out with, "in doubt a man of worth will trust to his own wisdom" (*LotR*, 500), which to me is a neat explication of a couple of lines from a closely similar situation in *Beowulf*, lines which have been much disputed by scholars: *æghwæþres sceal scearp scyldwiga gescad witan, worda ge weorca.*[12] More generally, Old English wisdom is marked by words like 'seldom' and 'often,' which by the habitual English understatement mean 'never' and 'always.' Théoden accordingly says, "news from afar is seldom sooth" – it is like "news from Bree," the opposite of "sure as Shire-talk" (*LotR*, 501, 632). Aragorn, who has done service with the Riders and knows how they talk, remarks sardonically, "seldom does

---

were essentially alien traditions of literature, were not good at dealing with native forms and genres, like folk-poetry and fantasy; and, worse, were liable to project their own inadequacy on to what they should have been studying. See, for instance, Nokes in *Smith of Wootton Major*, the critics in '*Beowulf*: The Monsters and the Critics,' and the 'misologists' in 'Valedictory Address.'

[12] Clark Hall 1940 – the translation which has a 'Preface' by Tolkien – translates (p. 35) "The bold shield-warrior, who judges well, must know the difference between these two – words and deeds." But this is nonsense. Any fool can tell the *difference* between the two: 'Actions speak louder than words' just reminds you which are more important. Tolkien's version implies that the coastguard is really saying, 'sometimes you have to make your mind up, regrettably, *from words alone*.'

thief ride home to the stable" (*LotR*, 497); Éomer says, "oft the unbidden guest proves the best company" (*LotR*, 522), and Théoden says, "oft evil will shall evil mar" (*LotR*, 581). I have not found close ancient parallels for these yet, but they are reminiscent in form of some examples in the collections mentioned earlier: more research is needed.

The same goes for something said twice by Aragorn, "dawn is ever the hope of men" (*LotR*, 524), and then "None knows what the new day shall bring him" (*LotR*, 527), echoed by Théoden, "in the morning counsels are best, and night changes many thoughts" (*LotR*, 783), and also by Legolas, in the traditional four-beat style and with Anglo-Saxon alliteration and wording, "Rede oft is found at the rising of the sun" (*LotR*, 419). Gandalf also plays the saying-exchange game with Théoden, answering "Faithful heart may have forward tongue" with, "say rather, to crooked eyes truth may wear a wry face" (*LotR*, 510).

I could continue about the Riders, who are the most insistently proverbial of all the peoples of Middle-earth, but time and space restrict me to saying only two things about them. One, like Tolkien's Anglo-Saxon riddles, their proverbs sometimes look as if they are the forgotten ancestors of ours, as with Éowyn's once more poetic and alliterative version of 'where there's a will there's a way': "Where will wants not, a way opens" (*LotR*, 787). And two, people like Éomer vary familiar proverbs like Gaffer Gamgee, as in words which Tolkien actually wrote to me long ago, this time with double and chiastic alliteration, 'n – l – l – n,' "Need brooks no delay, yet late is better than never" (*LotR*, 817). (Incidentally, at the end of my US citizenship interview I was told to write a sentence to prove I could speak English, and wrote that one, with sardonic reference to the years the whole process had taken: the interviewer rejected it as not proper English. But his objection failed, because as Théoden says, "Great heart will not be denied" (*LotR*, 824). Also I had taken care to have my lawyer sitting in.)

I must now pass over elvish and Gondorian wisdom, as also orcish, and get to what I earlier referred to as the proverbial core of *The Lord of the*

Rings. Tolkien, as we have seen, used proverbs for humour; and to set scenes; and to indicate cultural variation. He liked to use standard proverbs, but also to set up variations on them, and to bring in modern versions of ancient and forgotten ones. If we had an *Annotated The Lord of the Rings*, all this would become fairly clear. The proverbs I have mentioned also point in all kinds of directions: they are about appearances, and inevitability, and decision-making, and determination, and seeing how things go. After making all allowances for this kind of thing, though, one is left with a small body of proverbial statements which seem to me to be original to Tolkien, to be ascribed to different characters, but which nevertheless point in the same direction. These proverbs are about ignorance, about not knowing things.

Gandalf starts it off by saying to Frodo, in the early chapter 'The Shadow of the Past,' "even the very wise cannot see all ends." Frodo remembers it (without the word 'very') when he decides what to do about Gollum in 'The Taming of Sméagol' (*LotR*, 58, 601). In between Gandalf has varied it, in 'The Council of Elrond,' by saying, "despair is only for those who see the end beyond all doubt" (*LotR*, 262). If even the very wise cannot see all ends, this implies that those who see the end beyond all doubt are not wise, which I am sure is what Gandalf again means. Legolas meanwhile says, on the edge of Fangorn, "Few can foresee whither their road will lead them, till they come to its end" (*LotR*, 481). He means, in context, that he and Aragorn and Gimli have just come round in a big circle, and could have reached Fangorn much more easily if they had left the Great River two weeks earlier and struck west: in other words, they have been wasting their time. He and Aragorn and Gimli are very close to despair at this point – Aragorn has been concerned about making the wrong decisions for some time, and as for Gimli, he has been consistently negative for days. Those who have seen the first edition will perhaps remember that there Aragorn eventually loses his temper, and says, when Gimli asks him why he has been looking in the *palantír* and talking to Sauron: "What do you fear that I should say to him: that I had a rascal of a rebel dwarf here that I would gladly exchange for a serviceable orc?"[13] Tolkien cut this out later, but I think he should have left it in – the tension between the two has been building up for a while.

The point is, though, that while Legolas uses this proverb to say they have been wasting their time, the proverb is right, but Legolas's application of it is wrong. Gandalf is just about to appear and tell them so. He points out that "between them our enemies have contrived only to bring Merry and Pippin with marvellous speed, and in the nick of time, to Fangorn, where otherwise they would never have come at all!" – and with fortunate consequences which at that point even Gandalf cannot foresee (*LotR*, 486). Gandalf says again, "Strange are the turns of fortune" (*LotR*, 571),[14] and Treebeard, "things will go as they will" (*LotR*, 571).[15] Returning to the idea of Saruman succeeding only in sending Merry and Pippin to quite unpredictably stir up Treebeard, Aragorn comments, but with reference to Sauron, "the hasty stroke goes oft astray" (*LotR*, 763). Gandalf agrees, saying "a traitor may betray himself," to which he adds the explanatory gloss, "and do good that he does not intend" (*LotR*, 797). He puts it more briskly and more gnomically with "Often does hatred hurt itself," and elsewhere, "a treacherous weapon is ever a danger to the hand" (*LotR*, 571, 486).

What these wise people are telling us, then, is first, 'you never know your luck,' and second, something along the lines of 'the other side has problems too.' The moral of it all is perfectly clear, and can be summed up

---

[13] See Hammond and Anderson (1993: 131).

[14] To which he adds, "Often does hatred hurt itself," echoing Théoden's "Oft evil will shall evil mar," cited above. The two sayings show two common features in traditional proverbial language: Gandalf's shows 'pararhyme' (more marked in speech than in spelling) in 'hate/hurt,' while Théoden opposes two phrases which look the same in length and stress, but are quite different grammatically. Adjective ('evil') + Noun ('will') as against Noun ('evil') + Verb ('mar'). There is a concealed grammatical clash also in "will shall." Proverbs, like hobbits, are trickier than they look.

[15] Echoed by Elrond, "The years will bring what they will" (*LotR*, 1034).

in three words said to me by a West Indian gentleman not far from where we are here in Aston some forty-three years ago, when I was feeling rather like Aragorn at his low point: 'Keep punching, fella.' It is perhaps going a bit far to say, 'and that is Tolkien's message in *The Lord of the Rings*,' but one could do worse. Let me just finish by saying how I would relate this particular vein of proverbiality to the structure and, once again, the 'ideology' of *The Lord of the Rings*.

Structure: this is a point which struck me forcibly while watching the recent movies. In the books, one thing is quite clear to me, which is that guiding your actions by what you see in a *palantír* is invariably disastrous for someone – for Saruman, for Sauron, for Denethor. What you see in the *palantír* is true, for the *palantír* does not lie, but it is normal to draw from it a wrong conclusion: as Sauron does, for instance, when he concludes first that Saruman has a hobbit, Pippin, and therefore has the Ring, and second, that Aragorn now has the Orthanc-stone, and therefore has both the hobbit and the Ring. This is what makes him launch a premature attack, "the hasty stroke goes oft astray" (*LotR*, 763), and even more crucially fail to concentrate efforts on guarding Mordor and the Sammath Naur. Looking in the *palantír* of Minas Tirith is furthermore what drives Denethor to despair, ignoring Gandalf's statement about despair quoted above. I have expressed elsewhere[16] my conviction that what Denethor sees in the Stone on March 13th must be Frodo in the hands of the Enemy, and would point out here only that this is surely confirmed by Denethor's words, not to Gandalf in 'The Pyre of Denethor' (when he says he has seen the Black Fleet approaching), but to Pippin two chapters before, "The Enemy has found it" (*LotR*, 805). Denethor has made the same mistake as Sauron, seeing a hobbit in the Stone and assuming that since the other side has a, or the, hobbit, it must also have the Ring. The underlying point also remains the same: to quote Galadriel's words about her Mirror, "The mirror is

---

[16] See Shippey (2004: 249-54), repeated with slight updates in Shippey (2005c: 423-9).

dangerous as a guide of deeds" (*LotR*, 354), and so is the *palantír*, for even with a *palantír* "even the wise cannot see all ends."

Without labouring the point too far, this is not the case in the movies, which use *palantírs* essentially as a communication device, on occasion quite helpful, most markedly in scene 8 of the third extended movie DVD, where Pippin is made to see into Sauron's mind and identify the place where his attack will come. I think this is caused by the very different narrative possibilities of books and movies.[17] What gets lost, however, is the point Tolkien keeps on making, which is that you must not guide your actions by what you *think* is happening to other people, or what you *think* they are doing, or going to do. You will only get it wrong, because (to repeat the saying yet again) "even the very wise cannot see all ends," and 'second-guessing' others may persuade you to forget your own duty, or to fall into despair. The last two volumes of *The Lord of the Rings* are a series of separate strands, or threads, all of them with different 'ends,' and no-one ever knows how one will affect another.

But in the end there is a pattern which is both just and fair, and I would add, is Providential. And that, I would say, is the 'ideological core' of *The Lord of the Rings*. It tells you how Providence works, and it works of course through people, lots of them with different capacities and different intentions. The intentions, good and bad, are woven together by some superior Power. This Power does not affect free will, indeed it demands free will, but it allows free-will actions to weave together, in ways which not even the wisest can foresee. It is the height of wisdom, then, to know the limits of wisdom.

---

[17] Tolkien seems to deny this by his remark (*Letters*, 270) that "The canons of narrative art in any medium cannot be wholly different." They can, however, be quite markedly different, and the difference has on the whole been increased by modern technology, of which Tolkien could have had no foreknowledge.

Perhaps I could end with five attempts at wise sayings from different characters, final truth lying somewhere between them all. First, Gríshnakh the Mordor-orc, who says (*LotR*, 445):

> "Little people should not meddle in affairs that are too big for them."

This is quite false. Let us try Aragorn, speaking again about 'ends' (*LotR*, 430):

> "there are some things that it is better to begin than to refuse, even though the end may be dark."

That seems closer to true 'proverbiousness.' However, we must not forget that there are no guarantees, and we should remember Treebeard (*LotR*, 475):

> "songs like trees bear fruit only in their own time and their own way; and some are withered untimely."

Galadriel says (*LotR*, 359):

> "Maybe the paths that you each shall tread are already laid before your feet, though you do not see them."

This seems rather predestinarian. Does it offer a challenge to the idea of free will? Perhaps we should note that while the paths may be laid, one of the things about roads and paths is that you do not have to go down them[18] – and of course, unlike rings, they do not just go round and round, but fork all the time, as is said in the hobbits' 'Old Walking Song,' which

---

[18] Though Gandalf says earlier, "one must tread the path that need chooses" (*LotR*, 289). Proverbs, like elves, say both yes and no (*LotR*, 83). But that is because they deal with difficult issues, and when used properly are context-sensitive.

furthermore repeats the idea that no-one can predict the future or the result of any decision. See, however, Aragorn just above. Finally, though, one thing I think is quite unqualifiedly correct comes from Celeborn, and returns me to what I said initially about survivor-genres (*LotR*, 365):

> "it may chance that old wives keep in memory word of
> things that once were needful for the wise to know."

Celeborn is absolutely right. Jacob Grimm would have agreed with him, Tolkien agreed with him, and I agree with him too. 'Survivor-genres' are important, and deserve much more attention than they have commonly received from scholarship.

Twigs and Branches

Minor Works by Tolkien

Tolkien and
'The Homecoming of Beorhtnoth'[1]

I would like to begin with a few words on Tolkien's scholarly reputation, as it now stands. At present scholarly reputations are often assessed in this way. They rest on your scores in the Humanities Research Citations Index. This Index gives you two scores, a primary and a secondary. Under the primary you have listed all your scholarly publications. Under the secondary, you have listed all the references which other people make in their scholarly publications to your scholarly publications. It is possible clearly to have a high primary score, but a low secondary score, if you publish a lot but no-one takes any notice of it. It is also possible to have a low primary score and a high secondary score: and this, I think, would now be the case with Tolkien. He had a relatively small number of scholarly publications in his own right, and these cease to appear rather early on in his career. On the other hand, people have referred to his publications in very large numbers. A final point, though, is that the secondary citations rest almost entirely on only two or three of those academic publications: these are the essays on '*Beowulf*: The Monsters and the Critics,' and the essay which is the subject of my talk today, 'The Homecoming of Beorhtnoth.' One might ask why some of Tolkien's other publications, like his essay on dialect in Chaucer's 'Reeve's Tale,' have received so little later attention. But that is a matter for another occasion (see further the piece on 'Tolkien's Academic Reputation Now' in this volume). What I want to talk about now is why the two papers I have mentioned have proved particularly important in later studies, and what the later one especially means for the study of Tolkien's own work.

---

[1] This piece first appeared in *Leaves from the Tree: J.R.R. Tolkien's Shorter Fiction* (London: Tolkien Society, 1991), 5-16, where it was the transcript of a talk given to the Tolkien Society in Beverley, Yorkshire. I have removed some of the features of oral delivery, and added references where required.

One initial point is that 'The Homecoming of Beorhtnoth' hardly looks like a scholarly publication. It appears in a scholarly journal, namely *Essays and Studies*. However, I do not know what the editor of *Essays and Studies* must have thought when the copy reached him. I myself was the editor of *Essays and Studies* for 1990, and if I had received a piece like 'The Homecoming of Beorhtnoth,' I would at the least have been highly embarrassed, for 'The Homecoming of Beorhtnoth' is not an academic paper, it is in very large part a poem. Tolkien knew this perfectly well, and indeed at the start of section three of the piece – i.e. the note which follows the long poem – he begins by confessing what he has done, and in a sort of way apologising for it. He says:

> This piece [...] was composed primarily as verse, to be condemned or approved as such. But to merit a place in *Essays and Studies* it must, I suppose, contain at least by implication criticism of the matter and manner of the Old English poem (or of its critics).
> ('Homecoming,' in *Reader*, 21)

You can see this is a sort of an apology. Tolkien knew he had not written an academic paper as you are supposed to. Nevertheless this piece has been one of Tolkien's most successful in attracting later academic citations.

What kind of a piece, then, is 'The Homecoming of Beorhtnoth'? I can give a one-word answer to this, though I may not be able to persuade anybody to accept it. It seems to me that 'The Homecoming of Beorhtnoth' is in the same genre as several of Tolkien's other works: namely, 'Leaf by Niggle,' 'Smith of Wootton Major,' and 'Farmer Giles of Ham.' These pieces have all been described as allegories, but that is not the word which I had in mind. It seems to me that all four are what I would call 'authorisations.' In them Tolkien is writing about something in order to give himself permission to write fantasy. This means that they are all really rather peculiar works. To go back to the word I used earlier, can they be considered as allegories? Well, I am sure that 'Leaf by Niggle' is an allegory. I am pretty sure that 'Smith of Wootton Major' is an allegory, if only because there are too many things hanging round loose in it (see 'Allegory versus Bounce' in this volume, but also Doughan 1991, Flieger 2001b). On one occasion I made out what I thought was an excellent case for 'Farmer Giles of Ham' being an allegory (in ch. 4 of successive editions of *The Road to Middle-earth*), but I could never quite persuade myself to believe it. 'Farmer Giles' looks very like an allegory, but one of the weak points in the whole thing is that when I constructed the allegory of it, I found myself missing out the character of the grey mare; and since Tolkien indicated the grey mare as the hero or heroine from early on in the story, that is a damaging admission. So while the first two pieces I mentioned may be considered allegories, I think probably 'Farmer Giles' is not an allegory, nor is 'The Homecoming of Beorhtnoth.' Nevertheless, whether these pieces are low down or high up on the allegorical scale I think the thing which they have in common is, as I said before, that they all provide 'authorisation.'

Another point which they have in common is that they all contain within them a discussion of the relationship between the real world and another world – another world very clearly seen. The other world is very clear in 'Smith of Wootton Major,' and also in 'Leaf by Niggle,' because in both cases the main character actually goes into it. In 'Farmer Giles,' it seems to me that the other world there is the world of fantasy from which the giant and the dragons come. The farmer meanwhile lives in the real world but goes into the dragons' world as well, and also returns from it. Now in 'The Homecoming of Beorhtnoth' the other world is not a place you can go into. Nevertheless you do have a contrast between the real world of the battlefield, with the corpses lying on it, and in the background a fantasy world which goes on in the head of one of the *characters*. The poem section of 'The Homecoming' is then in many respects a dialogue between characters in the real world and a character who much of the time inhabits a fantasy world. In that respect 'The Homecoming' is like the other three pieces I mention: all four create a dialogue between a real world and a fantasy world; all end up giving permission in a sort of a way to use fantasy; but in the process they all indicate a kind of argument *against using fantasy.*

In other words, I think Tolkien had to have a dialogue with himself about whether it was permissible or not to use fantasy, before he could launch himself into it. It also seems to me that as you look at these four works in what appears to be their order of composition – though Tolkien's habits of rewriting over long periods make this especially difficult to ascertain – they seem to show increasing insecurity and increasing doubt as to whether the activity which Tolkien himself was carrying on was legitimate. 'The Homecoming of Beorhtnoth' is well towards the doubtful or insecure or illegitimate end of that continuum. Nevertheless 'The Homecoming' remains an authorisation. It is an authorisation to be an author.

Turning to the poem itself, one thing that is very evident – though not so evident that some people haven't got it wrong – is that it is a dialogue between two characters, whose names are Torhthelm and Tídwald. Torhthelm means 'bright helmet.' Tídwald means 'ruler of time.' This latter has been translated as 'time forest.' I don't know what a time forest might be, but in any case I am sure that the second element of the name comes from the Anglo-Saxon verb, in its West Saxon form (which Tolkien habitually corrected to the monophthongal Mercian form), *wealdan*, to wield: so, if you prefer, 'wielder of time.' But whatever the names mean, Tídwald represents the realistic side of the dialogue, Torhthelm the fantasy side of it.

The next thing to say is that the fantasy side of the dialogue, Torhthelm the minstrel's son, has very little to recommend him. He is in fact systematically blackened all the way through the piece. One can say straight off that Torhthelm is (1) cowardly. He is too easily frightened. When he sees shapes moving across the battlefield, he assumes immediately that they are hell walkers, bogeys, barrow-wights, or something of the sort. But they aren't. They are just sneak-thieves coming along to pick up what they can. Torhthelm is too easily frightened then, and one might note that in another little scenelet a page or two later he suddenly realises that the Danes who have won the battle and gone away might possibly come back, and immediately shows signs of fear. Tídwald on the other hand feels he has just come to do his job and so gets on with it. So Torhthelm is cowardly. He is also very evidently (2) boastful. He boasts about what he may do when he comes to it, but because of the evidence of cowardice shown elsewhere you are meant to realise immediately that these boasts will be as undeserved and as improper as the ones which he criticises in other people.

A third thing you can say about him is that he is (3) murderous. In one scene he finds the body of his master Beorhtnoth, and picks up the golden-hilted sword which is mentioned in *The Battle of Maldon* as being dropped. He picks the sword up and takes it away with him. But when he discovers the corpse-robbers snooping round the battlefield he strikes one of them with the sword and kills him. Tídwald immediately reproves him and says:

> That blade was made for better uses.
> You wanted no weapon: a wallop on the nose,
> or a boot behind, and the battle's over
> with the likes of these. Their life's wretched,
> but why kill the creatures, or crow about it?
> There are dead enough around. Were he a Dane, mind you,
> I'd let you boast [...] (*Reader*, 14)

But Torhthelm is frightened of the Danes. He is good only for attacking scavengers, and the scavengers are actually English, so there is no reason to kill them at all except for disgust. Nor is there any need for him to do it with Beorhtnoth's sword. There is indeed something degrading for the golden-hilted sword which the hero has dropped on the battlefield to be picked up and used for this act, I repeat, of murder.

There are still other places where Tolkien seems to go out of his way to blacken the character of Torhthelm. One is set up in the little factual introduction which Tolkien wrote for the piece, in which he remarks that:

> The 'Danes' – they were on this occasion probably for the most part Norwegians – were, according to one version of the Anglo-Saxon Chronicle, led by Anlaf, famous in Norse saga and history as Olaf Tryggvason, later to become King of Norway. (*Reader*, 3)

This is picked up later on in the poem section when Torhthelm, replying to Tídwald's remark about things being bad for the poor, says:

> But Æthelred'll prove less easy prey
> than Wyrtgeorn was; and I'll wager, too,
> this Anlaf of Norway will never equal
> Hengest or Horsa! (*Reader*, 17)

These names need a little glossing. Wyrtgeorn is an Anglo-Saxon version of Vortigern, the king of the British at the time of the invasion of Anglo-Saxons. Hengest and Horsa are the people who overcame him. Torhthelm is saying that the English Æthelred will not give way to the Norse Anlaf in the way that the Welsh Vortigern gave way to the English Hengest. This statement needs considering for a moment. In 991, when the Battle of Maldon itself was fought, Æthelred had not been on the throne for very long and his inadequacies had not yet been exposed. By the time his reign came to an end, however, his nickname probably already was, as it has remained ever since, Æthelred 'the Unready.' He was in the end one of the very few English kings who have ever been deposed by popular disgust. Torhthelm's prophecy then is entirely wrong. Æthelred did indeed prove just as easy prey as Vortigern; and as for "this Anlaf of Norway," he became in the end, as Tolkien had noted in his introduction, the great hero king of Norway, Olaf Tryggvason. He was then at least equal to Hengest or Horsa, and the second part even of Torhthelm's prophecy is wrong. So you could say that not only is Torhthelm cowardly, boastful and murderous, he is also a poor prophet; and our awareness of this latter point has been deliberately set up by Tolkien. Well, I have a horror of using colloquialisms, but I find it hard to forbear one at this moment. I fear that Tolkien has, as they say, gone over the top. In this poem he is making a dead set at one character, and that character, one has to say, is simply a stooge.

What is Tolkien attacking through the character of Torhthelm? It seems to me that he is attacking Old English poetry in itself. Torhthelm in a sense represents the tradition of Old English poetry. He is mesmerised by words. On at least two occasions he breaks into a chant while he is actually talking to Tídwald, and the chant seems to be an improvised poem (see *Reader*, 11 and 12). Tídwald responds to these with interest and approval, but on other occasions shows scepticism. There is a striking scene when the two have loaded the corpse of Beorhtnoth into the cart, and Torhthelm says something to the effect that he would like to get some sleep. Tídwald says the only place to get any sleep is in the bottom of the cart with the body. And Torhthelm says angrily, "You're a brute, Tída." But Tídwald replies "It's only plain language." And then he says "If a poet sang you" – and he gives a quick burst of five lines of Old English poetry done in Torhthelm's own style – you wouldn't call it cruel, you'd accept it (*Reader*, 18). The gist of all this is that Torhthelm's mind is presented as in some sense addled by Old English poetry. He is unable to understand plain language or to see events plainly because Old English poetry has confused him. Why, one must wonder, should Tolkien launch this attack on the traditions of Old English poetry – this pointed, careful and knowledgeable attack? It is unprovoked, and there is no doubt about it.

The only answer I can give to that at the moment is that Tolkien felt that Old English poetry should be attacked because it had provided the motivation for Beorhtnoth. Just to recap on the events of the historical battle itself: the Essex levy had the Danes bottled up on an island in the river Blackwater. You can get off this island at low tide when the river ebbs across a sort of bridge, or causeway. The poem makes it clear that to begin with the Vikings could not get off the island because the tide was too high, but that when the tide ebbed they tried to fight their way off but were unsuccessful because the Essex levy had the causeway blocked. The poem then says that the Vikings asked Beorhtnoth personally to let them cross the causeway on to level ground to fight the battle on even terms. They asked in fact for *upgang*, 'passage to land.' And Beorhtnoth conceded this to them, pulling his men back presumably fifty or a hundred yards and letting the Vikings across to fight it out.

Then, of course, he lost. The Anglo-Saxons broke, and the poem then commemorates the stand of Beorhtnoth's companions around his body. What Tolkien is saying here is that Beorhtnoth's decision to give the Vikings *upgang* was a disastrous error. One may say that everybody's hindsight is always 20/20, but I agree that it was a mistake. The question is, what caused the disastrous error? Tolkien again inserts a scene into his poem to exemplify his answer to this. Torhthelm and Tídwald come with the body of Beorhtnoth to the bridge or causeway, and Torhthelm says how strange it is that they managed to force a passage across without fierce battle. But, he remarks, there is little sign of heavy casualties for the heathens here where one would expect to find them. Tídwald then gets a long speech saying "No, more's the pity." And then he says:

> Alas, my friend, our lord was at fault,
> [...]
> He let them cross the causeway, so keen was he
> to give minstrels matter for mighty songs.
> Needlessly noble. It should never have been
> [...] (*Reader*, 16)

Tídwald's view, then, is that Beorhtnoth let the Vikings cross because his mind, like Torhthelm's, had been addled by listening to minstrels. He let the Vikings cross "to give minstrels matter for mighty songs." There is no sign of this in the original poem. It is purely a hypothesis or speculation by Tolkien without evidence to support it. The Anglo-Saxon poem of *The Battle of Maldon* never says anything like that at all. Tolkien obviously knew that perfectly well. Indeed, one of the main points of his final section in 'The Homecoming' is to draw attention to the fact that the poem only says three words about Beorhtnoth's motivation. These are now famous lines, and frequently cited by critics. But before the publication of this piece by Tolkien they had hardly ever been commented on at all. Indeed, Tolkien drawing attention to these lines is one of the main reasons for his very high secondary citation rate in the Humanities Index.

The two lines to which Tolkien drew attention are lines 89-90 of the original poem, and there has been continuing dissension ever since about how they should be translated. I would translate them as follows: 'then the earl began in his pride to hand over too much land to the hateful people.' Tolkien comments on the phrase 'too much land,' saying that if you allow for Old English idiom, 'too much' means that none should have been given up at all. I think that's probably right. The poet means that Beorhtnoth should not have allowed the Vikings to cross at all. The other question is what does the word *ofermód* mean? There is no doubt that *ofer* means 'over', while *mód* means 'courage.' *Ofermód* could then be easily translated as 'too much courage.' But there are other translations. In other Germanic languages similar words can for instance mean 'arrogance.' *Mód* can also mean 'pride' and *ofermód* could then mean 'too much pride.' Tolkien translated it "overmastering pride." That I think is going too far, but the suggestion clearly is that Beorhtnoth has been taken over by desire to excel, by some kind of selfishness. Tolkien is saying that the motivation for Beorhtnoth's admittedly disastrous error is "overmastering pride," which Tolkien goes on to suggest is actually diabolical. In a damaging footnote he remarks that "In verse the noun occurs only twice, once applied to Beorhtnoth, and once to Lucifer" (*Reader*, 24).

Summing up, Tolkien's suggestion is that Beorhtnoth made his mistake out of diabolical pride; but that that diabolical pride was actually created by heroic tradition as expressed in Old English poetry.[2] Beorhtnoth

---

[2] Honegger 2007 shows in detail how Tolkien's critique of pride developed over the years, as far as can be seen from the fragmentary surviving drafts.

wanted to be a hero. He was prepared to sacrifice his own life for that. But he was also prepared to sacrifice the lives of the Essex levy. Tolkien's view was that he had no right to expend the lives of his men as well as his own. But since piety prevents one from criticising the dead in Beorhtnoth, Tolkien has created a character to represent the bad qualities of Old English poetry in Torhthelm: and the criticism which might be directed at Beorhtnoth is directed at Torhthelm instead.

There is a further strange point in this argument, seen in the word which Tolkien uses early on to describe Beorhtnoth's error. He calls it "This act of pride and misplaced chivalry" (*Reader*, 4). He goes on immediately to say that Beorhtnoth's household "containing the picked knights and officers of his bodyguard" fought on until they were all dead beside him. These two words, 'chivalry' and 'knights' are clearly anachronisms. *Cniht* in Old English simply means 'boy.' Its sense of 'armed rider' is a much later development. Meanwhile, 'chivalry' comes from the French word *chevalerie* and is connected with the word for horse. But what do the Anglo-Saxons do at the start of the battle of Maldon? What the Anglo-Saxons always do – send the horses to the rear! There is no chivalry in the poem. In fact there are no horses there either. So chivalry is an anachronism, like knight, and this again is something which Tolkien knew as well as I do. Why did he do this? He is ascribing to Beorhtnoth an attitude for which there is no evidence in England for perhaps another 150 years.

And there is another point which has not been commonly seen. Tolkien was attacking Old English poetry. He was also, in a sense, attacking his old colleague and collaborator, E.V. Gordon. Gordon and Tolkien had of course collaborated many years before on their edition of *Sir Gawain and the Green Knight*. They had then intended to continue a collaboration on an edition of *Pearl*, which eventually came out under the editorship of Gordon's widow. Tolkien and Gordon clearly had a close working relationship for many years (for which see Anderson 2003). Nevertheless one thing which Gordon did on his own was to produce an edition of the Old English poem *The Battle of Maldon*, in 1937. In a way, Tolkien seems to me in 'The Homecoming' to be presenting a veiled attack on the opinions expressed in this edition. Yet in other ways it is quite clear that he is relying on it. Tolkien's remark in his first footnote that Beorhtnoth was in reality 6 foot 9 inches tall is taken from Gordon. Later on he mentions – and again this is taken from Gordon – that when Beorhtnoth's body was discovered, it was headless. There is a good deal, then, of Gordon's edition within 'The Homecoming of Beorhtnoth,' and yet the main drive of Tolkien's piece is to say that Gordon is wrong: wrong in seeing this poem as the supreme example of "the northern heroic spirit" (*Reader*, 21). Tolkien did not agree with that. But why did he feel this need to attack Gordon, to criticise Beorhtnoth, to mount an assault on the traditions of Old English poetry, and to base the whole thing on evident speculation and quite conscious anachronism?

Perhaps we should go back to the question of what Old English poetry in particular has been addling the mind of the stooge Torhthelm. It is all too clear within Tolkien's poem that Torhthelm has been reading *Beowulf*. How can this be? Tolkien had every respect for *Beowulf*. He should not have thought that it would be a mind-addling experience for Torhthelm. One of the answers, perhaps, is that Torhthelm has been reading a bad edition of *Beowulf*. He says very early on:

> [...] It's like the dim shadow
> of heathen hell, in the hopeless kingdom
> where search is vain. (*Reader*, 8)

It's a good rule in reading Anglo-Saxon poetry to ignore most of the words and concentrate only on the ones which carry alliteration. Here they are, 'heathen,' 'hell' and 'hope.' Now these three words are found together in a line in *Beowulf*, line 179. But it is a line *which Tolkien thought was spurious*. Appendix C of his piece on 'The Monsters and the Critics' is actually about this section and makes it clear that Tolkien would like to have it removed from the poem.

Why did Tolkien think that? I think I can answer that question quite easily. It is centred on the word 'heathen.' One should note that 'heathen' is a word only used by Christians. If you are a heathen you don't call yourself a heathen, it is only Christians who call you one. It is a word which was obviously used in Anglo-Saxon very early on, from the time of their conversion. Nevertheless it is a word used with great reluctance in *Beowulf*. *Beowulf* is all about heathens. All the characters in *Beowulf* were heathens, they couldn't have been anything else, nobody had ever offered them the chance of conversion. But the *Beowulf* poet is very reluctant to use the word heathen of his heroes. Indeed he uses the word in the poem only six times. On one occasion all editors have assumed that it is a mistake and have deleted it – following what appears to be an attempt at deletion or emendation by the Anglo-Saxon scribe, who was, however, not the original poet. So that takes us down to five uses in the poem. Of these five uses two are applied to Grendel, and two to the dragon, i.e. to the monsters. The only time when the word 'heathen' is definitely used in *Beowulf* of human beings is in line 179, the line just mentioned, and that is why Tolkien thought it was spurious. He thought that the *Beowulf*-poet did not want to say that his ancestors were heathen. But though this word is used rarely in *Beowulf*, it is used freely in *The Battle of Maldon*. It is used freely also in 'The Homecoming of Beorhtnoth,' and in fact – and this may not be an accident – in this much shorter piece Tolkien in fact uses it six times. What this suggests, I think, is that Tolkien did not want, on this occasion, to take the same line as his predecessor, the *Beowulf*-poet. The latter was very reluctant to condemn human beings by calling them heathens, while both the *Maldon*-poet and Tolkien himself, by contrast, were quite prepared to do so. The mistake which Gordon made, in Tolkien's opinion, was to fail to see this distinction between two Old English poems. He saw *Maldon* as a poem celebrating 'the northern heroic spirit,' but that spirit was essentially a heathen one. Compromise between heathens and Christians might take place in *Beowulf*, which Tolkien thought was earlier than *Maldon*, but after three centuries of heathen-Christian warfare in Britain it could not exist in *Maldon*; and Tolkien himself was also about to reject the compromise. This rejection however meant in some way sacrificing a part of himself. Like his collaborator Gordon, he admired 'the northern heroic spirit,' yet he felt it was inevitably on the other side of a line of legitimacy. The compromise was no longer legitimate, it had to be expelled. But how was this to be done?

The main problem which Tolkien faced here is that the *Maldon* poem is a very clear example of one aspect of "the northern heroic spirit" which everyone has noticed ever since the poem was rediscovered in modern times. This poem is one of the few cases in northern literature, and the only one in Old English poetry, where you find a motif mentioned by the Roman writer Tacitus almost a thousand years earlier: namely, the motif of non-survival of a leader's death. According to Tacitus, once a Germanic leader had been killed it was a disgrace for his personal followers to survive the battle unless they had avenged him. But although he says this, there are not many surviving examples where this belief seems to have been honoured. In *Maldon*, however, there is no doubt that the English members of Beorhtnoth's bodyguard had a chance to surrender, to leave, to quit, but they refused to take it – just because, as the speeches in the poem indicate, they felt that it was wrong for them to survive the death of their lord. This then is a very clear example of 'the northern heroic spirit.' The most famous statement of this is made in lines which Tolkien again referred to within his passage of critical commentary. They are lines 312-13, and Tolkien called them "the best-known lines of the poem, possibly of all Old English verse." Nevertheless he did not like them, he felt that too much attention had been paid to them, he wanted to redirect critical attention from lines 312-13 to lines 89-90. Yet it was difficult for Tolkien absolutely to leave these lines out, while if they were allowed in they allowed a re-entry for the heroic spirit which Tolkien so clearly thought was heathen and now illegitimate.

What do you do when you have to mention something but you want to diminish its force? The answer to this is clearly known, and we all do it. You introduce the words but you *put them in inverted commas* to show they are not to be taken absolutely straight. This is what Tolkien does in 'The Homecoming of Beorhtnoth' with the critical lines taken from the speech of the old retainer, Beorhtwold. What happens is that Torhthelm uses the lines, but uses them *when he is asleep*. He falls asleep in the wagon which is taking him and the body of Beorhtnoth back. He speaks "drowsily and half-dreaming," and apparently looking forward into the future. As he goes on his voice "becomes louder, but it is still the voice of one speaking in a dream." And in this dream, still looking forward into the future, Torhthelm hears voices chanting:

> stern words they sing with strong voices.
> (*He chants*) Heart shall be bolder, harder be purpose,
> more proud the spirit as our power lessens!
> Mind shall not falter nor mood waver,
> though doom shall come and dark conquer.
> (*Reader*, 19)

And with that Torhthelm wakes up. Now the second and third lines of the quotation just given are genuine, and come from *Maldon*, where they are spoken by the retainer Beorhtwold refusing to surrender and preferring to die with his master. But in Tolkien's piece they have in some way been transferred from the past to the future. The heroic spirit, in fact, is still in 'The Homecoming of Beorhtnoth': but it has been taken out of the past, transferred forward to the future, and has also had added to it lines of a more ominous nature about doom coming and dark conquering – statements which are not in the original Old English *Maldon* at all.

It seems to me that Tolkien has ceased at this point to write historically and is instead considering contemporary issues. What he means is that the world of the future which Torhthelm foresees in his dream – that is to say, our world – has once more grown heathen. At the time of *The Battle of*

Maldon people like Tídwald thought that whatever happened on this particular day the Christians in the end would be victorious. The next thing you would hear would be the voice of the monks singing in Latin, while Christianity would overwhelm the Danes and the Scandinavians and the whole of the northern world. For a while, indeed, it seemed to be like that; but now the tide is turning, the world has grown heathen again, and the spirit which Tídwald thought had been conquered – a heathen and heroic spirit – had once more returned to trouble us. In Tolkien's view the poem of *The Battle of Maldon* was an attack on the northern heroic spirit which had led to Beorhtnoth's act of disastrous folly; but this had not been understood by modern critics like Gordon, who had preferred in a way to revive that heroic spirit by praising retainers like Beorhtwold instead of criticising leaders like Beorhtnoth. Tolkien thought that might have been acceptable as a merely scholarly error if the matter had not been revived and become dangerous again in the twentieth century.

Why had it been allowed to revive in this way? Perhaps because what was missing was a picture of Christian heroism. Old literature had given us pictures of heathen heroism and these pictures had proved insidious, too powerful, too successful, too seductive to many people in the past (like Beorhtnoth) and to more people in the present (like Gordon). I am sure that Tolkien was also thinking in a way of the resurgence of self-consciously Nordic or Germanic attitudes in Nazi Germany.[3] He felt that the heathen spirit of the Vikings and the berserks had come back in his own time, and had to be fought once more. To fight it, two things had to be done: one, an acceptable image of heroism had to be created; and two, Tolkien had to commit an act of parricide. He had in fact to take 'the northern heroic spirit' and sacrifice it. That was what he was doing in 'The Homecoming of

---

[3] This brings up again the issue of date of composition. Hammond and Anderson (1993: 303) show that a version of the poetic part of the piece was in existence before World War II, in the early 1930s, see also *Treason* 106-7. Tolkien's fears may not have been much assuaged by the victory of the Allies (see *Letters*, 64).

Beorhtnoth.' He was taking the Old English poem on *Maldon* and converting it into a dialogue. And in this dialogue there was no doubt about who was right and who was wrong. Tídwald and Christianity and lines 89-90 of the poem were in the right, and Torhthelm and Beorhtwold and lines 312-13 and the critics including Gordon were in the wrong. They had to be put incontrovertibly in the wrong over the heroic spirit in order to give Tolkien himself permission to write a work embodying a different and non-heathen version of that heroic spirit.

Underlying all this, I think, is deep insecurity on Tolkien's part about the propriety of a believing and committed Christian writing an enormous, three-volume work in which there is no mention of Christ at all. Is *The Lord of the Rings* a heathen work? No, it isn't. But if you looked at it carelessly you might think it was. I think Tolkien was disturbed about the relationship between the heroic spirit and the Christian spirit and wanted to perform an act of ceremonial sacrifice, as it were, before he could allow himself to go forward and do what he in fact did, which is in a sense to reconcile them. I would say then that not only is 'The Homecoming of Beorhtnoth' a work of authorisation, it seems to me also to be a work of insecurity. I do not know when it was finished, and may be wrong in suggesting that Tolkien wrote it, or rewrote it, in order to give himself permission to go on to *The Lord of the Rings*. He may well have written some of it, or rewritten the whole, after he had finished *The Lord of the Rings*, or at least after he had got the latter into all but final shape. So perhaps as well as being a work of authorisation one could say that it was also a work of apology – a work of apology, which allowed him to do what he had done already. But it was also a way of clearing up a doubt in his own mind, of sorting something out in his own head so that he could go further forward. At the end we could probably say that what 'The Homecoming of Beorhtnoth' tells us is that what Tolkien very much wanted to do was to create a new image of a heroic style. He knew there were old images, very powerful images, so powerful that they had taken over far too much of the modern mentality. Was it possible to create an alternative and Christianised image of a heroic style? That was the question. And Tolkien set himself to answer it to give a sequence of new images of heroism in characters like Aragorn and Théoden, not forgetting Sam Gamgee.

In this he was very successful. Few if any people have been able in this to imitate him. Part of the reason why Tolkien has not been successfully imitated, I think, is that his imitators have lacked the spiritual tension which we see in 'The Homecoming,' and which creates at once insecurity, apology and power. Tolkien was aware of an attitude which he found immensely seductive. He tried very hard to reject it. Yet at the same time he could not help feeling it and you can still see him feeling it as he writes. I would suggest then that Tolkien was trying in his work to reconcile a Christian attitude and a heroic attitude, and would have liked very much to feel that his ancestors in the past had tried to do the same thing. He saw the author of *Maldon* as doing what he himself had done. I myself think this is a mistake, resting on a highly personalised interpretation of *Maldon* (for which see Shippey 1985). Nevertheless I can see why Tolkien needed to believe it, and why the only way he could explain one poem was by himself writing another.

The Versions of 'The Hoard'[1]

In 1923 Tolkien published a poem in *The Gryphon*, the Leeds University journal, with the title 'Iumonna Gold Galdre Bewunden': this form of the poem is now most easily to be found on pp. 335-7 of the revised edition of Douglas Anderson's *The Annotated Hobbit* (2002). In 1937 he republished the poem, with the same title, but in a significantly different version, eight lines longer and with a great deal of internal rewriting, in the March issue of *The Oxford Magazine* (vol. 55, no. 15, p. 473). Twenty-five years later this second version of the poem, with a few minor changes, was to be republished in *The Adventures of Tom Bombadil*, as 'The Hoard.' And in 1970 the same poem reappeared under the same title in Roger Lancelyn Green's *Hamish Hamilton Book of Dragons*, this time with only one change, an obvious typo (if a particularly bad one). We have in other words effectively two versions of one poem, with two different titles, the second version reprinted three times; but, rather confusingly, the three reprintings of the second version have two different titles, while the first version and the first printing of the second version have the same title.

With bibliographical confusions out of the way, one may ask what the poem, the rewritings, and the retitlings, have to tell us about Tolkien.

Beginning with the poem, its structure and its point remain much the same all the way through. It follows the progress of a hoard of gold and jewels: laid down by the elves, acquired by a dwarf, seized by a dragon who kills the dwarf, seized by a warrior who kills the dragon, lost forever when the human owner is killed by his enemies. The unhappy fate of the owners seems however to be caused by the hoard itself. In all versions the second, third and fourth stanzas begin, "There was an old dwarf/dragon/king," while the fifth begins "There is an old hoard." The old dragon was however

---

[1] This was first published in *Lembas* 100 (2001): 3-7. As always, I thank the editor and members of Unquendor for permission to reprint. The piece was translated into Spanish as 'Las Versiones de "El Tesoro".' *Mae Govannen* 2-3 (2002): 8-11.

a young one at the end of stanza 2, the old king a young warrior at the end of stanza 3. They have grown old in possession of the hoard, and the hoard has turned them into misers, obsessives, lonely, deaf to the noise of approaching danger, their death regretted by none. The story resembles the folk-tale of the men who went out to find Death, but found gold instead (not realising that gold = Death), which Chaucer told in his 'Pardoner's Tale,' and which is told in different and rather more Tolkienian form by Kipling as 'The King's Ankus' in *The Second Jungle Book* (1895). Its theme is important in *The Hobbit*, where Smaug resembles the dragon of stanza 3, but where Thorin also comes under the "bewilderment" of the hoard, which betrays him into injustice and almost into treachery, and the Master of Laketown also succumbs to the "dragon-sickness" and absconds with stolen gold, only to die of starvation in the Waste (*Hobbit*, 248, 272).

Tolkien however had a clearer source for the idea of 'dragon-sickness,' which is signalled by the original title, 'Iumonna Gold Galdre Bewunden.' This means 'the gold of men of former time (*iu-monna*) wound round (*bewunden*) with spell (*galdre*, dative form of *galdor*).' The language is Old English, and the four words form line 3052 of the poem *Beowulf*. There the gold belongs to a dragon: he has no name in the poem, but he is called *stearc-heort*, and I shall refer to him as Stark-heart. Stark-heart is killed by Beowulf, and his hoard rifled, corresponding in a way to the action of stanza 3 of the poem.

But where did Stark-heart get the hoard from? According to *Beowulf*, the hoard was once the property of 'the men of old,' one of whom, last of his race, hid it in the earth – at least, he definitely told the earth to hold it. But having made the speech which begins, 'Hold earth, now heroes cannot, the treasure of earls [...],' this Last Survivor very oddly leaves the treasure to be found standing open (*opene standan*) by Stark-heart (line 2271). This seems very strange. Anyone hiding a treasure surely knows that the important thing, having dug the hole and deposited the treasure, is to *fill the hole in again*! Not leave it standing open. The thought has accordingly occurred to many readers of *Beowulf*, who remember the motif in Scandinavian stories of warriors 'lying down on their gold and turning into dragons,' that maybe this is what was meant to have happened in *Beowulf* too. The Last Survivor, a man, put his treasure in a barrow, lay down on it himself, and became the dragon. That is 'dragon-sickness' for you. It is something which comes from gold, and from greed, and which in time will turn the most gallant of warriors into an old miser, or maybe even an old dragon.

This does not happen to Beowulf, for Beowulf is killed fighting the dragon. But perhaps it was starting to happen. As he lies dying, Beowulf asks his relative and follower Wiglaf to bring the gold out so that he can look at it and die easier. After he is dead, Wiglaf says that everyone tried to dissuade him from fighting the dragon, but he would not listen. Wiglaf also refuses to have anything to do with the hoard, and orders it to be burned with Beowulf, so that in the end what is left lies in the ground 'as useless to men as it was before' (*eldum swa unnyt swa hit ǣror wæs*, line 3168).

What then is the spell (*galdor*) with which the gold was wound round (*bewunden*)? If it was meant to protect the hoard, it doesn't seem to have worked: the dragon took it, Beowulf took it. But maybe it did work – if, that is, it was meant not to prevent the hoard from being rifled but to bring disaster on those who rifled it. There is another passage in the poem, just a few lines after Tolkien's title-line (3069-75) which says something about this, though it is very hard to understand. The gist of it is that the men of old who owned the hoard did indeed put a curse on whoever disturbed it; but the last two lines seem to be putting forward some kind of qualification, as if trying, uneasily and uncertainly, to exempt Beowulf himself from its effects.

The one line in the Old English epic which Tolkien took as his title, with its associated puzzles and problems, accordingly seems to provide many of the elements of his own poem's theme: change of ownership, transformation of the owner, 'dragon-sickness,' an inescapable (?) curse. One might even say that Wiglaf's determined rejection of the gold, in

Beowulf, provides a vital element in the basic plot of *The Lord of the Rings*: something which could apparently be used for good (the hoard, the Ring) nevertheless has to be rejected because of what it will do to the user. Certainly Tolkien never forgot the line and the scenario. In *The Hobbit* the dwarves bury the trolls' gold, but put spells over it to keep it safe; as has been said, Smaug, Thorin and the Master of Laketown are all smitten with 'dragon-sickness'; at the start of *The Two Towers* Aragorn says that Pippin and Merry's swords, taken from the wight's barrow, are "wound about with spells" for the defeat of Mordor (*LotR*, 405), as of course will be highly significant later on.

The first title for this poem, then, was a good one. Why did Tolkien change it? One can guess that it seemed too recondite for the wider audience of *The Adventures of Tom Bombadil*. But having dealt with the poem's theme, and its retitlings, one may ask what the rewritings have to tell us, especially the major rewriting of 1937.

I will begin by saying that, since the 1962 version of the poem in *The Adventures of Tom Bombadil* is the one most people are likely to have, I will use that as the base-text, and signal only changes from it. To put it briefly, the relatively minor differences between 1937 and 1962 are that in the former, line 7 has 'Elves' without a capital; line 10 lacks the first word, "and"; line 29 ends with a semi-colon not a full-stop; line 37 begins with "with," not "in"; line 60 begins with "whose," not "its"; and the last two lines, 75-6, are completely rewritten: in the 1937 version it is the earth that keeps the secret, not the night, see further below. Meanwhile, the 1970 version is the same as the 1962 one, with the exception of the rather disastrous typo in line 64 of "fold" for "gold." Tolkien had kept that line very much the same from 1923, but it did not survive the Roger Lancelyn Green printing. (With his experience of printers, it is not surprising that Tolkien was a daring emender of old texts like *Exodus*. He knew that accurate copying was the exception rather than the rule.)

Turning to the much larger differences between the 1923 version (which I shall call 'G' for Gryphon) and all others (from now on, 'AO'), the main one is that G has 68 lines, divided into five stanzas of 12/14/16/16 and 10 lines, while AO have 76, divided 16/16/20/16 and 8. I consider them now one stanza at a time.

Stanza 1: AO's 16 lines can be divided 4/6/6. In the first 4 lines, "the gods" seed the earth with silver and gold; in the next 6 the elves make treasures from the metal, in a time before the breeding of the dwarves; in the last 6 doom and the shadow come upon them. This stanza can be fitted into Tolkien's already (by 1937) developed mythology. The "gods" are the Valar, the time when sun and moon are new must be after the destruction of the Two Trees, and the elves making treasures in the green hills could well be the sons of Fëanor in their new realm of Eriador. Readers could be forgiven, however, for not understanding what happens to them, or how the treasures pass from the elves to the dwarf who possesses them in the next stanza. The elves have been cut down by "iron" and manacled by "steel," but the only agent identified is the abstraction "Greed," which could stand for anyone or anything: dragons, dwarves, agents of Melkor. The most relevant story in *The Silmarillion* is perhaps the tale of elf vs. dwarf warfare in chapter 22, in which dwarves steal the treasure of Thingol – though since they are later intercepted by Beren and the plunder is taken back, poem and narrative do not completely match.

G meanwhile divides this stanza 6/2/4. There is no mention of "the gods." The poem begins with the elves singing as they work their gold (in fact lines 1-2 of G are substantially the same as 7-8 of AO. G and AO 5-6 also express substantially the same idea). G 7-8 are slightly perfunctory: the lines say only that there were men who learned from the elves, though these men play no further part in the poem. The last four lines of both versions make it no clearer who or what it is that takes off the treasures to its "holes."

Stanza 2: In AO this divides 6/4/6. The old dwarf works in his cave; age begins to overpower him; he does not hear the "young dragon" coming. In G the division is 4/4/6. The first 4 lines make it much clearer that the dwarf's gold has been "stolen from men and elves." The middle 4 lines are generally similar in both versions. The last 6 lines at least tell the same story, though with considerable change of emphasis: G is more concerned to point the moral, that the dwarf is betrayed by his own obsession with what he stole, "His hope was in gold and in jewels his trust," so that he seems to be punished by the dragon for his crime against men and elves. In AO these lines are more laconic and non-committal.

Stanza 3: I would divide this stanza in AO 10/4/6. The first ten lines concentrate on the dragon, old, bent, wrinkled and losing his fire, very aware however of every single item he possesses. Lines 11-14 tell us of his fear and hatred of thieves. Lines 15-20 have the dragon, like the dwarf, not hearing the challenger who comes for his hoard. G is less easy to divide. The first 12 lines lead on more seamlessly from the image of the old dragon to the hatred of thieves; once again the moral is rather more pointed, with explicit comment on the dragon's smouldering "lust" for gold and his lack of "ruth." One feature which both versions share with *Beowulf* is that the challenger shouts to bring the dragon out of his den. On the other hand, unlike *Beowulf*, the warrior is young, is not deserted by his comrades, is not killed in the fight, and finally is motivated entirely by desire for the hoard, not by retaliation and the need to protect his people.

Stanza 4: This stanza is very much the same in G and AO. All the rhyme-words, for instance, are identical. There is however a run of verbal changes within the lines, as for instance in line 8, where G "mighty" becomes AO "strong," or line 10, G "tarnished" AO "fallen." In line 12 G "elfin" becomes AO "elvish": one sees Tolkien becoming more particular about the philology of his myth-making ('elfin,' or worse, 'elphin,' being non-medieval and historically incorrect forms). One other point of difference is that AO has become markedly shorter in line lengths than G, by the cutting out of words like "was" and "and." In AO also the last two lines of each of the middle three stanzas are almost completely monosyllabic and paratactic (i.e. connected only by "and" or "but"). G uses longer words, longer lines, and (twice) the connective "Yet." The effect created in AO is much more abrupt, marking the contrast between the riches hoarded and fought for and the careless discarding of their owners.

Stanza 5: The irony in stanza 4 is of course that the old king dies without telling anyone where his hoard has been hidden, so that this time it is not passed on. In stanza 5 G and AO differ again, G for once being longer, ten lines as against eight. G is also more optimistic and more cyclical. In AO the hoard waits in the mound, and will do so as long as the elves "sleep"; there is no hint of how long this will be or indeed whether there will be an awakening. In G the last four lines imagine a triumphant return, when the makers of the treasures come back, "The lights of Faery" burn again, "And songs long silent once more awake." The last word of G is, thus, "awake," while in the 1962 and 1970 versions it is "sleep." In the 1937 version, however, the change is less pronounced, for though the last rhyme-pair uses the same words, they are in reverse order from 1962/1970. 1937 reads, "While gods wait and the elves sleep, / its old secret shall the earth keep," while 1962/1970 have, "The old hoard the Night shall keep, / while earth waits and the Elves sleep." In 1962 and 1970, also, the "gods" have been eliminated. In 1937 it is the gods who wait and the earth that keeps the secret; in 1962/1970 it is the earth that waits and the night that keeps the secret.

Comparing the two versions closely brings out one further point, which is that, as so often, the metrical scheme of all versions of this poem is more complex than it appears. The poem is written in rhyming couplets, and at first glance one might think it is in iambic pentameter, the most common of English metres. But actually it is not in pentameters. Line lengths vary in AO from 6 to 10 syllables (11 in G), but the most common line-length is 9 syllables, followed in frequency by 8. Nine syllable lines are not usual in modern English poetry, especially as Tolkien here never uses 'feminine' rhyme, i.e. rhyme which operates on the last two syllables, as with 'tower/power' or 'nation/station.' It is probably a better description of the metre of this poem to say that (as with Old English poetry) each line consists of two half-lines, with a strongly marked break or caesura, each half-line consisting of four or five syllables (rarely, three), but each half-line also containing two strong stresses, often in consecutive syllables. It is in short based on counting stresses rather than syllables, and is in that way more like the native tradition of poetry than the tradition learned from French.

The advantages of this mode are: (1) greater flexibility and (2) greater concision. It is clear, if one compares the versions, that Tolkien worked deliberately to heighten the latter effect. The whole poem is quite unusually monosyllabic – AO contain only three rhyme-words which are not monosyllables, "unseen," "unjust," and "unlock," while G has seven. Just to complete the parallel with Old English, the 'un-' prefix in the three cases in AO would be regarded in Old English metrics as an 'anacrusis,' i.e. one of the small group of prefixes allowed under some circumstances 'not to count' metrically. Tolkien was writing an Old English theme with an Old English vocabulary, and something quite close to Old English metre, as if to show it could still be done.

Tolkien's rewritings of his early poems have several times seemed significant, to me and to other critics: I have commented for instance on the careful rewritings of 'Firiel' (1934) as 'The Last Ship' in *The Adventures of Tom Bombadil*, of 'Looney' (1934) as 'The Sea-bell' in the same collection, of 'Light as Leaf on Lindentree' (1925) as Aragorn's song of Beren in *The Fellowship of the Ring* (see Shippey 2003a: 281-5, 194-5). The rewritings of 'Iumonna Gold' seem to me to be of similar kind. Characteristic is the change of the last word from "awake" to its opposite "sleep" – compare the shift of the word "sorrowless" from the end of the penultimate stanza in 'Light as Leaf' to the very last word of the poem in Aragorn's song.

Tolkien's deep interest in metre, and his wish to revive lost native traditions which he regarded as better suited to the essential nature of the language than modern forms, are also visible. At the same time one can see how much better than G, in several respects, is the text of AO, and how Tolkien continued to improve the text of 1937 even in 1962.

One other entirely characteristic feature is the way in which Tolkien's imagination was triggered by a textual problem, or set of problems, already seen by many scholars, but treated by them as a textual problem alone, not one which also had both a mythical explanation (a man turning into a dragon) and a real-world meaning ('dragon-sickness' as a disease of ownership). A final conclusion one might draw is that while Tolkien always remained strongly faithful to his original conceptions, he also had the capacity to continue refining them in narrative and in poetry, as in this case for at least forty years.

Allegory versus Bounce: (Half of) an Exchange on *Smith of Wootton Major*[1]

My comments take off from the statement made by Roger Lancelyn Green in a review of *Smith* shortly after its publication – a statement endorsed by Tolkien and quoted with approval by Dr Flieger, and others.[2] Dr Flieger's paraphrase of Green runs as follows:

> Green observed that the effect of the story transcends any explicit reference and warned against looking too hard for a specific message. He wrote of it that "To seek for the meaning is to cut open the ball in search of its bounce." This may prove to be the best summation of the story's appeal. The bounce is clearly there, but to search for it is to defeat its effect; to allegorize it is to deaden the bounce completely. (Flieger 1997: 233)

I accept Flieger's paraphrase, but I reject Green's metaphor. More important, if 'the bounce' here is 'whatever it is that makes reading the story pleasurable,' then I can testify that as far as I am concerned Flieger's last phrase, "to allegorize it is to deaden the bounce completely," is not true of my experience at all. Much of the pleasure I take in the story comes from searching out allegory. This does not go away, but increases with re-reading, and re-searching. Green's metaphor, to use another metaphor, seems to me like saying 'put that ball on the mantelpiece, and for goodness' sake

---

[1] This piece began as a public debate between myself and Verlyn Flieger, at the International Society for the Fantastic in the Arts conference at Fort Lauderdale, Florida, on 22 March 2001. Our remarks were then published in *Journal for the Fantastic in the Arts* 12/2 (2001): 186-200, with my section running 191-200. Dr Flieger and I got quite different results from the same work, and the idea was to see why. My thanks go to Bill Senior, editor of *JFA*, for allowing reprint, and to Dr Flieger for generously accepting one more one-sided view.

[2] See Flieger (1997: 233) and Doughan (1991: 17).

don't bounce it, it will break!' But it doesn't break – or not when I bounce it.

I have no wish, accordingly, to try to confute Dr Flieger's reading, but I do have to record that my experience is not hers. We are clearly reading the same text (and I do not believe that either of us has much patience with mystical notions that there is no such thing as 'the same text'), but we are not reading it the same way. Is this the result of different initial presuppositions? Different areas of knowledge? Or perhaps we are reading it differently on a purely mechanical level, in the way our eyes move and we take in words?

I begin with a simple possibility: perhaps we have different views about allegory. What is an 'allegory'? This question, like almost all matters of definition, has been put to the Four Wise Men of Oxenford,[3] and as with 'blunderbuss' their answer is not especially helpful: the core of it runs "a figurative narrative [...] in which properties and circumstances attributed to the apparent subject really refer to the subject they are meant to suggest," a definition which leaves one wondering about words like 'really' and 'meant.'[4] I find it more useful to look at Tolkien's own theory and practice, and these are on the face of it incompatible. Tolkien wrote, for instance, "I cordially dislike allegory in all its manifestations, and always have done so since I grew old and wary enough to detect its presence."[5] I hesitate to say that this is not true (as stated above, you cannot tell people what they like or dislike), but the fact is that Tolkien was something of a serial allegorist. Much of the force of the opening of his famous lecture '*Beowulf*: The

---

[3] I refer here to Tolkien's joke about the word "blunderbuss," in *Farmer Giles of Ham* (*Reader*, 131). To him "the Four Wise Clerks of Oxenford" were the editors of *The Oxford English Dictionary* (see Kocher 1974: 161). There are more than four of them now, of course.

[4] See *The Oxford English Dictionary*, eds. J. Simpson and E.S.C. Weiner, 2nd ed. 1989: I, 333. The entry is substantially the same as that of the first edition (then *The New English Dictionary*) of 1884 onwards, I, 232.

[5] 'Foreword' to 2nd edition of *The Lord of the Rings* (xvii). Tolkien's remark, of course, is meant as a reply to a thoroughly shallow and unconvincing form of allegorisation.

Monsters and the Critics' comes from three short allegories in sequence: *Beowulf* seen as a child to whose christening one fairy (Poësis) has not been invited; the criticism of *Beowulf* viewed as a Babel of tongues; and most important and most extensive, the allegory of *Beowulf* as a tower. Tolkien explicitly identifies this long paragraph as "yet another allegory," and says at the end of it, "I hope I shall show that that allegory is just" (*Essays*, 7-8).

The idea of 'just-ness' seems to me important, and perhaps explains the contradiction indicated above. In Tolkien's view, allegory is essentially a set of equations. Each item in the surface narrative has to correspond to an item in the unstated meaning, and those items have to fit together in closely similar ways. It was this view that led him to reject the idea that *The Lord of the Rings* was an allegory of World War II (with the Ring implicitly as atomic power). If this had been the case, he pointed out in a scornful paragraph in the 'Foreword' already cited, the Ring would not have been destroyed, it would have been used; Saruman would have been enabled to make his own Ring; and so on. Amateur allegorists of his work, Tolkien felt, did not know their own business. Their allegory was not 'just.' By contrast, though, Tolkien in the *Beowulf* lecture did know his own business. Every item in the 'tower' allegory makes perfect sense if translated into the world of *Beowulf*-criticism, and so (I believe) does every item in the 'Babel' allegory.[6] The point of the allegories is also perfectly clear. They function as *reductio ad absurdum*: the image of the busy critics destroying the tower, then complaining what a mess it is in, and saying it was a silly idea to build it anyway, is evidently absurd, but bears a strong resemblance to what German critics of the poem actually did. They did not think what they did was absurd, but Tolkien's allegory tries to persuade one that it was.

---

[6] For an interpretation of the 'tower' allegory, see Shippey (2003a: 46-7). (I regret to say that in both earlier editions of this work there is a critical misprint – the "man's own descendants" question should read, "Why did not he restore the old house?") The 'Babel' allegory has never been explained in detail, though most of the evidence for such an explanation is to be found in Shippey and Haarder 1998. See also Drout (2002: 151, 255).

Allegory used this way, one can see, is a simplifying and argumentative mode.

This has made it unpopular in modern critical terms. Nowadays what is valued is complexity, diversity, dialogism, multiple meanings, freedom to interpret the inexhaustible text (etc.); and allegory, with its one-to-one correspondences and its strict discipline, is viewed as limited and pedantic. In the 'Foreword' already mentioned, Tolkien opposes it to 'applicability,' notes that many confuse the two, and expresses the distinction as "the one [applicability] resides in the freedom of the reader, and the other [allegory] in the purposed domination of the author" (*LotR*, xvii). It would be possible for me to avoid contradicting Tolkien by saying that I seek only for 'applicability' in *Smith*, not 'allegory.' But I would point out, first, that there is an extensive scale between perfect freedom and perfect domination; and second, that several major works of English literature (including ones which Tolkien respected, and ones he probably did not) are commonly taken to be allegories, which demand interpretation and will not work without it, but where the "domination of the author" has certainly not led to a final, deadened solution. I mean works like Langland's *Piers Plowman*, Spenser's *Faerie Queene*, Bunyan's *Pilgrim's Progress*, but, perhaps most strikingly in modern times, also Orwell's *Animal Farm*. It would be an extremely unambitious and unproductive procedure to read any of the three just mentioned 'just for the story,' though I can imagine there are some people who do so. Children, for instance, might read the Orwell story just as a sort of joke, though even they, I think, would feel some sense of fear, some awareness that this story is not just about animals. But in such cases the story, the attractive surface narrative, is there partly though not entirely to provoke a quest for a further meaning, clearly intended and sometimes indicated by the author; and no-one suggests that this quest should be abandoned, for fear of losing a hypothetical 'bounce.'[7] It is in this category of allegorical work that I would put *Smith*.

There are then two points that I would add. One is that I would put 'Leaf by Niggle' in the same, or a similar category. I think this is quite clearly an allegory, and an autobiographical one, and one of the signs of this is the work's extreme 'just-ness.' Many of the details in it, just as with Tolkien's allegory of the tower, can be given one-to-one correspondences with reality (in my view, Niggle's house, garden, paintings, potatoes, shed, journey, temperament, and much else). These details (rightly interpreted) make the story both funnier and more threatening – in my view, they add to the bounce.[8] But the second point is that, obviously with *The Faerie Queene* and even with the much shorter and clearer 'Leaf by Niggle,' no-one is ever going to catch every detail. Probably the authors themselves could not have done so. Allegories of an extended kind have a habit of getting away from their authors, as the surface narrative imposes its own logic. They are also clearly used by many authors (Langland and Bunyan prominent among them) as a way of trying to understand their own feelings and their own situation, as an investigative mode as well as an explanatory one. In only the shortest and simplest allegories does the author 'dominate' the reader (as Tolkien said) or even (and this is my addition) his/her own text. The advantage of all this is that it is quite possible to read an extended allegory, like *Smith*, or 'Leaf by Niggle,' or *Piers Plowman*, and find something new every time – but still something allegorical. Like tennis balls, they bounce higher the more you warm them up, and the way you warm them up is by playing with them.

---

[7] Quite a lot of people might like to argue that the quest should be turned in some other direction. The rather obvious equations of *Animal Farm* (old Major as Marx, Snowball as Trotsky, Napoleon as Stalin, Moses the raven as the clergy) have been repeatedly denied, usually by Marxists, Trotskyites, Stalinists, or their sympathizers. It is true that one wonders what happened to Lenin.

[8] For my reading of this story, see Shippey (2000a: 266-77). The reading there contains significant additions of detail to the original theory as advanced in Shippey (1982: 34-5 and 1992: 40-1).

To abandon metaphor and turn to reading *Smith*, it seems to me that my readings of the story depend on identifying details. It is amazing how easy these are to miss. Thus (and I owe the following identifications to Dr Flieger, who has had the advantage of reading Tolkien's own commentary on his text, from which I now quote): "The Great Hall is evidently in a way an 'allegory' of the village church; the Master Cook [...] is plainly the Parson and the priesthood." Cooking meanwhile equates to "personal religion and prayer" (Flieger 1997: 232). Tolkien here uses the words 'evidently' and 'plainly,' but I do not think I made these equations on first or even later reading. What the account of the Great Hall and its festivities told me was that I was reading an allegory of some kind: social behaviour in Wootton Major was too far removed from real-life behaviour at any period of English history for me to accept it as just surface narrative. However, once the equations between Hall and church, etc., have been made, several other details take on meaning. Rather late on in the tale, for instance, we are told that once Alf takes over as Master Cook from Nokes, the Hall was "re-glazed and re-painted." Some called this "new-fangled," but "some with more knowledge knew that it was a return to old custom" (*Smith*, 46). It is important to note that these sentences have no further narrative point. It makes no difference to the rest of the story what the Hall looks like. This rather extensive description is 'narratively redundant.' In an allegory, though, what is narratively redundant is likely to be allegorically especially significant. Here it seems to me that Tolkien is expressing approval of changes in church fashion in his own day, away from the careful sobriety, the 'Sunday suit' style of Victorian devotion, and towards a more cheerful and more dramatic attitude to worship, seen by many as disrespectful and modernistic, but by Tolkien as a return to the medieval integration of religion with everyday life and with imaginative richness (as in the carving and painting of gargoyles, which he mentions particularly).

The Hall/church identification may make one wonder, further, about the place Smith lives, Wootton Major. Why Wootton? Why Major? Here I agree with Dr Flieger that Wootton means, philologically, 'Wood-town,' the town in the wood; and the wood is a highly significant image. Dr Flieger suggests that woods are gateways to the other world, as in Dante, and this is so (Flieger 1997: 250). To it I would add that woods are for Tolkien ambiguous places (a point forcefully made in Flieger 2001a). He loved them as much as anyone, but he also saw them as places where travellers easily become confused, 'bewildered,' lose sight of the stars, lose their (physical and moral) bearings. They represent the world of reality, the mundane world, because in them it is so easy to forget that there is a world outside them, and to despair. Smith, of course, is above all the character with an available exit from Wootton, or the wood of the world, into Faërie. Meanwhile, why Major? Does the story need a Minor? In view of Tolkien's Catholicism, it is tempting to see the Church of Wootton Major as the Catholic Church, with Wootton Minor perhaps as its Anglican offshoot. An interesting detail here is that Nokes, not liked and not accepted as an apprentice by the previous Master Cook (so outside the 'apostolic succession,' so to speak) is "a solid sort of man with a wife and children" (*Smith*, 10). If he is 'plainly' a parson, then, as Tolkien declared, he must be a Protestant one. Possibly the Major/Minor suggestion made just above is the wrong way round – as in purely English terms would be the case.[9]

The question of names is especially relevant to allegory because, in normal life, names do not mean anything: surnames especially, as we all know, are not chosen but come by accident of birth; most people do not in fact know what their names 'mean' (i.e., what they used to mean long ago, before they became just names). In a story, though, the author chooses the names. In realistic stories they will be chosen to sound random, as in reality. In an allegory they are likely once again to have strong suggestion. Here, and speaking entirely for myself, I cannot get over the choice of the

---

[9] In Tolkien's lifetime Catholics were a minority in England as against Protestants and especially Anglicans. This balance has been steadily changing.

name 'Nokes.' There is a Noakes in *The Lord of the Rings*, "Old Noakes of Bywater," and in his 'Guide to the Names in *The Lord of the Rings*' Tolkien noted the derivation from Middle English *atten oke(s)*, 'at the oak(s),' and added, for the benefit of his translators, "since this is no longer recognized, this need not be considered. The name is in the tale unimportant" ('Guide,' 170). It is just a label, in other words, like most names; but that is in *The Lord of the Rings*, which is not an allegory, and which has hundreds of names without narrative meaning.

What I cannot forget, reading *Smith*, is that for Tolkien 'oak' had a clear private meaning, several times recalled.[10] 'Oak' in Old English is *ác*, and it is also the name for the rune representing 'A'. The name for 'B' in the Old English runic alphabet is *beorc*, or 'birch.' In the syllabus Tolkien devised at Leeds University, and which he tried with limited success to transplant to Oxford,[11] the 'B-scheme' was the one he controlled, the language-and-medieval scheme of study, and the 'A-scheme' was the one controlled by his colleague the Professor of Literature. These two schemes existed on terms of strong mutual ideological hostility, which it would take many pages to explain. I can only say here that to me (the inheritor of many of Tolkien's feuds), Alf Prentice's sharp rebuke to Nokes almost at the end has many resonances. "You are a vain old fraud," he says, "fat, idle, and sly. I did most of your work. Without thanks you learned all that you could from me except respect for Faery, and a little courtesy" (*Smith*, 57). Ignoring the first sentence, which is just rude, the next two seem to me to represent reasonably well the relationship between philology (the 'B-scheme') and literary studies (the 'A-scheme' represented by Nokes): English departments in universities were established by philologists, who created a discipline of vernacular literary study, and were then ungratefully

---

[10] It is most obvious in the Old English poem called 'Eadig Beo Thu!' in *Songs for the Philologists*, 13, translated Shippey (2003a: 355-6).

[11] See Tolkien, 'OES.' More than seventy years later, there is some doubt as to how far Tolkien did or did not succeed at Oxford. At Leeds, the 'B-scheme' survived till 1983.

pushed aside by critics who, notoriously, had no time for fantasy, or Faery, whether medieval or modern. If Tolkien did not intend this equation, why choose the names 'Nokes' rather than one of the many thousand neutral names available?

I have to accept, of course, that this is very largely a private symbolism, which Tolkien could not have expected more than a few of his readers to notice. Most of his readers, though, could still get the point, or most of the point: Nokes is annoying not just because he has only a feeble image of Faery himself, but because he insists that that is the only one there is. He is indeed absolutely precisely one of those "professional persons" who "suppose their dullness and ignorance to be a human norm," and whom Tolkien picked out for special assault in his 'Valedictory Address to the University of Oxford,' by which he clearly meant professors of literature (*Essays*, 225). And then we have the strange scene in which Smith is protected from the Wind by the weeping birch. I have said what I think about this elsewhere, and have clearly failed to convince Dr Flieger;[12] but this perhaps brings us close to one reason for our disagreements. It seems to me, as said above, that my readings depend above all on details, and on 'just-ness.' I can accept that I miss details, and equations, like the very obvious Hall/church one. One reason why the 'bounce' does not weaken, in my opinion, is that I hope to catch or identify a few more details on every new reading. What I do not think is that I am supposed just not to wonder about them, to accept them as part of surface narrative, as I might in a realistic novel. Dr Flieger, in a word, takes *Smith* holistically, while I take it bit by bit. There is no doubt that her way fits modern critical taste better than mine, as does a liking for dialogism, multiple meanings, freedom to interpret the inexhaustible text (etc.), as said above. Whether modern critical taste has much to do with Tolkien may, however, be doubted. I note

---

[12] See Shippey (1982: 206-7; 1992: 244-6, 320; 2003a: 278-80); and Flieger (1997: 243-4).

also, in Dr Flieger's analysis, a conviction that the whole text is somehow too fragile to be rudely disassembled. My 'oak-and-birch' theory is not rejected outright, but is felt to "place a heavy burden on a story whose effect depends not a little on its lightness of touch." Elsewhere and also in the context of rejecting autobiographical and allegorical elements we hear of its "gossamer appeal," its "unpretentious air" and "effortless ability to imply without stating" (Flieger 1997: 244, 231, 233). Light, gossamer, effortless: this is an image of Faery, but I have a feeling that it is a Shakespearean one rather than a Tolkienian one. As I have said elsewhere, Tolkien was in a technical sense one of the most 'tough-minded' of authors, not a holistic person at all.[13]

One does, of course, in the end have to consider the story as a whole, the story "in its own terms," as Dr Flieger insists, though for me one has to go through the bit-by-bit stage of considering details first: things like names are for me quite literally the story's carefully-selected 'own terms.' I can only say here that for me the critical facts about the story are that it is double-stranded; that it is about succession; and that Smith himself appears to fail, or to enjoy only temporary success, along both strands. The one strand is cooking. The succession of Master Cooks goes Rider – Nokes – Alf Prentice – Harper. The other is possession of the star, and its succession goes Rider – Smith – Nokes's Tim. According to Tolkien's own statement, the Hall, the Master Cooks, and cooking in general, are all to be equated with religion; while it seems obvious that the star which gives entry into Faery stands for something like Tolkien's own inspiration, a quality essentially literary and imaginative. This basic separation seems to me, however, hard to maintain in detail. For one thing, Nokes the Cook shows a revealingly shallow attitude to Faery, which seems to have more to do with literature

---

[13] I have to repeat that 'tough-mindedness' here has a special sense, of being concerned with details, single facts, rather than systems, see Shippey (2003a: 333-4). It is quite possible to be 'tough-minded' and 'tender-hearted' at once. The basic idea is William James's.

than with religion. For another, it is hard for me to see Alf, the elf-king (elves are proverbially soulless) simply as a parson, a representative of the Church. I conclude, therefore, that as one might expect these two strands are not readily separable, but relate to each other. The theme of *Smith* is the integration of fantasy with belief; the question it resolves is whether fantasy – the deliberate, imaginative, literary creation of myth by individuals – is compatible with belief in the myth created by God (the Christian myth). Strict views have long insisted that this is not the case. Tolkien took such strict views seriously, but he very much did not want to accept them. *Smith* works out that debate, and also makes the case for the autonomy of fantasy against the beef-witted, rigorously practical, 'stands to reason' attitude of Nokes (so often repeated since by 'modernist' critics).

Uncertainty is conveyed once more by redundancy, this time by 'redundant characters.' These are the characters introduced, it seems, so as to be *excluded* from both sequences of succession: Smith's son Ned, and his grandson Tomling. Neither becomes Cook, neither receives the star. Indeed, in one of the least expected strokes of the narrative, the star goes to a descendant of Nokes, Nokes of Townsend's Tim. These surprising introductions seem to me to be capable of interpretation, but perhaps the point to make here is that they seem to me to demand it. Surely Tolkien here is saying something at once pessimistic (no-one can control the future) and optimistic (inspiration may appear to be lost, but will return in some entirely unpredicted form): it reminds me of the debate between Legolas and Gimli in Minas Tirith, at the start of 'The Last Debate,' Gimli taking the pessimistic view (human works all fail), Legolas the optimistic one (but their seed does not fail).

My essential point about allegory and its 'bounciness' is however this: a full reading of *Smith*, for me, would look like a long edited text, with footnoted commentary on several score, or several hundred separate points. To name a very small selection of them, the character Rider, the Fairy Queen doll, and the contrast between it and the real Fairy Queen, the "old books of recipes" which Nokes can barely read, the strange sequence in Smith's family of Nokes-like names (Nell, Nan, Ned), the King's Tree, the Living Flower which *is* inherited by Smith's kin, the scented bell-flowers which go to Tomling, the story's forty-eight year time-span, the character Harper who "comes from your own village," the name Townsend (Nokes of Townsend is "quite different"), the word "nimble," almost the last word of the story and one marked like Ned, Nan, Nell and Nokes by the philological feature of 'nunnation.' What do all these mean? In some cases, I think I know, but it would take a long and separate comment to explain; in others I do not know, but am still thinking about it (which means that there is still 'bounce' in reserve). But it seems to me that that is the way complex allegories work. Their life is in detail. Their texture is not 'gossamer,' but surprisingly tough. The fear that their charm may be destroyed by too close an analysis is misplaced. They ask for careful thought, not just emotional response, because they have something serious and complex to express. This is emphatically not to say, however, that what they have to express can be reduced to some (once decoded) much simpler meaning. It is perhaps this last mistaken belief which has created the modern reaction against the allegorical mode. But that is not the way that medieval allegorists worked, nor necessarily modern ones.

Blunt Belligerence: Tolkien's *Mr. Bliss*[1]

It has long been thought that the Water Rat, in A.A. Milne's *The Wind in the Willows*, was modelled on F.J. Furnivall, rowing fanatic and founder of the Early English Text Society. Whether true or not, this is inappropriate. Clearly the real patron of philology should be Mr. Badger, if not for his surliness and his thick-stick policies, then for his belligerent defence of Toad's vulgar English, under attack from Ratty. "What's the matter with his English? It's the same what I use myself, and if it's good enough for me, it ought to be good enough for you!"

That's the spirit (Tolkien would certainly have agreed). And in much the same spirit he created *Mr. Bliss*, a work which celebrates at every point a vanished vulgar England where everybody did – and spoke – exactly as they pleased, and life was consequently a series of amiable abrupt collisions, feebly refereed by the police in the shape of Sergeant Boffin.

Nobody in this tale thinks twice or hesitates. Mr. Bliss is driving off in his new motorcar – yellow, inside and out, with red wheels, cost five shillings and sixpence, bought on impulse and on credit – before he thinks to ask where he is going. He only bought it because the Girabbit said it was going to be a fine day; and since the Girabbit is blind, sleeps all day, lives down a hole, and has a skin made of mackintosh, you would think its opinion hardly worth having if it could be induced to give one. But none of Professor Tolkien's characters would be so chicken-hearted as to admit a doubt. Mr. Bliss asks; so the Girabbit tells him; and off the story goes.

From then on characters erupt round every corner, each one blunter and more plain-spoken than the last, all dropping their aitches and mangling their syntax as if they had a bet on it. The bears may be marginally fiercer than the Dorkinses, but not greedier, and the Dorkinses have dogs to even

---

[1] This appeared first as a review in the *Times Literary Supplement*, 26 November 1982, 1306. I thank the editor for permission to reprint it here.

things up. However, neither dog nor donkey can be kept to its duty without added inducements; and soon, by contagion, the author starts to behave similarly. Each page of print has facing it a page of manuscript facsimile twined in medieval style round Tolkien's own drawings. But on page 26 the author has rebelled. "The car is just here," says a note – arrow pointing off – "but I am tired of drawing it."

How nice to have a really solid lead for shirking! As with Beatrix Potter, there is a fascination for the child reader in seeing naughtiness done thorough and got away with. Yet the child's desire for a precise and ultimate justice is satisfied too. At the end of all his adventures Mr. Bliss is faced with a bill, itemised and complete, depriving him of everything except the foreign coins he keeps for collections. Attempts to bill him for the Girabbit fail, though, because they aren't fair. Better to say "Well we're blowed" with the vulgar bears than go on finicking like the Dorkinses: they'll be holding elocution lessons next.

This is a book which ought to feel dated, from its currency (pounds, shillings and pence), its language-jokes, its assumptions about class, and its whole ethos of anarchic independence within a rigid framework of law, or convention. However, dating has done little harm to Tom Kitten or Mr. Badger, and there seems no reason why it should here. This is a classic like they don't write any more: and just to rub the point in about vulgar English, on page 37 the manuscript reading "Mr. Binks stepped back sudden" should have been allowed to stand. 'Suddenly' may be 'correct,' but 'sudden' is English and it's right.

Another Road to Middle-earth: Jackson's Movie Trilogy[1]

Fifty years after the first publication of *The Lord of the Rings*, the ironies pointed to twenty-five years ago in the first paragraph of the first edition of *The Road to Middle-earth* have only become more obvious. Far from passing into the "merciful oblivion" predicted by Philip Toynbee, far from being a work few adults will look at twice, as declared by Alfred Duggan, *The Lord of the Rings* has found a new and even larger audience in a new medium, the three films directed by Peter Jackson and released in successive years 2001-2003. These are arguably the most successful films ever made. As of January 2004 the three between them had taken some one and a quarter billion pounds (or over $2 billion) at the box office, a figure certainly multiplied by VHS and DVD sales, especially of the extended versions which give a final total running time of close on twelve hours.[2] It is impossible to estimate how many viewers this represents, since one DVD can be seen by many people, and conversely the box office takings are inflated by repeat viewers, but it is safe to say that hundreds of millions of people have seen or will see the films. There will almost certainly be more viewers than readers (though of course they are often the same people). And, of course, the figures keep on growing. The figure above is based on Kristin Thompson's article of 2003, but in the 'Introduction' to her book of

---

[1] This essay began as 'Another Road to Middle-earth: Jackson's Movie Trilogy,' in Neil D. Isaacs and Rose Zimbardo (eds.) 2004. *Understanding the Lord of the Rings*. Boston: Houghton Mifflin, pp. 233-54. Updated and expanded it became 'Appendix C' in the third (UK) edition of *The Road to Middle-earth* (London: HarperCollins, 2005), pp. 409-29. Here again I have updated figures and references. I am grateful to Drs. Isaacs and Zimbardo, and to Houghton Mifflin and HarperCollins for allowing me to repeat myself here.

[2] Some figures for video/DVD sales are given by Kristin Thompson 2003. Though such figures are always out-of-date, it is clear that the Tolkien films have unusually high cassette/DVD sales, especially of DVDs, though relatively low rentals (people want to keep them). Even in 2003 the return on such sales was approaching the figure for box office takings.

2006 she suggests that the takings from the movies and the franchising thereof could reach well over ten billion dollars – a truly amazing amount, especially if compared with professorial average lifetime salaries.

Yet, even more amazingly, the Toynbee/Duggan reaction continued to be powerful, even during the making of the films. I have to confess that for what immediately follows (as for what I have said elsewhere about Tolkien's local reputation, see Shippey (2003a: 44) and note) I can acknowledge no source other than gossip, though this time it is the gossip of Los Angeles, not Oxford. Perhaps one day the full story will be revealed. But it is said that while Peter Jackson was making the films, the moguls of Hollywood, alarmed at the ever-increasing scale and cost of the production, sent to New Zealand a 'script doctor,' whose job it was to get the films back on track. The 'script doctor' immediately saw the faults in the Tolkien plot. Having heroes riding (or in this case walking) to the rescue of a threatened people was of course perfectly familiar and acceptable, as in *The Magnificent Seven*: but there was no need to have *two* threatened peoples, Rohan and Gondor. One of them could be cut out, which meant that the battle of Helm's Deep could be amalgamated with the battle of the Pelennor Fields. A love-interest for Aragorn was also clearly vital, but once again there was no need for *two* of them: either Arwen or Éowyn should go, preferably Arwen, and Aragorn should then marry Éowyn instead of politely dissuading her. One could then make a further saving by eliminating the figure of Faramir. Meanwhile, though there was some doubt about the wisdom of having such small and unheroic figures as hobbits as heroes, they might be retained as a gimmick: but four of them were one too many. And it was absolutely vital that *one of the hobbits should die*. With changes like these, *The Lord of the Rings* could be converted into a perfectly acceptable, run-of-the-mill movie script, just like the other (and disastrously unsuccessful) screen epics being made at much the same time, like *Troy* and *Alexander* – all at the expense, of course, of cultural contrast, originality, emotional depth, and a few other inessentials.

The script doctor's advice was ignored – Thompson 2006 comments *passim* on the advantages of making the movie far away from Hollywood, in New Zealand – and Jackson's films perhaps convinced even the moguls in the end that there was something they did not know about popular appeal. Nevertheless, the changes proposed do say something about the individual and even eccentric nature of Tolkien's work. So often it does *not* do what one might expect. The thought occurs, indeed, that many of the criticisms made of it by Tolkien's many hostile reviewers from Muir 1955 to Griffin 2006 would be much more accurate if levelled at the stripped-down, dumbed-down version Hollywood would have preferred. As often, the critics were criticising what they pretended to have read, not engaging with the work itself. But the success of the films does raise a more important issue. For many people, *The Lord of the Rings* now means the film version, not the books. In what ways are the two versions different, and would Tolkien himself have approved of the difference?

It should be remembered that Tolkien did live long enough to see a film script and to comment on it – the script indeed survives, with Tolkien's marginal notations, in the archive at Marquette University, Milwaukee, while there are extensive selections from his letters of protest in *Letters*, 260-61, 266-67, 270-77. That 1957 script was beyond all question an extraordinarily bad one, unambitious and careless, and Tolkien's comments are appropriately blistering. Still, three points deserve to be extracted from them. First, Tolkien had no objection to a film version *per se*. Second, he realised straight away that for a film version his book would have to be cut; and he was sure that in such circumstances outright cutting would be preferable to compression. Better to take out entirely such semi-independent sections as the involvement with Tom Bombadil, or the Scouring of the Shire, or (he noted particularly, see *Letters*, 277) the return of Saruman, than to try to squeeze everything in at racing speed. What would happen if one chose that alternative would be, all too likely, that the Prime Action, Tolkien's term for Frodo and Sam making their way into Mordor, would be downgraded in favour of the Subsidiary Action, the wars and the battles and the heroes.

The third point is more debatable. Tolkien (writing it should be remembered with a degree of "resentment" about a confessedly poor script) protested that:

> The canons of narrative art in any medium cannot be wholly different; and the failure of poor films is often precisely in exaggeration, and in the intrusion of unwarranted matter owing to not perceiving where the core of the original lies. (*Letters*, 270)

Leaving aside for the moment the question of "the core of the original," one could query Tolkien's phrase "wholly different." The "canons of narrative art" may well not be *wholly* different, but in different media they could well be *substantially* different. But is this just a matter of a change of medium, or does it affect the nature of the entire work? In what follows I try to answer the question just put.

One very evident difference between writing a book and making a film is money. Someone like Tolkien, writing on his own in the spare time from his 'day job,' had no-one to consider but himself. All that he was investing was his spare time, and as Dáin says very appositely to the messenger of Mordor, "the time of my thought is my own to spend" (*LotR*, 235). Someone like Jackson, controlling a budget of many millions of dollars, had to think about producing a return on the investment, and so to consider popular appeal. Every now and then, accordingly, one can see him 'playing to the gallery.' Legolas skateboards down a flight of steps on a shield at the battle of Helm's Deep (*JTT* 51, 'The Breach of the Deeping Wall').[3] Gimli twice plays to a joke about 'dwarf-tossing,' once in the scene with the

---

[3] References to all three Jackson films are by scenes as numbered in the extended DVD versions put out by New Line Cinemas in 2002 (*The Fellowship of the Ring*, here *JFR*), 2003 (*The Two Towers*, here *JTT*), and 2004 (*The Return of the King*, here *JRK*).

Balrog, where Gimli refuses to be thrown across the chasm – "Nobody tosses a dwarf!" (*JFR* 36, 'The Bridge of Khazad-dum') – and once at Helm's Deep again, where this time he accepts the indignity in the cause of duty – "Toss me [...] Don't tell the elf!" (*JTT* 53, 'The Retreat to the Hornburg'). Tolkien would have understood neither addition: they are there for a teenage audience. Something similar could be said about the extra role given to Arwen in the first film, where she replaces Glorfindel in the scenes after Frodo is stabbed on Weathertop. This makes her into a better example of the strong active female character now preferred, but the rewriting rings a little hollow. In Tolkien it is Frodo who turns to defy the Ringwraiths at the edge of the ford of the Loudwater, but his defiance is weary, lonely and unsuccessful. Jackson has Arwen turning and defying the Ringwraiths, "If you want him, come and claim him!" (*JFR* 21, 'The Flight to the Ford'). Of course they do want him, they have every intention of claiming him, and Arwen's defiance actually makes no difference: not much is gained by introducing the stereotype of the 'warrior princess' – except that, as has been said, this is the kind of thing a modern audience expects, or may be thought to expect.

There are a number of insertions and alterations like this in the Jackson films, and they have caused a good deal of offence to lovers of the books: the first two essays in the recent collection on *Tolkien and Film* (Croft 2004a) are critical to the point of indignation, and set the tone for much of what follows in subsequent essays.[4] I would say only that the effect of these commercially-driven scenelets need not be exaggerated: they pass quickly. I would add, too, obvious as it may seem, that print and film are different media. Printing out movie dialogue in black and white on a page can easily make it seem flat, uninspiring, deeply inferior to the version as

---

[4] See Bratman 2004 and Croft 2004b. Bratman indeed refers to the first version of this essay as "Sarumanian accomodationism" (2004: 35), which is strong language! This essay and Bratman's however form a good example of the *sic et non* scholastic method, if I may bring in Abelard to counter Aquinas.

originally written. On the other hand, some of the long speeches in Tolkien's *The Lord of the Rings*, delivered orally, would overwhelm any actor's ability to hold audience attention. Orality and literacy demand substantially different forms even of language.[5]

Much more serious is the question of "the canons of narrative art," and here I cannot help thinking that there must have been several occasions where Jackson's scriptwriters[6] said, in effect, 'but we can't do that' – occasions where Tolkien himself seems to forget, or ignore, some of the very basic axioms of narrative. One of these is 'show, don't tell.' Tolkien's narrative is on occasion unusually talkative, ready to bypass major dramatic scenes, and quite ready to leave the reader, or viewer, 'up in the air' – as for instance with the Ring. The unquestioned "core of the original," to use Tolkien's term, is the Ring and what we are told about it: its effect is always corrupting, no-one can be trusted with it, it cannot be hidden, it must be destroyed and it must be destroyed in the place of its forging. Without these data the story cannot proceed. But though much of this is told by Gandalf to Frodo in the early chapter 'The Shadow of the Past,' full information and identification does not take place till twelve chapters later in 'The Council of Elrond,' while there is a full six months between the two events (April 13th to October 25th) – and seventeen years between 'The Shadow of the Past' and Bilbo's farewell party. This leisurely unrolling does not suit the narrative medium of film, and Jackson's solution is clear, direct, and arresting: much of the history of the Ring as conveyed tortuously by Gandalf and other speakers in 'The Council of Elrond' is taken out and told at the start, with a cool, quiet voice-over accompanying scenes of

---

[5] The point is regularly forgotten, especially in academia, and especially in American academia, where the practice of reading out one's paper at a conference is standard. But listeners simply cannot take in long and syntactically-complex sentences, though they may be able to read them with perfect ease. I would make this point with reference to some of the criticisms expressed, e.g., in Timmons 2004.

[6] Fran Walsh and Philippa Boyens are credited with the screenplay, along with Jackson himself.

extreme drama and violence on screen (*JFR* 1, 'Prologue: One Ring to Rule them All'). Far fewer 'talking heads,' and the viewer 'put in the picture' from the beginning. This change does indeed come with a price, as discussed further below, but it makes the action quicker and more visual.

Even more challenging for the scriptwriters, I would imagine, was Tolkien's handling of the destruction of Orthanc by the Ents. In his narrative we have a markedly slow build-up to the Ents' decision to march, broken by "a great ringing shout" (*LotR*, 473) and rapid movement to the end of the chapter 'Treebeard,' which closes with the Ents and the hobbits looking down into Nan Curunir, the Valley of Saruman. Attention then moves elsewhere for almost four full chapters, nearly seventy pages, and the next time Orthanc appears it is a ruin. What has happened in between? This is not explained for another ten pages, and then it is told in flashback by Merry and Pippin between them. Jackson's scriptwriters clearly could not repeat this. They had a choice between a scene with people talking ruminatively about something that had happened already, or a major action scene in chronological order (*JTT* 59, 'The Flooding of Isengard'). In a visual medium such a choice can only go one way. The same is true of Aragorn's journey from the Paths of the Dead to Pelargir, his rout of the Corsairs, and his arrival in the nick of time at the Pelennor Fields. In the book the Grey Company disappears from sight on page 773, and reappears almost sixty pages later (829), in a way which further remains unexplained until this time Legolas and Gimli start to tell the story, again in flashback, a further thirty pages later (856). Once more it is a choice between 'talking heads' and major action scenes with every opportunity for special effects, and the choice for a film-maker is just as inevitable, as one sees from the scenes in the film of *The Return of the King* – 31, 'Aragorn Takes the Paths of the Dead,' 33, 'Dwimorberg: the Haunted Mountain,' 35, 'The Paths of the Dead,' and 37, 'The Corsairs of Umbar,' set out in linear fashion, and close enough together to maintain continuity. It is hard to protest about any of these changes. In such cases the 'canons of narrative art' *are* different as between visual and verbal media, and Jackson surely had to do what he did.

Does it lead, however, to Tolkien's feared subordination of Prime Action to Subsidiary Action, taking one's attention off the Ring and on to the special effects? I would suggest that in fact Jackson restores any balance lost, several times, with rather deft transpositions which foreground or bring back quiet but important scenes which might otherwise have been suppressed. 'The Council of Elrond' is a case in point. In the film, much of its material has already been used, while it is quite clear that no film-maker could afford to spend a significant proportion of his running time on what is in effect a committee meeting, and one which ends moreover in exhaustion and prolonged silence: "All the Council sat with downcast eyes, as if in deep thought" (*LotR*, 263). In Jackson, by contrast, the much shorter meeting ends with all parties shouting and haranguing each other. Yet the vital words at the end are almost exactly the same in both versions, Frodo saying "I will take the Ring, though I do not know the way" (*LotR*, 264). In Tolkien these are dropped into a silence, in Jackson they have to penetrate a hubbub of voices. What happens in the film is that Frodo says "I will take the Ring," and is ignored. As he walks forward to say it a second time, Gandalf turns to listen. And as the others notice Gandalf listening and fall silent, he says it a third time,[7] this time completing it almost as in Tolkien: "I will take the Ring to Mordor. Though I do not know the way." The scene in the film makes a point vital to the story, and to the Prime Action, which is that it is the small and physically insignificant characters, the hobbits, who dominate the plot, though this is completely unexpected by anyone except Gandalf, the only one among the wise who ever pays any attention to them. Jackson's straightening and lightening of the plot finds a justification in just this moment.

---

[7] Possibly Frodo says the words four times. Only three are sub-titled, but Frodo appears to say "I will take the Ring" completely inaudibly, as if to himself, before trying to say it out loud.

Another transposition to which I would call attention comes from 'The Shadow of the Past.' In this chapter, in Tolkien, there is an especially resonant exchange between Frodo and Gandalf. Slowly realising what Gandalf is telling him, Frodo says reluctantly, "I wish it need not have happened in my time," and Gandalf answers:

> "So do I [...] and so do all who live to see such times. But that is not for them to decide. All we have to decide is what to do with the time that is given us." (*LotR*, 50)

For English people of Tolkien's generation, the words 'in my time' carry a powerful echo. In 1938, returning from the Munich conference where he gave way to Hitler, Neville Chamberlain notoriously and quite wrongly announced that he brought back 'peace in our time,' and the words (themselves taken from the Anglican liturgy) have become irrevocably tainted with appeasement, avoidance of duty, and failure. When Gandalf says "all who live to see such times," then, he could be taken as meaning, in unconscious prophecy, Tolkien's contemporaries and countrymen; and when he says "them," the pronoun includes Frodo and the Shire-hobbits, along with everyone in Middle-earth and indeed everyone at any time faced with the need for painful decision. Gandalf then softens the implied criticism slightly by changing his pronoun, including himself, and narrowing the focus: "All *we* have to decide is what to do with the time that is given *us*" (my emphasis). The echo of Chamberlain, however, might well slip past a twenty-first century audience almost a lifetime removed from 1938 and Munich. But Jackson gives the words a renewed emphasis by moving them to a different place and moment. In the first of his films, the words are still said by Gandalf to Frodo, but they are said in another notably quiet scene, in the dark, as the two characters talk in the Mines of Moria (*JFR* 34, 'A Journey in the Dark'). Their force is furthermore established by repetition. Almost at the very end of the movie, as Frodo prepares to leave the Fellowship and set out as he intends for Mordor on his own (*JFR* 46, 'The Road Goes Ever On'), he seems to hear Gandalf's words repeated, with the face of Gandalf (whom he and the viewers think at that moment to be dead) filling the screen. Only the words have once more had their pronouns changed. This time what Frodo hears is, "All *you* have to decide is what to do with the time that is given *you*." The statement has accordingly become entirely personal, directed precisely at Frodo's own single moment of decision.

This kind of switching between universal truth and individual application is entirely Tolkienian, exemplified several times in the hobbit-poetry which Jackson has cut out. Yet what is cut out in one place has a tendency to reappear in another. Bombadil has vanished entirely from Jackson's films, but some of his words are reallocated to Treebeard, and there is one moment where the third of the films shows a very careful reading of the original. At the start of the chapter 'Fog on the Barrow-Downs,' Frodo has a dream – except that we are told explicitly that it may not be a dream. In this dream, or vision, or moment of insight, Frodo sees "a far green country open[ing] before him under a swift sunrise" (*LotR*, 132). No more is said and nothing is made of this dream, or vision, but it returns almost nine hundred pages later. On the penultimate page Frodo, setting out from the Grey Havens, once again "beheld white shores and beyond them a far green country under a swift sunrise" (*LotR*, 1007). What is it that he sees? Is it Aman, the Undying Lands? Or is it something even beyond them, something which is not reserved for him alone? In one of the most violent sequences of the three films, *JRK* 49, 'A Far Green Country,' as the trolls are battering their way into Minas Tirith, Jackson surprisingly takes up the question. He shows Pippin sitting, frightened, a little way behind the front line, when Gandalf comes over to him and talks to him about death. Death is not the end, he says, smiling. When it comes we will find ourselves walking into the "far green country." Pippin is reassured, but the scene has a point well beyond the momentary reassurance. One feels that here the wise men, Tolkien or Gandalf or Jackson, are talking to everyone, and talking to them about death, a subject well beyond the range of most

Hollywood rhetoric. It is a good example of Jackson's readiness to hold the action and say something quietly, and it shows also at the very least a careful and thrifty reading of the original.

Less easy to explain are scenes which add complexity to a plot which (as the script doctor no doubt said) has quite enough movement in it already. The first substantial one of these occurs near the middle of the film of *The Two Towers*. Aragorn and Théoden are withdrawing towards Helm's Deep, when their column is attacked by orc warg-riders. This is itself an addition to the original text, but one has to admit that for Tolkien to mention warg-riders and then never foreground them was an intolerable provocation to any movie-maker. But as the attack is beaten off, Aragorn falls over a cliff and into a river, where he lies as if dead. He is then called back from death, seemingly, by a vision of Arwen and by the attentions of his horse, Brego (see *JTT* 34, 'The Wolves of Isengard,' and 37, 'The Grace of the Valar'), after which he returns to Helm's Deep and the action continues as before. Why build in what seems to be a narrative digression, a zig-zag? One motive must be to find, once more, a role for Arwen. Just as he is brought back to life by love of her, so she turns back to share his fate and that of Middle-earth – and that means, to die – for love of him (*JTT* 38, 'Arwen's Fate'). Her decision furthermore is echoed by the decision of her father Elrond to abandon his *fainéant* role and dispatch a surprisingly well-drilled elvish army to the rescue of Helm's Deep, another addition to the original.

I would suggest that a second motivation for this set of changes lies in the different politico-military expectations of a 21st century audience. Tolkien's English contemporaries could accept without trouble the idea that the forces of evil might just be stronger than those of good: it was part of their real-world experience. After sixty years of almost unchallenged military superiority, 21st century American viewers need another and less matter-of-fact explanation for failure, and it is given as disunity and despair. Jackson presents Théoden, not making a tactical withdrawal, but refusing to fight out of a kind of disillusionment. "The old alliances are dead," he says, "we are alone" (*JTT* 43, 'Aragorn's Return'). No help will come from Gondor (Tolkien's Théoden had not expected any), no help from the elves (in Tolkien, the Riders do not even know quite what elves are). There is indeed a slightly Churchillian suggestion in all this, with Théoden saying in the same scene, "If there is to be an end, I would have them make such an end as is worthy of remembrance," much like Churchill's famous 'finest hour' speech of 1940. But the sense of having been abandoned is set up, of course, only to be reversed, as the elvish army turns up to honour the Old Alliance and man the walls of the Hornburg. Jackson's version insists that the source of weakness is disunity, and Aragorn and Arwen are given an expanded role as the focus of union, reinforcing Elrond's words much earlier, "You will unite, or you will fall" (*JFR* 27, 'The Council of Elrond'). This, perhaps, is the main justification for the whole Aragorn-revival digression. It is there to show that "there is always hope" (Aragorn to the boy Haleth son of Háma, *JTT* 48, 'The Host of the Eldar'), that Théoden is wrong to think he has been abandoned.[8] The movie has been affected, one might say, by close on sixty years of NATO.

An even more marked plot-shift centres on Faramir. As everyone who has read Tolkien will remember, Faramir has every opportunity to strip Frodo of the Ring, about which he knows a great deal even before Sam's blundering admission, but rejects the temptation. Jackson has him succumb to it, declare "the Ring will go to Gondor," and march Frodo, Sam and Gollum off to Gondor as prisoners. In Jackson's version, Faramir intends to hand the Ring over to his father as "a mighty gift" (*JTT* 57, 'The Nazgûl Attack') – and the phrase is indeed Tolkien's, but in Tolkien it is said not

---

[8] Arwen says to Elrond, her father, "There is still hope" in *JTT* 38, 'Arwen's Fate,' and this conversation is what brings the elvish army to the rescue at Helm's Deep. There is a kind of symmetry, then, in three or four scenes: Arwen persuading her father in *JTT* 38, Aragorn encouraging Théoden in *JTT* 43 and Haleth in *JTT* 48, Sam re-motivating Frodo and at the same time convincing Faramir in *JTT* 60.

by Faramir deciding to seize the Ring but by Denethor, rebuking him for letting it go (*LotR*, 795). This digression too makes no real difference in the end, as Faramir is persuaded, seemingly by Sam, into letting the Ring and the hobbits go back into Mordor (and indeed anything else would have altered the plot terminally). So why introduce this second apparently unnecessary complication, which as with the Aragorn-digression above returns the characters to where they would have been anyway? One reason may well be to form a connection with the refashioning of Denethor in the third movie, which turns him into a thoroughly unpleasant character. It is true that even in Tolkien Denethor is cold, proud, ambitious, and misguided. It is his decision to defend the Rammas Echor, the wall which Gandalf thinks to be wasted labour, and this decision all but costs Faramir his life. It was his decision also to send Boromir to Rivendell rather than his brother, although the prophetic dream was clearly meant for the latter. It was this decision which meant that Faramir was the one to encounter the hobbits in Ithilien, as Faramir angrily if allusively reminds his father (*LotR*, 795) but Denethor refuses to take responsibility. Nevertheless, and in spite of his other disastrous errors, it is possible to feel a certain sympathy for Tolkien's Denethor: he makes his mistakes for Gondor. One cannot say the same of Jackson's Denethor. One of the more blatant uses of cinematic suggestion is the scene in the third movie in which Denethor, having sent his son out to fight, sits in his hall and gobbles a meal, tearing meat apart with his hands and munching till juice runs down his chin. He is made to look greedy, self-indulgent, the epitome of the 'château general' who sends men to their deaths while living himself in style and comfort. And in a repeat of the 'disunion' motif, he refuses to light the beacons to summon Rohan, till Pippin does so at Gandalf's direction – Tolkien's Denethor had lit the beacons and sent out the errand-riders before ever they arrived (see *LotR*, 748).

What the revised Faramir and Denethor interplay does is generate a theme particularly popular in recent (American) film, that of the son trying desperately to gain the love of his father, and of the father rejecting (till too late) the love of his son. It also appeals to American taste by making Denethor stand for old-world arrogance and hierarchy, while Faramir is converted from his obedience to his father by the intervention of the lower-class figure of Sam. What happens is that Sam, having dragged Frodo back from the winged Nazgûl, is given a long speech, transposed from its original place on the Stairs of Cirith Ungol, on "the great stories" and the heroes of old. "They kept going because they were holding on to something," he tells Frodo, because "there's some good in this world, and it's worth fighting for" (*JTT* 60, 'The Tales that Really Mattered'). His words are given total authority by being presented as a voice-over to images of victory at Helm's Deep and at Isengard, of which Sam at that moment knows nothing. For all his rustic accent, he has become a prophet, a spokesman for the movie's philosophic core, and Faramir, having overheard Sam talking to Frodo, is made to recognise this by giving way and changing his mind about the Ring.

The sequence indeed shows two general tendencies in the Jackson films, which I would label rather clumsily as 'democratisation' and 'emotionalisation.' One sees the former in the liking for enlarging the roles of relatively minor characters: just as Sam's stout heart converts Faramir, so Pippin's cunning diversion of Treebeard through the wasted groves near Orthanc converts Treebeard, in Jackson's version only, from neutrality to decision (*JTT* 54, 'Master Peregrin's Plan' and 56, 'The Last March of the Ents'). Meanwhile, the best example of the latter must be the way in which Jackson turns the journey of Gollum, Frodo, and Sam into a 'triangle' situation, in which Gollum (or rather Sméagol) competes with Sam for Frodo's love – a sequence which includes Gollum's trickery over the *lembas* and leads to Frodo actually dismissing Sam on the Stairs of Cirith Ungol. The Jackson handling of Gollum / Sméagol is masterful all through, with an especially good and original scene in which Sméagol argues with and exorcises his *alter ego* Gollum (*JTT* 29, 'Gollum and Sméagol'), only for Gollum to come back after the seeming betrayal at Henneth Annûn (*JTT* 42, 'The Forbidden Pool'). Jackson has a countervailing tendency, one might note, to iron out merely tactical complications, like the conflicting motives of the three groups of orcs who capture Merry and Pippin, Uglúk's Isengarders, Gríshnakh's Mordor-orcs, and the "mountain-maggots" from Moria. He makes motivation more understandable (for a 21st century audience) in terms of love given and love refused, faint-heartedness and mistaken loyalty.

One might say that there are no neutrals in Jackson's vision, or that those who wish to remain neutral, like Théoden, or the Ents, or the elves turning their backs on Middle-earth, are made to see the error of their ways. Jackson is also quicker than Tolkien to identify evil without qualification, and as a purely outside force (a failing of which Tolkien has often, but wrongly, been accused). In the opening voice-over we are told that after the battle of Dagorlad, Isildur had "this one chance to destroy evil for ever" (*JFR* 1, 'Prologue: One Ring to Rule Them All'). For ever? When Tolkien uses the phrase, it is marked immediately as mistaken. Elrond says he remembers the day "when Thangorodrim was broken, and the Elves deemed that evil was ended for ever, *and it was not so*" (*LotR*, 237, my emphasis), but there is no such qualification from Jackson. Jackson also has Elrond say to Gandalf that because of Isildur's error "evil was allowed to endure" (*JFR* 24, 'The Fate of the Ring'), but Tolkien's wise ones, I am sure, would be conscious that evil is always latent, and will exist whether humans and elves allow it to or not. There is the kernel here of a serious challenge to Tolkien's view of the world, with its insistence on the fallen nature even of the best, and its conviction that while victories are always worthwhile, they are also always temporary. And this could, at last, be a problem not created by any failure to perceive "the core of the original," but a grave and genuine difference between two different media, and their respective "canons of narrative art."

I come now to a matter which I have tried to elucidate before.[9] Tolkien, however, is an author one can never quite get to the bottom of, and viewing the Jackson films has once again generated a thought that had previously escaped me. This is that just as the complex structure of the middle sections of *The Lord of the Rings* is there to demonstrate the characters' natural feelings of 'bewilderment,' in two senses, the old, literal, and perfectly true sense of being 'lost in the Wild,' and the modern, metaphorical, and avoidable sense of being 'mentally confused,' so there is also a demonstration in them of another danger, which can also be summed up by one ambiguous word. The word is 'speculation,' and this is something to be avoided at all costs. 'Speculation' furthermore has two meanings, just as one might expect from Tolkien. Its modern and metaphorical sense is something like 'allowing one's actions to be guided by hypotheses about what will happen, or what is happening, or what other people are likely to do.' Its ancient and literal sense is, however, the practice of looking in a *speculum* – a mirror, a glass, a crystal ball. Frodo and Sam 'speculate' when they look in the Mirror of Galadriel, and it is a temptation to them. It tempts Sam to abandon his duty to Frodo and go home to rescue the Gaffer: this would be disastrous for the whole of Middle-earth. Fortunately Galadriel is there to counsel him and to point out "the Mirror is dangerous as a guide of deeds" (*LotR*, 354). It is that kind of reasoning from the mirror the witches show him that destroys Macbeth.[10] But the major source of dangerous 'speculation' in *The Lord of the Rings* is the *palantíri*, the Seeing Stones.

These are used four times in Tolkien's work, with a very consistent pattern. The first occasion is when Pippin picks up the *palantír* thrown from Orthanc by Gríma, and later sneaks a look at it when Gandalf is asleep. In

---

[9] See Shippey (2000a: 172-3) and (2003a: 160-7).
[10] For the importance of the play to Tolkien, see Shippey (2003a: 182-4). There is an old theatrical tradition that the 'glass' which Macbeth sees in Act IV, Scene 1, line 118ff. was, in the original first production, a mirror angled towards King James I in the audience so that the latter could see himself, as one of Banquo's descendants.

the Stone, he sees Sauron, and Sauron sees him. But though Sauron sees Pippin, he draws from this *a wrong conclusion*, namely that Pippin is the Ring-bearer, and has been captured by Saruman, who now has the Ring (*LotR*, 578-9). The next day Aragorn, who has been given the Stone by Gandalf, deliberately shows himself in it to Sauron, and once again Sauron draws *the wrong conclusion*: namely, that Aragorn has overpowered Saruman and that *he* is now the owner of the Ring. It is fear of this new power arising which makes Sauron launch his premature attack, and Gandalf indeed realises that this was all along Aragorn's intention (*LotR*, 797). Gandalf further surmises that it was the *palantír* which was Saruman's downfall. As he looked in it, he saw only what Sauron allowed him to see, and once more drew *the wrong conclusion*, losing heart and deciding that resistance would be futile (*LotR*, 584). Both Sauron and Saruman have allowed what they see in the Stones to guide their decisions, and what they have seen is true; but they have seen only fractions of the truth.

The most disastrous use of a *palantír* is however made by Denethor. The sequence of events is here made especially clear by Tolkien, though it is disguised by his own 'leapfrogging' style of narrative, which I have tried to describe in several places.[11] Aragorn shows himself to Sauron in the Orthanc Stone on 6th March. On the 7th and 8th Frodo and Sam are with Faramir in Ithilien. On the 9th Gandalf and Pippin reach Minas Tirith. On the 10th Faramir returns to Minas Tirith and reports to his father that he has met, and released, two hobbits, whom both he and his father know were carrying the Ring. The next day Denethor sends Faramir to defend Osgiliath, clearly a tactical error. On the 13th Faramir is brought back badly wounded, and Denethor retires to his secret chamber, from which people see "a pale light that gleamed and flickered [...] and then flashed and went out." When he comes down, "the face of the Lord was grey, more deathlike than his son's"

---

[11] Not entirely successfully, for it is very hard to convey in print. See in particular the diagram on Shippey (2000a: 104).

(*LotR*, 803). Clearly Denethor has been using his *palantír*, but what has he seen in it? Much later on, close to suicide, he will tell Gandalf that he has seen the Black Fleet approaching (as it is), though he does not know (though at that moment the reader does) that the Fleet now bears Aragorn and rescue, not a new army of enemies (*LotR*, 835). However, this does not seem quite enough to trigger Denethor's total despair. Surely we are meant to realise that what he has seen in the *palantír* is Frodo, whom he knows to be the Ring-bearer, *in the hands of Sauron*. Both Frodo's capture and Faramir's wounding take place on March 13th; and one may recall that Sauron plays a similar trick by showing Gandalf and the leaders of the West Frodo's *mithril*-coat and Sam's sword in the parley outside the Black Gate. The matter is put beyond doubt, however, by what Denethor says to Pippin as he prepares for suicide. "Comfort me not with wizards! [...] The fool's hope has failed. The Enemy has found it, and now his power waxes" (*LotR*, 805). "The fool's hope" is Gandalf's plan to destroy the Ring (see *LotR*, 795), and the "it" that "the Enemy" has found must be the Ring. Once again, then, Denethor has seen something true in a *palantír*, and has drawn from it *a wrong conclusion*.

What all these scenes do collectively is to indicate the dangers of 'speculating.' Speculating in the old sense (looking into crystal balls) is invariably disastrous in Tolkien's fictional world. Warning against the dangers of speculation in the modern sense, the way in which too much looking into the future can erode the will to action in the present, is however very much part of Tolkien's analysis of the real world.[12] The answer to speculation lies in the repeated scenes when we are made to realise that the fate of one character or group of characters depends on assistance coming from a

---

[12] To quote Hamlet's famous "To be or not to be" soliloquy, from Act III scene 1: "Thus conscience doth make cowards of us all, / And thus the native hue of resolution / Is sicklied o'er with the pale cast of thought, / And enterprises of great pitch and moment / With this regard their currents turn awry / And lose the name of action." For the importance of *Macbeth* to Tolkien, see the note above; Michael D.C. Drout (2004a) points out clear debts to *King Lear* in his article of 2004.

direction of which they are quite unaware. Sam and Frodo cross Gorgoroth unseen because Sauron is distracted, quite deliberately, by Aragorn. Théoden King is saved at Helm's Deep by the Huorns brought by Gandalf, but also by Merry and Pippin alerting Treebeard. Saruman is destroyed in a way by his own actions. For all Aragorn's doubts about his own decisions, Gandalf reminds him, "between them our enemies have contrived only to bring Merry and Pippin with marvellous speed, and in the nick of time, to Fangorn, where otherwise they would never have come at all" (*LotR*, 486). The *palantíri* mislead careless users by filling them with unjustified fear, but the whole structure of *The Lord of the Rings* indicates that decision and perseverance – not speculating on what is happening elsewhere, but doing your job and getting on with it, 'looking to your front' like a Lancashire Fusilier – that this mental attitude may be rewarded beyond hope. This, I would suggest, is Tolkien's philosophic core.[13] He believes in the workings of Providence – the Providence which 'sent' Gandalf back, and which 'meant' Frodo to have the Ring (*LotR*, 491, 55). But that Providence does not overrule free will, because it works only through the actions and decisions of the characters. In Tolkien there is no chance, no coincidence. What his 'bewildered' characters perceive as chance or coincidence is a result only of their inability to see how actions connect.

    The structure of *The Lord of the Rings*, then, does very much what John Milton said he was going to in *Paradise Lost* (Book I, 25-26): both authors, the arch-Protestant and the committed Catholic, mean to "assert eternal Providence, / And justify the ways of God to men." But to follow that structure one needs a very sure grasp both of the chronology of events, and the way in which events in one plot-strand (like the capture of Frodo) affect those in another (like the suicide of Denethor). It seems to me that the medium of film does not lend itself to this kind of intellectual connection.

---

[13] See further the essay on "'A Fund of Wise Sayings': Proverbiality in Tolkien' in this volume.

As noted above, Jackson diminishes the theme of 'bewilderment' from the start by explaining the history of the Ring start to finish, and by eliminating flashbacks: 'putting the viewer in the picture' is achieved at the cost of reducing the characters' (and the reader/viewer's) sense of uncertainty. Jackson furthermore does not use the *palantíri* much. In the first film we do indeed see Saruman looking into one (*JFR* 18, 'The Spoiling of Isengard'), but he uses it only to report and receive orders: there is no hint that he is being misled. Pippin later picks it up in the flotsam of Isengard (the explanation of how it comes there is rather different, a result of the early elimination of Saruman in Jackson's version) and as in Tolkien sneaks a look at it. But the important thing in Jackson's third film is not Sauron seeing Pippin, and drawing the wrong conclusion, but Pippin seeing Sauron, and being able, quite correctly, to guess some part of his plan – to assault Minas Tirith (*JRK* 8, 'The Palantir'). Aragorn uses the Stone later on in the film, (*JRK* 60, 'Aragorn Masters the Palantir'), but not as indicated by Tolkien. The theme of mistaken 'speculation' has been all but entirely removed.

Meanwhile the related theme of mis-diagnosed coincidence is indeed present, but relatively vestigially. In the shortened presentation of Sam and Frodo's approach to Mount Doom, the two look out across the plain of Gorgoroth, and see the camp-fires of the orcs going out as Sauron's armies move away to the Black Gate. Sam thinks and says that this is a stroke of luck ("Some luck at last," *JRK* 62, 'In the Company of Orcs'), but he is wrong, at least in the sense that he means it, because Aragorn and Gandalf have led their remaining forces to the Black Gate precisely in order to draw Sauron's attention.[14] But other 'coincidences' have been removed. In Tolkien, it was a fortunate coincidence that the sword with which Merry stabs the chief Nazgûl had been made long ago for use against "the dread realm of Angmar and its sorcerer king" (*LotR*, 826), who is now the

---

[14] Tolkien's point, to state it yet again, is that this is what 'luck' always is: the result of something which has happened elsewhere, without our knowledge, but which is nevertheless part of the Providential design.

Nazgûl; but the film, having eliminated the barrow-wight sequence, makes nothing of this. Similarly, there is no doubt in Tolkien that Denethor's attempted murder of Faramir is what dooms Théoden, for as Pippin draws Gandalf away, Gandalf says, "if I do [save Faramir], then others will die" (*LotR*, 832). But this demonstration that there is always a price to pay for weakness is also no longer visible. In general, Tolkien's painstaking double analysis both of the dangers of speculation and of the nature of chance, which between them express a highly traditional but at the same time markedly original view of the workings of Providence, is not reflected in Jackson's sequence of movies. In that sense, much of the philosophical "core of the original" has indeed been lost in the movie version.

However, and here I query Tolkien's statement cited at the start of this essay, this may be because the "canons of narrative art," while certainly not "wholly different" in a different medium, are identifiably different. For one thing, the film medium has more trouble dealing with distorted time sequences than does prose fiction. Film makers can easily cut from one scene to another, and Jackson often does so with strikingly contrastive effects.[15] The implication, though, is always that the different scenes (more of them, shorter, much more broken up)[16] are happening at more or less the same time. Simply by having chapter and book divisions, with all the familiar devices of chapter-titles and fresh-page starts, a novelist like Tolkien can in effect say to his reader, 'I am now taking you back to where I left off with this group of characters.' One result is that the reader is much more aware of what he or she knows, from another plot-strand, that the characters in the plot-strand being narrated do not know, with obvious resultant effects

---

[15] Jackson's own version of 'interlace' obviously deserves extended treatment of its own. See, again, Thompson 2003 and 2006, for extended and valuable comments on Jackson's debts to cinematic tradition.

[16] Against the 62 chapters of *The Lord of the Rings* (some ten of which are largely or completely cut out of the film versions), the extended version of *JFR* has 46 scenes, not counting credits, of *JTT* 66, of *JRK* 76, a total of 188: three or four scenes, then, for every one of Tolkien's chapters actually used.

of irony, or of reassurance. This is a major difference between the two versions we now have of *The Lord of the Rings*.

Does it matter? Jackson may not have been able to cope with all the ramifications of Tolkien on Providence, but then few if any readers do. It is very difficult to say whether some part of Tolkien's intention gets through even to careless or less-comprehending readers: he would have hoped so, but there is no guarantee that he was correct. And meanwhile Jackson has certainly succeeded in conveying much of the more obvious parts of Tolkien's narrative core, many of them quite strikingly alien to Hollywood normality – the difference between Prime and Subsidiary Action, the differing styles of heroism, the need for pity as well as courage, the vulnerability of the good, the true cost of evil. It was brave of him to stay with the sad, muted, ambiguous ending of the original, with all that it leaves unsaid. Perhaps the only person who could answer the question posed above – do the changes affect the nature of the entire work? – would be a person with an experience quite opposite to my own: someone who had seen the films, preferably several times over, and *only then* had read Tolkien's original. It would be interesting to gather from such a person a list of 'things I hadn't realised before,' as also 'things Tolkien left out.' Perhaps the most heartening thing one can say is that there will certainly now be many millions of people in exactly that position, new readers facing a new experience, and finding once again Tolkien's road to Middle-earth.

ABBREVIATIONS & REFERENCES

All works are by J.R.R. Tolkien, unless indicated otherwise.

'AW'	'*Ancrene Wisse* and *Hali Meiðhad*.' In *Essays and Studies* 14 (1929): 104-26.
BLT 1	*The Book of Lost Tales, Part One*. Edited by Christopher Tolkien. The History of Middle-earth I. London: HarperCollins, 1983.
BLT 2	*The Book of Lost Tales, Part Two*. Edited by Christopher Tolkien. The History of Middle-earth II. London: HarperCollins, 1984.
Bosworth-Toller	Bosworth, Joseph, ed. by T. Northcote Toller. *An Anglo-Saxon Dictionary*. 1898, with supplement 1921, revised by Alistair Campbell 1955. Oxford: Clarendon.
Essays	*The Monsters and the Critics and Other Essays*. Edited by Christopher Tolkien. London: George Allen & Unwin, 1983.
Exodus	*The Old English Exodus: Text, Translation and Commentary*. Edited by Joan Turville-Petre. Oxford: Clarendon, 1981.
Finn	*Finn and Hengest: The Fragment and the Episode*. Edited by Alan Bliss. London: George Allen & Unwin, 1982.
Giles	*Farmer Giles of Ham*. London: George Allen & Unwin, 1949. Reprinted in and here cited from *Reader*, pp. 121-87.
'Guide'	'Guide to the Names in *The Lord of the Rings*.' In Jared Lobdell (ed.). 1975. *A Tolkien Compass*. La Salle, Ill.: Open Court Press, pp. 153-201.
Hobbit	*The Hobbit: or There and Back Again*. First edition 1937. Cited here from the corrected edition, with 'Note on the Text' by Douglas A. Anderson, London: HarperCollins, 2002.
'Homecoming'	'The Homecoming of Beorhtnoth Beorhthelm's Son', *Essays and Studies*, N.S. 6 (1953): 1-18. Reprinted in and here cited from *Reader*, pp. 1-27.
Jewels	*The War of the Jewels: The Later Silmarillion, Part Two, The Legends of Beleriand*. Edited by Christopher Tolkien. The History of Middle-earth XI. London: HarperCollins, 1994.
Lays	*The Lays of Beleriand*. Edited by Christopher Tolkien. The History of Middle-earth III. London: HarperCollins, 1985.

'Leaf'	'Leaf by Niggle.' First published in *Dublin Review* for Jan. 1945, pp. 46-61. Reprinted in *Reader* as the second part of 'Tree and Leaf', pp. 100-120, and cited from there.
Letters	*Letters of J.R.R. Tolkien*. Edited by Humphrey Carpenter with the assistance of Christopher Tolkien. London: George Allen & Unwin, 1981.
Lost Road	*The Lost Road and Other Writings: Language and Legend before The Lord of the Rings*. Edited by Christopher Tolkien. The History of Middle-earth V. London: HarperCollins, 1987.
LotR	*The Lord of the Rings*. Frst printed in three vols., 1954-5. 2nd ed. 1966; cited here from the corrected one-volume edition, with 'Note on the Text' by Douglas A. Anderson, London: HarperCollins, 2001, by page, or by book and chapter.
'Monsters'	'Beowulf: The Monsters and the Critics', *Proceedings of the British Academy* vol. 22 (1936), pp. 245-95. Reprinted in and here cited from *Essays*, pp. 5-48.
Morgoth	*Morgoth's Ring: The Later Silmarillion, Part One, The Legends of Aman*. Edited by Christopher Tolkien. The History of Middle-earth X. London: HarperCollins, 1993.
OED	*The Oxford English Dictionary*. 1st edn. 13 vols., Oxford: Clarendon Press, 1933. Reprints *The New English Dictionary on Historical Principles*, 10 vols., 1884-1928. With Supplement in 4 vols, 1972-86. 2nd edn., prepared by J.A. Simpson and E.S.C. Weiner. 20 vols. Oxford: Clarendon Press, 1989.
'OES'	'The Oxford English School.' *Oxford Magazine* 48.21 (29 May 1930): 778-80, 782.
'OFS'	'On Fairy-Stories.' First printed in *Essays Presented to Charles Williams*. London: Oxford University Press, 1947, pp. 38-89. Reprinted in *Essays*, pp. 109-61, and as the first part of 'Tree and Leaf' in *Reader*, pp. 33-99, and here cited from the former.
Reader	*The Tolkien Reader*. New York: Ballantine, 1966. Contains *Giles*, 'Homecoming', 'Leaf' and 'OFS' together as 'Tree and Leaf', and *TB*.
Sauron	*Sauron Defeated: The End of the Third Age. (The History of the Lord of the Rings, Part Four)*. Edited by Christopher Tolkien. The History of Middle-earth IX. London: HarperCollins, 1991.
SGGK	*Sir Gawain and the Green Knight*. Edited by J.R.R. Tolkien and E.V. Gordon. Oxford: Clarendon Press, 1925.

SGPO	*Sir Gawain and the Green Knight, Pearl and Sir Orfeo.* Translated by J.R.R. Tolkien, edited and with an introduction by Christopher Tolkien. London: George Allen & Unwin, 1975.
Shaping	*The Shaping of Middle-earth: The Quenta, the Ambarkanta and the Annals.* Edited by Christopher Tolkien. The History of Middle-earth IV. London: HarperCollins, 1986.
Silm	*The Silmarillion.* Edited by Christopher Tolkien. London: George Allen & Unwin, 1977.
'Sir Gawain'	'Sir Gawain and the Green Knight'. Lecture first delivered 1953. First printed in and cited from *Essays*, pp. 72-108.
Smith	*Smith of Wootton Major.* London: George Allen & Unwin, 1967.
Songs	*Songs for the Philologists*, by J.R.R. Tolkien, E.V. Gordon and others. Privately printed at the Dept. of English, University College, London, 1936.
TB	*The Adventures of Tom Bombadil and Other Verses from The Red Book.* London: George Allen & Unwin, 1962. Reprinted in and here cited from *Reader*, pp. 189-251.
Treason	*The Treason of Isengard (The History of The Lord of the Rings, Part Two).* Edited by Christopher Tolkien. The History of Middle-earth VII. London: HarperCollins, 1989.
UT	*Unfinished Tales of Númenor and Middle-earth.* Edited by Christopher Tolkien. London: George Allen & Unwin, 1981.
'Valedictory'	'Valedictory Address to the University of Oxford.' Lecture delivered 1959. Cited from *Essays*, 224-40.

Allchin, A.M., et al. (eds.). 1994. *Heritage and Prophecy: Grundtvig and the English-Speaking World*. Norwich: Canterbury Press.

Anderson, J.J. (ed.). 1977. *Cleanness*. Manchester: Manchester University Press.

Anderson, Douglas. (ed.). 2002. *The Annotated Hobbit*. Revised and Expanded edition. Boston: Houghton Mifflin.

----- 2003. '"An Industrious Little Devil": E.V. Gordon as Friend and Collaborator with Tolkien.' In Chance (ed.) 2003, pp. 15-25.

Andersson, Theodore M. 1980. *The Legend of Brynhild*. (Islandica XIII.) Ithaca and London: Cornell University Press.

Arngart, O.S. (ed.). 1981. 'The Durham Proverbs.' *Speculum* 56: 288-300.

Auden, W.H. 1956. 'At the End of the Quest, Victory.' Review of *Return of the King*. *New York Times Book Review*, January 22: 5.

----- 1968. 'Good and Evil in *The Lord of the Rings*.' In C.B. Cox and A.E. Dyson (eds.). 1968. *Word in the Desert: The Critical Quarterly Tenth Anniversay Number*. London: Oxford University Press, pp. 138-42.

Baird, Ian F. (ed.). 1982. *Scotish Feilde and Flodden Feilde*. New York and London: Garland.

Björnsson, Árni. 2003. *Wagner and the Volsungs: Icelandic Sources of 'Der Ring des Nibelungen'*. London: Viking Society for Northern Research.

Björnsson, Stefán. (ed. and trans.). 1785. *Hervararsaga ok Heidrekskongs*. Copenhagen.

Blackwelder, Richard E. 1990. *A Tolkien Thesaurus*. New York: Garland.

Blackham, Robert S. 2006. *The Roots of Tolkien's Middle-earth*. Stroud: Tempus Publishing.

Bloch, Howard, and Stephen G. Nichols (eds.). 1996. *Medievalism and the Modernist Temper*. Princeton, NJ: Princeton University Press.

Bosworth-Toller. See 'Abbreviations.'

Bown, Nicola. 2001. *Fairies in Nineteenth-Century Art and Literature*. Cambridge: Cambridge University Press.

Brady, Caroline. 1943. *The Legends of Ermanaric*. Berkeley: University of California Press.

Bratman, David. 1999. 'Tolkien and the Counties of England.' *Mallorn* 37 (December issue): 5-13.

----- 2004. 'Summa Jacksonica: A Reply to Defenses of Peter Jackson's *Lord of the Rings* Films, after St Thomas Aquinas.' In Croft (ed.) 2004a, pp. 27-62.

Burns, Marjorie. 2004. 'Norse and Christian Gods: The Integrative Theology of J.R.R. Tolkien.' In Chance (ed.) 2004, pp. 163-78.

----- 2005. *Perilous Realms: Celtic and Norse in Tolkien's Middle-earth.* Toronto: University of Toronto Press.

Busby, Keith (ed.). 1993. *Essays on the New Philology.* Amsterdam: Rodopi.

Byock, Jesse (trans.). 1990. *The Saga of the Volsungs.* Berkeley: University of California Press.

Cameron, M.L. 1993. *Anglo-Saxon Medicine.* Cambridge: Cambridge University Press.

Carey, John, 1992. *The Intellectuals and the Masses: Pride and Prejudice among the Literary Intelligentsia, 1880-1939.* London: Faber & Faber.

Carpenter, Humphrey. 1977/2000. *J.R.R. Tolkien: A Biography.* London: George Allen & Unwin. Revised edn. Boston: Houghton Mifflin, 2000.

----- see also 'Abbreviations,' *Letters*.

Carroux, Margaret (trans.). 1972. *Der Herr der Ringe*. 3 vols. Stuttgart: Klett-Cotta.

Chance, Jane (ed.). 2003. *Tolkien the Medievalist.* London: Routledge.

----- (ed.). 2004. *Tolkien and the Invention of Myth: A Reader.* Lexington, KY: University of Kentucky Press.

----- 2006. 'Subversive Fantasist: Tolkien on Class Difference.' In Hammond and Scull (eds.) 2006, pp. 153-68.

Clark, George, and Daniel Timmons (eds.). 2001. *J.R.R. Tolkien and His Literary Resonances: Views of Middle-earth.* Westport, Conn. and London: Greenwood.

Clark Hall, John R. (trans., rev. by C.L. Wrenn). 1940. *Beowulf and the Finnsburg Fragment.* London: George Allen & Unwin.

Collingwood, R.G. 2005. *The Philosophy of Enchantment: Studies in Folktale, Cultural Criticism, and Anthropology.* Edited by David Boucher, Wendy James, and Philip Smallwood. London: Oxford University Press.

Cooke, Deryck. 1979. *I Saw the World End: A Study of Wagner's 'Ring.'* London: Oxford University Press.

Crawford, S.J. (ed.). 1922. *The Old English Heptateuch.* Early English Text Society, Original Series 160. London: Oxford University Press.

Croft, Janet Brennan (ed.). 2004a. *Tolkien on Film: Essays on Jackson's Lord of the Rings*. Mythopoeic Press: Altadena, CA.

----- 2004b. 'Mithril Coats and Tin Ears: 'Anticipation' and 'Flattening' in Peter Jackson's *Lord of the Rings* Trilogy.' In Croft (ed.) 2004a, pp. 63-80.

Curry, Patrick. 1997. *Defending Middle-Earth: Tolkien, Myth and Modernity.* New York: St Martin's Press.

----- 1999. 'Tolkien and his Critics: A Critique.' In Honegger (ed.) 1999a, pp. 81-148.

D'Ardenne, Simone (ed.). 1961. *Þe Liflade ant te Passiun of Seinte Iuliene*. Early English Text Society Original Series 248. London: Oxford University Press.

Darwin, Charles. 1968. *The Origin of Species*. Edited by J.W. Burrow. Harmondsworth: Penguin.

Delbanco, Andrew. 1999. 'The Decline and Fall of Literature.' *New York Review of Books* 46.17 (November 4): 32-8.

Detter, Ferdinand, and Richard Heinze (eds.). 1903. *Saemundar Edda*. Leipzig: Wigand.

Dickerson, Matthew T., and Jonathan Evans. 2006. *Ents, Elves and Eriador: the Environmental Vision of J.R.R. Tolkien*. Louisville, KY: University Press of Kentucky.

Dobson, Eric. 1976. *The Origins of Ancrene Wisse*. Oxford: Clarendon.

Doughan, David. 1991. 'In Search of the Bounce: Tolkien Seen through Smith.' In *Leaves from the Tree: Tolkien's Shorter Fiction* [no editor]. London: The Tolkien Society, pp. 17-22.

Dronke, Ursula (ed. and trans.). 1969. *The Poetic Edda*, Vol. 1, 'Heroic Poems.' Oxford: Clarendon.

Drout, Michael C. (ed.). 2002. *J.R.R. Tolkien: Beowulf and the Critics*. Medieval and Renaissance Texts and Studies 248. Tempe: Arizona Center for Medieval and Renaissance Studies.

----- 2004a. 'Tolkien's Prose Style and its Literary and Rhetorical Effects.' *Tolkien Studies* 1: 137-62.

----- 2004b. 'A Mythology for Anglo-Saxon England.' In Chance (ed.) 2004, pp. 229-47

----- 2007, forthcoming (ed.). *J.R.R. Tolkien Encyclopedia: Scholarship and Critical Assessment*. London and New York: Routledge.

Duggan, Hoyt. 1997. 'Meter, Stanza, Vocabulary, Dialect.' In D.S. Brewer and Jonathan Gibson (eds.). 1997. *A Companion to the Gawain-Poet*. Brewer: Woodbridge, pp. 221-42.

Ekwall, Eilert (ed.). 1977. *The Concise Oxford Dictionary of English Place-Names*. 4th edn. Reprint from 1960. Oxford: Clarendon.

Elliott, R.W.V. 1984. *The Gawain Country: Essays on the Topography of Middle English Alliterative Poetry*. Leeds Texts and Monographs No. 8. Leeds: University of Leeds School of English.

Ettmüller, Ludwig (ed.). 1875. *Carmen de Beovvulfi Gautarum regis rebus praeclare gestis atque interitu, quale fuerit antequam in manus interpolatoris, monachi Vestsaxonici, inciderat*. Zürich.

Faulkes, Anthony. (ed.). 1982. *Snorri Sturluson, Edda: Prologue and Gylfaginning*. Oxford: Clarendon Press.

----- (trans.). 1987. *Snorri Sturluson: Edda*. London: Dent.

Fick, August. 1874. *Vergleichendes Wörterbuch der Indogermanischen Sprachen*. 3rd edn. 4 vols. Göttingen: Vandenhoeck and Ruprecht.

Fimi, Dimitra. 2006. ''Come Sing ye Light Fairy Things Tripping so Gay': Victorian Fairies and the Early Work of J.R.R. Tolkien.' In *Working with English: Medieval and Modern Language, Literature and Drama* 2.

----- 2007. 'Victorian Fairyology.' In Drout 2007: 691-2.

Flieger, Verlyn. 1983. *Splintered Light: Logos and Language in Tolkien's World*. Grand Rapids, MI: Eerdmans.

----- 1997. *A Question of Time: J.R.R. Tolkien's Road to Faerie*. Kent, OH: Kent State University Press.

----- 2001a. 'Taking the Part of Trees: Eco-Conflict in Middle-earth.' In Clark and Timmons (eds.) 2001, pp. 147-58.

----- 2001b. 'Allegory versus Bounce: Tolkien's *Smith of Wootton Major*,' *Journal of the Fantastic in the Arts* 12.2: 186-91.

----- 2004. 'A Mythology for Finland: Tolkien and Lönnrot as Mythmakers.' In Chance (ed.) 2004, pp. 277-83.

----- and Carl F. Hostetter (eds.). 2000. *Tolkien's Legendarium: Essays on The History of Middle-earth*. Westport, CT: Greenwood.

Foote, Peter G., and Randolph Quirk (eds.). 1974. *Gunnlaugssaga Ormstungu*. London: Viking Society for Northern Research.

Freud, Sigmund. 1929. *Zur Psychopathologie des Alltagslebens*. Vienna: Internationaler Psychoanalytischer Verlag.

Garth, John. 2003. *Tolkien and the Great War: The Threshold of Middle-earth*. London: HarperCollins.

Gaskill, Howard (ed.). 1996. *James Macpherson: The Poems of Ossian and Related Works*. Edinburgh: Edinburgh University Press.

Gee, Henry. 2004. *The Science of Middle-earth*. Cold Spring Harbor, NY: Cold Spring Press.

Gibbon, Edward. 1776-88. *The History of the Decline and Fall of the Roman Empire*. Edited by David Womersley 1994. London: Allen Lane.

Gilliver, Peter, Jeremy Marshall and Edmund Weiner. 2006. *The Ring of Words: Tolkien and the Oxford English Dictionary*. London: Oxford University Press.

Gordon, E.V. (ed.). 1927. *An Introduction to Old Norse*. 2nd edn. revised by A.R. Taylor 1957. Oxford: Clarendon.

----- (ed.). 1953. *Pearl*. Oxford: Clarendon.

Green, Martin. 1977. *Children of the Sun: A Narrative of Decadence in England after 1918*. New York: Basic Books.

Greer, Germaine. 1997. *Waterstone's Magazine* (Winter/Spring): 4.

Griffin, Jasper. 2006. 'The True Epic Vision.' Review of Stephen Mitchell (trans.). *Gilgamesh: A New English Translation. New York Review of Books* 53.4 (March 9): 25-26.

Grimm, Jacob. 1879-90. *Kleinere Schriften*, 8 vols. Berlin: Dümmler.

----- 1875-8. *Deutsche Mythologie*, 4th edn. Berlin: Dümmler. Reprint in 2 vols. with original pagination, Wiesbaden: Fourier, 2003.

Grimm, Wilhelm. 1829. *Die Deutsche Heldensage*. Gütersloh: Bertelsmann.

Grimm, Jacob and Wilhelm. 1999. *Deutsches Worterbuch*. Originally 16 vols. 1854-1960. Reprint in 33 vols. Munich: Deutscher Taschenbuch Verlag.

Gross, Michael. 1999. 'Lewis and Cambridge.' *Modern Philology* 96: 439-84.

Grundtvig, N.F.S. 1832. *Nordens Mythologi*. Copenhagen: Schubothes Buchhandlung.

Haarder, Andreas. 1975. *Beowulf: The Appeal of a Poem.* Copenhagen: Akademisk Forlag.

----- (ed.). 1982. *The Medieval Legacy: A Symposium*. Odense: Odense University Press.

Haigh, Walter E. 1928. *A New Glossary of the Dialect of the Huddersfield District*. London: Oxford University Press.

Hammond, Wayne G., with Douglas A. Anderson. 1993. *J.R.R. Tolkien: A Descriptive Bibliography*. Winchester: St Paul's Bibliographies; New Castle, DL: Oak Knoll Books.

----- and Christina Scull (eds.). 2006. *The Lord of the Rings 1954-2004: Scholarship in Honor of Richard E. Blackwelder*. Milwaukee, WI: Marquette University Press.

Hanson, Victor D., John Heath, and Bruce S. Thornton. 2001. *Bonfire of the Humanities*. Wilmington, DL: ISI Press.

Hathaway, E.J. *et al.* (eds.). 1975. *Fouke le Fitz Waryn*. Anglo-Norman Text Society. Oxford: Blackwell.

Hatto. A.T. (trans.). 1965. *The Nibelungenlied*. Harmondsworth: Penguin.

Heinzel, Richard. 1887. *Über die Hervararsaga.* Sitzungsberichte der Kaiserlichen Akademie der Wissenschaften (Vienna) 114: 475.

Hirst, S.M. 1985. 'An Anglo-Saxon Inhumation Cemetery at Sewerby, East Yorkshire.' *University Archaeological Reports* 4: York.

Honegger, Thomas (ed.). 1999a. *Root and Branch: Approaches towards Understanding Tolkien*. Zurich and Berne: Walking Tree Publishers.

----- 1999b. 'The Monster, the Critics, and the Public: Literary Criticism after the Poll.' In Honegger (ed.). 1999a, pp. 1-5.

----- (ed.). 2003. *Tolkien in Translation*. Zurich and Berne: Walking Tree Publishers.

----- 2007 (forthcoming). '*The Homecoming of Beorhtnoth*: Philology and the Literary Muse.' *Tolkien Studies* 4.

Horobin, Simon C.P. 2001. 'J.R.R. Tolkien as a Philologist: A Reconsideration of the Northernisms in Chaucer's Reeve's Tale.' *English Studies* 82.2: 97-105.

Hostetter, Carl F., and Arden Smith. 1995. 'A Mythology for England.' In Reynolds and GoodKnight (eds.) 1995, pp. 281-90.

Houghton, Joe. 1983. Review of J.R.R. Tolkien (ed. and trans.), *Finn and Hengest*. *Amon Hen* (May issue) 61: 4.

Høverstad, Torstein Bugge (trans.). 1980. *Ringenes Herre*. 3 vols. Oslo: Tiden Norsk Forlag.

Hult, David F. 1996. 'Gaston Paris and the Invention of Courtly Love.' In Bloch and Nichols (eds.) 1996, pp. 192-224.

Hutton, Ronald. 2003. *Witches, Druids and King Arthur*. Hambledon and London: London and New York, esp. pp. 98-106.

----- 2007 (forthcoming). 'The Pagan Tolkien.' Paper delivered at Aston 50th anniversary conference, August 12, 2005; to appear in conference proceedings.

Johannesson, Nils-Lennart. 1997. 'The Speech of the Individual and of the Community in *The Lord of the Rings*.' In Peter Buchs and Thomas Honegger (eds.). 1997. *News from the Shire and Beyond*. Zurich and Berne: Walking Tree Publishers, pp. 11-47.

Jónsson, Guthni (ed.). 1984. *Þiðreks saga af Bern*. 2 vols. Reykjavik: Íslendingasagnaútgáfan.

Kamenkovich, Maria. 1992. 'The Secret War and the End of the First Age: Tolkien in the Former USSR.' *Mallorn* 29: 33-8.

Kirby, W. F. (trans.). 1907. *Kalevala: The Land of Heroes*. 2 vols. London: Dent; New York: Dutton.

Kocher, Paul. 1974. *Master of Middle-earth: The Achievement of J.R.R. Tolkien in Fiction*. Harmondsworth: Penguin.

Krege, Wolfgang (trans.). 2000. *Der Herr der Ringe*. Stuttgart: Klett-Cotta.

Kroesen, R. 1982. 'The Enmity between Thorgrímr and Vésteinn in the *Gísla saga Súrssonar*.' *Neophilologus* 66: 386-90.

Kuteeva, Maria (ed.). 2000. *The Ways of Creative Mythologies: Imagined Worlds and their Makers*. 2 vols. Telford: The Tolkien Society.

Laing, Lloyd, and Jennifer Laing. 1979. *Anglo-Saxon England*. London: Routledge Kegan Paul.

Lewis, C.S. 1938. *Out of the Silent Planet*. London: Bodley Head.

----- 1945. *That Hideous Strength*. London: Bodley Head.

----- 1955. *Mere Christianity*. Reprint. London: Fontana.

----- 1961. *The Screwtape Letters, with Screwtape Proposes a Toast*. Reprint. London: Fontana.

----- 1969. 'The Anthropological Approach.' In Walter Hooper (ed.). 1969. *Selected Literary Essays of C.S. Lewis*. Cambridge: Cambridge University Press, pp. 301-11,

----- 1970. 'Evil and God.' In Walter Hooper (ed.). 1970. *God in the Dock: Essays on Theology and Ethics*. Grand Rapids, MI: Eerdmans, pp. 21-4.

----- 1990. *Studies in Words*. Reprint of 2nd edition (1967). Cambridge: Cambridge University Press.

Littledale, R.F. 1909. 'The Oxford Solar Myth.' In Palmer (ed.) 1909, pp. xxxi-xlviii.

Louis, Cameron. 1993. 'Proverbs, Precepts, and Monitory Pieces.' In J. Burke Severs and Albert E. Hartung (eds.). 1993. *A Manual of Writings in Middle English 1050-1500*. 10 vols. to date, IX: 2957-3048. New Haven: Connecticut Academy of Arts and Sciences.

Lucas, P.J. (ed.). 1977. *Exodus*. London: Methuen.

McIntosh, Angus, M.L. Samuels and Michael Benskin (eds.). 1986. *A Linguistic Atlas of Late Medieval English*. 4 vols. Aberdeen: Aberdeen University Press.

Mackail, J.W. 1899. *The Life of William Morris*. 2 vols. London and New York: Longmans, Green.

Macpherson, James, see Gaskill.

Maenchen-Helfen, J. Otto. 1973. *The World of the Huns*. Berkeley and Los Angeles: University of Cailfornia Press.

Menand, Louis. 2001. 'College: The End of the Golden Ages.' *New York Review of Books* 48.16, October 18: 44-47.

Mierow, C.C. (trans.). 1915. *The Gothic History of Jordanes*. 2nd edn. Princeton: Princeton University Press.

Mitchell, Bruce. 1995. 'J.R.R. Tolkien and Old English Studies: An Appreciation." In Reynolds and GoodKnight (eds.) 1995, pp. 206-12

Mommsen, Theodor (ed.). 1882. *Jordanes: Romana et Getica*. Monumenta Germaniae Historica, Auctores Antiquissimi 5.1. Berlin: Weidmann.

Moore, G.E. 1903. *Principia Ethica*. Cambridge: Cambridge University Press.

Morris, William. 1910-12. *Collected Works*. London: Longmans, Green.

Morris, May. 1912. 'Introduction' to vol. 14 of *The Collected Works of William Morris*, above, *The House of the Wolfings, and The Story of the Glittering Plain*, pp. xv-xxix.

----- 1912. 'Introduction' to vol. 15 of *The Collected Works of William Morris*, above, *The Roots of the Mountains*, pp. xi-xxxii.

Muir, Edwin. 1955. 'A Boy's World.' Review of *The Return of the King*. *Observer* (November 27): 11.

Müller, Max. 1880. 'Comparative Mythology.' In Max Müller. 1880. *Chips from a German Workshop*. 4 vols. London: Longmans, II: 1-126. Also in Palmer (ed.) 1909, pp. 1-178.

Neckel, Gustav, and Hans Kuhn. 1962, 1968. *Edda: Die Lieder des Codex Regius nebst verwandten Denkmälern*. 2 vols. Heidelberg: Carl Winter.

Nichols, Stephen G. (ed.). 1990. 'The New Philology.' *Speculum* 65/1: 1-108.

Nicholson, Lewis E. (ed.). 1963. *An Anthology of Beowulf Criticism*. South Bend, IN: Notre Dame University Press.

Niles, John D, *et al.* 2007, forthcoming. *Beowulf and Lejre*. Tempe: Arizona Center for Medieval and Renaissance Studies.

Noad, Charles. 2000. 'On the Construction of 'The Silmarillion'.' In Flieger and Hostetter (eds.) 2000, pp. 31-68.

Omberg, Margaret. 1976. *Scandinavian Themes in English Poetry, 1760-1800*. Studia Anglistica Upsaliensis 29. Stockholm: Almqvist and Wiksell.

Onions, C.T., with G.W.S. Friedrichsen and R.W. Burchfield (eds.). 1969. *The Oxford Dictionary of English Etymology*. Revised edn. Oxford: Clarendon Press.

The Oxford English Dictionary. See 'Abbreviations,' *OED*.

Palmer, A. Smythe (ed.). 1909. *Comparative Mythology: An Essay by Max Müller*. London: Routledge; New York: Dutton. Reprint 1977.

Pálsson, Hermann, and Paul Edwards (trans.). 1976. *The Saga of Egil Skallagrimsson*. Harmondsworth: Penguin.

Porter, Andrew (trans.) 1977. *Richard Wagner: The Ring of the Nibelung*. German text with English translation. London: Faber Music.

Putter, Ad. 1996. *An Introduction to the Gawain-poet*. London and New York: Addison Wesley Longman.

Quint, David. 1993. *Epic and Empire: Politics and Generic Form from Virgil to Milton*. Princeton: Princeton University Press.

Rateliff, John D. 2000. '*The Lost Road, The Dark Tower*, and *The Notion Club Papers*: Tolkien and Lewis's Time Travel Triad.' In Flieger and Hostetter (eds.) 2000, pp. 199-218.

Revard, Carter. 2000. 'Scribe and Provenance.' In Susanna Fein (ed.). 2000. *Studies in the Harley Manuscript: The Scribes, Contents, and Social Contexts of BL MS Harley 2253*. Kalamazoo, MI.: Medieval Institute Publications, pp. 21-109.

Reynolds, Patricia, and Glen H. GoodKnight (eds.). 1995. *Proceedings of the J.R.R. Tolkien Centenary Conference*. Milton Keynes: Tolkien Society; Altadena, CA: Mythopoeic Press.

Rosebury, Brian. 1992. *Tolkien: A Critical Assessment*. Revised edn. 2002. Basingstoke and New York: Palgrave.

Salu, Mary (trans.). 1955. *The Ancrene Riwle*. London: Burns and Oates.

Schneider, Hermann. 1928-34. *Germanische Heldensage*. 2 vols. Berlin and Leipzig: de Gruyter.

Schuchart, Max (trans.). 1956. *In de Ban van de Ring*. 3 vols. Utrecht: Het Spectrum.

Scragg, Don G. (ed.). 1981. *The Battle of Maldon*. Manchester: Manchester University Press.

Senior, William A. 2000. 'Loss Eternal in Tolkien's Middle-earth.' In Clark and Timmons (eds.) 2000, pp. 173-82.

Shepherd, G.T. (ed.). 1959. *Ancrene Wisse, Parts Six and Seven*. London: Nelson.

Shippey, Tom. 1971. 'The Uses of Chivalry: *Erec* and *Gawain*.' *Modern Language Review* 66: 241-50.

----- 1972. *Old English Verse*. London: Hutchinson.

----- (ed. and trans.). 1976. *Poems of Wisdom and Learning in Old English*. Cambridge: Brewer.

----- 1977. 'Maxims in Old English Narrative: Literary Art or Traditional Wisdom?' In Hans Bekker-Nielsen (ed.). 1977. *Oral Tradition, Literary Tradition: A Symposium*. Odense: Odense University Press, pp. 28-46.

----- 1978. *Beowulf*. London: Edward Arnold.

----- 1980. 'Introduction' to William Morris, *The Wood beyond the World*. World's Classics Series. London: Oxford University Press, pp. v-xix.

----- 1982. *The Road to Middle-earth*. London: George Allen & Unwin; Boston: Houghton Mifflin, 1983.

----- 1985. 'Boar and Badger: An Old English Heroic Antithesis?' *Leeds Studies in English* 16: 220-39.

----- 1992. *The Road to Middle-earth*. 2nd expanded edn. London: HarperCollins.

----- 1997a. 'Langland, the Scribes and the Editors.' Review of George Russell and George Kane (eds.). 1997. *Piers Plowman: The C-Text*. London: Athlone Press, and Charlotte Brewer. 1996. *Editing Piers Plowman*. Cambridge:

Cambridge University Press; in *Times Literary Supplement* (August 22): 12-13.

----- 1997b. Review of Howard Bloch and Stephen Nichols (eds.). 1995. *Medievalism and the Modernist Temper*. Baltimore and London: Johns Hopkins University Press; in *Envoi* 6.2 (Fall issue): 161-70.

----- 1999a. '"The Death-Song of Ragnar Lodbrog': A Study in Sensibilities.' In Richard Utz and Tom Shippey (eds.). 1999. *Medievalism in the Modern World: Essays in Honour of Leslie Workman*. Turnhout: Brepols, pp. 155-72.

----- 1999b. Review of Steven Justice and Kathryn Kirby-Fulton (eds.). 1997. *Written Work: Langland, Labor and Authorship*. Philadelphia: University of Philadelphia Press; in *Albion* 30: 666-8.

----- 2000a. *J.R.R. Tolkien: Author of the Century*. London: HarperCollins; Boston: Houghton Mifflin, 2001.

----- 2000b. 'The Undeveloped Image: Anglo-Saxons in Popular Consciousness from Turner to Tolkien.' In Don Scragg and Carole Weinberg (eds.). 2000. *Literary Appropriations of the Anglo-Saxons from the Thirteenth to the Twentieth Century*. Cambridge: Cambridge University Press, pp. 215-36.

----- 2000c. '*The Tale of Gamelyn*: Class Warfare and the Embarrassments of Genre.' In Ad Putter and Jane Gilbert (eds.). 2000. *The Spirit of Medieval English Popular Romance*. London: Longman, pp. 78-96.

----- 2003a. *The Road to Middle-earth*, 3rd expanded edn. Boston: Houghton Mifflin.

----- 2003b. 'Bilingualism and Betrayal in Chaucer's Summoner's Tale.' In Jean Godsall-Myers (ed.). 2003. *Speaking in the Medieval World*. Leiden and Boston: Brill, pp. 125-44.

----- 2004. 'Another Road to Middle-earth: Jackson's Movie Trilogy.' In Rose A. Zimbardo and Neil D. Isaacs (eds). 2004. *Understanding the Lord of the Rings: The Best of Tolkien Criticism*. Boston: Houghton Mifflin, pp. 233-54.

----- 2005a. 'A Revolution Reconsidered: Mythography and Mythology in the Nineteenth Century.' In Tom Shippey (ed.). 2005. *The Shadow-walkers: Jacob Grimm's Mythology of the Monstrous*. Tempe: Arizona Center for Medieval Studies; Turnhout: Brepols, pp. 1-28.

----- 2005b. '*Alias Oves Habeo*: The Elves as a Category Problem.' In *The Shadow-walkers*, above, pp. 157-88.

----- 2005c. 'Appendix C: Peter Jackson's Film Versions.' In *The Road to Middle-earth*, 3rd expanded edn., with added appendix. London: HarperCollins, pp. 409-29.

----- 2005d. 'The Merov(ich)ingian Again: *damnatio memoriae* and the *usus scholarum*.' In Andy Orchard (ed.). 2005. *Latin Learning and English Lore: Essays in Honor of Michael Lapidge*. Toronto: University of Toronto Press, pp. 389-406.

----- 2006. 'The Wrong Sow.' *New York Review of Books* 53.9 (May 25): 53.

----- 2007 (forthcoming). 'Imagined Cathedrals: Retelling Myth in the Twentieth Century.' In Stephen Glosecki (ed.). 2007. *Myth in Early North-West Europe*. Tempe: Arizona Center for Medieval and Renaissance Studies.

----- and Andreas Haarder. 1998. *Beowulf: The Critical Heritage*. London and New York: Routledge.

Simpson, Jacqueline (trans.). 2005. *Icelandic Folktales and Legends*. Revised edn. Stroud: Tempus.

Simrock, Karl (trans.). 1859. *Beowulf: das älteste deutsche Epos, übersetzt und erläutert*. Stuttgart and Augsburg.

Sisam, Kenneth. 1953. 'The Beowulf Manuscript.' In Kenneth Sisam. 1953. *Studies in the History of Old English Literature*. Oxford: Clarendon, pp. 61-4.

Skeat, W.W. 1892. *Principles of English Etymology*. 2 vols. Oxford: Clarendon Press.

Snorri Sturluson, see Faulkes.

Solzhenitsyn, Alexander. 1974. *The Gulag Archipelago: 1918-1956*. Translated by Thomas P. Whitney. London: Collins/Fontana.

Sparling, H.H. 1924. *The Kelmscott Press and William Morris, Master Craftsman*. London: Macmillan.

Stafford, Fiona. 1996, 'Introduction: The Ossianic Poems of James Macpherson.' In Gaskill (ed.) 1996, pp. v-xxi.

Stallybrass, J. S. (trans.). 1882-8. *Teutonic Mythology*. 4 vols. London: George Bell.

Stanley, Eric G. 1975. *The Search for Anglo-Saxon Paganism*. Cambridge: Brewer.

Stenström, Anders. 1984. Review of J.R.R. Tolkien (ed.). 1981. *The Old English Exodus*. Oxford: Clarendon; in *Amon Hen* (March issue) 66: 5-7.

----- 1995. 'A Mythology? For England?' In Reynolds and GoodKnight (eds.) 1995 1995, pp. 310-14.

Stevenson, Robert Louis. 1924. *Ethical Studies and Edinburgh: Picturesque Notes*. London: Heinemann.

Stuart, Heather. 1976. 'The Anglo-Saxon Elf.' *Studia Neophilologica* 48: 313-20.

Thompson, E.P. 1955. *William Morris: Romantic to Revolutionary*. London: Lawrence and Wishart.

Thompson, Kristin. 2003. 'Fantasy, Franchises, and Frodo Baggins: *The Lord of the Rings* and Modern Hollywood.' *The Velvet Light Trap* 32 (Fall issue): 45-63.

----- 2006. *Frodo, Fantasy and Franchises: The Lord of the Rings and Modern Hollywood*. Berkeley and Los Angeles: University of California Press.

Thompson, Paul. 1967. *The Work of William Morris*. London: Heinemann.

Thorarensen, Thorstein (trans.). 2001. *Hringadróttinssaga*. Reykjavik: Fjölvaútgáfan.

Thorkelin, Grímur, *et al.* (eds.). 1818. *Edda Sæmundar*. 2 vols. Copenhagen.

Thun, Nils. 1969. 'The Malignant Elves.' *Studia Neophilologica* 41: 378-96.

Timmons, Dan. 2004. 'Frodo on Film: Peter Jackson's Problematic Portrayal.' In Croft (ed.) 2004, pp. 123-48.

Tolkien, Christopher. 1953-7. 'The Battle of the Goths and Huns.' *Saga-Book of the Viking Society* 14: 141-63.

----- (ed. and trans.). 1960. *The Saga of King Heidrek the Wise*. London: Nelson.

Tolkien, J.R.R. For works by Professor Tolkien, other than those referenced in full in footnotes, see 'Abbreviations.'

Turner, Allan. 2005. *Translating Tolkien: Philological Elements in 'The Lord of the Rings'*. Frankfurt: Peter Lang.

Vigfusson, Gudbrand, and F. York Powell (eds.). 1883. *Corpus Poeticum Boreale*. 2 vols. Oxford: Clarendon.

Wagner, Richard, see Porter.

Walde, Alois (ed. Julius Pokorny). 1930. *Vergleichendes Wörterbuch der Indogermanischen Sprachen*. 2 vols. Berlin: de Gruyter.

Wallace, David (ed.). 1999. *Medieval English Literature*. Cambridge History of English Literature I. Cambridge: Cambridge University Press.

Waugh, Auberon. *The Times*, 20 Jan. 1997.

Wawn, Andrew. 2002. *The Vikings and the Victorians: Inventing the Old North in Nineteenth-Century Britain*. Cambridge: Brewer.

West, Richard C. 2003. 'Real-world Myth in a Secondary World: Mythological Aspects in the Story of Beren and Lúthien.' In Chance (ed.) 2003, pp. 259-67.

Wilson, A.N. 1990. *C.S. Lewis: A Life*. London and New York: Norton.

Wolfe, Gene. 1981. *A Book of Days*. New York: Doubleday.

Zettersten, Arne. 2006. 'The AB Language Lives.' In Hammond and Scull (eds.) 2006, pp. 13-24.

Index

A

Aelfwine
   'Elf-friend', 270
Aesc
   as anglicization of Old Norse *Askr*, 271
Aethelred, 328
Alalminorë
   as Warwickshire, 57
Alberich
   father of Hagen in *Der Ring des Nibelungen*, 109
Alboin
   Lombard form of Old English Ælfwine. see Aelfwine
   prince of the Lombards, son of Audoin, 269
Alexander, 366
allegories
   used by Tolkien, 353
allegory, 97
   definition attempted, 352
   Tolkien's understanding of it, 353
Alliterative Revival, 51
Ancrene Wisse, 47, 52, 211
Anderson, Douglas
   The Annotated Hobbit (2002), 307, 341

Anderson, Poul, 131
Andvaranaut
   Ring of the Nibelung, 102, 103, 106, 108, 112
Andvari, 100, 111
Anglo-Saxon Chronicle, 116
applicability, 354
Árnason, Jón, 188
Atlakviða, 109, 124, 126, 128
   tale of Gunnar and Högni, 273
Attila, 121, 132, 133, 149
   Gothic for 'little father', 133
Austen, Jane, 267

B

Barfield, Owen, 217
Bartholinus, Thomas
   Antiquitatum Danicarum de Causis Contempt & Mortis a Danis adhuc gentilibus libri tres ex vetustis codicis & monumentis hactenus ineditis congesti (1689), 189
Battle of Flodden Field, 45
Battle of Hastings, 45
Battle of Maldon, 116, 206, 274, 330
   and the 'northern heroic spirit', 335
   as an attack on the northern heroic spirit, 337
'Battle of the Goths and Huns', 127

Battle of the Somme, 199
Beleg, 110
Benford, Greg
  Timescape (1980), 267
Beorhtwold, 275
Beowulf, 1, 3, 4, 5, 6, 9, 10, 11, 12, 13, 14, 15, 17, 18, 19, 23, 27, 69, 82, 91, 93, 119, 134, 176, 178, 181, 192, 194, 210, 261, 342, 343
  and dragon-sickness, 343
  and paganism, 9
  as inspiration of Torhthelm, 333
  edited by Grímur Thorkelin (1815), 81
  edited by Jacob Grimm, 87
  Finnsburg Episode, 183
  proverbial and gnomic sayings, 312
Beren
  and question of nobility, 297
Beren and Lúthien, 4
black-elves
  in Snorri Sturluson, 220
Blackwelder, Richard
  Tolkien Thesaurus (1990), 157, 164, 165
Bliss, Alan, 175
Brady, Caroline
  The Legends of Ermanaric (1943), 132
Bratman, David, 42, 43, 47
Brodeur, A.G., 25

Brunhild
  in the *Nibelungenlied*, 104, 108. See also Brynhild
Brünnhilde. See also Brunhild and Brynhild
  in *Der Ring des Nibelungen*, 108
Brut
  by Layamon, 48
Brynhild, 101
  in Snorri's *Prose Edda*, 101, 102
  in the *Þiðreks saga af Bern*, 105, 106
  in the *Völsunga saga*, 102, 103, 108
Brynjólfsson, Gísli, 193
Bunyan, John
  Pilgrim's Progress (as allegory), 354
Burgdalers
  as Goths, 121
Byggviskviða Grindilsbana, 7

C

Carpenter, Humphrey
  J.R.R. Tolkien
    A Biography (1977), 62
Chamberlain, Neville
  'peace in our time', 373
Chanson de Roland
  edited 1837, 81
courage, theory of, 27, 191
Crankshaw, Edward, 40
Croker, Thomas
  Irische Elfenmärchen, 188

Curry, Patrick, 80, 95

D

d'Ardenne, Simonne
    edition of *Seinte Iuliene*, 53
Dáin Ironfoot
    as 'traditional Germanic' hero, 279, 280
dark-elves
    in Snorri Sturluson, 220
Darmston
    derived from *Déormódes-tún*, 17
Darwin, Charles
    Origin of Species (1859), 160
Dasent, George, 25
Davis, Norman, 62
Denkspruch
    as origin of proverb, 307
Dickens, Charles, 267
    Great Expectations, 295
Distichs of Cato, 304
Douglas, Gavin
    translation of the *Aeneid* (1513), 253
dragon-sickness, 13, 14, 15, 342, 344
drihtneas, 181
Dronke, Ursula, 132
Drout, Michael, 3
Dualism, 245
Duggan, Alfred, 365
Durham Proverbs, 304

Durin
    the Deathless, 1
Dusky Men
    as Huns, 121
Dvergatal
    in *Völuspá*, 195
Dwarves
    and reincarnation, 1
dwimmerlaik
    its etymology and derivation, 169

E

Eastemnet. See emnet
Edda, 124
    Elder Edda (also called *Poetic Edda*), 20, 28, 99, 189, 192, 219
    Elder Edda (also called *Poetic Edda*), edited by Jacob and Wilhelm Grimm (1812), 81
    Gylfaginning in the *Prose Edda* by Snorri Sturluson, 20
    Hattatal in the *Prose Edda* by Snorri Sturluson, 20
    Prose Edda by Snorri Sturluson, 20, 21, 24, 26, 29, 30, 99, 171, 189, 220
    Skáldskaparmál in the *Prose Edda* by Snorri Sturluson, 20
'Elbereth Gilthoniel'
    as index entry, 238
    language of the song discussed, 239

elf
- as discussed by Jacob Grimm, 90
- in Old English, 218
- in the Eddas, 219
- origin and etymology, 216
- Tolkien and the different categories of elves in Germanic mythology, 226

Eliot, George, 84
- *Middlemarch*, 84

Eliot, T.S., 199

emnet, 116, 117

England
- as geographical vs. cultural designation, 92
- cultural and national identity, 90
- The Shire and The Mark as national self-images, 92

Eöl
- the Dark Elf, 229

Eormenric. See Ermanaric

Eota
- OE 'Jute', 182

eoten
- OE 'giant', 182

Erik the Viking
- by Monty Python, 94

Ermanaric, 121

Exodus, 175, 178, 180, 182, 185, 210, 221

F

Fafnir, 100, 103

fairy-tales, 238

fantasy trilogy, 40

Farmer Giles of Ham
- as allegory, 325

fatalism
- in Norse tradition, 26

Finn, 183

Finn and Hengest, 17, 175, 184, 186

'Finnsburg Episode', 17, 183

Finnsburg Fragment, 17, 18, 176, 183, 186

Flieger, Verlyn, 351

folk-poetry
- vs. literary poetry, 238

Forster, E.M., 199
- and the Bloomsbury group, 263

Fragment of a Sigurd-Lay, 99

Furnivall, F.J., 363

G

Gamgees
- as lower class of the Shire, 290

Gandalf
- inspired by Old Norse *Gandálfr*, 196

Garulf, 17
- as misspelling for Gefwulf, 184

Gefwulf. See Garulf

gentlehobbit, 288, 294, 296
gentleman
    definition of what makes a gentleman, 294
Gibbon, Edward
    Decline and Fall of the Roman Empire, 80, 135
Glorfindel
    and reincarnation, 1
Goethe, Johann Wolfgang von, 82
Golding, William, 257, 263
    Lord of the Flies, 201
Gorbag, 243, 244, 247, 248
Gordon, E.V., 49, 61, 77, 206, 332
    editor of *The Battle of Maldon* (1937), 333
    Introduction to Old Norse (1927), 25, 94, 190
Gordon, Ida L., 62, 77
Goths
    as 'horse-people', 118
Götterdämmerung, 108
Green, Martin, 80
Green, Roger Lancelyn, 351
    Hamish Hamilton Book of Dragons (1970), 341
Greer, Germaine, 79
Grendel, 16, 17
Grimhild
    in the *Þiðreks saga af Bern*. See also Kriemhild.

Grimm, Jacob, 22, 81, 124, 127, 131, 135, 303
    definition of 'philolog', 119
    Deutsche Grammatik (1819-1837), 85, 160
    Deutsche Mythologie (1835), 85, 87, 187, 223
    Deutsches Wörterbuch (1838-), 85
Grimm, Jacob and Wilhelm
    Kinder- und Hausmärchen (1812), 87, 188
Grimm, Wilhelm
    Die deutsche Heldensage (1829), 131
Grishnákh, 247, 248
Grundtvig, Nikolai Frederik Severus, 88, 222
    Nordens Mythologi (1832), 222
    Nordens Mytologi (1808), 88, 187, 222
Grundtvig, Sven
    Danske Folkeviser, 88
Gudrun, 101
    in Snorri's *Prose Edda*, 101, 102
    in the *Völsunga saga*, 102
Gunnar. See also Gunther
    in the *Atlakviða*, 109
    in the *Völsunga saga*, 103
Gunnlaugs saga Ormstunga, 45
Gunther. See also Gunnar
    in *Der Ring des Nibelungen*, 108

H

Hagen
  son of Alberich in *Der Ring des Nibelungen*, 108
Haigh, Walter E.
  A New Glossary of the Dialect of the Huddersfield District (1928), 64, 164, 168
Hamlet, 19
Hamðismál, 132
Harley 2253
  Middle English poems, 49
Hávamál, 305
heathen
  in *Beowulf* and *The Lord of the Rings*, 11
  in *Beowulf*, *The Battle of Maldon* and 'The Homecoming of Beorhtnoth', 334
Heimskringla
  translated by Laing (1834), 81
Heinzel, R.
  Über die Hervararsage (1887), 132
Heithrek, 127, 129
Heiðreks Saga, 131
Heliand
  edited by J.A. Schmeller (1830), 81
Helm Hammerhand
  as 'traditional Germanic' hero, 278, 279
Hengest, 6, 17, 183, 184
Hengest and Horsa, 91, 328
Herefordshire
  as The Shire, 47
Hervarar saga, 122, 128, 130
Hinksey
  derived from *hengestes-ieg*, 17, 185
Hlöðskviða, 128, 133
  in *Hervarar saga*, 127
Hnæf, 17, 183
'Hoard'
  different versions in *Gryphon* (1923; older title 'Iumonna Gold Galdre Bewunden'), *The Oxford Magazine* (1937), 341
hobbit-poetry, 236
Höfuðlausn, 271
Högni, 31
  in *Atlakviða*, 109
Högni / Hagen
  brother of Gunnar / Gunther, 108
'Homecoming of Beorhtnoth'
  as authorisation to write *The Lord of the Rings*, 324, 338
  as discussion of realism vs. fantasy, 326
  as reaction to Gordon's edition of *The Battle of Maldon*, 333
Hostetter, Carl, 92
Houghton, Joe, 184
Hrólfs saga Kraka, 131, 196

Hrothgar, 16
Hugsvinnsmál, 305
Humanities Citations Index, 203, 323
Huxley, Aldous, 79

I

Ingeld
    son of Froda, 3

J

Jackson, Peter, 365
    changes due to 'democratisation' and 'emotionalisation', 378
    changes due to constraints of medium (film vs. book), 370
    changes due to politico-military expectations of a 21st century audience, 375
    changes made due to meet expectations of film-audience, 368
James, Henry, 267
Jónsson, Finnur, 25
Jordanes, 122
    Historia Getica, 121
Jörmunrekkr, 135

K

Kalevala, 21, 24, 32, 34, 35
    'The Tale of Kullervo', 32
    edited by Elias Lönnrot (1835), 20, 81
    translated by W.F. Kirby, 31
Kamenkovich, Maria, 95
Katharine group
    Middle English female saints' lives and other devotional works, 47
King Lear, 19
Kipling, Ruyard
    'The King's Ankus' in *The Second Jungle Book* (1895), 342
Kirby, W.F., 35
Königsproblem, 98, 101
Kortirion
    as Warwick, 57
Krakumál
    Death-song of Ragnar Lodbrog, 29, 94, 189
Kriemhild, 101
    in the *Nibelungenlied*, 104, 108. See also Gudrun

L

Lafferty, R.A.
    The Fall of Rome (1971), 131
Lancashire Fusiliers, 4, 42, 180, 185, 199, 383
Langland, William
    Piers Plowman, 51, (as allegory) 354
Laxness, Halldór
    Gerpla, 191, 202
Layamon, 37

Le Guin, Ursula K., 263
Lejre, 9
Lewis, C.S., 8, 74, 97, 245, 252
   Mere Christianity, 245
   Out of the Silent Planet (1938), 215
   That Hideous Strength (1945), 249, 257
   The Great Divorce (1946), 251
   The Last Battle, 8
   The Screwtape Letters, 246
   The Voyage of the Dawn Treader, 261
   Till We Have Faces, 8
light-elves
   in Snorri Sturluson, 220
Little Kingdom
   in *Farmer Giles of Ham*, 44
Longfellow, Henry Wadsworth
   The Song of Hiawatha, 34
Lönnrot, Elias, 23
   Kalevala, 222
   Suomen Kansan Vanhat Runot, 23
Lucas, Peter J., 177

M

Mabinogion
   translated by Lady Charlotte Guest (1836), 81
Macaulay, Thomas
   Lays of Ancient Rome, 23
Macpherson, James
   'Ossian', 21, 81

Magnificent Seven, 366
Mallet, Paul Henri
   Introduction à l'histoire de Danemarck, 24
   Monumens de la mythologie et de la poésie des Celtes et particulièrement des anciens Scandinaves (1755-56), 24, 189
Málshattakvæði, 305
Manichaeanism, 245, 260, 263
Marhwini, 118
Mark
   as 'borderland, frontier', 125
   as 'land, our land', 126
   in Morris' *The House of the Wolfings*, 286
   of the Riders of Rohan identified with Mercia, 54
McIntosh, Angus et. al.
   Linguistic Atlas of Late Medieval English (1986), 209
Mercia
   Anglo-Saxon kingdom, 43
Meyer, Elard Hugo, 86
Middle English Cato, 304
Milne, A.A.
   The Wind in the Willows, 363
Milton, John
   Comus, 52

Mîm
   in 'Tale of Túrin' inspired by
      Wagner's Mime, 110
Mime
   in *Der Ring des Nibelungen*, 110, 111.
      See also Regin
   in the *Þiðreks saga af Bern*, 110.
      See also Regin
Mirkwood, 123, 124, 126, 127, 128, 130
modernist poetry, 238
Moorcock, Michael, 285
Morris, May, 286
Morris, William, 120, 123, 127, 128, 131, 134, 135, 285
   The House of the Wolfings (1888), 119, 285
   The Roots of the Mountains (1889), 119
MS. Nero A.X, 61
Müller, Max, 159
Müller, Peter Erasmus, 88
mythology
   comparative, 85, 217
   dedicated to England, 92
   for England, 187, 192
   Old Norse, 191
mythopoeia, 19

N

Neave
   derived from Hnæf, 17, 184

Nibelungenlied, 23, 98, 100, 103, 104, 107, 108, 111, 134
   edited by von Hagen (1810), 81
Niggle, 10
ninnyhammer
   etymology and derivation, 167
Nokes
   origin and etymology, 358
noodle
   etymology and derivation, 64, 167, 168
Norse mythology
   in contrast to Classical or Biblical mythology, 83
nursery-rhymes, 237

O

Oakenshield
   inspired by Old Norse *Eikinskjaldi*, 195
ofermód, 331
Offa, 6
Olaf Tryggvason, 328
Old English
   its relationship to Old Norse, 192, 194
Old English poetry
   to be blamed for Beorhtnoth's decision, 329
Old Norse literature
   and *The Lord of the Rings*, 200
Old Walking Song, 235

Onions, Charles T., 161
> relationship to Tolkien, 158
> *The Oxford Dictionary of English Etymology* (1969), 157, 167

Opie, Iona and Peter
> *Language and Lore of Schoolchildren*, 308

Orwell, George, 252, 263
> *1984*, 201
> *Animal Farm* (as allegory), 354

Ottor
> father of Hengest and Horsa, 194

Oxford English Dictionary, 159, 253

P

palantíri
> use of the Seeing Stones in book and movies, 380

'Papelard Priest'
> alliterative poem edited by A.H. Smith, 51, 53

Paris, Gaston, 83

Patience, 61

Paul the Deacon, 270

Pearl, 61, 76
> edited by E.V. Gordon, 62
> translated by Tolkien, 63

Percy, Thomas
> *Five Pieces of Runic Poetry, translated from the Islandic Language* (1763), 81, 189

Northern Antiquities (1770), 189. see Mallet, *Monumens*, of which it is a translation

Reliques of Ancient English Poetry (1765), 51, 81

philology
> and the roots of Tolkien's romance, 41, 55
> as inspirational principle, 198

Poema Morale, 305

Potter, Beatrix, 364

Pratt, Fletcher
> *The Well of the Unicorn* (1948), 131

proverbs, 237

Proverbs of Alfred, 304

Proverbs of Hendyng, 304

Providence
> in *The Lord of the Rings* and Jackson's movies, 383

Purity, 61, 76

R

Ragnar Lóthbrok, 108

Ragnarök, 27

Ransom, Elwin
> in Lewis's *Out of the Silent Planet* as an affectionate portrait of Tolkien, 216

Regin
> brother of Fafnir in the Old Norse tradition, 109, 110. See also Mime

reincarnation, 1, 2
Revard, Carter, 48, 51, 53
riddles, 238
Riders of Rohan, 116
    as 'reconstructed' Germanic culture, 118
Ring
    Andvaranaut in the *Völsunga saga*, 101
    significance in Wagner and Tolkien, 98, 112
Ring of the Nibelung. See Andvaranaut
Road goes ever on and on, 236
Roman de Fouke Fitz Warin, 49
romance
    The Lord of the Rings as romance, 40
Russell, Bertrand
    and the Bloomsbury group, 264

S

Saga of Egil Skalla-Grimsson
    translated by Hermann Pálsson and Paul Edwards (1976), 271
Saga of Gísli Súrsson, 2
Saga of the Volsungs, 100
Salu, Mary
    translation of *Ancrene Wisse*, 53
Sarehole, 42
Sarehole Mill, 15, 56
Saruman
    Old Mercian form of *searuman*, 15

Schneider, Hermann, 135
    Germanische Heldensage (1928), 132
Scott, Walter, 23, 267, 295
'Scottish Field'
    poem about the Battle of Flodden Field, 53
Scyld Scefing, 12
shadow
    in *Beowulf* and *The Lord of the Rings*, 15, 16
shadow-helm, 181
Shagrat, 243, 244, 247, 248
Shakespeare, William, 50
    A Midsummer Night's Dream, 97
    King Lear, 50
    Love's Labours Lost, 51
    Macbeth, 51, 97
    Midsummer Night's Dream, 50
    The Tempest, 50
Shire, 54
Siegfried, 98. See also Sigurd
    compared to and contrasted with Túrin, 111
    in *Der Ring des Nibelungen*, 108, 109
Sigelwara land, 179
Sigurd. See also Siegfried
    in the *Völsunga saga*, 103
Sigurðarkviða inn meiri
    the Great Lay of Sigurd in the *Elder Edda*, 99
Simrock, Karl, 82

Sir Gawain and the Green Knight, 19,
   49, 61, 296
   dialect of the poem, 63, 66
   dreped in *SGGK*, 68
   edited by Tolkien and Gordon, 332
   etayn in *SGGK*, 69
   naunt ('aunt') in *SGGK*, 65
   rochereʒ, rocher, the Roaches in
      SGGK, 67
   wodwos in *SGGK*, 70
Sir Orfeo
   translated by Tolkien, 63
Sisam, Kenneth
   Fourteenth-Century Verse and Prose
      (1922), 164, 205
Skeat, Walter
   Principles of English Etymology
      (1892), 159
Smaug
   its derivation from **sméogan*, 196
Smith, A.H., 51
Smith, Arden, 92
Snaga, 247
Snorri Sturluson, 20, 26, 28, 194, 231
   version of the Sigurd-Lay in the *Prose
      Edda*, 99
Sólarljóð, 190
Solzhenitsyn, Alexander, 257
Song of Igor, 81
Sonnenkinder

the Children of the Sun (literary
   group), 80
speculation
   in its ancient and literal sense of
      'looking into a *speculum* = mirror',
      380
Spenser, Edmund
   The Faerie Queen, 97, (as allegory)
      354
St. Erkenwald, 61
Stanley, E.G., 115
   *The Search for Anglo-Saxon
      Paganism* (1975), 115
Stenström, Anders, 184
Stephens, George
   Er Engelsk en tysk sprog?, 193
   Thunor the Thunderer (1878), 88
Stevenson, Robert Louis, 295
Suffields
   Tolkien's maternal ancestors, 3
survivor-genres, 303
Sveinsson, Brynjófr, 189

T

Tavrobel
   as Great Haywood, 57
'The Battle of the Goths and Huns', 128
Théoden, 9
Thiðreks saga af Bern
   The Saga of Theodoric of Verona,
      100, 105, 107, 111

Thompson, E.P., 285
Thompson, Kristin, 365, 367
Thorkelín, Grímur Jónsson, 192, 222
Thrymskviða, 28, 189
Tol Eressëa, 56
    as England, 56
Tolkien, J.R.R.
    'A Secret Vice', 204
    '*Ancrene Wisse* and *Hali Meiðhad*' (1929), 61, 204, 206, 208
    '*Beowulf* – The Monsters and the Critics', 89, 204, 206, 209, 323
    chapters in *Year's Work* (1923 & 1924 & 1925), 204
    'Chaucer as a Philologist', 204, 207
    edition of *Ancrene Riwle*, 204
    edition of *Sir Gawain and the Green Knight* (together with E.V. Gordon), 204
    'English and Welsh', 204
    'Enigmata Anglo-Saxonica Nuper Inventa Duo', 303
    Exodus, edited by Joan Turville-Petre, 204
    Finn and Hengest, edited by A.J. Bliss, 204
    'Foreword' to Haigh's *Huddersfield Glossary*, 204
    glossary to Tolkien and Gordon's edition of *Sir Gawain and the Green Knight* (1925), 164
    Gollum as self-image, 163
    'Iumonna Gold Galdre Bewunden' (1923 in The *Gryphon* and 1937 in *The Oxford Magazine*). See 'Hoard'
    'Leaf by Niggle' as allegory, 355
    'M.E. Lexicography', 204
    'M.E. Losenger', 204
    Middle English Vocabulary, being a glossary to Kenneth Sisam's *Fourteenth-Century Verse and Prose*, 164, 204, 205
    Mr. Bliss, 363
    'Mythopoeia', 192
    'On Fairy-Stories', 204, 206
    'On Translating *Beowulf*', 4
    parson in *Farmer Giles of Ham* as self-image, 162
    'Preface' to *Beowulf* translation by Clark Hall and Wrenn, 204
    re-writing of nursery-rhyme 'The Cat and the Fiddle', 303
    re-writing of nursery-rhyme 'The Man in the Moon', 303
    '*Sigelwara land*', 89, 204
    Smith of Wootton Major, 167, (as allegory) 356
    'The Devil's Coach-Horses', 204
    'The Hoard'. See also 'Hoard' and 'Iumonna Gold Galdre Bewunden'

'The Homecoming of Beorhtnoth
  Beorhthelm's Son', 204, 206, 209,
  274, 276, 324
'The name Nodens', 204
'Valedictory Address', 204
Volsungakviða en nyja, 99, 192
W.P. Ker Memorial Lecture 1953 on
  Sir Gawain and the Green Knight,
  62, 204
Tooks
  as vestigial upper class of the Shire,
  290
Torhthelm
  characterisation, 326
Toynbee, Philip, 365
Trevino, Lee, 307
Troy, 366
Tulkas
  derivation of the word from *tulkas,
  193
Túrin, 110
  and question of nobility, 298
  compared to and contrasted with
    Wagner's Siegfried, 111
Turville-Petre, Joan, 175
Tyr
  equivalent of Tulkas, 26

U

Uglúk, 246, 247, 248
Unwin, Stanley, 40

V

Vidugavia, 117
Vidumavi, 117
Vinitharya, 117
virtuous paganism, 8, 9, 12, 192, 201
Völsunga saga, 102, 108, 111
Völuspá, 190
Vonnegut, Kurt, 263
Vortigern, 328

W

Wagner, Richard, 107, 109, 113
  Der Ring des Nibelungen, 97
  Götterdämmerung, 109
  Siegfried, 109
  Tolkien's attitude towards Wagner, 97
Walking Song, 236
Waugh, Auberon, 79
Waugh, Evelyn, 199, 200
Wawn, Andrew
  The Vikings and the Victorians
    (2002), 189
West Midlands, 42, 43, 44
  literary tradition, 44, 59
Westemnet. See emnet
White, Terence H., 263
  The Sword in the Stone, 285
Widsith, 134, 270
wight, barrow-wight

origin and etymology, 260
Williams, Charles, 217
Wither
    Deputy Director of N.I.C.E. in C.S. Lewis' *That Hideous Strength* as wraith, 258
wodwos
    derived from *wudu-wása*. See woses
Wolf, F.A.
    Liedertheorie, 23
Wolfe, Gene
    'Forlesen' (1981), 260

Woodhouse Lane, 56
Woolf, Virginia, 200
    and the Bloomsbury Group, 199, 263
Worm, Ole
    Runer, seu Danica Literatura Antiquissima vulgo Gothica dicta hic reddita opera (1636), 189
woses, 54, 55, 56, 70, 74, 165, 184
    'Wild Men of the Woods' of Druadan Forest.
wraith
    origin and etymology, 253

Walking Tree Publishers was founded in 1997 as a forum for publication of material (books, videos, CDs, etc.) related to Tolkien and Middle-earth studies. Manuscripts and project proposals can be submitted to the board of editors (please include an SAE):

Walking Tree Publishers
CH-3052 Zollikofen
Switzerland
e-mail: walkingtree@go.to
http://go.to/walkingtree

Cormarë Series

News from the Shire and Beyond. Studies on Tolkien.
    Edited by Peter Buchs and Thomas Honegger. Zurich and Berne 2004. Reprint. 1st edition 1997. (Cormarë Series 1)

Root and Branch. Approaches Towards Understanding Tolkien.
    Edited by Thomas Honegger. Zurich and Berne 2005. Reprint. 1st edition 1999. (Cormarë Series 2)

Richard Sturch. *Four Christian Fantasists. A Study of the Fantastic Writings of George MacDonald, Charles Williams, C. S. Lewis and J.R.R. Tolkien.* Zurich and Berne 2001. (Cormarë Series 3)

Tolkien in Translation.
    Edited by Thomas Honegger. Zurich and Berne 2003. (Cormarë Series 4)

Mark T. Hooker. *Tolkien Through Russian Eyes*. Zurich and Berne 2003. (Cormarë Series 5)

Translating Tolkien: Text and Film.
    Edited by Thomas Honegger. Zurich and Berne 2004. (Cormarë Series 6)

Christopher Garbowski. *Recovery and Transcendence for the Contemporary Mythmaker: The Spiritual Dimension in the Works of J.R.R. Tolkien.* Zurich and Berne 2004. Reprint. 1st edition by Marie Curie Sklodowska University Press, Lublin 2000. (Cormarë Series 7)

Reconsidering Tolkien.
    Edited by Thomas Honegger. Zurich and Berne 2005. (Cormarë Series 8)

Tolkien and Modernity 1.
    Edited by Frank Weinreich & Thomas Honegger. Zurich and Berne 2006. (Cormarë Series 9)

Tolkien and Modernity 2.
    Edited by Thomas Honegger & Frank Weinreich. Zurich and Berne 2006. (Cormarë Series 10)

Ross Smith. *Inside Language. Linguistic and Aesthetic Theory in Tolkien*. Zurich and Berne 2007. (Cormarë Series 12)

www.ingramcontent.com/pod-product-compliance
Lightning Source LLC
Chambersburg PA
CBHW071941220426
43662CB00009B/948